THOMAS REID'S INQUIRY AND ESSAYS

THOMAS REID'S

EDITED BY Ronald E. Beanblossom

AND Keith Lehrer

ISBN 0–915145–85–5 (pbk)
       0–915145–86–3 (cloth)

Previously published by
Bobbs-Merrill as ISBN 0–672–61173–2 (pbk)

INQUIRY AND ESSAYS

INTRODUCTION BY *Ronald E. Beanblossom*

Published by HACKETT PUBLISHING COMPANY, INC.
INDIANAPOLIS

THOMAS REID: 1710-1796

Hackett Publishing Company
Box 44937
Indianapolis, Indiana 46244-0937

First Edition
99 98 97 96 95   4 5 6 7 8 9 10
Cover design by Richard L. Listenberger

Library of Congress Cataloging in Publication Data

Reid, Thomas, 1710-1796.
    Thomas Reid's Inquiry and essays.
    Reproduced from The work of Thomas Reid, ed.
William Hamilton, 6th ed. Edinburgh, Maclachlan and
Stewart . . . 1863''—P.
    Bibliography: p.
    1. Philosophy.   I. Beanblossom, Ronald E., 1941–
II. Lehrer, Keith.   III. Title.   IV. Title: Inquiry and
essays.
B1532.A5 1983   192   83-22864
ISBN 0-915145-86-3
ISBN 0-915145-85-5 (pbk.)

The paper used in this publication meets the minimum requirements of
American National Standard for Information Sciences—Permanence of
Paper for Printed Library Materials, ANSI Z39.48-1984.

∞

CONTENTS

INTRODUCTION

1

Although the writings of Thomas Reid are very fertile and interesting, his life is biographically barren in comparison to such seventeenth- and eighteenth-century philosophers as Locke and Hume. What little is known about the life of Thomas Reid is due primarily to the efforts of his student and follower, Dugald Stewart (1753–1828). Reid was born April 26, 1710, at Strachan in Kincardinshire, Scotland, where his father, Lewis, served as a minister for fifty years. Many of the Reids had served as clergymen since the time of the Protestant Reformation in Scotland and others held various posts in government. One was a tutor for King James I and Alexander Reid was the personal physician of King Charles I. Reid's mother was a Gregory—a prominent family in Scottish intellectual life. Reid's uncle, David Gregory, was professor of astronomy at Oxford and was an intimate friend of Isaac Newton; and two of his uncles were professors of mathematics.

Reid's formal education began in the local parish school. After two years he was sent to the University of Aberdeen to pursue his studies; and at the age of twelve or thirteen, he was admitted to Marischal College where he studied under George Turnbull. Following graduation, Reid accepted an appointment as librarian at the university. Though Reid was a good student (he was not exceptional), the fact that one of his ancestors had long ago endowed this position of librarian may have encouraged the authorities to offer Reid the post. It afforded Reid the opportunity to pursue his scholarly interests, and he spent a great deal of time in the study of mathematics. This endeavor was encouraged to no small extent through Reid's close association with John Stewart who later became professor of mathematics at Marischal. Both men were involved in a study of Newton's *Principia*. Reid's appreciation of Newton's efforts is reflected throughout Reid's writings. In 1736 he resigned his post at Marischal and accompanied Stewart to England. It was while visiting Cambridge that he met Dr. Saunderson, a blind mathematician. As evidenced by the references to Saunderson in Reid's writings, their discussions apparently influenced Reid's views on, and may have aroused his interest in, problems of perception.

In the tradition of other members of the Reid family, Thomas Reid entered the ministry in 1737 at New Machar near Aberdeen. Reid's reception into his parish was not a warm one. He apparently received his post via the patronage system. This understandably aroused the anger of the previous minister and, subsequently, the congregation Reid was to serve. Nonetheless, Reid's popularity increased, especially after his marriage in 1740 to his cousin Elizabeth who gained the respect of the parishoners by her work among the sick. The modest and humble character of Reid is supposedly attested to by the fact that he preached the sermons of Dr. Tillotson and Dr. Evans rather than trust his own powers. This view should be tempered by the fact that the greater part of Reid's time during this period was spent in the study of external perception and other philosophical problems. It was during his stay at New Machar that Reid wrote "An Essay on Quantity," his first published paper, which appeared in 1748. The full title of this essay is "An Essay on Quantity, Occasioned by Reading a Treatise in Which Simple and Compound Ratios Are Applied to Our Ideas of Beauty and Virtue." According to Dugald Stewart, the treatise referred to is Hutchinson's *Inquiry into the Origin of Our Ideas of Beauty and Virtue.* In his essay Reid argues against attempts to apply mathematics, that is, the "doctrine" of measure or quantity, to that which does not admit of quantification. Reid outlines the conditions for quantification and concludes that virtue and beauty, like sensations, for example, pains, cannot be measured quantitatively.[1]

Though Reid had only this one published paper to his credit, in 1752 he was appointed professor of philosophy at Kings College in Aberdeen. The only explanation that Dugald Stewart offers for this appointment is that the professors had a high opinion of Reid's intellectual abilities. In addition to fulfilling the rigorous teaching requirements of the day (he taught mathematics, physics, logic, and ethics), Reid founded the Aberdeen Philosophical Society. This organization served as a forum for the presentation of papers written by members of the group that included George Campbell, Alexander Gerard, and James Beattie whose *Essay on Truth* did much to popularize common-sense philosophy (however, Beattie's vulgarizing of Reid also helped to discredit the common-sense doctrine among philosophers such as Kant).

It was before this society that Reid presented most of the papers that now compose *An Inquiry into the Human Mind on the Principles of Common Sense.* Although Reid did not publish the *Inquiry* until 1764, he states in the dedication that the rethinking of his views on the theory of ideas commenced in 1739 with the publication of Hume's *Treatise of Human Nature.* Reid acknowledges in the *Inquiry* that prior to that time he was a follower of Bishop Berkeley. Before publishing the *Inquiry*, Reid requested that Dr. Blair, a mutual friend of Hume's and

Reid's, persuade Hume to read the manuscript. It was in view of this request that Hume made his well known comment to the effect that "parsons" should mind their own business and leave philosophical controversies to philosophers. However, in a letter to Reid, Hume commends the manuscript as a serious challenge to his ideas.

In 1764 Reid succeeded Adam Smith as professor of moral philosophy at the University of Glasgow. This lectureship afforded Reid the opportunity to devote more time to his writing. However, Reid began to fear that he would not be able to complete his writings and wanted to devote full time to this work. In 1781, having previously resigned his post at Glasgow, he realized this desire. In 1785 Reid published the *Essays on the Intellectual Powers of Man* and this was followed in 1788 by his *Essays on the Active Powers of Man.* Though Reid remained intellectually active until his death in October of 1796, the *Essays* marked the end of his publications.

In what follows, I shall discuss Reid's views on various philosophical problems of current interest. Accordingly, I will first discuss Reid's attack on the theory of ideas; this will also touch upon Reid's views on conception, the problem of false memories, and misperception. Second, I will consider Reid's description of perception. Third, I will discuss the role of common sense in Reid's philosophy. Next, I will examine Reid's common-sense belief in the freedom of human actions. Then, I will discuss Reid's views on moral knowledge and his attack on Hume's emotive theory of moral beliefs. Finally, I will briefly discuss Reid's influence on Scottish, French, British, and American philosophy.

2

One of the major thrusts of Thomas Reid's *Inquiry* and *Essays on the Intellectual Powers* is an attack upon the theory of ideas. In fact, one of Reid's letters to James Gregory indicates that Reid regards this attack as his major philosophical contribution.

> The merit of what you are pleased to call *my philosophy*, lies, I think, chiefly, in having called in question the common theory of ideas, or images of things in the mind, being the only objects of thought; a theory founded on natural prejudices, and so universally received as to be interwoven with the structure of language.[2]

There is no date on this letter, but Reid may again be displaying his modesty in this passage, because he makes some interesting and positive contributions in his remarks on perception, memory, imagination and conception, personal identity, moral liberty, esthetics, and morals. Reid does devote a good deal of space to his attack on the theory of ideas, a philosophical view that he alleges Socrates and other philosophers held in various forms through the ages. In its "new" form, which Reid thinks begins with Descartes, the theory of ideas is the view that what we immediately think about or perceive is not an actual physical object but a mental surrogate. This surrogate for Locke is an idea or image in the mind that represents the real object. As Reid views the history of philosophy, Locke's theory of ideas ultimately results in Humean scepticism in which all that is left is the mental surrogate.

Reid acknowledges:

> I once believed this doctrine of ideas so firmly as to embrace the whole of Berkeley's system in consequence of it; till, finding other consequences to follow from it, which gave me more uneasiness than the want of a material world, it came into my mind, more than forty years ago, to put the question, What evidence have I, for this doctrine, that all the objects of my knowledge are ideas in my own mind?[3]

Reid's answer to his question is that he can find no evidence for the theory of ideas. Not only does the theory lead to absurdities such as there being no qualities in objects and there being thoughts without a thinker, but Reid claims, "No solid proof has been advanced of the existence of ideas . . . they are a mere fiction and hypothesis, contrived to solve the phaenomena of the human understanding [and] . . . they do not answer this end."[4]

As noted earlier, Hume took Reid seriously on these points, because in Hume's *Inquiry*, his "compleat answer to Dr. Reid," Hume attempts to prove that the theory of ideas is true and, hence, is not a mere hypothesis. Hume argues that "the table which we see seems to diminish as we remove further from it; but the real table, which exists independent of us, suffers no alteration. It was, therefore, nothing but its image which was present to the mind."[5] Reid's reply is:

> Let us suppose, for a moment, that it is the real table we see: Must not this real table seem to diminish as we remove farther from it? It is demonstrable that it must. How then can this apparent diminution be an argument that it is not the real table?[6]

If it is the real table we see, the table would *appear* to have different qualities from different positions even though its real qualities remain unchanged. The table we see would have a different apparent magnitude; that is, the table would *appear* to have a different magnitude from different distances; but the actual magnitude may remain unchanged. Hence, we are left with Reid's claim in the *Inquiry* that there is no evidence for the theory of ideas. Moreover, as we shall now see, the theory is also useless as an explanatory hypothesis.

The theory of ideas developed, according to Reid, because "Philosophers must have some system, some hypothesis, that shews the manner in which our senses make us acquainted with external things."[7] Reid also makes this point in the *Intellectual Powers* where he claims that the philosophers' attempts to account for this intercourse between a physical object and the mind have been based upon the analogy of the interaction between two physical objects. The principle of "no action at a distance" had been used by philosophers to account for the interaction between objects. The problem for perception is how an object at some distance from a mind "makes" the mind perceive it. Thus, Locke says:

> I cannot . . . conceive how bodies without us can any ways affect our senses, but by the immediate contact of the sensible bodies themselves, as in tasting and feeling, or the impulse of some sensible particles coming from them, as in seeing, hearing, and smelling; by the different impulse of which parts, caused by their different size, figure, and motion, the variety of sensations is produced in us.[8]

The particles transmitted by the object bridge the gap between the physical object and our physical body or sense organ. Ideas bridge the gap between the sense organ and the mind; the mind is in direct contact with a present or current idea. This is the principle of cognitive contact.[9]

Philosophers such as Locke profess to be followers of Newton. Yet, according to Reid, in using the theory of ideas to explain the operations of the mind, philosophers are employing precisely the sort of hypothesis that Newton rejects as inappropriate for science. In the first place, the theory of ideas is an illegitmate hypothesis, because it does not explain how we perceive objects. Is the image on the retina somehow transferred to the brain? How, then, does the mind perceive such images? "In a word, the manner and mechanism of the mind's perception is quite beyond our comprehension."[10] Not only does the theory of ideas fail as an explanatory hypothesis, but it also fails Newton's second requirement of a legitimate hypothesis, namely, there is no evidence that it is true. The theory of ideas is not proven by Hume's argument, nor is the theory a discovery of attentive reflection, that is, empirical investigation. It is based upon an analogy with the way one body acts upon another. But how are we to know that the mind works as physical objects do unless we discover this by experience?

Not only is there no evidence that the theory of ideas is true, but there is good reason to believe it is false. Reid contends that proponents of the theory not only claim that a present idea is always the immediate object of thought or perception but also that every object of thought must either be an idea or like an idea. To refute this claim, Reid makes use of Berkeley's discovery that nothing can be like a sensation or idea but an idea. Reid's *experimentum crucis* exemplifies his frequently employed strategy of "standing your opponent on his head;" this strategy involves adopting a claim of your opponent and using it to derive a different conclusion. Berkeley's discovery shows we *can* think of something besides ideas or sensations and, hence, the theory of ideas is false. Reid argues:

> I have as clear a conception of extension, hardness, and motion, as I have of the point of a sword; and, with some pains and practice, I can form as clear a notion of the other sensations of touch as I have of pain. When I do so, and compare them together [i.e., compare my concept of extension and hardness with my sensations], it appears to me as clear as daylight, that the former are not of kin to the latter, nor resemble them in any one feature.[11]

The sensation of pain one feels upon striking his head against an object cannot resemble the quality of hardness, that is, the impenetrability of the object. Moreover, in line with his comments in the "Essay on Quantity," Reid notes that mental occurrences, sensations, for example, differ from qualities, because sensations are intensive and non-measurable, whereas qualities are extensive and measurable. Locke couldn't measure his contrary *feelings* or *sensations* of hot and cold, but he could measure the *quality* of heat by placing a thermometer in a pan of water.[12]

Another objection Reid raises against the theory of ideas is that the theory is committed to the thesis that if an agent thinks about x, then there exists an x, namely an idea, which is the object of the agent's thought. This thesis contradicts the commonsense belief that we can think about nonexistent objects, for example, a unicorn. Reid agrees that we cannot think about nothing; there must be an object of thought. But to think about something such as a unicorn is not to say that the object exists.

> The philosopher says, I cannot conceive a centaur without having an idea of it in my mind. I am at a loss to understand what he means. He surely does not mean that I cannot conceive it without conceiving it. This would make me no wiser. What then is this idea? Is it an animal, half horse and half man? No. Then I am certain it is not the thing I conceive. Perhaps he will say, that the idea is an image of the animal. . . .

But this too is unsatisfactory for:

> I know what it is to conceive an image of an animal, and what it is to conceive an animal; and I can distinguish the one of these from the other without any danger of mistake.[13]

Reid's point is that to have an image of a unicorn as the object of thought would be like having a drawing of a unicorn for the object of thought. But a unicorn is not the same thing as the image of the unicorn any more than it is the same thing as a drawing of a unicorn. Though we can conceive of unicorns without forming an image, Reid would grant that we may conceive of the unicorn pictorially by forming an image. However, the image is *not* the object of thought, but is a *way* or *manner* of thinking. Thinking is a mental act, but the thing conceived of, that is, a unicorn, is not a mental act.

Moreover, the correct analysis of misperception and misremembering does not require the theory of ideas. We may explain such errors by saying that the agent *thought* he saw water in the desert but was mistaken. It is what Reid calls a "seeming perception."[14] Moreover, this is the way we ordinarily speak when we are not certain about what we are perceiving or remembering. In such cases we say "I *think* I see

an x," or "I *seem* to see an x," or "I *seem* to remember that x."
We need not postulate an idea as the object of misperception
or false memory, because in such cases there may be nothing
perceived or remembered.

In describing the perceptual experience, Reid notes that,
aside from the role played by our sensations, perception involves the conception of and belief in the present existence of
an object. The only difference in this respect between perception and memory is that "The belief which we have in perception, is a belief of the present existence of the object;
that which we have in memory, is a belief of its past existence. . . ."[15] But, as Reid has argued, surely we can conceive
of and believe in what does not exist. Hence, there need not
be a presently existing object of our perceptual experiences;
our memory experiences need not have as an object something that exists or has ever existed.

Finally, the theory of ideas, as an attempt to account for
misperception and other false beliefs, creates more problems
than it solves. For example, the claim that we always think
about a present idea eliminates memory in the ordinary sense,
for there is no *re*calling of an idea.[16] You cannot bring before
the mind numerically the same images or sensations you previously experienced. Thus, proponents of the theory of ideas are
committed to the view that you don't think again of something
you've thought of before, and this view is contrary to the
opinion of common sense.[17]

The representative theory or double object theory contends
that, as in perception, where the physical object is only a mediate object of thought, in memory the past event is only a
mediate object of thought, whereas a present idea is the immediate object of thought. It may seem that this double-object
theory of perception and memory does in some sense allow us
to think again of something past, for the past event is the
mediate object of thought. But Reid can make no sense out of
this second object of thought: "It seems very hard, or rather
impossible, to understand what is meant by an object of

thought that is not an immediate object of thought."[18] Reid can find no empirical evidence to support the claim that there are two objects of thought and that the mediate object of thought never becomes immediate.

Not only does the theory of ideas do away with memory in the strict sense of thinking again about a past event or object, but, "It may be observed, that the common system, that ideas are the only immediate objects of thought, leads to scepticism with regard to memory, as well as with regard to the objects of sense."[19] Berkeley had already shown that in perception you cannot prove that a present idea is like some object not present to the mind. Assuming the theory of ideas, there is the same need to prove that the present idea in memory is like some past occurrence. "But what is there in the idea that can lead me to this conclusion? What mark does it bear of the date of its archetype? Or what evidence have I that it had an archetype, and that it is not the first of its kind?"[20]

To summarize, in his attack on the theory of ideas, Reid has claimed that he can think of something quite unlike an idea. Unless his opponents can refute this claim, there is no reason to accept their hypothesis. Second, the theory of ideas contradicts the commonsense view that we can think of nonexistent objects. Third, the theory of ideas in attempting to account for misperception and other false beliefs, leads to disaster, namely, scepticism with regard to memory and perception. Finally, Reid accounts for perception and mistaken memory experiences without appeal to the theory of ideas.

3

We now turn to Reid's own theory of perception. Reid contends that those espousing to theory of ideas have been misled, because they failed to distinguish between sensing and perceiving—between having a sensation and perceiving something. "All the systems of philosophers about our senses and their objects have split upon this rock, of not distinguishing properly sensations which can have no existence but when they are felt, from the things suggested by them."[21] Reid thinks they may have been misled by customary forms of expression. He says:

> The same mode of expression is used to denote sensation and perception; and, therefore, we are apt to look upon them as things of the same nature. Thus, *I feel a pain ; I see a tree :* the first denoteth a sensation, the last a perception. The grammatical analysis of both expressions is the same. . . . But, if we attend to the things signified by these expressions, we shall find that, in the first, the distinction between the act and the object is not real but grammatical; in the second, the distinction is not only grammatical but real.
>
> The form of the expression, *I feel a pain,* might seem to imply that the feeling is something distinct from the pain felt; yet, in reality, there is no distinction. As *thinking a thought* is an expression which could signify no more than *thinking,* so *feeling a pain* signifies no more than *being pained.* What we have said of pain is applicable to every other mere sensation.[22]

Living a life signifies no more than living; there is no object called life that one lives. The same is true of sensations, which for Reid are merely ways of experiencing. Though it is a strange way of speaking, "I have a pain" might be translated adverbially "I am sensing painfully."

Our sensations play an important role in perception. Indeed, Reid believes this is one reason why the two acts have been confused. Reid describes three elements in the act of perception that are discoverable when one reflects upon his perceptual experience:

1. We have sensations.
2. These sensations suggest the conception of an object and lead to
3. The *immediate* conviction or belief in the present existence of that object.

By 'immediate' Reid means noninferential. Perceptions are in this respect like the axioms of mathematics.

> When I hear a certain sound, I conclude immediately, without reasoning, that a coach passes by. There are no premises from which this conclusion is inferred by any rules of logic.[23]

Given this distinction between sensing, which has no object or content distinct from the feeling, and perceiving, which in veridical instances has an existent object, Reid may explain cases of misperception by nothing that the agent has a sensation. For example, the agent senses redly, and erroneously takes there to be an external red object before him. This interpretation of Reid is supported by the fact that he talks of appearances as sensations. "When I see an object, the appearance which the colour of it makes, may be called *the sensation*, which suggests to me some external thing as its cause."[24] He also sometimes substitutes 'taking' for 'perceiving': "A sphere may be painted upon a plane, so exactly, as to be taken for a real sphere."[25] There are also cases of misperception in which the agent takes there to be an external object before him when no such object exists. As in the case of memory, this mistaking can occur, because we can conceive of what does not exist or did not exist.

What Reid says about 'visible figure' and 'original perception' may seem to commit him to the view that even when one mistakenly believes he is perceiving a real or material object, there is always *some* existent object he mistakes for the real one. For example, in speaking of the original perception of visible objects, which consist of color as well as what Reid calls visible figure and visible magnitude, Reid sometimes calls these proper objects of sight "real and external" objects. In the *Essays*, he says we cannot mistake our original perceptions.[26] Therefore, in our original perception of visible objects (which are two dimensional) there must exist such visible shapes and magnitudes even when they are not identical to the real or material object. Though we mistakenly believe that an object is elliptical, there does exist an elliptical shape, which is the visible object of our original perception. This is the view that A.D. Woozley attributes to Reid.[27]

In using the terms 'visible figure' and 'tangible figure' Reid is again exhibiting the influence of Berkeley and, like Berkeley, is attempting to distinguish between what is presented in a visual experience and a tactile experience. Though space will not permit a full defense of the claim, I will give some textual evidence to show that Reid uses 'visible object' in three different senses and that he also uses 'original perception' in three different senses. Since Reid does not specify the sense of these terms when he uses them, this can lead to a great deal of confusion. Once the various senses of 'visible object' and 'original perception' are pointed out, then we may claim that Reid does not posit an existent object in mistaken or non-veridical perceptual experiences; hence, Reid could analyze these experiences as proposed earlier, namely, in terms of sensing and mistaking.

Reid sometimes uses 'visible figure' to mean (1) the shape of the real object as seen by the eye, (2) the visible appearance or sensation, and (3) the retinal image. For example, Reid appears to be using the first meaning when he says, "The visible figure *of bodies* is a *real* and external object to the eye, as their tangible figure is to the touch."[28] Clearly Reid does not mean that the real object has two different figures, visible and tangible, for that is absurd, "nor was it ever maintained by any man, that the same object has two kinds of extension and figure totally dissimilar."[29]

Having said that the visible figure is something extended and shaped and having said that it is *real* and *external* to the eye (and, hence, that it is not a sensation), Reid also says in the *Inquiry* that the visible figure is at *"no distance* from the eye."[30] Here Reid appears to be talking of retinal images. It is the visible figure that a blind man can determine if:

. . . he can project the outline of a given body, upon the surface of a hollow sphere, whose centre is in the eye. This projection is the visible figure he wants: for it is the same figure with that which is projected upon the *tunica retina* in vision.[31]

It is this sense of visible figure that Reid uses when he says that given the real figure, we can demonstrate its visible figure.

However, Reid also uses 'visible figure' in a third sense. When speaking of the "perspective appearance," he sometimes uses 'visible figure' to mean the sensation or appearance rather than the retinal image. According to Reid, we cannot perceive the retinal image or the angles of the rays of light striking the retina (a point made by Berkeley in his *Essay towards a New Theory of Vision*). Perceiving is an act of the mind—a matter of conceiving and believing in the existence of an object.[32] What the agent conceives of and believes he is experiencing is not a retinal image but an external object. Moreover, the agent does not and indeed cannot attend to his retinal image. Thus, when Reid says these visible appearances are not attended to—though *they* can be—he is not using "appearance" to mean retinal image but rather to mean the sensation by means of which we conceive of the object.

> Thus, the visible appearance of things in my room varies almost every hour. . . . A book has a different appearance to the eye, in every distance and position; yet we conceive it to be still the same; and overlooking the appearance, we immediately conceive the real figure, distance, and position of the body, of which its visible or perspective appearance is a sign and indication.[33]

There is an intimate connection between the sensation or appearance and the retinal image; namely, there is a causal connection (though Reid claims he cannot tell how the one causes the other) between the physiological function of the sense organ and the mental act of sensing. Thus, even a blind man could "conceive that the length of the object will appear greater or less, in proportion to the angle which it subtends at the eye."[34]

Another aspect of Reid's account of perception is what he calls original, as opposed to acquired, perception. 'Original perception' generally means the perception of the "proper objects" of the various senses. Thus, the visual perception of color, which is a proper object of sight, would be an original perception. Seeing a sphere would be an acquired perception because the proper objects of sight are only two dimensional. However, two different senses of 'original perception' emerge when one considers the nature of proper objects. Thus, in one sense of original perception the proper object of sight, that is, the visible object, sometimes refers to the retinal image as when Reid says, "the objects which we see naturally and originally . . . have length and breadth, but no thickness *nor distance from the eye.*"[35]

At other times original perception involves the perception of those qualities of the objects that are properly discovered by each sense. "By this sense [i.e., sight] we perceive originally the visible figure and colour of *bodies* only. . . ."[36] Seemingly, Reid would want to say, for example, in the case of a penny, originally our sight tells us that there is a circular shape but not that the shape has thickness. Only through the experience of seeing and touching the penny do we learn to see it as a three dimensional object (which is a proper object of touch). We can have this acquired perception, because we have learned to associate our visual cues or sensations with this additional quality.

I noted earlier that Reid says in the *Essays* we cannot be mistaken in our original perceptions. Here Reid misuses 'perceive,' because he is not referring to the perception of an object but to our sensations or appearances; which, according to Reid, should not be spoken of as being perceived. Reid's discussion of original perception is one in which the agent mistakes a circle for a sphere. "We say in this case, that the eye is deceived, that the *appearance* is fallacious. But there is no fallacy in the original perception, but only in that which is acquired by custom."[37] Here Reid is using 'original perception' to mean appearance. The agent cannot be mistaken as to what sensations or appearances he is having, but he can misinterpret those sensations.

> The appearance of things to the eye always corresponds to the fixed laws of Nature; therefore, if we speak properly, there is no fallacy in the senses. . . . but we sometimes mistake the meaning of the signs, either through ignorance of the laws of Nature, or through ignorance of the circumstance which attend the signs.[38]

I have argued that when Reid says we cannot be mistaken in our *original perception*, for example, of *visible objects*, he is using those terms to mean sensations. Furthermore, according to Reid, sensations have no existent object, but are a mode of sensing. Hence, Reid is not committed to the thesis that misperception must always have an existent object.

4

Reid distinguishes between sensations in the mind and qualities in objects. He then faces the question as to whether or not such qualities exist. His answer, simply put, is that it is a matter of common sense that they do exist. The apparent simplicity of this answer has subjected Reid to a great deal of misunderstanding and unjust criticism. For example, Kant views Reid's appeal to common sense as, "but an appeal to the opinion of the multitude, of whose applause the philosopher is ashamed, while the popular charlatan glories and boasts in it."[39] Some of Reid's own countrymen viewed his work as an appeal to the vulgar. For example, the poet Robert Burns states in his letter "to James Tennant of Glenconner:"

> I've sent you . . . twa sage philosophers to glimpse on:
> Smith wi' his sympathetic feeling,
> An' Reid to common sense appealing.
> Philosophers have fought and wrangled,
> An' meikle Greek an' Latin mangled,
> Till, wi' their logic-jargon tir'd
> And in the depth of science mir'd
> To common sense they now appeal-
> What wives and wabsters see and feel![40]

There is reason for interpreting Reid's appeal to common sense as an appeal to the masses. For example, Reid says that in matters of common sense, "the learned and the unlearned, the philosopher and the day-labourer, are upon a level, and will pass the same judgment, when they are not misled by some bias."[41] And in the *Inquiry* Reid consistently casts his lot with the vulgar. In fact, Reid, especially in the *Inquiry*, seems to drive a wedge between reason and common sense. Philosophers attempt, by the use of reason, to destroy the dictates of common sense; yet common sense, "declines the tribunal of reason, and laughs at all the artillery of the logician."[42] On the other hand, in this same passage Reid also speaks of trying to reconcile reason and common sense. A reconciliation is possible because they are not really incompatible; by adopting false principles, philosophers have made it appear that the dictates of reason are at odds with the dictates of common sense. A reconciliation is possible because common sense judges of things self-evident; common sense is thus "only another name for one branch or one degree of reason."[43]

As for 'common sense,' Reid sometimes means, as in the above passage, that common sense is a power of the mind (common to all or most men) that judges what beliefs are self-evidently true. Sometimes Reid uses 'common sense' to mean the body of beliefs commonly accepted as true; it is those "principles which irresistibly govern the belief and the conduct of all mankind in the common concerns of life."[44]

Though it is doubtful that Kant ever read Reid, this latter interpretation of common sense may have been the view that Kant attacks in the *Prolegomena*. A third meaning of 'common sense' seems to be the principle of self-evidence that underlies these commonly held beliefs.

> The evidence of sense, the evidence of memory, and the evidence of the necessary relations of things, are all distinct and original kinds of evidence, equally grounded on our constitution.
> . . . To reason against any of these kinds of evidence, is absurd; nay, to reason for them is absurd. They are first principles; and such fall not within the province of reason, but of common sense.[15]

In this last passage Reid uses 'reason' to mean reasoning. We can't by reasoning directly establish the self-evidence of a belief; if we could do so, it would not be *self*-evident. Here Reid seems to be anticipating Bentham who was later to claim that the utilitarian principle, as the fundamental ethical principle, cannot be established by means of a direct proof. Self-evident principles function like the axioms of mathematics. A self-evident belief cannot itself be proven to be true, but it serves as the basis for reasoning. As we shall see later, however, Reid seems to reject this line of argument for some of his first principles.

How are we to determine which are the commonsense beliefs? Reid appeals to various criteria or tests for determining these fundamental beliefs of mankind. One test of course is to appeal to mankind. Whatever can be found to be a universally held belief—or nearly so—is a candidate for a commonsense belief. We need not conduct an exhaustive poll to determine what mankind believes. For first, "the universality of these opinions . . . is sufficiently evident, from the whole tenor of human conduct. . . ." Moreover, "there are other opinions that appear to be universal, from what is common in the structure of all languages." For example, "the distinction between substances, and the qualities belonging to them; between thought and the being that thinks; between thought and the objects of thought; is to be found in the structure of all languages."[46] Unless we can discover some error or prejudice responsible for these universally held beliefs, they are candidates for first principles.

Reid does not restrict the marks of self-evident beliefs to universality of opinion. In addition the contradictory of a first principle is not only false but absurd. Commonsense beliefs are irresistible; even the philosopher who calls them into question is compelled to believe them, when he leaves his study.[47]

Though reasoning cannot establish the truth of a common-sense belief, and though there are various tests for determining which are the commonsense beliefs, there may yet be disputes about such matters.[48] Among the means available to settle such disputes are a determination of what the bulk of mankind believes; determining whether that which contradicts the supposed first principle is absurd; and showing that "a first principle which a man rejects, stands upon the same footing with others which he admits."[49]

Reid uses these first principles or fundamental beliefs to combat scepticism. Philosophers have argued that there can be no perceptual knowledge, because it is always possible that we are mistaken in our perceptual beliefs. Because of this possibility, Descartes resolved not to believe in the existence of external objects, until he could prove that such objects existed. If, however, the Cartesian program fails—and Reid claims that it does—we are left with scepticism. According to Reid, scepticism is the result of Descartes' fatal legacy, to wit, that our perceptual beliefs are unjustified until sufficient evidence is produced to *prove* them true. When no proof is forthcoming, scepticism prevails.

In opposition, Reid argues that the faculties of the mind, for example, the faculties of reason, perception, memory, etc. should be placed on an equal footing. "Why, sir, should I

believe the faculty of reason more than that of perception?"[50]
In "A Brief Account of Aristotles Logic" Reid extends this
equality of the faculties to cover consciousness. "It is difficult
to give any reason for distrusting our other faculties, that will
not reach consciousness itself."[51] Neither Descartes nor Hume
called into question the testimony of consciousness. Descartes
regarded the testimony of consciousness as something that
cannot be doubted. Hume nowhere questions whether he has
impressions and ideas. They are guilty of an inconsistency. In
the case of perceptual knowledge, Hume and Descartes proceed on the assumption that perceptual beliefs are neither
certain nor known to be true until sufficient evidence is produced to *prove them true*. However, in the case of sensations or
consciousness, they regard beliefs as certain even though they
are not proven to be true. Instead of regarding the testimony
of consciousness as guilty until proven innocent, which the
sceptic does in the case of perception; the sceptic, like Reid,
regards it as innocent until proven guilty.

> I beg, therefore, to have the honour of making an addition to the
> sceptical system, without which I conceive it cannot hang to-
> gether. I affirm, that the belief of the existence of impressions
> and ideas, is as little supported by reason, as that of the existence
> of minds and bodies.[52]

What if the sceptic argues that first person sensory reports
are certain, not just because they can't be proven to be mistaken, but rather because it is logically impossible for them to
be mistaken; they are incorrigible? Reid does not specifically
address himself to this position; however, the sort of reply he
might make can be constructed in the light of what he says
about Descartes' *cogito ergo sum*. Reid takes Descartes to be
arguing that because he is conscious that he is thinking, he is
certain that he is thinking. Second, thinking cannot exist without a mind and, hence, a thinking being or mind exists. Reid
argues that these premises cannot prove the truth of the con-

clusion, because the premises are no more evident than what is to be proved by them. Likewise, Reid might argue, the claim "I feel pain" is at *least* as certain as the belief that all such beliefs are incorrigible. Thus, the thesis of incorrigibility cannot be used to prove that first person sensory beliefs are evident, because ". . . its evidence [in this case, the evidence for the thesis of incorrigibility] is no clearer, nor more immediate, than that of the proposition to be proved by it [e.g., 'I am thinking' or 'I feel pain']."[53] If the incorrigibility of the testimony of consciousness does not make such beliefs evident, then the sceptic is again in the position of arbitrarily accepting the testimony of one faculty, consciousness, as evident.

Thus Reid argues that to be consistent, we should treat the testimony of all our faculties in the same way we treat consciousness. Given Reid's frequent use of the court metaphor in which he compares the mind to a judge,[54] another way of stating his position on the evidence of common sense beliefs is in terms of that theory of jurisprudence that regards a man as innocent until proven guilty. According to Reid, our commonsense beliefs, for example, first person sensory beliefs, perceptual beliefs, and memory beliefs, should be regarded as epistemically justified or innocent until proven guilty, even though we cannot offer any reasons on their behalf. Thus, "I shall take it for granted that the evidence of sense, when the proper circumstances concur, is good evidence, and a just ground of belief."[55]

5

Reid uses the term 'active power' not in contradistinction to 'passive power', which is a contradiction in terms, but in contradistinction to 'speculative power'. "The powers of seeing, hearing, remembering, distinguishing, judging, reasoning, are speculative powers; the power of executing any work of art or labour is active power."[56] A crucial question concerning active powers is whether or not any of our actions are in "our own power." This is an important question, according to Reid, because it is only these actions for which an agent can be held morally responsible; *ought* implies *can*.

Reid begins his discussion with a relative conception of active power. "It is an attribute in a being by which he can do certain things if he wills. This . . . is only a relative conception. It is relative to the effect, and to the will of producing it."[57] Reid finds difficulty with the notion of active power. First, he notes that in common language we refer to reasons and motives as causes; we call gravity a cause. Yet, strictly speaking only *agents* can be said to act or cause things to occur; the only cause is efficient cause. Tables and chairs, for example, are inert or passive. Therefore, they cannot be said to act, for action requires the exertion of some power or force. Likewise, motives and reasons may serve as an influence for what we will to do, but they are not causes.

> We cannot, without absurdity, suppose a motive either to act or to be acted upon. . . . They may be compared to advice . . . , which leaves a man still at liberty. For in vain is advice given when there is not a power either to do or to forbear what it recommends.[58]

Having removed motives and reasons as the causes of our actions—having said what active power is not, it is difficult to say what it is.

The second reason for the difficulty in coming to grips with the meaning of 'active power' emerges in Reid's discussion of free will. Reid has said that active power is that attribute of an agent by which he can do a thing if he wills. This would seem to conform to the notion of an agent acting of his own free will, to wit, it is the capacity of an agent to either do or refrain from doing *x* if he chooses or wills to do so. However, Reid adds to this notion of liberty the requirement that the agent determines his will (presumably because the will is not itself an agent and, hence, cannot act). "By the *Liberty of a Moral Agent*, I understand, *a power over the determinations of his own Will.*"[59] Reid is saying that an action done of the agent's own willing or choosing is *not* uncaused, for every event has a cause. Rather, the agent's action is self-caused; the *agent* is the cause of his own action. Not only is it the *agent* who has wants or desires, but also it is the *agent* who determines what *he* wills to do. What is this power by means of which the agent exerts force on his will? Is it another sort of willing? This is the answer that Reid puts in the mouth of his opponents:

> Liberty, they say, consists only in a power to act as we will. . . . Hence, it follows, that liberty does not extend to the determinations of the will, but only to the actions consequent to its determination. . . . To say that we have power to will such an action, is to say, that we may will it, if we will. This supposes the will to be determined by a prior will; and, for the same reason, that will must be determined by a will prior to it, and so on in an infinite series of wills, which is absurd.[60]

Reid claims this variation of the third man argument does not apply to his definition of moral liberty.

> I consider the determination of the will as an effect. This effect must have a cause which had power to produce it; and the cause must be either the person himself, whose will it is, or some other being.[61]

In the first instance, the agent's action is free; and in the second, it is determined; but in neither case is the action uncaused. But, one might ask Reid, if this power to determine what is willed is not itself a matter of willing, what is it? Reid's answer is that we have only a relative conception of it; we conceive of this power only by means of its effects in the same way that we conceive of mind and material substance.

Reid lists the belief that man has some degree of power over his actions and his will as a contingent first principle. Having said that we cannot *prove* such principles to be true, Reid offers three arguments to prove that man has a degree of power over his will, that is, that man has "moral liberty."[62] A closer examination of these arguments reveals that, in reality, the first two are elaborations of his justification for listing the belief in our moral liberty as a first principle. Indeed, in the discussion of his first argument, Reid claims:

> This natural conviction of our acting freely, which is acknowledged by many who hold the doctrine of necessity, ought to throw the whole burden of proof upon that side; for, by this, the side of liberty has what lawyers call a *jus quaesitum*, or a right of ancient possession, which ought to stand good till it is overturned. If it cannot be proved that we always act from necessity, there is no need of arguments on the other side to convince us that we are free agents.[63]

Thus, Reid's first argument for moral liberty should be interpreted in the following way: we are conscious of deliberating about whether or not to perform various actions; this deliberation provides adequate evidence for the claim that we also believe in our moral liberty. "Deliberation about an action . . . implies a conviction that it is in our power."[64] A man does not deliberate about whether he will *do x* if he believes that he cannot do *x;* he may deliberate about whether he would do *x if* he could, but he is not deliberating about whether he *will do x.* Thus, because we are sometimes conscious of deliberating about what courses of action to take, we thereby have evidence that we believe in our moral liberty; it is an irresistible belief.

> It resembles, in this respect, our belief of the existence of a material world; our belief that those we converse with are living and intelligent beings; our belief that those things did really happen, which we distinctly remember; and our belief that we continue [to be] the same identical persons.[65]

In short what the argument shows is that the belief in moral liberty is a commonsense belief, a belief that is self-evident, and hence, a belief we are justified in believing. It is up to those who argue that we never act freely, to show that this belief is always mistaken.

I will not pursue Reid's second argument for moral liberty, because it employs the same strategy as the first. Reid's second argument is that we are conscious of the belief that we are morally accountable for some of our actions. If this is the case, then we must also believe that we had the power to perform these actions and, hence, we have introspective evidence for our claim that the belief in our moral liberty is a commonsense belief.

The third argument, however, is not based upon introspective evidence. Rather, Reid argues that the actions of *other* men give *us* reason to believe *they* are acting freely and, *a fortiori*, gives us reason to believe there are free actions. The same actions, which justify our belief that we are dealing with intelligent beings rather than machines, also serve as reasons for believing that these men act freely.

> All the reason we can assign for believing that our fellow-men think and reason, is grounded upon their actions and speeches. . . .
>
> The conclusion of this argument is—that, if the actions and speeches of other men give us sufficient evidence that they are reasonable beings, they give us the same evidence . . . that they are free agents.[66]

Reid's argument seems to be as follows:

1. If from the actions and speeches of the agent we can infer that he is an intelligent being, then his actions and speeches provide sufficient evidence to show that he is conducting a planned or purposive action, *x*.

2. If the agent's actions and speeches provide sufficient evidence to show that the agent is conducting a planned action, *x*, then from these same actions and speeches we can infer that *x* is in his power to perform.

3. Therefore, if from the actions and speeches of the agent

we can infer that he is an intelligent being, then from these actions and speeches we can infer that x is in his power to perform; that is, we can infer that he is a free agent.

Presumably, Reid's justification for the first premise is that an involuntary action, such as the twitching of an eyelid, gives no evidence of intelligence. It is only because some of the agent's actions appear purposive that we can infer he is an intelligent being. Likewise, if the agent never had the power to execute his plan, there would be no reason to regard him as a man rather than a machine or a puppet.

> If we can believe that an extensive series of means may conspire to promote an end without a cause that intended the end, and had power to choose and apply those means for the purpose, we may as well believe that this world was made by a fortuitous concourse of atoms, without an intelligent and powerful cause.[67]

Perhaps more interesting than the argument itself is the fact that Reid offers it. If the belief in moral liberty is a self-evident first principle, why does Reid attempt to *prove* it is a reasonable belief? The answer lies in Reid's views about God. Note that Reid nowhere lists belief in the existence of God as a first principle. Yet, he clearly commits himself to the argument from design as the best reason to believe in the existence of God. He grounds this argument on the necessary first principle, *"that design and intelligence in the cause may be inferred, with certainty, from marks or signs of it in the effect."*[68] Reid believes this argument for God is on the same footing as one we might offer for belief in finite intelligent beings; if the latter argument is inadequate, so is the argument from design. Thus, in his discussion of the first principle that there are finite, thinking beings, Reid notes that not only is this a natural conviction, it is also a belief that may be established by reasoning. Yet, before they are able to reason in this way, men often find themselves compelled to believe that some fellow beings are intelligent. "This knowledge, therefore, must be antecedent to reasoning, and therefore, must be a first principle."[69]

Thus, Reid feels he is able to offer a proof for this self-evident belief, even though he may still feel no need to do so. In this respect he contradicts what he has said about first principles in general and the first principles of morals in particular. Reid rejects the demand for a justification of the first principles of morals, because "this is to demand a reason for what does not exist. The first principles of morals are not deductions. They are self-evident; and their truth, like that of other axioms, is perceived without reasoning or deduction."[70] Apparently Reid is willing to offer proof for the belief in finite intelligent beings, because he needs to *prove* the existence of God—an intelligent being; for that proof he needs the necessary first principle, which permits the inference of intelligence in the cause on the basis of signs of intelligence in the effect. Likewise, Reid wants to infer from these signs of intelligence that God has the power or moral liberty to create those things that serve as signs of his intelligence. Reid sees no way of offering proof for the existence of an intelligent God who has moral liberty without applying these proofs to finite beings.

6

As is indicated by his inclusion of the first principles of morals, Reid believes there is moral knowledge. Moral reasoning, as does all reasoning, begins with self-evident first principles. Moral knowledge, as does all knowledge, involves acts of judgment and, hence, propositions that are either true or false.[71]

According to Reid, the theory of ideas results in the view that there is no moral knowledge. Reid thinks that Hume's system is the logical consequence of the theory of ideas. Hume's hypothesis that belief is a sensitive rather than a cogitative act results in the claim that "morality, therefore, is more properly felt than judg'd of."[72] According to Hume, there are moral sentiments but not moral judgments, and these sentiments or feelings can be neither true nor false.[73] Thus, Hume is committed to the view that there is no moral knowledge, because moral beliefs are not acts of judgment and, hence, there are no corresponding propositions which are either true or false. As Reid points out, there can be no knowledge without truth: "What is not true cannot be known."[74]

According to Hume, moral pronouncements merely express an agent's agreeable or disagreeable feelings, which are aroused either by his conduct or the conduct of others. In rejecting this emotive theory of morality, Reid offers two types of arguments. First, Reid invokes an empirical or introspective argument. Reid does not deny that there are feelings involved in our beliefs about moral conduct. However, he does deny that the presence of such feelings excludes the presence of reason or cogitative acts. Indeed, a belief may result from ". . . the sensation and . . . be regulated by it. In other in stances, the sensation is the consequence of it [that is, the belief]."[75] Perceptual beliefs are examples of the former, and moral beliefs are examples of the latter. Reid is aware that, for example, moral approval may evoke the agreeable feeling to which Hume refers. However, Reid's awareness or consciousness also reveals that this agreeable feeling depends upon his favorable *judgment* of the agent's conduct. Thus, if Hume's view that there are moral sentiments rather than moral judgments is an empirical claim, then he is mistaken, because some agents do make moral judgments. "That I ought not to steal, or to kill. . . . I am conscious that I judge them to be true propositions; and my consciousness makes all other arguments unnecessary, with regard to the operations of my own mind."[76]

Reid's empirical argument is another example of his frequently employed strategy of using a claim of his opponent to refute his opponent. Consciousness, according to Hume, can't deceive us about the actions or sentiments of our mind; what is revealed by consciousness must be what it appears to be (compare *Treatise*, p. 190). If one adopts Hume's view on consciousness, then Reid must be correct in his claim that he makes moral judgments and that his sentiments of approval or disapproval depend upon, or are caused by, those judgments.

Next, Reid rejects Hume's theory of morals on linguistic grounds. If, as Hume claims, an agent's moral approbation is merely an agreeable feeling, then the agent's expression of approval does not express a judgment about someone's conduct; rather the agent is only expressing something about himself, namely, that he has an agreeable feeling. Thus, "Such a man did well and worthily, his conduct is highly approvable" means the same as "the man's conduct gave me a very agreeable feeling."[77] Reid offers two arguments for thinking these two expressions do not mean the same thing.

First, "Such a man did well and worthily, his conduct is highly approvable" is ordinarily used to express a judgment about the conduct of an agent. Although this expression may be used to express something either about the speaker or someone else, "the man's conduct gave me a very agreeable feeling," can only be used to express something about the speaker. Hence, the two expressions cannot mean the same thing.[78]

Finally, Reid argues that if we consider the contradictories of the two expressions, it can again be seen that the expressions do not mean the same thing. Consider the contradictory of the first expression—"his conduct is not highly approvable." If an agent made such a claim, we would ordinarily take him to be expressing a different opinion about someone's conduct; but nothing whatever is implied about the integrity of the agent expressing the opposing view. However, this is not the case in the second expression. Assuming we cannot be mistaken about our own feelings, an agent cannot contradict the original speaker without implying that the original speaker is lying.[79] Hence, because the denials of the two expressions may be characterized in incompatible ways, the expressions cannot mean the same thing.

7

The influence of Thomas Reid has been far reaching. However, I will only briefly deal with those countries where Reid's influence has been most notable, to wit, France, Great Britain, the United States, and, of course, Scotland. Reid is often pictured as the founder of the Scottish school of common sense philosophy. Some of the major figures of this school were James Beattie (1735–1802) and Reid's student, Dugald Stewart (1753–1828). Because of his extravagant claims for common sense, there is some difference of opinion as to whether James Oswald (?–1793) should be considered a member of this school of philosophy. However, there is no doubt about Reid's influence on all of these figures. Moreover, though Beattie and Oswald were both somewhat more extravagant than Reid in their claims for common sense and though Stewart offered some minor amendments to Reid's views, they were essentially noncritical proponents of his views.

There is another group of Scottish philosophers, however, who though they were influenced by Reid, were nonetheless much more critical of his views and attempted major revisions. One of Reid's most vociferous critics was Thomas Brown (1778–1820), a student of Dugald Stewart. Brown claimed that the theory of ideas, which Reid attacked, was not held by any philosopher except possibly Malebranche and Berkeley. Instead, the theory of ideas is precisely the sort of view that Reid himself adopts.

So far is Dr. Reid from having the merit of confuting the universal, or even general illusion of philosophers with respect to ideas
in the mind, as images or separate things, distinct from the perception itself, that his own opinions as to perception, on this
point at least, are precisely the same as those which generally
prevailed before.[80]

Brown, on the other hand, did not disagree with Reid over
the existence of commonsense beliefs. He did contend, however, that we need to reduce these principles to as few as
possible.

William Hamilton (1791–1856) often assumed the burden
of defending Thomas Reid. Nonetheless, Hamilton's marked
differences with Reid emerge in the footnotes of his edition of
Reid and in his notes at the end of Reid's works. Hamilton was
faced with the dilemma of, on the one hand, holding on to
Reid's common sense philosophy and, on the other hand,
utilizing the insights of the newly discovered Kantian philosophy. The result was a claim that our knowledge is relative. We
cannot know things as they are in themselves; we can only
know things as they appear to our individual faculties. This
attempt to straddle these two metaphysical horses (as well as
Hamilton's view of conscious reflection as an inductive
method of investigating the mind—a view inherited from
Reid) provided the fodder for J. S. Mill's attack on common
sense in *Examination of the Philosophy of Sir William Hamilton*
(1865).

Mill, a Scottish gift to England, was not the only one attack-
ing common sense philosophy. For example, the Scottish
philosopher, James Ferrier (1808–1864), is often portrayed as
a foe of Reid's commonsense philosophy. In particular Ferrier
criticizes Reid's uncritical acceptance of commonsense beliefs.
However, it is in part this line of attack that leads George Davie
to argue that Ferrier is not a foe of common sense per se.
Rather, as a rationalistic product of the commonsense school,
Ferrier seeks an analysis and justification of the beliefs of com-

mon sense. Thus, Davie argues, Ferrier is not abandoning common sense but is seeking a reconciliation between philosophy and common sense.[81] This attempt to justify commonsense beliefs became a major point of contention between Ferrier and his teacher, William Hamilton.

Reid, like Hamilton, faced criticism from without as well as from within Scotland. One of his severest critics in England was Joseph Priestley, who, like Thomas Brown, charges that Reid completely misunderstood the theory of ideas. Philosophers do not literally mean that there are images of external things, but rather they use such expressions metaphorically to mean that "impressions of some kind or other were conveyed to the mind by means of the organs of sense."[82] Priestley's attack, however, is not confined to the charge that Reid misunderstood the theory of ideas. The doctrine of common sense is dismissed as no answer at all to the problem of scepticism. Reid claims that there really are such things as material objects and minds. According to Priestley, in support of this claim, Reid says no more than that these things *"are so because they are so,* which is Dr. Reid's common sense, and his short irrefragable argument."[83]

Priestley's rejection of common sense is instructive, because it is a common criticism of commonsense philosophy—whether it be the philosophy of Thomas Reid or G. E. Moore. What this criticism overlooks is the theory of evidence—the view that some beliefs are justified until proven guilty—inherent in the commonsense doctrine. Reid would reply that Priestley asks for a proof where none can be given and then criticizes common sense, because it does not provide one.

France and Scotland had strong cultural and political ties during this period—ties promoted by their common opposition to England's hegemony. This may help to account for the ready acceptance of Reid's work in France. However, Reid also served the purpose of those looking for an answer to the sensationalist philosophy of Condillac. Royer-Collard is regarded as the philosopher responsible for introducing Reid's work to France. Collard lectured on Reid at the Sorbonne from 1811–1814. Both Collard and Jouffrey, whose translation of Reid's work became the standard edition in France, hailed Reid's application of the inductive method in the study of the mind.

Though Condillac professes to agree with the Baconian inductive method, Collard, Jouffrey, and V. Cousin regard Condillac's philosophy as a deductive system that uncritically accepts the Lockean doctrine that nothing is in the intellect that is not first in the senses; Condillac uses this presupposition to develop a system that has no basis in experience.

> The whole of English and French philosophy in the eighteenth century comes from Locke and its principle is the *tabula rasa.* Reid grounded Scottish philosophy on the contrary principle. . . . Kant in fact proposed, as Reid did, to establish in metaphysics and morals speculative and practical laws which depend on the constitution of human reason itself, laws which are not derived from experience and which alone make experience possible. It is the same enterprise differently carried out.[84]

Cousin, a student of Collard's, was able to use his position as minister of public instruction to make Reid's commonsense philosophy standard material in the French schools. Reid's philosophy continued to be standard fare in the French schools until the late nineteenth century.

Reid's commonsense philosophy was likewise not without advocates among the British in the late nineteenth century. One of the most notable of these was Henry Sidgwick. There have also been more recent British philosophers who, though they differ from him in significant respects, have been influenced by Reid. For example, H. H. Price states that:

> The position maintained in this chapter with regard to the nature and the validity of perceptual consciousness is in essence identical with that maintained by Reid against Hume.[85]

Undoubtedly a case could be made for claiming that other contemporary British philosophers (for example, C. D. Broad and J. L. Austin) have been influenced by Reid, but I will here restrict my comments to one of Sidgwick's more famous students, G. E. Moore. No doubt Moore came in contact with Reid's views while under the tutelage of Sidgwick. In any event we do know that very early in his career Moore was aware of Reid, because in "The Nature and Reality of Objects of Perception" (1905–1906) Moore criticizes Reid's use of 'perception'.[86]

In addition to Moore's knowledge of Reid, there are several striking similarities in what they say. There is of course the common insistence that some terms or concepts are unanalyzable. For Reid, these terms include 'belief', 'willing', and 'duty'; for Moore, of course, 'good' is unanalyzable. Both Reid and Moore distinguish between mental acts and the actuality of physical objects. Indeed both argue, there may be confusion about whether or not there is a distinction, for example, between sensations and objects, because the same word is used to denote both sensations and physical qualities—the object is hot, and one may have a hot sensation upon touching that object. Confusion may also arise because of the difficulty of attending to our sensations, which become transparent as we become familiar with them; upon touching a familiar object, one does not usually attend to his tactile sensations but instead attends to the object causing those sensations.[87] For these reasons, it is possible to mistakenly believe either, as the idealists do, that only sensations exist or, as others do, that only physical objects exist.

Additional similarities between the views of Reid and Moore are their mutual appeals to common sense and their arguments against scepticism and idealism. Both Reid and Moore agree that scepticism and idealism go hand in hand: if all that an agent is aware of is his own ideas or sensations, then he has, "no *reason* for holding that anything does exist except himself."[88] Other objects and persons may exist, but the idealist committed to *esse est percipi* has no evidence for such a belief and cannot legitimately infer that such objects exist.

Reid and Moore also agree that idealism is committed to the mistaken view that we cannot think about nonexistent objects, for example, unicorns, because the object of thought is always a present idea in the mind. Moore considers this unacceptable consequence in his discussion of F. H. Bradley's view that time is unreal. According to Moore, Bradley commits himself to the view that things, for example, time, can exist even though they are unreal. Thus, it would seem that we can think about unreal objects that are nonetheless existent. Moore finds it difficult to understand what is meant by saying that this unreal object exists, for "the fact that we can think of unicorns is not sufficient to prove that, in any sense at all, there *are* any unicorns." Whatever it is that we mean when we say that we are imagining a unicorn, "it is certainly *not* that I am conceiving with regard to the property of 'being a unicorn', that there is something which possesses it."[89]

In "Some Judgements of Perception," Moore argues that the sceptic cannot prove that we have no knowledge of material objects; the sceptic cannot show that we lack such knowledge, because his arguments will always "rest upon some premise which is, beyond comparison, less certain than is the proposition which it is designed to attack."[90] It is for this same reason that Reid says the beliefs of common sense "disdain the trial of reasoning, and disown its authority"[91] and that "he must either be a fool, or want to make a fool of me, that would reason me out of my reason and senses."[92] The beliefs of common sense are more certain than the arguments the philosopher offers against these beliefs; that is why the philosopher cannot convince Reid to give up such beliefs or convince him that his beliefs are unreasonable.

In his discussion of probable reasoning Reid rejects the claim that we can only be said to know for certain in those cases where it is logically impossible to be mistaken; it is not the case that the only demonstrative knowledge constitutes knowledge.

"Philosophers consider probable evidence, not as a degree, but as a species of evidence, which is opposed, not to certainty, but to another species of evidence, called demonstration."[93] Reid is concerned to reject the claim that "probable knowledge" does not constitute knowledge, because Hume attempts to reduce all of our knowledge claims to mere probability; hence, according to Hume, there would be no cases of knowing for certain. In "Four Forms of Scepticism," Moore makes a claim similar to Reid's (though he dislikes the term "probable knowledge").

> I am inclined to think that what is 'based on' an analogical or inductive argument, in the sense in which my knowledge or belief that this is a pencil is so, may nevertheless be certain knowledge and *not* merely more or less probable belief.[94]

Moore and Reid make two other claims that relate to the above discussion. The sceptic might argue that the reason we can't be said to know unless it is logically impossible that we're mistaken is that of the problem of deception. If, as Descartes thought, it is always possible that we are merely dreaming that we're sitting by the fire, how do we know that we are not being deceived. In short the sceptic may claim that whenever it is possible that we are being deceived, before we can know that p we must know *how* we know that p. How does the agent know he is not being deceived?

In opposition to this view, both Reid and Moore claim that we can know that p *without* knowing how we know that p.

> If, for instance, I do know that the earth had existed for many years before I was born, I certainly only know this because I have known other things in the past which were evidence for it. And I certainly do not know exactly what the evidence was. Yet all this seems to me to be no good reason for doubting that I do know it. We are all, I think, in this strange position that we do *know* many things, with regard to which we *know* further that we must have evidence for them, and yet we do not know *how* we know them.[95]

Secondly, the sceptic might argue that because of the possibility of mistake, we can't be said to know that *p* unless we can prove that *p* is true. Moore rejects this claim in "Proof of an External World."

> They would say: "If you cannot prove your premise that here is one hand and here is another, then you do not know it. . . ." This view that, if I cannot prove such things as these, I do not know them, is, I think, the view which Kant was expressing. . . . Such a view, though it has been very common among philosophers, can, I think, be shown to be wrong.[96]

Though Moore thinks this view can be shown to be wrong, he does not attempt to do so. Reid, however, as noted earlier, argues that the sceptic is inconsistent in requiring proofs for our perceptual beliefs but not for first person sensory beliefs.

Finally, Reid and Moore agree that the ordinary man as well as the philosopher is able to know such things as, "This is my hand that I see," without being able to give an analysis of what this means. Such propositions have an ordinary, though perhaps an unanalyzed or unanalyzable, meaning. Reid is for this reason concerned with the ordinary meaning of terms and philosophers' violation of this usage as a means of creating sceptical problems. Similarly, in "A Defense of Common Sense," Moore objects to those philosophers who make it appear that they believe there are real objects when they do not. Berkeley, for example, professes to agree with common sense that the things we see and feel are real objects. However, what he means by 'real object' is not what we ordinarily mean. Thus, some philosophers:

> . . . use the expression "The earth has existed for many years past" to express, not what it would ordinarily be understood to express, but the proposition that some proposition, related to this in a certain way, is true; when all the time they believe that the proposition, which this expression would ordinarily be understood to express, is, at least partially, false.[97]

Thus, both Reid and Moore agree that there is an ordinary meaning of the expression "the earth has existed for many years past," which both the philosopher and nonphilosopher understand.

What I have given here in the way of similarities between Reid and Moore is necessarily merely a sketch. However, these similarities, together with the fact that Moore was familiar with Reid's works, make it reasonable to believe that Moore was influenced by Reid.

Reid's influence in American philosophy has also been great. His influence first emerged in the "free will" controversy in the early 1800's. Jonathan Edwards argued that all acts are motivated and, hence, are necessary actions. In support of the opposing view that men act freely, philosophers such as Samuel West appealed to empirical evidence, to wit, the testimony of consciousness. In conjunction with this latter view, there was a new emphasis upon "mental philosophy" as exemplified in Asa Burton's *Essays on Some of the First Principles of Metaphysiks, Ethicks, Theology* (1824). Schneider contends that the work indicates "the general influence of Reid and the Scottish school."[98] This claim is supported by the fact that Reid's *Essays* together with Dugald Stewart's *Elements of Philosophy* created quite a stir in America about 1820. Philosophy prior to that time had been divided into natural and moral philosophy; but with this new Scottish influence, philosophy was divided into mental, or intellectual and moral, philosophy. Among those philosophers who were influenced by this Scottish emphasis upon mental philosophy were the president of Yale, Noah Porter, who published *The Human Intellect* (1868), and the president of Princeton, James McCosh, who published *Psychology* (1886).

During the latter stages of the nineteenth century idealism began to supplant commonsense realism as the dominant philosophical force in America. But in the early part of the twentieth century (1905), realism began to reassert itself through a group of philosophers who were called the "new realists."[99] Proponents of the new realism, which might better be called "naive realism revisited," included H. B. Holt, Walter T. Marvin, William P. Montague, Ralph Barton Perry, and E. G. Spaulding. These realists were familiar with Reid as evidenced in *The New Realism* where Perry conducts a lengthy attack on Reid's doctrine of substance.

The new realists, like Reid, claimed that we have immediate perceptual knowledge of external objects; that is, no reasoning is involved. Unlike Reid, they rejected the traditional role of sensations as the means for knowing about external objects. Reid's doctrine of sensations had been criticized by people like Hamilton on the grounds that, by regarding sensations as the means for perceiving external objects, Reid had in fact not gotten rid of Locke's doctrine of mediate perception—a doctrine which Reid severely criticized. The new realists likewise felt that sensations had no role to play in the immediate perception of external objects. "Nothing intervenes between the knower and the world external to him. Objects are not represented to consciousness by ideas; they are themselves directly presented."[100] Thus, unlike Reid, the new realist claimed that things are what they appear to be. This consequence was obviously unsatisfactory. The movement of new realism passed from the American scene about 1930.

Among those critical of the new realists were proponents of a "new" type of realism. In 1920 Durant Drake, J. B. Pratt, A. K. Rogers, George Santayana, Roy Wood Sellars, C. A. Strong, and A. O. Lovejoy published *Essays in Critical Realism*. This group was also familiar with Reid's work. Rogers speaks of Reid in *A Student's History of Philosophy*. These "critical realists," like the new realists, were concerned with the apparent incompatibility between that theory of perception in which sensations play a role and the claim for immediate knowledge of external objects. Thus, in discussing Reid's attack on the theory of ideas as the friend of scepticism, Lovejoy poses the answer of the critical realists to this problem. "What the epistemological dualist is most certain about, in short, is that physical realism is incompatible with the hypothesis of the immediacy of knowledge."[101]

The critical realists, then, opt for a dualistic theory of perception. To avoid Berkeley's criticism, which noted that we cannot, on the basis of our sensations, *infer* the existence of external objects, the critical realists adopted various versions of Reid's doctrine of suggestion. Something about the character of our sensations "somehow" conveys information about the character of the physical objects. Whatever the way the sensations convey this information, it is not by inference. Moreover, there need be no exact resemblance between the sensation and the physical object signified. When the round object appears elliptical, the elliptical appearance conveys the information that a round object is before us. There is no elliptical object present. This is the amendment which Drake offers to Lovejoy's position.[102]

The problem remains, however, as to how we are to know that there is a round object or an elliptical object? What is there about the appearance that justifies accepting either of these answers? Santayana concludes that it is merely a matter of animal faith. "That such external things exist, that I exist myself . . . is a faith not founded on reason."[103] In short we lack evidence for our belief and, hence, it is unjustified.

C. J. Ducasse, who had also read Reid, follows a strategy that Reid and Kant both used; find out wherein two opposing views agree, and attack that point of agreement. Accordingly, Ducasse rejects the claim that if sensations convey information, then we can only have immediate knowledge of our sensations. We need give up neither Reid's claim that we have immediate knowledge of the external world nor his claim that our sensations convey information about the external world. In *Nature, Mind and Death* Ducasse, like Reid, claims we should not say that we perceive sensations or appearances. Sensing is a way of experiencing—a mental process in which there is no object distinct from the experience. "What this means is perhaps made clearest by saying that to sense blue is then to sense *bluely*, just as to dance the waltz is to dance 'waltzily' *(i.e.* in the manner called 'to waltz'). . . . Sensing . . . is a mental process."[104] Sensing is a state of the observer and, hence, is not an intermediate *object* between the subject and the real object.

R. M. Chisholm follows Ducasse's and Reid's analysis of the role of sensations. Chisholm, analyzes 'taking' as follows:

> "There is something that S *perceives* to be *f*" means: there is an *x* which is *f* and which appears in some way to S; S takes *x* to be *f*; and S has adequate evidence for the proposition that *x* is *f*.[105]

Like Reid, Chisholm contends that Hume is correct in maintaining that on the basis of our sensations, we cannot infer the existence of an external object. And, like Reid, Chisholm maintains that our perceptual beliefs are evident. Contrary to what Santayana and Hume say, belief in the existence of an external object is not merely a matter of animal faith. Rather, our perceptual beliefs are epistemically justified until proven otherwise.[106]

I have focused upon Reid's epistemological views in order to illustrate his influence upon American philosophy. However, Reid's influence has not been limited to his epistemological views. For example, Reid's agency theory of causation has influenced Chisholm's views on the "free will" controversy. Like Reid, Chisholm maintains that a man acts freely just in case his action is caused not by other events but by that man instead. This would be an instance of "agent causation". The question of liberty is not really a question of free will, that is, whether the will is free to choose; rather the question of liberty is whether the *man* is free to choose. Actions in which the agent is free to choose are not uncaused actions but are self or agent-caused actions.[107]

Reid's influence has not always been so obvious as that of

Kant and other great philosophers. He has nonetheless had a significant influence in his own country and in France, Britain, and the United States.[108] In spite of his influence on many philosophical figures and movements and in spite of his fresh approach to the philosophical disputes of his day, Thomas Reid has been one of the most neglected figures in the study of the modern period. Hopefully, the availability of Reid's most important works will lead to a reevaluation of his place in the history of philosophy.

RONALD E. BEANBLOSSOM

NOTES

1. *The Works of Thomas Reid,* ed. Wm. Hamilton, Sixth Ed. (Edinburgh, 1863), pp. 715–719. This discussion provides one basis for Reid's claim for the nonresemblance between sensations and qualities in objects, namely, whereas our sensations, e.g., of hot and cold, cannot be measured, the qualities of hot and cold can be measured. Cf. *Works,* p. 119.

2. *Works,* p. 88.

3. *Ibid.,* p. 283.

4. *Ibid.,* p. 106.

5. David Hume, *An Inquiry Concerning Human Understanding,* ed. Charles W. Hendel (Indianapolis, 1955), p. 161.

6. *Works,* p. 304.

7. *Ibid.,* p. 140.

8. John Locke, *An Essay Concerning Human Understanding,* ed. Alexander Campbell Fraser (New York, 1959), V. 2, p. 184.

9. *Works,* pp. 368–369. Cf. p. 302.

10. *Ibid.,* p. 157. Cf. pp. 236; 305.

11. *Ibid.,* pp. 127–128.

12. *Ibid.,* p. 119.

13. *Works,* p. 373.

14. *Ibid.,* p. 320.

15. *Ibid.,* p. 198.

16. *Ibid.,* p. 355. Cf. p. 344.

17. *Ibid.,* p. 106.

18. *Ibid.,* p. 278. Cf. pp. 355; 427.

19. *Ibid.,* p. 357.

20. *Ibid.,* p. 445.

21. *Ibid.,* pp. 130–131.

22. *Ibid.,* pp. 182–183.

23. *Ibid.,* p. 117.

24. *Ibid.*, p. 145.

25. *Ibid.*, p. 332. Cf. R. M. Chisholm, *Perceiving*, (Ithaca, 1957), pp. 77–78. Chisholm analyzes perceiving in terms of taking.

26. *Ibid.*, p. 332; cf. p. 146.

27. *Essays on the Intellectual Powers*, ed. A. D. Woozley (London, 1941), p. xxi. fn. Woozley claims Reid must distinguish between perceptual objects and material objects and that both are different from sensations. He apparently bases this claim on the fact that even in cases of misperception, there is a conception of and belief in the existence of an object. What Woozley apparently failed to consider is that, according to Reid, an agent can conceive of and believe in what does not exist.

28. *Works*, p. 146, italics mine.

29. *Ibid.*, p. 326.

30. *Ibid.*, p. 193.

31. *Ibid.*, p. 143.

32. *Ibid.*, p. 246: "The eye is not that which sees; it is only the organ by which we see." Cf. p. 257.

33. *Ibid*, p. 135. There does seem to be a fourth meaning of 'visible' and 'tangible', namely, they refer to the different *conceptions* we have of the object by means of sight and touch. Cf. p. 326.

34. *Ibid.*, p. 143.

35. *Ibid.*, p. 182, italics mine. Here Reid misuses 'see'.

36. *Ibid.*, p. 185, italics mine. Cf. p. 188.

37. *Ibid.*, p. 332, italics mine.

38. *Ibid.*, p. 194.

39. Immanuel Kant, *Prolegomena to Any Future Metaphysics*, ed. L. W. Beck, (New York, 1950), p. 7.

40. *The Complete Poetical Works of Robert Burns*, (Boston and New York, 1897), p. 143.

41. *Works*, p. 438. Note that Reid acknowledges that the masses are not an infallible guide in matters of common sense.

They may be misled by bias or even by lacking a clear understanding of what is at issue.

42. *Ibid.*, p. 127.
43. *Ibid.*; p. 425.
44. *Ibid.*, p. 102. Cf. pp. 110–111.
45. *Ibid.*, p. 108.
46. *Ibid.*, p. 440–441.
47. *Ibid.*, pp. 108, 438, 443, 640.
48. *Ibid.*, p. 437.
49. *Ibid.*, p. 439.
50. *Ibid.*, p. 183.
51. *Ibid.*, p. 713.
52. *Ibid.*, p. 129.
53. *Ibid.*, p. 100.
54. *Ibid.*, p. 413: "As a judge, after taking the proper evidence, passes sentence in a cause, and that sentence is called his judgment, so the mind, with regard to whatever is true or false, passes sentence, or determines according to the evidence that appears."
55. *Ibid.*, p. 328.
56. *Ibid.*, p. 515.
57. *Ibid.*, p. 524.
58. *Ibid.*, pp. 608–609. Cf. pp. 301; 525.
59. *Ibid.*, p. 599.
60. *Ibid.*, p. 601.
61. *Ibid.*, p. 602.
62. *Ibid.*, pp. 616f.
63. *Ibid.*, p. 620.
64. *Ibid.*, p. 617. Cf. Keith Lehrer, "Can We Know that We Have Free Will By Introspection?", *The Journal of Philosophy* (March, 1960), p. 145.
65. *Ibid.*, p. 618.
66. *Ibid.*, p. 623.
67. *Ibid.*, p. 623.
68. *Ibid.*, p. 457.

69. *Ibid.*, p. 449.

70. *Ibid.*, p. 675. Cf. pp. 590–591.

71. *Ibid.*, pp. 670–671. Cf. p. 590: "The truths immediately testified by our moral faculty, are the first principles of all moral reasoning from which all our knowledge of duty must be deduced."

72. David Hume, *A Treatise of Human Nature*, ed. L. A. Selby-Bigge (Oxford, 1967), p. 470.

73. *Ibid.*, p. 458.

74. *Works*, p. 633.

75. *Ibid.*, p. 672.

76. *Ibid.*, p. 673. There is reason to regard Hume's claim as an empirical one. In addition to claiming in the title of the *Treatise* that he is using the experimental method, Hume also claims that you will never discover vice in an action. "You never can find it, till you turn your reflexion into your own breast, and find a sentiment of disapprobation, which arises in you, towards this action." (*Treatise*, pp. 468–469).

77. One might argue in defense of Hume that the two expressions do not mean the same thing. Rather, the first expression is meaningless. Reid rejects this alternative view on the grounds that we are able to understand these expressions when they are used in ordinary discourse; thus, they are not meaningless. Cf. p. 673.

78. *Ibid.*, p. 673.

79. *Ibid.*, p. 673. It should be pointed out that an agent need not be saying the speaker is lying. Rather, the agent may be accusing the speaker of making a verbal mistake in the way that he labels his feelings. However, Reid's point would still be that we characterize this contradictory expression differently than we characterize the contradictory of the first expression.

80. Thomas Brown, *Lectures on the Philosophy of the Human Mind*, 14th ed. (Edinburgh, 1844), p. 174. Quoted by S. A. Grave, *The Scottish Philosophy of Common Sense*, (Oxford, 1960), p. 20. Reid might agree that Hume used 'ideas' in the way that

he (Reid) uses 'sensations'. "It is often impossible, from the tenor of his [Hume's] discourse, to know whether, by those ideas, he means the operations of the mind, or the objects about which they are employed. And, indeed, according to his system, there is no distinction between the one and the other." Reid, *Works*, p. 224.

81. George Davie, *The Democratic Intellect*, 2nd ed. (Edinburgh, 1964), pp. 275–285.

82. Joseph Priestley, *An Examination of Dr. Reid's Inquiry*, 2nd ed. (London, 1775), p. 30.

83. *Ibid.*, p. 64.

84. Victor Cousin, *Cours de l'historie de la philosophie Moderne*, Nouvelle ed. (Paris, 1846–47), p. 581. Quoted by S. A. Grave, *The Scottish Philosophy of Common Sense*, (Oxford, 1960), p. 3.

85. H. H. Price, *Perception*, (London, 1933), p. 203.

86. G. E. Moore, *Philosophical Studies*, (New Jersey, 1968), p. 57.

87. *Ibid.*, pp. 19–20; Cf. Reid, *Works*, pp. 113; 120.

88. *Ibid.*, pp. 28–29. Cf. Reid, *Works*, p. 285: The theory of ideas ". . . seems to take away all the evidence we have of other intelligent beings like ourselves. What I call a father, a brother, or a friend, is only a parcel of ideas in my own mind."

89. *Ibid.*, pp. 216–217. Cf. Reid, *Works*, pp. 373: ". . . there appears to me no contradiction in his conceiving an object that neither does nor ever did exist."

90. *Ibid.*, p. 228.

91. Reid, *Works*, p. 101.

92. *Ibid.*, p. 104.

93. *Ibid.*, p. 482.

94. G. E. Moore, *Philosophical Papers*, (New York, 1962), p. 222.

95. *Ibid.*, pp. 43–44. Cf. Reid, *Works*, p. 107: "I know it is said, that, in a delirium, or in dreaming, men are apt to mistake one for the other [i.e. sensation, memory, and imagination]. But does it follow from this, that men who are neither dream-

ing nor in a delirium cannot distinguish them? But how does a man know that he is not in a delirium? I cannot tell: neither can I tell how a man knows that he exists."

96. *Ibid.*, p. 148.

97. *Ibid.*, p. 36.

98. Herbert W. Schneider, *A History of American Philosophy*, (New York, 1946), p. 233.

99. In what follows I am indebted to Keith Lehrer's article, "Scottish influences on Contemporary American Philosophy," *The Philosophical Journal*, (1968), pp. 34–42.

100. E. B. Holt and others, *The New Realism*, (New York, 1912), p. 2.

101. Arthur O. Lovejoy, *The Revolt Against Dualism*, (La Salle, Illinois, 1929), p. 67.

102. Durant Drake and others, *Essays in Critical Realism* (London, 1920), pp. 29–30.

103. George Santayana, *Scepticism and Animal Faith*, (U.S.A., 1955), p. 106.

104. C. J. Ducasse, *Nature, Mind, and Death* (La Salle, Illinois, 1951), p. 259.

105. R. M. Chisholm, *Perceiving* (Ithaca, New York, 1957), p. 3.

106. *Ibid.*, p. 77f.

107. R. M. Chisholm, "Human Freedom and the Self," in *Reason and Responsibility*, ed. Joel Feinberg, 2nd ed. (Encino, California, 1971), pp. 362; 364.

108. Reid's influence in America is not limited to the movements I have mentioned. Pragmatism also was influenced by him. C. S. Pierce, for example, admired Reid. Like Reid, Pierce held that reasoning must begin with common sense beliefs. Cf. John Passmore, *A Hundred Years of Philosophy* (London, 1957), p. 261.

BIBLIOGRAPHY

*Barker, Stephen F. and Tom L. Beauchamp, (eds.). *Thomas Reid: Critical Interpretations. Philosophical Monographs,* 3 (1976).

Beanblossom, Ronald E. "In Defense of Thomas Reid's Use of 'Suggestion'." *Grazer Philosophische Studien,* 1 (1975), pp. 19–24.

Beanblossom, Ronald E. "Russell's Indebtedness to Reid." *The Monist,* 6 (April 1978), pp. 192–204.

Bozeman, Theodore D. *Protestants in an Age of Science: The Baconian Ideal and Antebellum Religious Thought.* Chapel Hill: University of North Carolina Press, 1977.

Brody, Baruch. "Reid and Hamilton on Perception." *Monist,* 55 (1971), pp. 423–441.

Daniels, Norman. "Thomas Reid's Discovery of a Non-Euclidean Geometry." *Philosophy of Science,* 39 (1972), pp. 219–234.

Duggan, Timothy. "Thomas Reid's Theory of Sensation." *Philosophical Review,* 69 (1960), pp. 90–100.

Ellos, William J. *Thomas Reid's Newtonian Realism.* Lanham, Maryland: University Press of America, 1981.

Flower, Elizabeth and Murphey, Murray G. *A History of Philosophy in America.* 2 vols. Indianapolis: Hackett Publishing Company, Inc., 1977.

Grave, S. A. *The Scottish Philosophy of Common Sense.* Oxford: Oxford University Press, 1960.

Jones, O. M. *Empiricism and Intuitionism in Reid's Common Sense Philosophy.* Princeton: Princeton University Press, 1927.

Kivy, Peter. "Lectures on the Fine Arts." *Journal of History of Ideas,* 31 (1970), pp. 17–32.

*These volumes contain extensive bibliographies in addition to their articles about Reid.

Kuklick, Bruce. *The Rise of American Philosophy: Cambridge, Massachusetts, 1860–1930*. New Haven: Yale University Press, 1977.

Laudan, L. L. "Thomas Reid and the Newtonian Turn of British Methodological Thought." *The Methodological Heritage of Newton.* ed. Robert E. Butts and John W. Davis. Toronto: University of Toronto Press, 1970, pp. 103–131.

Lehrer, Keith. "Can We Know that We Have Free Will by Introspection?" *The Journal of Philosophy*, 57 (1960), pp. 145–157.

Lehrer, Keith. "Scottish Influences on Contemporary American Philosophy." *The Philosophical Journal*, 5 (1968), pp. 34–42.

Madden, Edward H. "The Metaphilosophy of Commonsense." *American Philosophical Quarterly*, 20 (1983), pp. 23–36.

Marcil-LaCoste, Louise. *Claude Buffier and Thomas Reid: Two Common-Sense Philosophers*. Kingston, Ontario: McGill-Queens University Press, 1982.

Meyer, D. H. *The Instructed Conscience: The Shaping of the American National Ethic*. Philadelphia: University of Pennsylvania Press, 1972.

The Philosophy of Thomas Reid. The Monist, 61, (April 1978).

Segerstedt, T. T. *The Problem of Knowledge in Scottish Philosophy.* Lunds, Sweden: Lund's University Press, 1935.

Shoemaker, Sydney. *Self-Knowledge and Self-Identity*. Ithaca: Cornell University Press, 1972.

Sidgwick, Henry, "The Philosophy of Common Sense." *Mind*, 4 (1895), pp. 145–158.

Sloan, Douglas. *Scottish Enlightenment and the American College Ideal.* New York: Teachers College Press, Columbia University, 1971.

Strasser, Johano. "Lumen Naturale-Sens Commun-Common Sense." *Die Zeitschrift Fuer Philosophisthe Forshung*, 23 (1969), pp. 177–198.

Taylor, Richard and Timothy Duggan. "On Seeing Double." *Philosophical Quarterly*, 8 (1958), pp. 171–174.

Winch, P. G. "The Notion of 'Suggestion' in Thomas Reid's Theory of Perception." *Philosophical Quarterly*, 3 (1953), pp. 327–341.

Recent Books on Thomas Reid:
  Thomas Reid and 'the Way of Ideas' by Roger D. Gallie (Kluwer, 1989).
  The Philosophy of Thomas Reid, a collection of new essays edited by Melvin Dalzamo and Eric Matthews (Kluwer, 1989).
  Thomas Reid, by Keith Lehrer (Routledge, 1989).

NOTE ON THE TEXT

Hamilton's sixth edition is generally regarded as the definitive edition of Reid's works. In keeping with this judgment the present text is reproduced from *The Works of Thomas Reid*, ed. William Hamilton, 6th ed. Edinburgh: Maclachlan and Stewart; London: Longman, Green, Longman, Roberts, and Green, 1863. Hamilton's editions use old British spellings that have been retained in the text, but obsolete spellings within quotes have been updated in the introduction to this volume.

One of the more controversial aspects of the present text is the deletion of many of Hamilton's footnotes. It is our judgment that while Hamilton's critical and expository footnotes may be of historical interest, they are generally based upon a misinterpretation of Reid and are primarily a vehicle for presenting Hamilton's views. The present edition is an attempt to "let Reid speak for himself." Some of Hamilton's footnotes have been retained and these are identified by "H".

R.E.B.

For the second printing of this volume the bibliography has been updated. However, the text is essentially unchanged.

R.E.B.
1983

AN INQUIRY INTO
THE HUMAN MIND
ON THE PRINCIPLES
OF COMMON SENSE

CHAPTER 1 / INTRODUCTION.

Section III: The Present State of This Part of Philosophy—of
Des Cartes, Malebranche, and Locke

That our philosophy concerning the mind and its faculties
is but in a very low state, may be reasonably conjectured even
by those who never have narrowly examined it. Are there any
principles, with regard to the mind, settled with that perspicuity and evidence which attends the principles of mechanics, astronomy, and optics? These are really sciences built
upon laws of nature which universally obtain. What is discovered in them is no longer matter of dispute: future ages may
add to it; but, till the course of nature be changed, what is
already established can never be overturned. But when we
turn our attention inward, and consider the phaenomena of
human thoughts, opinions, and perceptions, and endeavour
to trace them to the general laws and the first principles of our
constitution, we are immediately involved in darkness and per-
plexity; and, if common sense, or the principles of education,
happen not to be stubborn, it is odds but we end in absolute
scepticism.

Des Cartes, finding nothing established in this part of
philosophy, in order to lay the foundation of it deep, resolved
not to believe his own existence till he should be able to give
a good reason for it. He was, perhaps, the first that took up
such a resolution; but, if he could indeed have effected his
purpose, and really become diffident of his existence, his case

3

would have been deplorable, and without any remedy from reason or philosophy. A man that disbelieves his own existence, is surely as unfit to be reasoned with as a man that believes he is made of glass. There may be disorders in the human frame that may produce such extravagancies, but they will never be cured by reasoning. Des Cartes, indeed, would make us believe that he got out of this delirium by this logical argument, *Cogito, ergo sum;* but it is evident he was in his senses all the time, and never seriously doubted of his existence; for he takes it for granted in this argument, and proves nothing at all. I am thinking, says he—therefore, I am. And is it not as good reasoning to say, I am sleeping—therefore, I am? or, I am doing nothing—therefore, I am? If a body moves, it must exist, no doubt; but, if it is at rest, it must exist likewise.

Perhaps Des Cartes meant not to assume his own existence in this enthymeme, but the existence of thought; and to infer from that the existence of a mind, or subject of thought. But why did he not prove the existence of his thought? Consciousness, it may be said, vouches that. But who is voucher for consciousness? Can any man prove that his consciousness may not deceive him? No man can; nor can we give a better reason for trusting to it, than that every man, while his mind is sound, is determined, by the constitution of his nature, to give implicit belief to it, and to laugh at or pity the man who doubts its testimony. And is not every man, in his wits, as much determined to take his existence upon trust as his consciousness?

The other proposition assumed in this argument, That thought cannot be without a mind or subject, is liable to the same objection: not that it wants evidence, but that its evidence is no clearer, nor more immediate, than that of the proposition to be proved by it. And, taking all these propositions together—I think; I am conscious; Everything that thinks, exists; I exist—would not every sober man form the same opinion of the man who seriously doubted any one of them? And if he was his friend, would he not hope for his cure from physic and good regimen, rather than from metaphysic and logic?

But supposing it proved, that my thought and my consciousness must have a subject, and consequently that I exist, how do I know that all that train and succession of thoughts which I remember belong to one subject, and that the I of this moment is the very individual I of yesterday and of times past?

Des Cartes did not think proper to start this doubt; but Locke has done it; and, in order to resolve it, gravely determines that personal identity consists in consciousness—that is, if you are conscious that you did such a thing a twelvemonth ago, this consciousness makes you to be the very person that did it. Now, consciousness of what is past can signify nothing else but the remembrance that I did it; so that Locke's principle must be, That identity consists in remembrance; and, consequently, a man must lose his personal identity with regard to everything he forgets.

Nor are these the only instances whereby our philosophy concerning the mind appears to be very fruitful in creating doubts, but very unhappy in resolving them.

Des Cartes, Malebranche, and Locke, have all employed their genius and skill to prove the existence of a material world; and with very bad success. Poor untaught mortals believe undoubtedly that there is a sun, moon, and stars; an earth, which we inhabit; country, friends, and relations, which we enjoy; land, houses, and moveables, which we possess. But philosophers, pitying the credulity of the vulgar, resolve to have no faith but what is founded upon reason.[1] They apply to philosophy to furnish them with reasons for the belief of those things which all mankind have believed, without being able to give any reason for it. And surely one would expect, that, in matters of such importance, the proof would not be difficult; but it is the most difficult thing in the world. For these three great men, with the best good will, have not been able, from all the treasures of philosophy, to draw one argument that is fit to convince a man that can reason, of the existence of any one thing without him. Admired Philosophy! daughter of light! parent of wisdom and knowledge! if thou art she, surely thou hast not yet arisen upon the human mind, nor blessed us with more of thy rays than are sufficient to shed a darkness visible upon the human faculties, and to disturb that repose and security which happier mortals enjoy, who never approached thine altar, nor felt thine influence! But if, indeed, thou hast not power to dispel those clouds and phantoms which thou hast discovered or created, withdraw this penurious and malignant ray; I despise Philosophy, and renounce its guidance—let my soul dwell with Common Sense.

Section IV: Apology for Those Philosophers

But, instead of despising the dawn of light, we ought rather to hope for its increase: instead of blaming the philosophers I have mentioned for the defects and blemishes of their system, we ought rather to honour their memories, as the first discoverers of a region in philosophy formerly unknown; and, however lame and imperfect the system may be, they have opened the way to future discoveries, and are justly entitled to a great share in the merit of them. They have removed an infinite deal of dust and rubbish, collected in the ages of scholastic sophistry, which had obstructed the way. They have put us in the right road—that of experience and accurate reflection. They have taught us to avoid the snares of ambiguous and ill-defined words, and have spoken and thought upon this subject with a distinctness and perspicuity formerly unknown. They have made many openings that may lead to the discovery of truths which they did not reach, or to the detection of errors in which they were involuntarily entangled.

It may be observed, that the defects and blemishes in the received philosophy concerning the mind, which have most exposed it to the contempt and ridicule of sensible men, have chiefly been owing to this—that the votaries of this Philosophy, from a natural prejudice in her favour, have endeavoured to extend her jurisdiction beyond its just limits, and to call to her bar the dictates of Common Sense. But these decline this jurisdiction; they disdain the trial of reasoning, and disown its authority; they neither claim its aid, nor dread its attacks.

In this unequal contest betwixt Common Sense and Philosophy, the latter will always come off both with dishonour and loss; nor can she ever thrive till this rivalship is dropt, these encroachments given up, and a cordial friendship restored: for, in reality, Common Sense holds nothing of Philosophy, nor needs her aid. But, on the other hand, Philosophy (if I may be permitted to change the metaphor) has no other root but the principles of Common Sense; it grows out of them, and draws its nourishment from them. Severed from this root, its honours wither, its sap is dried up, it dies and rots.

The philosophers of the last age, whom I have mentioned, did not attend to the preserving this union and subordination so carefully as the honour and interest of philosophy required: but those of the present have waged open war with Common Sense, and hope to make a complete conquest of it by the subtilties of Philosophy—an attempt no less audacious and vain than that of the giants to dethrone almighty Jove.

Section V: Of Bishop Berkeley—The "Treatise of Human Nature"—And of Scepticism

The present age, I apprehend, has not produced two more acute or more practised in this part of philosophy, than the Bishop of Cloyne, and the author of the "Treatise of Human Nature." The first was no friend to scepticism, but had that warm concern for religious and moral principles which became his order: yet the result of his inquiry was a serious conviction that there is no such thing as a material world—nothing in nature but spirits and ideas; and that the belief of material substances, and of abstract ideas, are the chief causes of all our errors in philosophy, and of all infidelity and heresy in religion. His arguments are founded upon the principles which were formerly laid down by Des Cartes, Malebranche, and Locke, and which have been very generally received.

And the opinion of the ablest judges seems to be, that they neither have been, nor can be confuted; and that he hath proved by unanswerable arguments what no man in his senses can believe.

The second proceeds upon the same principles, but carries them to their full length; and, as the Bishop undid the whole material world, this author, upon the same grounds, undoes the world of spirits, and leaves nothing in nature but ideas and impressions, without any subject on which they may be impressed.

It seems to be a peculiar strain of humour in this author, to set out in his introduction by promising, with a grave face, no less than a complete system of the sciences, upon a foundation entirely new—to wit, that of human nature—when the intention of the whole work is to shew, that there is neither human nature nor science in the world. It may perhaps be unreasonable to complain of this conduct in an author who neither believes his own existence nor that of his reader; and therefore could not mean to disappoint him, or to laugh at his credulity. Yet I cannot imagine that the author of the "Treatise of Human Nature" is so sceptical as to plead this apology. He believed, against his principles, that he should be read, and that he should retain his personal identity, till he reaped the honour and reputation justly due to his metaphysical *acumen*. Indeed, he ingeniously acknowledges, that it was only in solitude and retirement that he could yield any assent to his own philosophy; society, like day-light, dispelled the darkness and fogs of scepticism, and made him yield to the dominion of common sense. Nor did I ever hear him charged with doing anything, even in solitude, that argued such a degree of scepticism as his principles maintain. Surely if his friends apprehended this, they would have the charity never to leave him alone.

Pyrrho the Elean, the father of this philosophy, seems to have carried it to greater perfection than any of his successors: for, if we may believe Antigonus the Carystian, quoted by Diogenes Laertius, his life corresponded to his doctrine. And, therefore, if a cart run against him, or a dog attacked him, or if he came upon a precipice, he would not stir a foot to avoid the danger, giving no credit to his senses. But his attendants, who, happily for him, were not so great sceptics, took care to keep him out of harm's way; so that he lived till he was ninety years of age. Nor is it to be doubted but this author's friends would have been equally careful to keep him from harm, if ever his principles had taken too strong a hold of him.

It is probable the "Treatise of Human Nature" was not written in company; yet it contains manifest indications that the author every now and then relapsed into the faith of the vulgar, and could hardly, for half a dozen pages, keep up the sceptical character.

In like manner, the great Pyrrho himself forgot his principles on some occasions; and is said once to have been in such a passion with his cook, who probably had not roasted his dinner to his mind, that with the spit in his hand, and the meat upon it, he pursued him even into the marketplace.

It is a bold philosophy that rejects, without ceremony, principles which irresistibly govern the belief and the conduct of all mankind in the common concerns of life; and to which the philosopher himself must yield, after he imagines he hath confuted them. Such principles are older, and of more authority, than Philosophy: she rests upon them as her basis, not they upon her. If she could overturn them, she must be buried in their ruins; but all the engines of philosophical subtilty are too weak for this purpose; and the attempt is no less ridiculous than if a mechanic should contrive an *axis in peritrochio* to remove the earth out of its place; or if a mathematician should pretend to demonstrate that things equal to the same thing are not equal to one another.

Zeno endeavoured to demonstrate the impossibility of motion; Hobbes, that there was no difference between right and wrong; and this author, that no credit is to be given to our senses, to our memory, or even to demonstration. Such philosophy is justly ridiculous, even to those who cannot detect the fallacy of it. It can have no other tendency, than to shew the acuteness of the sophist, at the expense of disgracing reason and human nature, and making mankind Yahoos.

Section VII: The System of All These Authors is The Same, and Leads to Scepticism

But what if these profound disquisitions into the first principles of human nature, do naturally and necessarily plunge a man into this abyss of scepticism? May we not reasonably judge so from what hath happened? Des Cartes no sooner began to dig in this mine, than scepticism was ready to break in upon him. He did what he could to shut it out. Malebranche and Locke, who dug deeper, found the difficulty of keeping out this enemy still to increase; but they laboured honestly in the design. Then Berkeley, who carried on the work, despairing of securing all, bethought himself of an expedient:—By giving up the material world, which he thought might be spared without loss, and even with advantage, he hoped, by an impregnable partition, to secure the world of spirits. But, alas! the "Treatisé of Human Nature" wantonly sapped the foundation of this partition, and drowned all in one universal deluge.

These facts, which are undeniable, do, indeed, give reason to apprehend that Des Cartes' system of the human understanding, which I shall beg leave to call *the ideal system,* and which, with some improvements made by later writers, is now generally received, hath some original defect; that this scepticism is inlaid in it, and reared along with it; and, therefore, that we must lay it open to the foundation, and examine the materials, before we can expect to raise any solid and useful fabric of knowledge on this subject.

Section VIII: We Ought Not to Despair of a Better

But is this to be despaired of, because Des Cartes and his followers have failed? By no means. This pusillanimity would be injurious to ourselves and injurious to truth. Useful discoveries are sometimes indeed the effect of superior genius, but more frequently they are the birth of time and of accidents. A traveller of good judgment may mistake his way, and be unawares led into a wrong track; and, while the road is fair before him, he may go on without suspicion and be followed by others; but, when it ends in a coal-pit, it requires no great judgment to know that he hath gone wrong, nor perhaps to find out what misled him.

In the meantime, the unprosperous state of this part of philosophy hath produced an effect, somewhat discouraging indeed to any attempt of this nature, but an effect which might be expected, and which time only and better success can remedy. Sensible men, who never will be sceptics in matters of common life, are apt to treat with sovereign contempt everything that hath been said, or is to be said, upon this subject. It is metaphysic, say they: who minds it? Let scholastic sophisters entangle themselves in their own cobwebs; I am resolved to take my own existence, and the existence of other things, upon trust; and to believe that snow is cold, and honey sweet, whatever they may say to the contrary. He must either be a fool, or want to make a fool of me, that would reason me out of my reason and senses.

I confess I know not what a sceptic can answer to this, nor by what good argument he can plead even for a hearing; for either his reasoning is sophistry, and so deserves contempt; or there is no truth in human faculties—and then why should we reason?

If, therefore, a man find himself intangled in these metaphysical toils, and can find no other way to escape, let him bravely cut the knot which he cannot loose, curse metaphysic, and dissuade every man from meddling with it; for, if I have been led into bogs and quagmires by following an *ignis fatuus*, what can I do better than to warn others to beware of it? If philosophy contradicts herself, befools her votaries, and deprives them of every object worthy to be pursued or enjoyed, let her be sent back to the infernal regions from which she must have had her original.

But is it absolutely certain that this fair lady is of the party? Is it not possible she may have been misrepresented? Have not men of genius in former ages often made their own dreams to pass for her oracles? Ought she then to be condemned without any further hearing? This would be unreasonable. I have found her in all other matters an agreeable companion, a faithful counsellor, a friend to common sense, and to the happiness of mankind. This justly entitles her to my correspondence and confidence, till I find infallible proofs of her infidelity.

CHAPTER 2 / OF SMELLING.

Section II: The Sensation Considered Abstractly

. . . let us now attend carefully to what the mind is conscious of when we smell a rose or a lily; and, since our language affords no other name for this sensation, we shall call it a *smell* or *odour,* carefully excluding from the meaning of those names everything but the sensation itself, at least till we have examined it.

Suppose a person who never had this sense before, to receive it all at once, and to smell a rose—can he perceive any similitude or agreement between the smell and the rose? or indeed between it and any other object whatsoever? Certainly he cannot. He finds himself affected in a new way, he knows not why or from what cause. Like a man that feels some pain or pleasure formerly unknown to him, he is conscious that he is not the cause of it himself, but cannot, from the nature of the thing, determine whether it is caused by body or spirit, by something near, or by something at a distance. It has no similitude to anything else, so as to admit of a comparison; and, therefore, he can conclude nothing from it, unless, perhaps, that there must be some unknown cause of it.

It is evidently ridiculous to ascribe to it figure, colour, extension, or any other quality of bodies. He cannot give it a place, any more than he can give a place to melancholy or joy; nor can he conceive it to have any existence, but when it is smelled. So that it appears to be a simple and original affection or feeling of the mind, altogether inexplicable and unaccountable. It is, indeed, impossible that it can be in any body: it is a sensation, and a sensation can only be in a sentient thing. . . .

Section III: Sensation and Remembrance, Natural Principles of Belief

So far we have considered this sensation abstractly. Let us next compare it with other things to which it bears some relation. And first I shall compare this sensation with the remembrance, and the imagination of it.

I can think of the smell of a rose when I do not smell it; and it is possible that when I think of it, there is neither rose nor smell anywhere existing. But when I smell it, I am necessarily determined to believe that the sensation really exists. This is common to all sensations, that, as they cannot exist but in being perceived, so they cannot be perceived but they must exist. I could as easily doubt of my own existence, as of the existence of my sensations. Even those profound philosophers who have endeavoured to disprove their own existence, have yet left their sensations to stand upon their own bottom, stript of a subject, rather than call in question the reality of their existence.

Here, then, a sensation, a smell for instance, may be presented to the mind three different ways: it may be smelled, it may be remembered, it may be imagined or thought of. In the first case, it is necessarily accompanied with a belief of its present existence; in the second, it is necessarily accompanied with a belief of its past existence; and in the last, it is not accompanied with belief at all, but is what the logicians call *a simple apprehension.*

Why sensation should compel our belief of the present existence of the thing, memory a belief of its past existence, and imagination no belief at all, I believe no philosopher can give a shadow of reason, but that such is the nature of these operations: they are all simple and original, and therefore inexplicable acts of the mind.

Suppose that once, and only once, I smelled a tuberose in a certain room, where it grew in a pot, and gave a very grateful perfume. Next day I relate what I saw and smelled. When I attend as carefully as I can to what passes in my mind in this case, it appears evident that the very thing I saw yesterday, and the fragrance I smelled, are now the immediate objects of my mind, when I remember it. Further, I can imagine this pot and flower transported to the room where I now sit, and yielding the same perfume. Here likewise it appears, that the individual thing which I saw and smelled, is the object of my imagination.

Philosophers indeed tell me, that the immediate object of my memory and imagination in this case, is not the past sensation, but an idea of it, an image, phantasm, or species, of the odour I smelled: that this idea now exists in my mind, or in my sensorium; and the mind, contemplating this present idea, finds it a representation of what is past, or of what may exist; and accordingly calls it memory, or imagination. This is the doctrine of the ideal philosophy; which we shall not now examine, that we may not interrupt the thread of the present investigation. Upon the strictest attention, memory appears to me to have things that are past, and not present ideas, for its object. We shall afterwards examine this system of ideas, and endeavour to make it appear, that no solid proof has ever been advanced of the existence of ideas; that they are a mere fiction and hypothesis, contrived to solve the phaenomena of the human understanding; that they do not at all answer this end; and that this hypothesis of ideas or images of things in the mind, or in the sensorium, is the parent of those many paradoxes so shocking to common sense, and of that scepticism which disgrace our philosophy of the mind, and have brought upon it the ridicule and contempt of sensible men.

In the meantime, I beg leave to think, with the vulgar, that, when I remember the smell of the tuberose, that very sensation which I had yesterday, and which has now no more any existence, is the immediate object of my memory; and when I imagine it present, the sensation itself, and not any idea of it, is the object of my imagination. But, though the object of my sensation, memory, and imagination, be in this case the same, yet these acts or operations of the mind are as different, and as easily distinguishable, as smell, taste, and sound. I am conscious of a difference in kind between sensation and memory, and between both and imagination. I find this also, that the sensation compels my belief of the present existence of the smell, and memory my belief of its past existence. There is a smell, is the immediate testimony of sense; there was a smell, is the immediate testimony of memory. If you ask me, why I believe that the smell exists, I can give no other reason, nor shall ever be able to give any other, than that I smell it. If you ask, why I believe that it existed yesterday, I can give no other reason but that I remember it.

Sensation and memory, therefore, are simple, original, and

perfectly distinct operations of the mind, and both of them are original principles of belief. Imagination is distinct from both, but is no principle of belief. Sensation implies the present existence of its object, memory its past existence, but imagination views its object naked, and without any belief of its existence or nonexistence, and is therefore what the schools call *Simple Apprehension.* [2]

Section IV: Judgment and Belief in Some Cases Precede Simple Apprehension

But here, again, the ideal system comes in our way: it teaches us that the first operation of the mind about its ideas, is simple apprehension—that is, the bare conception of a thing without any belief about it: and that, after we have got simple apprehensions, by comparing them together, we perceive agreements or disagreements between them; and that this perception of the agreement or disagreement of ideas, is all that we call belief, judgment, or knowledge. Now, this appears to me to be all fiction, without any foundation in nature; for it is acknowledged by all, that sensation must go before memory and imagination; and hence it necessarily follows, that apprehension, accompanied with belief and knowledge, must go before simple apprehension, at least in the matters we are now speaking of. So that here, instead of saying that the belief or knowledge is got by putting together and comparing the simple apprehensions, we ought rather to say that the simple apprehension is performed by resolving and analysing a natural and original judgment. And it is with the operations of the mind, in this case, as with natural bodies, which are, indeed, compounded of simple principles or elements. Nature does not exhibit these elements separate, to be compounded by us; she exhibits them mixed and compounded in concrete bodies, and it is only by art and chemical analysis that they can be separated.

Section V: Two Theories of the Nature of Belief Refuted—
Conclusions From What Hath Been Said

But what is this belief or knowledge which accompanies
sensation and memory? Every man knows what it is, but no
man can define it. Does any man pretend to define sensation,
or to define consciousness? It is happy, indeed, that no man
does. And if no philosopher had endeavoured to define and
explain belief, some paradoxes in philosophy, more incredible
than ever were brought forth by the most abject superstition
or the most frantic enthusiasm, had never seen the light. Of
this kind surely is that modern discovery of the ideal philosophy, that sensation, memory, belief, and imagination, when
they have the same object, are only different degrees of
strength and vivacity in the idea.[3] Suppose the idea to be that
of a future state after death: one man believes it firmly—this
means no more than that he hath a strong and lively idea of
it; another neither believes nor disbelieves—that is, he has a
weak and faint idea. Suppose, now, a third person believes
firmly that there is no such thing, I am at a loss to know
whether his idea be faint or lively: if it is faint, then there may
be a firm belief where the idea is faint; if the idea is lively, then
the belief of a future state and the belief of no future state must
be one and the same. The same arguments that are used to
prove that belief implies only a stronger idea of the object than
simple apprehension, might as well be used to prove that love
implies only a stronger idea of the object than indifference.
And then what shall we say of hatred, which must upon this
hypothesis be a degree of love, or a degree of indifference? If
it should be said, that in love there is something more than an
idea—to wit, an affection of the mind—may it not be said with
equal reason, that in belief there is something more than an
idea—to wit, an assent or persuasion of the mind?

But perhaps it may be thought as ridiculous to argue against
this strange opinion, as to maintain it. Indeed, if a man should

maintain that a circle, a square, and a triangle differ only in magnitude, and not in figure, I believe he would find nobody disposed either to believe him or to argue against him; and yet I do not think it less shocking to common sense, to maintain that sensation, memory, and imagination differ only in degree, and not in kind. I know it is said, that, in a delirium, or in dreaming, men are apt to mistake one for the other. But does it follow from this, that men who are neither dreaming nor in a delirium cannot distinguish them? But how does a man know that he is not in a delirium? I cannot tell: neither can I tell how a man knows that he exists. But, if any man seriously doubts whether he is in a delirium, I think it highly probable that he is, and that it is time to seek for a cure, which I am persuaded he will not find in the whole system of logic.

I conclude, then, that the belief which accompanies sensation and memory, is a simple act of the mind, which cannot be defined. It is, in this respect, like seeing and hearing, which can never be so defined as to be understood by those who have not these faculties; and to such as have them, no definition can make these operations more clear than they are already. In like manner, every man that has any belief—and he must be a curiosity that has none—knows perfectly what belief is, but can never define or explain it. I conclude, also, that sensation, memory, and imagination, even where they have the same object, are operations of a quite different nature, and perfectly distinguishable by those who are sound and sober. A man that is in danger of confounding them, is indeed to be pitied; but whatever relief he may find from another art, he can find none from logic or metaphysic. I conclude further, that it is no less a part of the human constitution, to believe the present existence of our sensations, and to believe the past existence of what we remember, than it is to believe that twice two make four. The evidence of sense, the evidence of memory, and the evidence of the necessary relations of things, are all distinct and original kinds of evidence, equally grounded on our constitution: none of them depends upon, or can be resolved into another. To reason against any of these kinds of evidence, is absurd; nay, to reason for them is absurd. They are first principles; and such fall not within the province of reason,[4] but of common sense.

Section VI: Apology For Metaphysical Absurdities—
Sensation Without a Sentient, a Consequence of the
Theory of Ideas—Consequences of This Strange Opinion

Having considered the relation which the sensation of smelling bears to the remembrance and imagination of it, I proceed to consider what relation it bears to a mind, or sentient principle. It is certain, no man can conceive or believe smelling to exist of itself, without a mind, or something that has the power of smelling, of which it is called a sensation, an operation, or feeling. Yet, if any man should demand a proof, that sensation cannot be without a mind or sentient being, I confess that I can give none; and that to pretend to prove it, seems to me almost as absurd as to deny it.

This might have been said without any apology before the "Treatise of Human Nature" appeared in the world. For till that time, no man, as far as I know, ever thought either of calling in question that principle, or of giving a reason for his belief of it. Whether thinking beings were of an ethereal or igneous nature, whether material or immaterial, was variously disputed; but that thinking is an operation of some kind of being or other, was always taken for granted, as a principle that could not possibly admit of doubt.

However, since the author above mentioned, who is undoubtedly one of the most acute metaphysicians that this or any age hath produced, hath treated it as a vulgar prejudice, and maintained that the mind is only a succession of ideas and impressions without any subject; his opinion, however contrary to the common apprehensions of mankind, deserves respect. I beg therefore, once for all, that no offence may be taken at charging this or other metaphysical notions with absurdity, or with being contrary to the common sense of mankind. No disparagement is meant to the understandings of the authors or maintainers of such opinions. Indeed, they commonly proceed, not from defect of understanding, but from an excess of refinement the reasoning that leads to them often gives new light to the subject, and shews real genius and deep penetration in the author; and the premises do more than atone for the conclusion.

If there are certain principles, as I think there are, which the constitution of our nature leads us to believe, and which we are under a necessity to take for granted in the common concerns of life, without being able to give a reason for them—these are what we call the principles of common sense; and what is manifestly contrary to them, is what we call absurd.

Indeed, if it is true, and to be received as a principle of philosophy, that sensation and thought may be without a thinking being, it must be acknowledged to be the most wonderful discovery that this or any other age hath produced. The received doctrine of ideas is the principle from which it is deduced, and of which indeed it seems to be a just and natural consequence. And it is probable, that it would not have been so late a discovery, but that it is so shocking and repugnant to the common apprehensions of mankind, that it required an uncommon degree of philosophical intrepidity to usher it into the world. It is a fundamental principle of the ideal system, that every object of thought must be an impression or an idea —that is, a faint copy of some preceding impression. This is a principle so commonly received, that the author above mentioned, although his whole system is built upon it, never offers the least proof of it. It is upon this principle, as a fixed point, that he erects his metaphysical engines, to overturn heaven and earth, body and spirit. And, indeed, in my apprehension, it is altogether sufficient for the purpose. For, if impressions and ideas are the only objects of thought, then heaven and earth, and body and spirit, and everything you please, must signify only impressions and ideas, or they must be words without any meaning. It seems, therefore, that this notion, however strange, is closely connected with the received doctrine of ideas, and we must either admit the conclusion, or call in question the premises. . . .

However this may be, it is certainly a most amazing discovery that thought and ideas may be without any thinking being —a discovery big with consequences which cannot easily be traced by those deluded mortals who think and reason in the common track. We were always apt to imagine, that thought supposed a thinker, and love a lover, and treason a traitor: but this, it seems, was all a mistake; and it is found out, that there may be treason without a traitor, and love without a lover, laws without a legislator, and punishment without a sufferer, succession without time, and motion without anything moved, or space in which it may move: or if, in these cases, ideas are the lover, the sufferer, the traitor, it were to be wished that the author of this discovery had farther condescended to acquaint us whether ideas can converse together, and be under obligations of duty or gratitude to each other; whether they can make promises and enter into leagues and covenants, and fulfil or break them, and be punished for the breach. If one set of ideas makes a covenant, another breaks it, and a third is punished for it, there is reason to think that justice is no natural virtue in this system.

It seemed very natural to think, that the "Treatise of Human Nature" required an author, and a very ingenious one too; but now we learn that it is only a set of ideas which came together and arranged themselves by certain associations and attractions.

After all, this curious system appears not to be fitted to the present state of human nature. How far it may suit some choice spirits, who are refined from the dregs of common sense, I cannot say. It is acknowledged, I think, that even these can enter into this system only in their most speculative hours, when they soar so high in pursuit of those self-existent ideas as to lose sight of all other things. But when they condescend to mingle again with the human race, and to converse with a friend, a companion, or a fellow-citizen, the ideal system vanishes; common sense, like an irresistible torrent, carries them along; and, in spite of all their reasoning and philosophy, they believe their own existence, and the existence of other things. . . .

Section VII: The Conception and Belief of a Sentient Being or Mind is Suggested by Our Constitution—The Notion of Relations Not Always Got by Comparing the Related Ideas

Leaving this philosophy, therefore, to those who have occasion for it, and can use it discreetly as a chamber exercise, we may still inquire how the rest of mankind, and even the adepts themselves, except in some solitary moments, have got so strong and irresistible a belief, that thought must have a subject, and be the act of some thinking being; how every man believes himself to be something distinct from his ideas and impressions—something which continues the same identical self when all his ideas and impressions are changed. It is impossible to trace the origin of this opinion in history; for all languages have it interwoven in their original construction. All nations have always believed it. The constitution of all laws and governments, as well as the common transactions of life, suppose it.

It is not less impossible for any man to recollect when he himself came by this notion; for, as far back as we can remember, we were already in possession of it, and as fully persuaded of our own existence, and the existence of other things, as that one and one make two. It seems, therefore, that this opinion preceded all reasoning, and experience, and instruction; and this is the more probable, because we could not get it by any of these means. It appears, then, to be an undeniable fact, that, from thought or sensation, all mankind, constantly and invariably, from the first dawning of reflection, do infer a power or faculty of thinking, and a permanent being or mind to which that faculty belongs; and that we as invariably ascribe all the various kinds of sensation and thought we are conscious of, to one individual mind or self.

But by what rules of logic we make these inferences, it is impossible to shew; nay, it is impossible to shew how our sensations and thoughts can give us the very notion and conception either of a mind or of a faculty. The faculty of smelling is something very different from the actual sensation of smelling; for the faculty may remain when we have no sensation. And the mind is no less different from the faculty; for it continues the same individual being when that faculty is lost. Yet this sensation suggests to us both a faculty and a mind; and not only suggests the notion of them, but creates a belief of their existence; although it is impossible to discover, by reason, any tie or connection between one and the other.

What shall we say, then? Either those inferences which we draw from our sensations—namely, the existence of a mind, and of powers or faculties belonging to it—are prejudices of philosophy or education, mere fictions of the mind, which a wise man should throw off as he does the belief of fairies; or they are judgments of nature—judgments not got by comparing ideas, and perceiving agreements and disagreements, but immediately inspired by our constitution.

If this last is the case, as I apprehend it is, it will be impossible to shake off those opinions, and we must yield to them at last, though we struggle hard to get rid of them. And if we could, by a determined obstinacy, shake off the principles of our nature, this is not to act the philosopher, but the fool or the madman. It is incumbent upon those who think that these are not natural principles, to shew, in the first place, how we can otherwise get the notion of a mind and its faculties; and then to shew how we come to deceive ourselves into the opinion that sensation cannot be without a sentient being.

It is the received doctrine of philosophers, that our notions of relations can only be got by comparing the related ideas: but, in the present case, there seems to be an instance to the contrary. It is not by having first the notions of mind and sensation, and then comparing them together, that we perceive the one to have the relation of a subject or substratum, and the other that of an act or operation: on the contrary, one of the related things—to wit, sensation—suggests to us both the correlate and the relation.

I beg leave to make use of the word *suggestion*, because I know not one more proper, to express a power of the mind, which seems entirely to have escaped the notice of philosophers, and to which we owe many of our simple notions which are neither impressions nor ideas, as well as many original principles of belief. I shall endeavour to illustrate, by an example, what I understand by this word. We all know that a certain kind of sound suggests immediately to the mind, a coach passing in the street; and not only produces the imagination, but the belief, that a coach is passing. Yet there is here no comparing of ideas, no perception of agreements or disagreements, to produce this belief: nor is there the least similitude between the sound we hear and the coach we imagine and believe to be passing.[5]

It is true that this suggestion is not natural and original; it is the result of experience and habit. But I think it appears from what hath been said, that there are natural suggestions: particularly, that sensation suggests the notion of present existence, and the belief that what we perceive or feel does now exist; that memory suggests the notion of past existence, and the belief that what we remember did exist in time past; and that our sensations and thoughts do also suggest the notion of a mind, and the belief of its existence, and of its relation to our thoughts. By a like natural principle it is, that a beginning of existence, or any change in nature, suggests to us the notion of a cause, and compels our belief of its existence. And, in like manner, as shall be shewn when we come to the sense of touch, certain sensations of touch, by the constitution of our nature, suggest to us extension, solidity, and motion, which are nowise like to sensations, although they have been hitherto confounded with them.

Section VIII: There is a Quality or Virtue in Bodies, Which We Call Their Smell—How This is Connected in The Imagination With The Sensation

We have considered smell as signifying a sensation, feeling, or impression upon the mind; and in this sense, it can only be in a mind, or sentient being: but it is evident that mankind give the name of *smell* much more frequently to something which they conceive to be external, and to be a quality of body: they understand something by it which does not at all infer a mind; and have not the least difficulty in conceiving the air perfumed with aromatic odours in the deserts of Arabia, or in some uninhabited island, where the human foot never trod. Every sensible day-labourer hath as clear a notion of this, and as full a conviction of the possibility of it, as he hath of his own existence; and can no more doubt of the one than of the other.

Suppose that such a man meets with a modern philosopher, and wants to be informed what smell in plants is. The philosopher tells him, that there is no smell in plants, nor in anything but in the mind; that it is impossible there can be smell but in a mind; and that all this hath been demonstrated by modern philosophy. The plain man will, no doubt, be apt to think him merry: but, if he finds that he is serious, his next conclusion will be that he is mad; or that philosophy, like magic, puts men into a new world, and gives them different faculties from common men. And thus philosophy and common sense are set at variance. But who is to blame for it? In my opinion the philosopher is to blame. For if he means by smell, what the rest of mankind most commonly mean, he is certainly mad. But if he puts a different meaning upon the word, without observing it himself, or giving warning to others, he abuses language and disgraces philosophy, without doing any service to truth: as if a man should exchange the meaning of the words *daughter* and *cow*, and then endeavour to prove to his plain neighbour, that his cow is his daughter, and his daughter his cow.

I believe there is not much more wisdom in many of those paradoxes of the ideal philosophy, which to plain sensible men appear to be palpable absurdities, but with the adepts pass for profound discoveries. I resolve, for my own part, always to pay a great regard to the dictates of common sense, and not to depart from them without absolute necessity: and, therefore, I am apt to think that there is really something in the rose or lily, which is by the vulgar called *smell*, and which continues to exist when it is not smelled: and shall proceed to inquire what this is; how we come by the notion of it; and what relation this quality or virtue of smell hath to the sensation which we have been obliged to call by the same name, for want of another.

Let us therefore suppose, as before, a person beginning to exercise the sense of smelling; a little experience will discover to him, that the nose is the organ of this sense, and that the air, or something in the air, is a medium of it. And finding, by farther experience, that, when a rose is near, he has a certain sensation, when it is removed, the sensation is gone, he finds a connection in nature betwixt the rose and this sensation. The rose is considered as a cause, occasion, or antecedent of the sensation; the sensation as an effect or consequence of the presence of the rose; they are associated in the mind, and constantly found conjoined in the imagination. . . .

Section IX: That There is a Principle in Human Nature, From Which The Notion of This, as Well as All Other Natural Virtues or Causes, is Derived

In order to illustrate further how we come to conceive a quality or virtue in the rose which we call *smell,* and what this smell is, it is proper to observe, that the mind begins very early to thirst after principles which may direct it in the exertion of its powers. The smell of a rose is a certain affection or feeling of the mind; and, as it is not constant, but comes and goes, we want to know when and where we may expect it; and are uneasy till we find something which, being present, brings this feeling along with it, and, being removed, removes it. This, when found, we call the cause of it; not in a strict and philosophical sense, as if the feeling were really effected or produced by that cause, but in a popular sense; for the mind is satisfied if there is a constant conjunction between them; and such causes are in reality nothing else but laws of nature. Having found the smell thus constantly conjoined with the rose, the mind is at rest, without inquiring whether this conjunction is owing to a real efficiency or not; that being a philosophical inquiry, which does not concern human life. But every discovery of such a constant conjunction is of real importance in life, and makes a strong impression upon the mind. . . .

As it is experience only that discovers these connections between natural causes and their effects; without inquiring further, we attribute to the cause some vague and indistinct notion of power or virtue to produce the effect. And, in many cases, the purposes of life do not make it necessary to give distinct names to the cause and the effect. Whence it happens, that, being closely connected in the imagination, although very unlike to each other, one name serves for both; and, in common discourse, is most frequently applied to that which, of the two, is most the object of our attention. This occasions an ambiguity in many words, which, having the same causes in all languages, is common to all, and is apt to be overlooked even by philosophers. Some instances will serve both to illustrate and confirm what we have said. . . .

Heat signifies a sensation, and *cold* a contrary one; but *heat* likewise signifies a quality or state of bodies, which hath no contrary, but different degrees. When a man feels the same water hot to one hand and cold to the other, this gives him occasion to distinguish between the feeling and the heat of the body; and, although he knows that the sensations are contrary, he does not imagine that the body can have contrary qualities at the same time. And when he finds a different taste in the same body in sickness and in health, he is easily convinced, that the quality in the body called *taste* is the same as before, although the sensations he has from it are perhaps opposite.

The vulgar are commonly charged by philosophers, with the absurdity of imagining the smell in the rose to be something like to the sensation of smelling; but I think unjustly; for they neither give the same epithets to both, nor do they reason in the same manner from them. What is smell in the rose? It is a quality or virtue of the rose, or of something proceeding from it, which we perceive by the sense of smelling; and this is all we know of the matter. But what is smelling? It is an act of the mind, but is never imagined to be a quality of the mind. Again, the sensation of smelling is conceived to infer necessarily a mind or sentient being; but smell in the rose infers no such thing. We say, this body smells sweet, that stinks; but we do not say, this mind smells sweet and that stinks. Therefore, smell in the rose, and the sensation which it causes, are not conceived, even by the vulgar, to be things of the same kind, although they have the same name.

From what hath been said, we may learn that the smell of a rose signifies two things: *First,* a sensation, which can have no existence but when it is perceived, and can only be in a sentient being or mind; *Secondly,* it signifies some power, quality, or virtue, in the rose, or in effluvia proceeding from it, which hath a permanent existence, independent of the mind, and which, by the constitution of nature, produces the sensation in us. By the original constitution of our nature, we are both led to believe that there is a permanent cause of the sensation, and prompted to seek after it; and experience determines us to place it in the rose. The names of all smells, tastes, sounds, as well as heat and cold, have a like ambiguity in all languages; but it deserves our attention, that these names are but rarely, in common language, used to signify the sensations; for the most part, they signify the external qualities which are indicated by the sensations—the cause of which phaenomenon I take to be this. Our sensations have very different degrees of strength. Some of them are so quick and lively as to give us a great deal either of pleasure or of uneasiness. When this is the case, we are compelled to attend to the sensation itself, and to make it an object of thought and discourse; we give it a name, which signifies nothing but the sensation; and in this case we readily acknowledge, that the thing meant by that name is in the mind only, and not in anything external. Such are the various kinds of pain, sickness, and the sensations of hunger and other appetites. But, where the sensation is not so interesting as to require to be made an object of thought, our constitution leads us to consider it as a sign of something external, which hath a constant conjunction with it; and, having found what it indicates, we give a name to that: the sensation, having no proper name, falls in as an accessory to the thing signified by it, and is confounded under the same name. So that the name may, indeed, be applied to the sensation, but most properly and commonly is applied to the thing indicated by that sensation. The sensations of smell, taste, sound, and colour, are of infinitely more importance as signs or indications, than they are upon their own account; like the words of a language, wherein we do not attend to the sound but to the sense.

Section X: Whether in Sensation The Mind is Active or Passive?

There is one inquiry remains, Whether, in smelling, and in other sensations, the mind is active or passive? This possibly may seem to be a question about words, or, at least, of very small importance; however, if it leads us to attend more accurately to the operations of our minds than we are accustomed to do, it is, upon that very account, not altogether unprofitable. I think the opinion of modern philosophers is, that in sensation the mind is altogether passive. And this undoubtedly is so far true, that we cannot raise any sensation in our minds by willing it; and, on the other hand, it seems hardly possible to avoid having the sensation when the object is presented. Yet it seems likewise to be true, that, in proportion as the attention is more or less turned to a sensation or diverted from it, that sensation is more or less perceived and remembered. Every one knows that very intense pain may be diverted by a surprise, or by anything that entirely occupies the mind. When we are engaged in earnest conversation, the clock may strike by us without being heard; at least, we remember not, the next moment, that we did hear it. The noise and tumult of a great trading city is not heard by them who have lived in it all their days; but it stuns those strangers who have lived in the peaceful retirement of the country. Whether, therefore, there can be any sensation where the mind is purely passive, I will not say; but I think we are conscious of having given some attention to every sensation which we remember, though ever so recent.

No doubt, where the impulse is strong and uncommon, it is as difficult to withhold attention as it is to forbear crying out in racking pain, or starting in a sudden fright. But how far both might be attained by strong resolution and practice, is not easy to determine. So that, although the Peripatetics had no good reason to suppose an active and a passive intellect, since attention may be well enough accounted an act of the will, yet I think they came nearer to the truth, in holding the mind to be in sensation partly passive and partly active, than the moderns, in affirming it to be purely passive. Sensation, imagination, memory, and judgment, have, by the vulgar in all ages, been considered as acts of the mind. The manner in which they are expressed in all languages, shews this. When the mind is much employed in them, we say it is very active; whereas, if they were impressions only, as the ideal philosophy would lead us to conceive, we ought, in such a case, rather to say, that the mind is very passive; for, I suppose, no man would attribute great activity to the paper I write upon, because it receives variety of characters.

The relation which the sensation of smell bears to the memory and imagination of it, and to a mind or subject, is common to all our sensations, and, indeed, to all the operations of the mind: the relation it bears to the will is common to it with all the powers of understanding; and the relation it bears to that quality or virtue of bodies which it indicates, is common to it with the sensations of taste, hearing, colour, heat, and cold— so that what hath been said of this sense, may easily be applied to several of our senses, and to other operations of the mind; and this, I hope, will apologize for our insisting so long upon it.

CHAPTER 4 / OF HEARING

Section II: Of Natural Language

One of the noblest purposes of sound undoubtedly is language, without which mankind would hardly be able to attain any degree of improvement above the brutes. Language is commonly considered as purely an invention of men, who by nature are no less mute than the brutes; but, having a superior degree of invention and reason, have been able to contrive artificial signs of their thoughts and purposes, and to establish them by common consent. But the origin of language deserves to be more carefully inquired into, not only as this inquiry may be of importance for the improvement of language, but as it is related to the present subject, and tends to lay open some of the first principles of human nature. I shall, therefore, offer some thoughts upon this subject.

By language I understand all those signs which mankind use in order to communicate to others their thoughts and intentions, their purposes and desires. And such signs may be conceived to be of two kinds: First, such as have no meaning but what is affixed to them by compact or agreement among those who use them—these are artificial signs; Secondly, such as, previous to all compact or agreement, have a meaning which every man understands by the principles of his nature. Language, so far as it consists of artificial signs, may be called *artificial;* so far as it consists of natural signs, I call it *natural.*

Having premised these definitions, I think it is demonstrable, that, if mankind had not a natural language, they could never have invented an artificial one by their reason and ingenuity. For all artificial language supposes some compact or agreement to affix a certain meaning to certain signs; therefore, there must be compacts or agreements before the use of artificial signs; but there can be no compact or agreement without signs, nor without language; and, therefore, there must be a natural language before any artificial language can be invented: which was to be demonstrated.

Had language in general been a human invention, as much as writing or printing, we should find whole nations as mute as the brutes. Indeed, even the brutes have some natural signs by which they express their own thoughts, affections, and desires, and understand those of others. A chick, as soon as hatched, understands the different sounds whereby its dam calls it to food, or gives the alarm of danger. A dog or a horse understands, by nature, when the human voice caresses, and when it threatens him. But brutes, as far as we know, have no notion of contracts or covenants, or of moral obligation to perform them. If nature had given them these notions, she would probably have given them natural signs to express them. And where nature has denied these notions, it is as impossible to acquire them by art, as it is for a blind man to acquire the notion of colours. Some brutes are sensible of honour or disgrace; they have resentment and gratitude; but none of them, as far as we know, can make a promise or plight their faith, having no such notions from their constitution. And if mankind had not these notions by nature, and natural signs to express them by, with all their wit and ingenuity they could never have invented language.

The elements of this natural language of mankind, or the signs that are naturally expressive of our thoughts, may, I think, be reduced to these three kinds: modulations of the voice, gestures, and features. By means of these, two savages who have no common artificial language, can converse together; can communicate their thoughts in some tolerable manner; can ask and refuse, affirm and deny, threaten and supplicate; can traffic, enter into covenants, and plight their faith. This might be confirmed by historical facts of undoubted credit, if it were necessary.

Mankind having thus a common language by nature, though a scanty one, adapted only to the necessities of nature, there is no great ingenuity required in improving it by the addition of artificial signs, to supply the deficiency of the natural. These artificial signs must multiply with the arts of life, and the improvements of knowledge. The articulations of the voice seem to be, of all signs, the most proper for artificial language; and as mankind have universally used them for that purpose, we may reasonably judge that nature intended them for it. But nature probably does not intend that we should lay aside the use of the natural signs; it is enough that we supply their defects by artificial ones. A man that rides always in a chariot, by degrees loses the use of his legs; and one who uses artificial signs only, loses both the knowledge and use of the natural. Dumb people retain much more of the natural language than others, because necessity obliges them to use it. And for the same reason, savages have much more of it than civilized nations. It is by natural signs chiefly that we give force and energy to language; and the less language has of them, it is the less expressive and persuasive. Thus, writing is less expressive than reading, and reading less expressive than speaking without book; speaking without the proper and natural modulations, force, and variations of the voice, is a frigid and dead language, compared with that which is attended with them; it is still more expressive when we add the language of the eyes and features; and is then only in its perfect and natural state, and attended with its proper energy, when to all these we superadd the force of action.

Where speech is natural, it will be an exercise, not of the voice and lungs only, but of all the muscles of the body; like that of dumb people and savages, whose language, as it has more of nature, is more expressive, and is more easily learned.

Is it not pity that the refinements of a civilized life, instead of supplying the defects of natural language, should root it out and plant in its stead dull and lifeless articulations of unmeaning sounds, or the scrawling of insignificant characters? The perfection of language is commonly thought to be, to express human thoughts and sentiments distinctly by these dull signs; but if this is the perfection of artificial language, it is surely the corruption of the natural.

Artificial signs signify, but they do not express; they speak to the understanding, as algebraical characters may do, but the passions, the affections, and the will, hear them not: these continue dormant and inactive, till we speak to them in the language of nature, to which they are all attention and obedience.

It were easy to shew, that the fine arts of the musician, the painter, the actor, and the orator, so far as they are expressive —although the knowledge of them requires in us a delicate taste, a nice judgment, and much study and practice—yet they are nothing else but the language of nature, which we brought into the world with us, but have unlearned by disuse, and so find the greatest difficulty in recovering it.

Abolish the use of articulate sounds and writing among mankind for a century, and every man would be a painter, an actor, and an orator. We mean not to affirm that such an expedient is practicable; or, if it were, that the advantage would counterbalance the loss; but that, as men are led by nature and necessity to converse together, they will use every mean in their power to make themselves understood; and where they cannot do this by artificial signs, they will do it, as far as possible, by natural ones: and he that understands perfectly the use of natural signs, must be the best judge in all the expressive arts.

CHAPTER 5 / OF TOUCH

Section I: Of Heat and Cold

The senses which we have hitherto considered, are very simple and uniform, each of them exhibiting only one kind of sensation, and thereby indicating only one quality of bodies. By the ear we perceive sounds, and nothing else; by the palate, tastes; and by the nose, odours. These qualities are all likewise of one order, being all secondary qualities; whereas, by touch we perceive not one quality only, but many, and those of very different kinds. The chief of them are heat and cold, hardness and softness, roughness and smoothness, figure, solidity, motion, and extension. We shall consider these in order.

As to heat and cold, it will easily be allowed that they are secondary qualities, of the same order with smell, taste, and sound. And, therefore, what hath been already said of smell, is easily applicable to them; that is, that the words *heat* and *cold* have each of them two significations; they sometimes signify certain sensations of the mind, which can have no existence when they are not felt, nor can exist anywhere but in a mind or sentient being; but more frequently they signify a quality in bodies, which, by the laws of nature, occasions the sensations of heat and cold in us—a quality which, though connected by custom so closely with the sensation, that we cannot, without difficulty, separate them, yet hath not the least resemblance to it, and may continue to exist when there is no sensation at all.

The sensations of heat and cold are perfectly known; for they neither are, nor can be, anything else than what we feel them to be; but the qualities in bodies which we call *heat* and *cold*, are unknown. They are only conceived by us, as unknown causes or occasions of the sensations to which we give the same names. But, though common sense says nothing of the nature of these qualities, it plainly dictates the existence of them; and to deny that there can be heat and cold when they are not felt, is an absurdity too gross to merit confutation. For what could be more absurd, than to say, that the thermometer cannot rise or fall, unless some person be present, or that the coast of Guinea would be as cold as Nova Zembla, if it had no inhabitants? . . .

But, whatever be the nature of that quality in bodies which we call *heat*, we certainly know this, that it cannot in the least resemble the sensation of heat. It is no less absurd to suppose a likeness between the sensation and the quality, than it would be to suppose that the pain of the gout resembles a square or a triangle. The simplest man that hath common sense, does not imagine the sensation of heat, or anything that resembles that sensation, to be in the fire. He only imagines that there is something in the fire which makes him and other sentient beings feel heat. Yet, as the name of *heat,* in common language, more frequently and more properly signifies this unknown something in the fire, than the sensation occasioned by it, he justly laughs at the philosopher who denies that there is any heat in the fire, and thinks that he speaks contrary to common sense.

Section II: Of Hardness and Softness

Let us next consider hardness and softness; by which words we always understand real properties or qualities of bodies of which we have a distinct conception.

When the parts of a body adhere so firmly that it cannot easily be made to change its figure, we call it *hard;* when its parts are easily displaced, we call it *soft.* This is the notion which all mankind have of hardness and softness; they are neither sensations, nor like any sensation; they were real qualities before they were perceived by touch, and continue to be so when they are not perceived; for if any man will affirm that diamonds were not hard till they were handled, who would reason with him?

There is, no doubt, a sensation by which we perceive a body to be hard or soft. This sensation of hardness may easily be had, by pressing one's hand against the table, and attending to the feeling that ensues, setting aside, as much as possible, all thought of the table and its qualities, or of any external thing. But it is one thing to have the sensation, and another to attend to it, and make it a distinct object of reflection. The first is very easy; the last, in most cases, extremely difficult.

We are so accustomed to use the sensation as a sign, and to pass immediately to the hardness signified, that, as far as appears, it was never made an object of thought, either by the vulgar or by philosophers; nor has it a name in any language. There is no sensation more distinct, or more frequent; yet it is never attended to, but passes through the mind instantaneously, and serves only to introduce that quality in bodies, which, by a law of our constitution, it suggests.

There are, indeed, some cases, wherein it is no difficult matter to attend to the sensation occasioned by the hardness of a body; for instance, when it is so violent as to occasion considerable pain: then nature calls upon us to attend to it, and then we acknowledge that it is a mere sensation, and can only be in a sentient being. If a man runs his head with violence against a pillar, I appeal to him whether the pain he feels resembles the hardness of the stone, or if he can conceive anything like what he feels to be in an inanimate piece of matter.

The attention of the mind is here entirely turned towards the painful feeling; and, to speak in the common language of mankind, he feels nothing in the stone, but feels a violent pain in his head. It is quite otherwise when he leans his head gently against the pillar; for then he will tell you that he feels nothing in his head, but feels hardness in the stone. Hath he not a sensation in this case as well as in the other? Undoubtedly he hath; but it is a sensation which nature intended only as a sign of something in the stone; and, accordingly, he instantly fixes his attention upon the thing signified; and cannot, without great difficulty, attend so much to the sensation as to be persuaded that there is any such thing distinct from the hardness it signifies.

But, however difficult it may be to attend to this fugitive sensation, to stop its rapid progress, and to disjoin it from the external quality of hardness, in whose shadow it is apt immediately to hide itself; this is what a philosopher by pains and practice must attain, otherwise it will be impossible for him to reason justly upon this subject, or even to understand what is here advanced. For the last appeal, in subjects of this nature, must be to what a man feels and perceives in his own mind.

It is indeed strange that a sensation which we have every time we feel a body hard, and which, consequently, we can command as often and continue as long as we please, a sensation as distinct and determinate as any other, should yet be so much unknown as never to have been made an object of thought and reflection, nor to have been honoured with a name in any language; that philosophers, as well as the vulgar, should have entirely overlooked it, or confounded it with that quality of bodies which we call *hardness*, to which it hath not the least similitude. May we not hence conclude, that the knowledge of the human faculties is but in its infancy?—that we have not yet learned to attend to those operations of the mind, of which we are conscious every hour of our lives?—that there are habits of inattention acquired very early, which are as hard to be overcome as other habits? For I think it is probable, that the novelty of this sensation will procure some attention to it in children at first; but, being in nowise interesting in itself, as soon as it becomes familiar, it is overlooked, and the attention turned solely to that which it signifies. Thus, when one is learning a language, he attends to the sounds; but when he is master of it, he attends only to the sense of what he would express. If this is the case, we must become as little children again, if we will be philosophers; we must overcome this habit of inattention which has been gathering strength ever since we began to think—a habit, the usefulness of which, in common life, atones for the difficulty it creates to the philosopher in discovering the first principles of the human mind.

The firm cohesion of the parts of a body, is no more like that sensation by which I perceive it to be hard, than the vibration of a sonorous body is like the sound I hear: nor can I possibly perceive, by my reason, any connection between the one and the other. No man can give a reason, why the vibration of a body might not have given the sensation of smelling, and the effluvia of bodies affected our hearing, if it had so pleased our Maker. In like manner, no man can give a reason why the sensations of smell, or taste, or sound, might not have indicated hardness, as well as that sensation which, by our constitution, does indicate it. Indeed, no man can conceive any sensation to resemble any known quality of bodies. Nor can any man shew, by any good argument, that all our sensations might not have been as they are, though no body, nor quality of body, had ever existed.

Here, then, is a phaenomenon of human nature, which comes to be resolved. Hardness of bodies is a thing that we conceive as distinctly, and believe as firmly, as anything in nature. We have no way of coming at this conception and belief, but by means of a certain sensation of touch, to which hardness hath not the least similitude; nor can we, by any rules of reasoning, infer the one from the other. The question is, How we come by this conception and belief?

First, as to the conception: Shall we call it an idea of sensation, or of reflection? The last will not be affirmed; and as little can the first, unless we will call that an idea of sensation which hath no resemblance to any sensation. So that the origin of this idea of hardness, one of the most common and most distinct we have, is not to be found in all our systems of the mind: not even in those which have so copiously endeavoured to deduce all our notions from sensation and reflection.

But, secondly, supposing we have got the conception of hardness, how come we by the belief of it? Is it self-evident, from comparing the ideas, that such a sensation could not be felt, unless such a quality of bodies existed? No. Can it be proved by probable or certain arguments? No; it cannot. Have we got this belief, then, by tradition, by education, or by experience? No; it is not got in any of these ways. Shall we then throw off this belief as having no foundation in reason? Alas! it is not in our power; it triumphs over reason, and laughs at all the arguments of a philosopher. Even the author of the "Treatise of Human Nature," though he saw no reason for this belief, but many against it, could hardly conquer it in his speculative and solitary moments; at other times, he fairly yielded to it, and confesses that he found himself under a necessity to do so.

What shall we say, then, of this conception, and this belief, which are so unaccountable and untractable? I see nothing left, but to conclude, that, by an original principle of our constitution, a certain sensation of touch both suggests to the mind the conception of hardness, and creates the belief of it: or, in other words, that this sensation is a natural sign of hardness. And this I shall endeavour more fully to explain.

Section III: Of Natural Signs

As in artificial signs there is often neither similitude between the sign and thing signified, nor any connection that arises necessarily from the nature of the things, so it is also in natural signs. The word *gold* has no similitude to the substance signified by it; nor is it in its own nature more fit to signify this than any other substance; yet, by habit and custom, it suggests this and no other. In like manner, a sensation of touch suggests hardness, although it hath neither similitude to hard ness, nor, as far as we can perceive, any necessary connection with it. The difference betwixt these two signs lies only in this —that, in the first, the suggestion is the effect of habit and custom; in the second, it is not the effect of habit, but of the original constitution of our minds.

It appears evident from what hath been said on the subject of language, that there are natural signs as well as artificial; and particularly, that the thoughts, purposes, and dispositions of the mind, have their natural signs in the features of the face, the modulation of the voice, and the motion and attitude of the body: that, without a natural knowledge of the connection between these signs and the things signified by them, language could never have been invented and established among men: and, that the fine arts are all founded upon this connection, which we may call *the natural language of mankind.* It is now proper to observe, that there are different orders of natural signs, and to point out the different classes into which they may be distinguished, that we may more distinctly conceive the relation between our sensations and the things they suggest, and what we mean by calling sensations signs of external things.

The first class of natural signs comprehends those whose connection with the thing signified is established by nature, but discovered only by experience. The whole of genuine philosophy consists in discovering such connections, and reducing them to general rules. The great Lord Verulam had a perfect comprehension of this, when he called it *an interpretation of nature.* No man ever more distinctly understood or happily expressed the nature and foundation of the philosophic art. What is all we know of mechanics, astronomy, and optics, but connections established by nature, and discovered by experience or observation, and consequences deduced from them? All the knowledge we have in agriculture, gardening, chemistry, and medicine, is built upon the same foundation. And if ever our philosophy concerning the human mind is carried so far as to deserve the name of science, which ought never to be despaired of, it must be by observing facts, reducing them to general rules, and drawing just conclusions from them. What we commonly call natural *causes* might, with more propriety, be called natural *signs*, and what we call *effects*, the things signified. The causes have no proper efficiency or casuality, as far as we know; and all we can certainly affirm is, that nature hath established a constant conjunction between them and the things called their effects; and hath given to mankind a disposition to observe those connections, to confide in their continuance, and to make use of them for the improvement of our knowledge, and increase of our power.

A second class is that wherein the connection between the sign and thing signified, is not only established by nature, but discovered to us by a natural principle, without reasoning or experience. Of this kind are the natural signs of human thoughts, purposes, and desires, which have been already mentioned as the natural language of mankind. An infant may be put into a fright by an angry countenance, and soothed again by smiles and blandishments. A child that has a good musical ear, may be put to sleep or to dance, may be made merry or sorrowful, by the modulation of musical sounds. The principles of all the fine arts, and of what we call *a fine taste*, may be resolved into connections of this kind. A fine taste may be improved by reasoning and experience; but if the first principles of it were not planted in our minds by nature, it could never be acquired. Nay, we have already made it appear, that a great part of this knowledge which we have by nature, is lost by the disuse of natural signs, and the substitution of artificial in their place.

A third class of natural signs comprehends those which, though we never before had any notion or conception of the thing signified, do suggest it, or conjure it up, as it were, by a natural kind of magic, and at once give us a conception and create a belief of it. I shewed formerly, that our sensations suggest to us a sentient being or mind to which they belong —a being which hath a permanent existence, although the sensations are transient and of short duration—a being which is still the same, while its sensations and other operations are varied ten thousand ways—a being which hath the same relation to all that infinite variety of thoughts, purposes, actions, affections, enjoyments, and sufferings, which we are conscious of, or can remember. The conception of a mind is neither an idea of sensation nor of reflection; for it is neither like any of our sensations, nor like anything we are conscious of. The first conception of it, as well as the belief of it, and of the common relation it bears to all that we are conscious of, or remember, is suggested to every thinking being, we do not know how.

The notion of hardness in bodies, as well as the belief of it, are got in a similar manner; being, by an original principle of our nature, annexed to that sensation which we have when we feel a hard body. And so naturally and necessarily does the sensation convey the notion and belief of hardness, that hitherto they have been confounded by the most acute inquirers into the principles of human nature, although they appear, upon accurate reflection, not only to be different things, but as unlike as pain is to the point of a sword.

It may be observed, that, as the first class of natural signs I have mentioned is the foundation of true philosophy, and the second the foundation of the fine arts, or of taste—so the last is the foundation of common sense—a part of human nature which hath never been explained.[6]

I take it for granted, that the notion of hardness, and the belief of it, is first got by means of that particular sensation which, as far back as we can remember, does invariably suggest it; and that, if we had never had such a feeling, we should never have had any notion of hardness. I think it is evident, that we cannot, by reasoning from our sensations, collect the existence of bodies at all, far less any of their qualities. This hath been proved by unanswerable arguments by the Bishop of Cloyne, and by the author of the "Treatise of Human Nature." It appears as evident that this connection between our sensations and the conception and belief of external existences cannot be produced by habit, experience, education, or any principle of human nature that hath been admitted by philosophers. At the same time, it is a fact that such sensations are invariably connected with the conception and belief of external existences. Hence, by all rules of just reasoning, we must conclude, that this connection is the effect of our constitution, and ought to be considered as an original principle of human nature, till we find some more general principle into which it may be resolved.[7]

Section IV: Of Hardness, and Other Primary Qualities

Further, I observe that hardness is a quality, of which we have as clear and distinct a conception as of anything whatsoever. The cohesion of the parts of a body with more or less force, is perfectly understood, though its cause is not; we know what it is, as well as how it affects the touch. It is, therefore, a quality of a quite different order from those secondary qualities we have already taken notice of, whereof we know no more naturally than that they are adapted to raise certain sensations in us. If hardness were a quality of the same kind, it would be a proper inquiry for philosophers, what hardness in bodies is? and we should have had various hypotheses about it, as well as about colour and heat. But it is evident that any such hypothesis would be ridiculous. If any man should say, that hardness in bodies is a certain vibration of their parts, or that it is certain effluvia emitted by them which affect our touch in the manner we feel—such hypotheses would shock common sense; because we all know that, if the parts of a body adhere strongly, it is hard, although it should neither emit effluvia nor vibrate. Yet, at the same time, no man can say, but that effluvia or the vibration of the parts of a body, might have affected our touch, in the same manner that hardness now does, if it had so pleased the Author of our nature; and, if either of these hypotheses is applied to explain a secondary quality—such as smell, or taste, or sound, or colour, or heat—there appears no manifest absurdity in the supposition.

The distinction betwixt primary and secondary qualities hath had several revolutions. Democritus and Epicurus, and their followers, maintained it. Aristotle and the Peripatetics abolished it. Des Cartes, Malebranche, and Locke, revived it, and were thought to have put it in a very clear light. But Bishop Berkeley again discarded this distinction, by such proofs as must be convincing to those that hold the received doctrine of ideas.[8] Yet, after all, there appears to be a real foundation for it in the principles of our nature.

What hath been said of hardness, is so easily applicable, not only to its opposite, softness, but likewise to roughness and smoothness, to figure and motion, that we may be excused from making the application, which would only be a repetition of what hath been said. All these, by means of certain corresponding sensations of touch, are presented to the mind as real external qualities; the conception and the belief of them are invariably connected with the corresponding sensations, by an original principle of human nature. Their sensations have no name in any language; they have not only been overlooked by the vulgar, but by philosophers; or, if they have been at all taken notice of, they have been confounded with the external qualities which they suggest.

Section V: Of Extension

It is further to be observed, that hardness and softness, roughness and smoothness, figure and motion, do all suppose extension, and cannot be conceived without it; yet, I think it must, on the other hand, be allowed that, if we had never felt any thing hard or soft, rough or smooth, figured or moved, we should never have had a conception of extension; so that, as there is good ground to believe that the notion of extension could not be prior to that of other primary qualities, so it is certain that it could not be posterior to the notion of any of them, being necessarily implied in them all.

Extension, therefore, seems to be a quality *suggested* to us, by the very same sensations which suggest the other qualities above mentioned. When I grasp a ball in my hand, I perceive it at once hard, figured, and extended. The feeling is very simple, and hath not the least resemblance to any quality of body. Yet it suggests to us three primary qualities perfectly distinct from one another, as well as from the sensation which indicates them. When I move my hand along the table, the feeling is so simple that I find it difficult to distinguish it into things of different natures; yet, it immediately suggests hardness, smoothness, extension, and motion—things of very different natures, and all of them as distinctly understood as the feeling which suggests them.

We are commonly told by philosophers, that we get the idea of extension by feeling along the extremities of a body, as if there was no manner of difficulty in the matter. I have sought, with great pains, I confess, to find out how this idea can be got by feeling; but I have sought in vain. Yet it is one of the clearest and most distinct notions we have; nor is there anything whatsoever about which the human understanding can carry on so many long and demonstrative trains of reasoning.

The notion of extension is so familiar to us from infancy, and so constantly obtruded by everything we see and feel, that we are apt to think it obvious how it comes into the mind; but upon a narrower examination we shall find it utterly inexplicable. It is true we have feelings of touch, which every moment present extension to the mind; but how they come to do so, is the question; for those feelings do no more resemble extension, than they resemble justice or courage—nor can the existence of extended things be inferred from those feelings by any rules of reasoning; so that the feelings we have by touch, can neither explain how we get the notion, nor how we come by the belief of extended things.

What hath imposed upon philosophers in this matter is, that the feelings of touch, which suggest primary qualities, have no names, nor are they ever reflected upon. They pass through the mind instantaneously, and serve only to introduce the notion and belief of external things, which, by our constitution, are connected with them. They are natural signs, and the mind immediately passes to the thing signified, without making the least reflection upon the sign, or observing that there was any such thing. Hence it hath always been taken for granted, that the ideas of extension, figure, and motion, are ideas of sensation, which enter into the mind by the sense of touch, in the same manner as the sensations of sound and smell do by the ear and nose.[9] The sensations of touch are so connected, by our constitution, with the notions of extension, figure, and motion, that philosophers have mistaken the one for the other, and never have been able to discern that they were not only distinct things, but altogether unlike. However, if we will reason distinctly upon this subject, we ought to give names to those feelings of touch; we must accustom ourselves to attend to them, and to reflect upon them, that we may be able to disjoin them from, and to compare them with, the qualities signified or suggested by them.

The habit of doing this is not to be attained without pains and practice; and till a man hath acquired this habit, it will be impossible for him to think distinctly, or to judge right, upon this subject.

Let a man press his hand against the table—*he feels it hard.* But what is the meaning of this?—The meaning undoubtedly is that he hath a certain feeling of touch, from which he concludes, without any reasoning, or comparing ideas, that there is something external really existing, whose parts stick so firmly together, that they cannot be displaced without considerable force.

There is here a feeling, and a conclusion drawn from it, or some way suggested by it. In order to compare these, we must view them separately, and then consider by what tie they are connected, and wherein they resemble one another. The hardness of the table is the conclusion, the feeling is the medium by which we are led to that conclusion. Let a man attend distinctly to this medium, and to the conclusion, and he will perceive them to be as unlike as any two things in nature. The one is a sensation of the mind, which can have no existence but in a sentient being; nor can it exist one moment longer than it is felt; the other is in the table, and we conclude, without any difficulty, that it was in the table before it was felt, and continues after the feeling is over. The one implies no kind of extension, nor parts, nor cohesion; the other implies all these. Both, indeed, admit of degrees, and the feeling, beyond a certain degree, is a species of pain; but adamantine hardness does not imply the least pain.

And as the feeling hath no similitude to hardness, so neither can our reason perceive the least tie or connection between them; nor will the logician ever be able to shew a reason why we should conclude hardness from this feeling, rather than softness, or any other quality whatsoever. But, in reality, all mankind are led by their constitution to conclude hardness from this feeling.

The sensation of heat, and the sensation we have by pressing a hard body, are equally feelings; nor can we, by reasoning, draw any conclusion from the one but what may be drawn from the other: but, by our constitution, we conclude from the first an obscure or occult quality, of which we have only this relative conception, that it is something adapted to raise in us the sensation of heat; from the second, we conclude a quality of which we have a clear and distinct conception—to wit, the hardness of the body.

Section VI: Of Extension

To put this matter in another light, it may be proper to try, whether from sensation alone we can collect any notion of extension, figure, motion, and space. I take it for granted, that a blind man hath the same notions of extension, figure, and motion, as a man that sees; that Dr Saunderson had the same notion of a cone, a cylinder, and a sphere, and of the motions and distances of the heavenly bodies, as Sir Isaac Newton.

As sight, therefore, is not necessary for our acquiring those notions, we shall leave it out altogether in our inquiry into the first origin of them; and shall suppose a blind man, by some strange distemper, to have lost all the experience, and habits, and notions he had got by touch; not to have the least conception of the existence, figure, dimensions, or extension, either of his own body, or of any other; but to have all his knowledge of external things to acquire anew, by means of sensation, and the power of reason, which we suppose to remain entire.

We shall, first, suppose his body fixed immovably in one place, and that he can only have the feelings of touch, by the application of other bodies to it. Suppose him first to be pricked with a pin—this will, no doubt, give a smart sensation: he feels pain; but what can he infer from it? Nothing, surely, with regard to the existence or figure of a pin. He can infer nothing from this species of pain, which he may not as well infer from the gout or sciatica. Common sense may lead him to think that this pain has a cause; but whether this cause is body or spirit, extended or unextended, figured or not figured, he cannot possibly, from any principles he is supposed to have, form the least conjecture. Having had formerly no notion of body or of extension, the prick of a pin can give him none.

Suppose, next, a body not pointed, but blunt, is applied to his body with a force gradually increased until it bruises him. What has he got by this, but another sensation or train of sensations, from which he is able to conclude as little as from the former? A scirrhous tumour in any inward part of the body, by pressing upon the adjacent parts, may give the same kind of sensation as the pressure of an external body, without conveying any notion but that of pain, which, surely, hath no resemblance to extension.

Suppose, thirdly, that the body applied to him touches a larger or a lesser part of his body. Can this give him any notion of its extension or dimensions? To me it seems impossible that it should, unless he had some previous notion of the dimensions and figure of his own body, to serve him as a measure. When my two hands touch the extremities of a body, if I know them to be a foot asunder, I easily collect that the body is a foot long; and, if I know them to be five feet asunder, that it is five feet long; but, if I know not what the distance of my hands is, I cannot know the length of the object they grasp; and, if I have no previous notion of hands at all, or of distance between them, I can never get that notion by their being touched.

Suppose, again, that a body is drawn along his hands or face, while they are at rest. Can this give him any notion of space or motion? It no doubt gives a new feeling; but how it should convey a notion of space or motion to one who had none before, I cannot conceive. The blood moves along the arteries and veins, and this motion, when violent, is felt: but I imagine no man, by this feeling, could get the conception of space or motion, if he had it not before. Such a motion may give a certain succession of feelings, as the colic may do; but no feelings, nor any combination of feelings, can ever resemble space or motion.

Let us next suppose, that he makes some instinctive effort to move his head or his hand; but that no motion follows, either on account of external resistance, or of palsy. Can this effort convey the notion of space and motion to one who never had it before? Surely it cannot.

Last of all, let us suppose that he moves a limb by instinct, without having had any previous notion of space or motion. He has here a new sensation, which accompanies the flexure of joints, and the swelling of muscles. But how this sensation can convey into his mind the idea of space and motion, is still altogether mysterious and unintelligible. The motions of the heart and lungs are all performed by the contraction of muscles, yet give no conception of space or motion. An embryo in the womb has many such motions, and probably the feelings that accompany them, without any idea of space or motion.

Upon the whole, it appears that our philosophers have imposed upon themselves and upon us, in pretending to deduce from sensation the first origin of our notions of external existences, of space, motion, and extension, and all the primary qualities of body—that is, the qualities whereof we have the most clear and distinct conception. These qualities do not at all tally with any system of the human faculties that hath been advanced. They have no resemblance to any sensation, or to any operation of our minds; and, therefore, they cannot be ideas either of sensation or of reflection. The very conception of them is irreconcilable to the principles of all our philosophic systems of the understanding. The belief of them is no less so.

Section VII: Of The Existence of a Material World

It is beyond our power to say when, or in what order, we came by our notions of these qualities. When we trace the operations of our minds as far back as memory and reflection can carry us, we find them already in possession of our imagination and belief, and quite familiar to the mind: but how they came first into its acquaintance, or what has given them so strong a hold of our belief, and what regard they deserve, are, no doubt, very important questions in the philosophy of human nature.

Shall we, with the Bishop of Cloyne, serve them with a *quo warranto*, and have them tried at the bar of philosophy, upon the statute of the ideal system? Indeed, in this trial they seem to have come off very pitifully; for, although they had very able counsel, learned in the law—viz., Des Cartes, Malebranche, and Locke, who said everything they could for their clients— the Bishop of Cloyne, believing them to be aiders and abetters of heresy and schism, prosecuted them with great vigour, fully answered all that had been pleaded in their defense, and silenced their ablest advocates, who seem, for half a century past, to decline the argument, and to trust to the favour of the jury rather than to the strength of their pleadings.

Thus, the wisdom of *philosophy* is set in opposition to the *common sense* of mankind. The first pretends to demonstrate, *a priori,* that there can be no such thing as a material world; that sun, moon, stars, and earth, vegetable and animal bodies, are, and can be nothing else, but sensations in the mind, or images of those sensations in the memory and imagination; that, like pain and joy, they can have no existence when they are not thought of. The last can conceive no otherwise of this opinion, than as a kind of metaphysical lunacy, and concludes that too much learning is apt to make men mad; and that the man who seriously entertains this belief, though in other respects he may be a very good man, as a man may be who believes that he is made of glass; yet, surely he hath a soft place in his understanding, and hath been hurt by much thinking.

This opposition betwixt philosophy and common sense, is apt to have a very unhappy influence upon the philosopher himself. He sees human nature in an odd, unamiable, and mortifying light. He considers himself, and the rest of his species, as born under a necessity of believing ten thousand absurdities and contradictions, and endowed with such a pittance of reason as is just sufficient to make this unhappy discovery; and this is all the fruit of his profound speculations. Such notions of human nature tend to slacken every nerve of the soul, to put every noble purpose and sentiment out of countenance, and spread a melancholy gloom over the whole face of things.

If this is wisdom, let me be deluded with the vulgar. I find something within me that recoils against it, and inspires more reverent sentiments of the human kind, and of the universal administration. Common Sense and Reason[10] have both one author; that Almighty Author in all whose other works we observe a consistency, uniformity, and beauty which charm and delight the understanding: there must, therefore, be some order and consistency in the human faculties, as well as in other parts of his workmanship. A man that thinks reverently of his own kind, and esteems true wisdom and philosophy, will not be fond, nay, will be very suspicious, of such strange and paradoxical opinions. If they are false, they disgrace philosophy; and, if they are true, they degrade the human species, and make us justly ashamed of our frame.

To what purpose is it for philosophy to decide against common sense in this or any other matter? The belief of a material world is older, and of more authority, than any principles of philosophy. It declines the tribunal of reason, and laughs at all the artillery of the logician. It retains its sovereign authority in spite of all the edicts of philosophy, and reason itself must stoop to its orders. Even those philosophers who have disowned the authority of our notions of an external material world, confess that they find themselves under a necessity of submitting to their power.

Methinks, therefore, it were better to make a virtue of necessity; and, since we cannot get rid of the vulgar notion and belief of an external world, to reconcile our reason to it as well as we can; for, if Reason should stomach and fret ever so much at this yoke, she cannot throw it off; if she will not be the servant of Common Sense, she must be her slave.

In order, therefore, to reconcile Reason to Common Sense in this matter, I beg leave to offer to the consideration of philosophers these two observations. First, That, in all this debate about the existence of a material world, it hath been taken for granted on both sides, that this same material world, if any such there be, must be the express image of our sensations; that we can have no conception of any material thing which is not like some sensation in our minds; and particularly that the sensations of touch are images of extension, hardness, figure, and motion. Every argument brought agains the existence of a material world, either by the Bishop of Cloyne, or by the author of the "Treatise of Human Nature," supposeth this. If this is true, their arguments are conclusive and unanswerable; but, on the other hand, if it is not true, there is no shadow of argument left. Have those philosophers, then, given any solid proof of this hypothesis, upon which the whole weight of so strange a system rests. No. They have not so much as attempted to do it. But, because ancient and modern philosophers have agreed in this opinion, they have taken it for granted. But let us, as becomes philosophers, lay aside authority; we need not, surely, consult Aristotle or Locke, to know whether pain be like the point of a sword. I have as clear a conception of extension, hardness, and motion, as I have of the point of a sword; and, with some pains and practice, I can form as clear a notion of the other sensations of touch as I have of pain. When I do so, and compare them together, it appears to me clear as daylight, that the former are not of kin to the latter, nor resemble them in any one feature. They are as unlike, yea as certainly and manifestly unlike, as pain is to the point of a sword. It may be true, that those sensations first introduced the material world to our acquaintance; it may be true that it seldom or never appears without their company; but, for all that, they are as unlike as the passion of anger is to those features of the countenance which attend it.

So that, in the sentence those philosophers have passed against the material world, there is an *error personae*. Their proof touches not matter, or any of its qualities; but strikes directly against an idol of their own imagination, a material world made of ideas and sensations, which never had, nor can have an existence.

Secondly, The very existence of our conceptions of extension, figure, and motion, since they are neither ideas of sensation nor reflection, overturns the whole ideal system, by which the material world hath been tried and condemned; so that there hath been likewise in this sentence an *error juris*.

It is a very fine and a just observation of Locke, that, as no human art can create a single particle of matter, and the whole extent of our power over the material world consists in compounding, combining, and disjoining the matter made to our hands; so, in the world of thought, the materials are all made by nature, and can only be variously combined and disjoined by us. So that it is impossible for reason or prejudice, true or false philosophy, to produce one simple notion or conception, which is not the work of nature, and the result of our constitution. The conception of extension, motion, and the other attributes of màtter, cannot be the effect of error or prejudice; it must be the work of nature. And the power or faculty by which we acquire those conceptions, must be something different from any power of the human mind that hath been explained, since it is neither sensation nor reflection.

This I would, therefore, humbly propose, as an *experimentum crucis,* by which the ideal system must stand or fall; and it brings the matter to a short issue: Extension, figure, motion, may, any one, or all of them, be taken for the subject of this experiment. Either they are ideas of sensation, or they are not. If any one of them can be shewn to be an idea of sensation, or to have the least resemblance to any sensation, I lay my hand upon my mouth, and give up all pretence to reconcile reason to common sense in this matter, and must suffer the ideal scepticism to triumph. But if, on the other hand, they are not ideas of sensation, nor like to any sensation, then the ideal system is a rope of sand, and all the laboured arguments of the sceptical philosophy against a material world, and against the existence of every thing but impressions and ideas, proceed upon a false hypothesis. . . .

Bishop Berkeley hath proved, beyond the possibility of reply, that we cannot by reasoning infer the existence of matter from our sensations; and the author of the "Treatise of Human Nature" hath proved no less clearly, that we cannot by reasoning infer the existence of our own or other minds from our sensations. But are we to admit nothing but what can be proved by reasoning? Then we must be sceptics indeed, and believe nothing at all. The author of the "Treatise of Human Nature" appears to me to be but a half-sceptic. He hath not followed his principles so far as they lead him; but, after having, with unparalleled intrepidity and success, combated vulgar prejudices, when he had but one blow to strike, his courage fails him, he fairly lays down his arms, and yields himself a captive to the most common of all vulgar prejudices—I mean the belief of the existence of his own impressions and ideas.

I beg, therefore, to have the honour of making an addition to the sceptical system, without which I conceive it cannot hang together. I affirm, that the belief of the existence of impressions and ideas, is as little supported by reason, as that of the existence of minds and bodies. No man ever did or could offer any reason for this belief. Des Cartes took it for granted, that he thought, and had sensations and ideas; so have all his followers done. Even the hero of scepticism hath yielded this point, I crave leave to say, weakly and imprudently. I say so, because I am persuaded that there is no principle of his philosophy that obliged him to make this concession. And what is there in impressions and ideas so formidable, that this all-conquering philosophy, after triumphing over every other existence, should pay homage to them? Besides, the concession is dangerous: for belief is of such a nature, that, if you leave any root, it will spread; and you may more easily pull it up altogether, than say, Hitherto shalt thou go and no further: the existence of impressions and ideas I give up to thee; but see thou pretend to nothing more. A thorough and consistent sceptic will never, therefore, yield this point; and while he holds it, you can never oblige him to yield anything else.

To such a sceptic I have nothing to say; but of the semisceptics, I should beg to know, why they believe the existence of their impressions and ideas. The true reason I take to be, because they cannot help it; and the same reason will lead them to believe many other things.

All reasoning must be from first principles; and for first principles no other reason can be given but this, that, by the constitution of our nature, we are under a necessity of assenting to them. Such principles are parts of our constitution, no less than the power of thinking: reason can neither make nor destroy them; nor can it do anything without them: it is like a telescope, which may help a man to see farther, who hath eyes; but, without eyes, a telescope shews nothing at all. A mathematician cannot prove the truth of his axioms, nor can he prove anything, unless he takes them for granted. We cannot prove the existence of our minds, nor even of our thoughts and sensations. A historian, or a witness, can prove nothing, unless it is taken for granted that the memory and senses may be trusted. A natural philosopher can prove nothing, unless it is taken for granted that the course of nature is steady and uniform.

How or when I got such first principles, upon which I build all my reasoning, I know not; for I had them before I can remember: but I am sure they are parts of my constitution, and that I cannot throw them off. That our thoughts and sensations must have a subject, which we call *ourself,* is not therefore an opinion got by reasoning, but a natural principle. That our sensations of touch indicate something external, extended, figured, hard or soft, is not a deduction of reason, but a natural principle. The belief of it, and the very conception of it, are equally parts of our constitution. If we are deceived in it, we are deceived by Him that made us, and there is no remedy.

I do not mean to affirm, that the sensations of touch do, from the very first, suggest the same notions of body and its qualities which they do when we are grown up. Perhaps Nature is frugal in this, as in her other operations. The passion of love, with all its concomitant sentiments and desires, is naturally suggested by the perception of beauty in the other sex; yet the same perception does not suggest the tender passion till a certain period of life. A blow given to an infant, raises grief and lamentation; but when he grows up, it as naturally stirs resentment, and prompts him to resistance. Perhaps a child in the womb, or for some short period of its existence, is merely a sentient being; the faculties by which it perceives an external world, by which it reflects on its own thoughts, and existence, and relation to other things, as well as its reasoning and moral faculties, unfold themselves by degrees; so that it is inspired with the various principles of common sense, as with the passions of love and resentment, when it has occasion for them.

Section VIII: Of The Systems of Philosophers Concerning the Senses[11]

All the systems of philosophers about our senses and their objects have split upon this rock, of not distinguishing properly sensations which can have no existence but when they are felt, from the things suggested by them. Aristotle—with as distinguishing a head as ever applied to philosophical disquisitions—confounds these two; and makes every sensation to be the form, without the matter, of the thing perceived by it. As the impression of a seal upon wax has the form of the seal but nothing of the matter of it, so he conceived our sensations to be impressions upon the mind, which bear the image, likeness, or form of the external thing perceived, without the matter of it. Colour, sound, and smell, as well as extension, figure, and hardness, are, according to him, various forms of matter: our sensations are the same forms imprinted on the mind, and perceived in its own intellect. It is evident from this, that Aristotle made no distinction between primary and secondary qualities of bodies, although that distinction was made by Democritus, Epicurus, and others of the ancients.[12]

Des Cartes, Malebranche, and Locke, revived the distinction between primary and secondary qualities; but they made the secondary qualities mere sensations, and the primary ones resemblances of our sensations. . . .

Bishop Berkeley gave new light to this subject, by shewing that the qualities of an inanimate thing, such as matter is conceived to be, cannot resemble any sensation; that it is impossible to conceive anything like the sensations of our minds, but the sensations of other minds. Every one that attends

properly to his sensations must assent to this; yet it had escaped all the philosophers that came before Berkeley. . . .

But let us observe what use the Bishop makes of this important discovery. Why, he concludes, that we can have no conception of an inanimate substance, such as matter is conceived
to be, or of any of its qualities; and that there is the strongest
ground to believe that there is no existence in nature but
minds, sensations, and ideas: if there is any other kind of
existence, it must be what we neither have nor can have any
conception of. But how does this follow? Why, thus: We can
have no conception of anything but what resembles some sensation or idea in our minds; but the sensations and ideas in our
minds can resemble nothing but the sensations and ideas in
other minds; therefore, the conclusion is evident. This argument, we see, leans upon two propositions. The last of them
the ingenious author hath, indeed, made evident to all that
understand his reasoning, and can attend to their own sensations: but the first proposition he never attempts to prove; it
is taken from the doctrine of ideas, which hath been so universally received by philosophers, that it was thought to need no
proof.

We may here again observe, that this acute writer argues
from a hypothesis against fact, and against the common sense
of mankind. That we can have no conception of anything,
unless there is some impression, sensation, or idea, in our
minds which resembles it, is indeed an opinion which hath
been very generally received among philosophers; but it is
neither self-evident, nor hath it been clearly proved; and
therefore it hath been more reasonable to call in question this
doctrine of philosophers, than to discard the material world,
and by that means expose philosophy to the ridicule of all men
who will not offer up common sense as a sacrifice to metaphysics.

We ought, however, to do this justice both to the Bishop of
Cloyne and to the author of the "Treatise of Human Nature,"
to acknowledge, that their conclusions are justly drawn from

the doctrine of ideas, which has been so universally received. On the other hand, from the character of Bishop Berkeley, and of his predecessors, Des Cartes, Locke, and Malebranche, we may venture to say, that, if they had seen all the consequences of this doctrine, as clearly as the author before mentioned did, they would have suspected it vehemently, and examined it more carefully than they appear to have done.

The theory of ideas, like the Trojan horse, had a specious appearance both of innocence and beauty; but if those philosophers had known that it carried in its belly death and destruction to all science and common sense, they would not have broken down their walls to give it admittance.

That we have clear and distinct conceptions of extension, figure, motion, and other attributes of body, which are neither sensations, nor like any sensation, is a fact of which we may be as certain as that we have sensations. And that all mankind have a fixed belief of an external material world—a belief which is neither got by reasoning nor education, and a belief which we cannot shake off, even when we seem to have strong arguments against it and no shadow of argument for it—is likewise a fact, for which we have all the evidence that the nature of the thing admits. These facts are phaenomena of human nature, from which we may justly argue against any hypothesis, however generally received. But to argue from a hypothesis against facts, is contrary to the rules of true philosophy.

CHAPTER 6 / OF SEEING

Section II: Sight Discovers Almost Nothing Which the Blind May Not Comprehend—The Reason of This

Notwithstanding what hath been said of the dignity and superior nature of this faculty, it is worthy of our observation, that there is very little of the knowledge acquired by sight, that may not be communicated to a man born blind. One who never saw the light, may be learned and knowing in every science, even in optics; and may make discoveries in every branch of philosophy. He may understand as much as another man, not only of the order, distances, and motions of the heavenly bodies; but of the nature of light, and of the laws of the reflection and refraction of its rays. He may understand distinctly how those laws produce the phaenomena of the rainbow, the prism, the camera obscura, and the magic lanthorn, and all the powers of the microscope and telescope. This is a fact sufficiently attested by experience.

In order to perceive the reason of it, we must distinguish the appearance that objects make to the eye, from the things suggested by that appearance: and again, in the visible appearance of objects, we must distinguish the appearance of colour from the appearance of extension, figure, and motion. First, then, as to the visible appearance of the figure, and motion, and extension of bodies, I conceive that a man born blind may have a distinct notion, if not of the very things, at least of something extremely like to them. May not a blind man be made to conceive that a body moving directly from the eye, or directly towards it, may appear to be at rest? and that the same motion may appear quicker or slower, according as it is nearer to the eye or farther off, more direct or more oblique? May he not be made to conceive, that a plain surface, in a certain position, may appear as a straight line, and vary its visible figure, as its position, or the position of the eye, is varied?—that a circle seen obliquely will appear an ellipse; and a square, a rhombus, or an oblong rectangle? . . .

We have seen how far a blind man may go in the knowledge of the appearances which things make to the eye. As to the things which are suggested by them or inferred from them, although he could never discover them of himself, yet he may understand them perfectly by the information of others. And everything of this kind that enters into our minds by the eye, may enter into his by the ear. Thus, for instance, he could never, if left to the direction of his own faculties, have dreamed of any such thing as light; but he can be informed of everything we know about it. He can conceive, as distinctly as we, the minuteness and velocity of its rays, their various degrees of refrangibility and reflexibility, and all the magical powers and virtues of that wonderful element. He could never of himself have found out, that there are such bodies as the sun, moon, and stars; but he may be informed of all the noble discoveries of astronomers about their motions, and the laws of nature by which they are regulated. Thus, it appears, that there is very little knowledge got by the eye, which may not be communicated by language to those who have no eyes. . . .

The distinction we have made between the visible appearances of the objects of sight, and things suggested by them, is necessary to give us a just notion of the intention of nature in giving us eyes. If we attend duly to the operation of our mind in the use of this faculty, we shall perceive that the visible appearance of objects is hardly ever regarded by us. It is not at all made an object of thought or reflection, but serves only as a sign to introduce to the mind something else, which may be distinctly conceived by those who never saw.

Thus, the visible appearance of things in my room varies almost every hour, according as the day is clear or cloudy, as the sun is in the east, or south, or west, and as my eye is in one part of the room or in another; but I never think of these variations, otherwise than as signs of morning, noon, or night, of a clear or cloudy sky. A book or a chair has a different appearance to the eye, in every different distance and position; yet we conceive it to be still the same; and, overlooking the appearance, we immediately conceive the real figure, distance, and position of the body, of which its visible or perspective appearance is a sign and indication.

When I see a man at the distance of ten yards, and afterwards see him at the distance of a hundred yards, his visible appearance, in its length, breadth, and all its linear proportions, is ten times less in the last case than it is in the first; yet I do not conceive him one inch diminished by this diminution of his visible figure. Nay, I do not in the least attend to this diminution, even when I draw from it the conclusion of his being at a greater distance. For such is the subtilty of the mind's operation in this case, that we draw the conclusion, without perceiving that ever the premises entered into the mind. A thousand such instances might be produced, in order to shew that the visible appearances of objects are intended by nature only as signs or indications; and that the mind passes instantly to the things signified, without making the least reflection upon the sign, or even perceiving that there is any such thing. It is in a way somewhat similar, that the sounds of a language, after it is become familiar, are overlooked, and we attend only to the things signified by them.

It is therefore a just and important observation of the Bishop of Cloyne, That the visible appearance of objects is a kind of language used by nature, to inform us of their distance, magnitude, and figure. And this observation hath been very happily applied by that ingenious writer, to the solution of some phaenomena in optics, which had before perplexed the greatest masters in that science. The same observation is further improved by the judicious Dr Smith, in his Optics, for explaining the apparent figure of the heavens, and the apparent distances and magnitudes of objects seen with glasses, or by the naked eye.

Avoiding as much as possible the repetition of what hath been said by these excellent writers, we shall avail ourselves of the distinction between the signs that nature useth in this visual language, and the things signified by them. . . .

Section IV: That Colour is a Quality of Bodies, Not a
Sensation of the Mind

By colour, all men, who have not been tutored by modern
philosophy, understand, not a sensation of the mind, which
can have no existence when it is not perceived, but a quality
or modification of bodies, which continues to be the same
whether it is seen or not. The scarlet-rose which is before me,
is still a scarlet-rose when I shut my eyes, and was so at mid-
night when no eye saw it. The colour remains when the appearance ceases; it remains the same when the appearance
changes. For when I view this scarlet-rose through a pair of
green spectacles, the appearance is changed; but I do not
conceive the colour of the rose changed. To a person in the
jaundice, it has still another appearance; but he is easily convinced that the change is in his eye, and not in the colour of
the object. Every different degree of light makes it have a
different appearance, and total darkness takes away all appearance, but makes not the least change in the colour of the body.
We may, by a variety of optical experiments, change the appearance of figure and magnitude in a body, as well as that of
colour; we may make one body appear to be ten. But all men
believe, that, as a multiplying glass does not really produce ten
guineas out of one, nor a microscope turn a guinea into a
ten-pound piece, so neither does a coloured glass change the
real colour of the object seen through it, when it changes the
appearance of that colour.

The common language of mankind shews evidently, that we
ought to distinguish between the colour of a body, which is
conceived to be a fixed and permanent quality in the body, and
the appearance of that colour to the eye, which may be varied
a thousand ways, by a variation of the light, of the medium, or
of the eye itself. The permanent colour of the body is the cause
which, by the mediation of various kinds or degrees of light,
and of various transparent bodies interposed, produces all this

variety of appearances. When a coloured body is presented, there is a certain apparition to the eye, or to the mind, which we have called *the appearance of colour.* Mr Locke calls it *an idea;* and, indeed, it may be called so with the greatest propriety. This idea can have no existence but when it is perceived. It is a kind of thought, and can only be the act of a percipient or thinking being. By the constitution of our nature, we are led to conceive this idea as a sign of something external, and are impatient till we learn its meaning. A thousand experiments for this purpose are made every day by children, even before they come to the use of reason. They look at things, they handle them, they put them in various positions, at different distances, and in different lights. The ideas of sight, by these means, come to be associated with, and readily to suggest, things external, and altogether unlike them. In particular, that idea which we have called *the appearance of colour,* suggests the conception and belief of some unknown quality in the body which occasions the idea; and it is to this quality, and not to the idea, that we give the name of *colour.* The various colours, although in their nature equally unknown, are easily distinguished when we think or speak of them, by being associated with the ideas which they excite. In like manner, gravity, magnetism, and electricity, although all unknown qualities, are distinguished by their different effects. As we grow up, the mind acquires a habit of passing so rapidly from the ideas of sight to the external things suggested by them, that the ideas are not in the least attended to, nor have they names given them in common language.

When we think or speak of any particular colour, however simple the notion may seem to be which is presented to the imagination, it is really in some sort compounded. It involves an unknown cause and a known effect. The name of *colour* belongs indeed to the cause only, and not to the effect. But, as the cause is unknown, we can form no distinct conception of it but by its relation to the known effect; and, therefore, both go together in the imagination, and are so closely united, that they are mistaken for one simple object of thought. When I would conceive those colours of bodies which we call *scarlet* and *blue*—if I conceived them only as unknown qualities, I could perceive no distinction between the one and the other. I must, therefore, for the sake of distinction, join to each of them, in my imagination, some effect or some relation that is peculiar; and the most obvious distinction is, the appearance which one and the other makes to the eye. Hence the appearance is, in the imagination, so closely united with the quality called *a scarlet-colour*, that they are apt to be mistaken for one and the same thing, although they are in reality so different and so unlike, that one is an idea in the mind, the other is a quality of body.

I conclude, then, that colour is not a sensation, but a secondary quality of bodies, in the sense we have already explained; that it is a certain power or virtue in bodies, that in fair daylight exhibits to the eye an appearance which is very familiar to us, although it hath no name. Colour differs from other secondary qualities in this, that, whereas the name of the quality is sometimes given to the sensation which indicates it, and is occasioned by it, we never, as far as I can judge, give the name of *colour* to the sensation, but to the quality only. Perhaps the reason of this may be, that the appearances of the same colour are so various and changeable, according to the different modifications of the light, of the medium, and of the eye, that language could not afford names for them. And, indeed, they are so little interesting, that they are never attended to, but serve only as signs to introduce the things signified by them. Nor ought it to appear incredible, that appearances so frequent and so familiar should have no names, nor be made objects of thought; since we have before shewn that this is true of many sensations of touch, which are no less frequent nor less familiar.

Section V: An Inference From the Preceding

From what hath been said about colour, we may infer two things. The first is, that one of the most remarkable paradoxes of modern philosophy, which hath been universally esteemed as a great discovery, is, in reality, when examined to the bottom, nothing else but an abuse of words. The paradox I mean is, That colour is not a quality of bodies, but only an idea in the mind. We have shewn, that the word *colour*, as used by the vulgar, cannot signify an idea in the mind, but a permanent quality of body. We have shewn, that there is really a permanent quality of body, to which the common use of this word exactly agrees. Can any stronger proof be desired, that this quality is that to which the vulgar give the name of *colour?* If it should be said, that this quality, to which we give the name of *colour*, is unknown to the vulgar, and, therefore, can have no name among them, I answer, it is, indeed, known only by its effects—that is, by its exciting a certain idea in us; but are there not numberless qualities of bodies which are known only by their effects, to which, notwithstanding, we find it necessary to give names? Medicine alone might furnish us with a hundred instances of this kind. Do not the words *astringent, narcotic, epispastic, caustic,* and innumerable others, signify qualities of bodies, which are known only by their effects upon animal bodies? Why, then, should not the vulgar give a name to a quality, whose effects are every moment perceived by their eyes? We have all the reason, therefore, that the nature of the thing admits, to think that the vulgar apply the name of *colour* to that quality of bodies which excites in us what the philosophers call the *idea of colour.* And that there is such a quality in bodies, all philosophers allow, who allow that there is any such thing as body. Philosophers have thought fit to leave that quality of bodies which the vulgar call *colour*, without a name, and to give the name of *colour* to the idea or appearance, to which, as we have shewn, the vulgar give no name, because they never make it an object of thought or reflection. Hence it appears, that, when philosophers affirm that colour is not in bodies, but in the mind, and the vulgar affirm that colour is not in the mind, but is a quality of bodies, there is no difference between them about things, but only about the meaning of a word.

The vulgar have undoubted right to give names to things which they are daily conversant about; and philosophers seem justly chargeable with an abuse of language, when they change the meaning of a common word, without giving warning.

If it is a good rule, to think with philosophers and speak with the vulgar, it must be right to speak with the vulgar when we think with them, and not to shock them by philosophical paradoxes, which, when put into common language, express only the common sense of mankind.

If you ask a man that is no philosopher, what colour is, or what makes one body appear white, another scarlet, he cannot tell. He leaves that inquiry to philosophers, and can embrace any hypothesis about it, except that of our modern philosophers, who affirm that colour is not in body, but only in the mind. . . .

We desire, therefore, with pleasure, to do justice to the doctrine of Locke, and other modern philosophers, with regard to colour and other secondary qualities, and to ascribe to it its due merit, while we beg leave to censure the language in which they have expressed their doctrine. When they had explained and established the distinction between the appearance which colour makes to the eye, and the modification of the coloured body which, by the laws of nature, causes that appearance, the question was, whether to give the name of *colour* to the cause or to the effect? By giving it, as they have done, to the effect, they set philosophy apparently in opposition to common sense, and expose it to the ridicule of the vulgar. But had they given the name of *colour* to the cause, as they ought to have done, they must then have affirmed, with the vulgar, that colour is a quality of bodies; and that there is neither colour nor anything like it in the mind. Their language, as well as their sentiments, would have been perfectly agreeable to the common apprehensions of mankind, and true Philosophy would have joined hands with Common Sense. As Locke was no enemy to common sense, it may be presumed, that, in this instance, as in some others, he was seduced by some received hypothesis. . . .

Section VII: Of Visible Figure and Extension

Although there is no resemblance, nor, as far as we know, any necessary connection, between that quality in a body which we call its *colour,* and the appearance which that colour makes to the eye, it is quite otherwise with regard to its *figure* and *magnitude.* There is certainly a resemblance, and a necessary connection, between the visible figure and magnitude of a body, and its real figure and magnitude; no man can give a reason why a scarlet colour affects the eye in the manner it does; no man can be sure that it affects his eye in the same manner as it affects the eye of another, and that it has the same appearance to him as it has to another man;—but we can assign a reason why a circle placed obliquely to the eye, should appear in the form of an ellipse. The visible figure, magnitude, and position may, by mathematical reasoning, be deduced from the real; and it may be demonstrated, that every eye that sees distinctly and perfectly, must, in the same situation, see it under this form, and no other. Nay, we may venture to affirm, that a man born blind, if he were instructed in mathematics would be able to determine the visible figure of a body, when its real figure, distance, and position, are given. Dr Saunderson understood the projection of the sphere, and perspective. Now, I require no more knowledge in a blind man, in order to his being able to determine the visible figure of bodies, than that he can project the outline of a given body, upon the surface of a hollow sphere, whose centre is in the eye. This projection is the visible figure he wants: for it is the same figure with that which is projected upon the *tunica retina* in vision.

A blind man can conceive lines drawn from every point of the object to the centre of the eye, making angles. He can conceive that the length of the object will appear greater or less, in proportion to the angle which it subtends at the eye; and that, in like manner, the breadth, and in general the distance, of any one point of the object from any other point, will appear greater or less, in proportion to the angles which those distances subtend. He can easily be made to conceive, that the visible appearance has no thickness, any more than a projection of the sphere, or a perspective draught. He may be informed, that the eye, until it is aided by experience, does not represent one object as nearer or more remote than another. Indeed, he would probably conjecture this of himself, and be apt to think that the rays of light must make the same impression upon the eye, whether they come from a greater or a less distance.

These are all the principles which we suppose our blind mathematician to have; and these he may certainly acquire by information and reflection. It is no less certain, that, from these principles, having given the real figure and magnitude of a body, and its position and distance with regard to the eye, he can find out its visible figure and magnitude. He can demonstrate in general, from these principles, that the visible figure of all bodies will be the same with that of their projection upon the surface of a hollow sphere, when the eye is placed in the centre. And he can demonstrate that their visible magnitude will be greater or less, according as their projection occupies a greater or less part of the surface of this sphere.

To set this matter in another light, let us distinguish betwixt the *position* of objects with regard to the eye, and their *distance* from it. Objects that lie in the same right line drawn from the centre of the eye, have the same position, however different their distances from the eye may be: but objects which lie in different right lines drawn from the eye's centre, have a different position; and this difference of position is greater or less in proportion to the angle made at the eye by the right lines mentioned. Having thus defined what we mean by the position of objects with regard to the eye, it is evident that, as the real figure of a body consists in the situation of its several parts with regard to one another, so its visible figure consists in the position of its several parts with regard to the eye; and, as he that hath a distinct conception of the situation of the parts of the body with regard to one another, must have a distinct conception of its real figure; so he that conceives distinctly the position of its several parts with regard to the eye, must have a distinct conception of its visible figure. Now, there is nothing, surely, to hinder a blind man from conceiving the position of the several parts of a body with regard to the eye, any more than from conceiving their situation with regard to one another; and, therefore, I conclude, that a blind man may attain a distinct conception of the visible figure of bodies. . . .

Section VIII: Some Queries Concerning Visible Figure Answered

It may be asked, What kind of thing is this visible figure? Is it a Sensation, or an Idea? If it is an idea, from what sensation is it copied? These questions may seem trivial or impertinent to one who does not know that there is a tribunal of inquisition erected by certain modern philosophers, before which everything in nature must answer. The articles of inquisition are few indeed, but very dreadful in their consequences. They are only these: Is the prisoner an Impression or an Idea? If an idea, from what impression copied? Now, if it appears that the prisoner is neither an impression, nor an idea copied from some impression, immediately, without being allowed to offer anything in arrest of judgment, he is sentenced to pass out of existence, and to be, in all time to come, an empty unmeaning sound, or the ghost of a departed entity.

Before this dreadful tribunal, cause and effect, time and place, matter and spirit, have been tried and cast: how then shall such a poor flimsy form as visible figure stand before it? It must even plead guilty, and confess that it is neither an impression nor an idea. For, alas! it is notorious, that it is extended in length and breadth; it may be long or short, broad or narrow, triangular, quadrangular, or circular; and, therefore, unless ideas and impressions are extended and figured, it cannot belong to that category.

If it should still be asked, To what category of beings does visible figure then belong? I can only, in answer, give some tokens, by which those who are better acquainted with the categories, may chance to find its place. It is, as we have said, the position of the several parts of a figured body with regard to the eye. The different positions of the several parts of the body with regard to the eye, when put together, make a real figure, which is truly extended in length and breadth, and which represents a figure that is extended in length, breadth, and thickness. In like manner, a projection of the sphere is a real figure, and hath length and breadth, but represents the sphere, which hath three dimensions. A projection of the sphere, or a perspective view of a palace, is a representative in the very same sense as visible figure is; and wherever they have their lodgings in the categories, this will be found to dwell next door to them.

It may farther be asked, Whether there be any sensation proper to visible figure, by which it is suggested in vision?— or by what means it is presented to the mind?

This is a question of some importance, in order to our having a distinct notion of the faculty of seeing; and to give all the light to it we can, it is necessary to compare this sense with other senses, and to make some suppositions, by which we may be enabled to distinguish things that are apt to be confounded, although they are totally different.

There are three of our senses which give us intelligence of things at a distance: smell, hearing, and sight. In smelling and in hearing, we have a sensation or impression upon the mind, which, by our constitution, we conceive to be a sign of something external: but the position of this external thing, with regard to the organ of sense, is not presented to the mind along with the sensation. When I hear the sound of a coach, I could not, previous to experience, determine whether the sounding body was above or below, to the right hand or to the left. So that the sensation suggests to me some external object as the cause or occasion of it; but it suggests not the position of that object, whether it lies in this direction or in that. The same thing may be said with regard to smelling. But the case is quite different with regard to seeing. When I see an object, the appearance which the colour of it makes, may be called *the sensation*, which suggests to me some external thing as its cause; but it suggests likewise the individual direction and position of this cause with regard to the eye. I know it is precisely in such a direction, and in no other. At the same time, I am not conscious of anything that can be called *sensation*, but the sensation of colour. The position of the coloured thing is no sensation; but it is by the laws of my constitution presented to the mind along with the colour, without any additional sensation.

Let us suppose that the eye were so constituted that the rays coming from any one point of the object were not, as they are in our eyes, collected in one point of the *retina*, but diffused over the whole: it is evident to those who understand the structure of the eye, that such an eye as we have supposed, would shew the colour of a body as our eyes do, but that it would neither shew figure nor position. The operation of such an eye would be precisely similar to that of hearing and smell; it would give no perception of figure or extension, but merely of colour. Nor is the supposition we have made altogether imaginary: for it is nearly the case of most people who have cataracts, whose crystalline, as Mr Cheselden observes, does not altogether exclude the rays of light, but diffuses them over the *retina*, so that such persons see things as one does through a glass of broken gelly: they perceive the colour, but nothing of the figure or magnitude of objects. . . .

We have reason to believe, that the rays of light make some impression upon the *retina;* but we are not conscious of this impression; nor have anatomists or philosophers been able to discover the nature and effects of it; whether it produces a vibration in the nerve, or the motion of some subtile fluid contained in the nerve, or something different from either, to which we cannot give a name. Whatever it is, we shall call it the *material impression;* remembering carefully, that it is not an impression upon the mind, but upon the body; and that it is no sensation, nor can resemble sensation, any more than figure or motion can resemble thought. Now, this material impression, made upon a particular point of the *retina*, by the laws of our constitution, suggests two things to the mind—namely, the colour and the position of some external object. No man can give a reason why the same material impression might not have suggested sound, or smell, or either of these, along with the position of the object. That it should suggest colour and position, and nothing else, we can resolve only into our constitution, or the will of our Maker. And since there is no necessary connection between these two things suggested by this material impression, it might, if it had so pleased our Creator, have suggested one of them without the other. Let us suppose, therefore, since it plainly appears to be possible, that our eyes had been so framed as to suggest to us the position of the object, without suggesting colour, or any other quality: What is the consequence of this supposition? It is evidently this, that the person endued with such an eye, would perceive the visible figure of bodies, without having any sensation or impression made upon his mind. The figure he perceives is altogether external; and therefore cannot be called an impression upon the mind, without the grossest abuse of language. If it should be said, that it is impossible to perceive a figure, unless there be some impression of it upon the mind, I beg leave not to admit the impossibility of this without some proof: and I can find none. Neither can I conceive what is meant by an impression of figure upon the mind. I can conceive an impression of figure upon wax, or upon any body that is fit to receive it; but an impression of it upon the mind, is to me quite unintelligible; and, although I form the most distinct conception of the figure, I cannot, upon the strictest examination, find any impression of it upon my mind.

If we suppose, last of all, that the eye hath the power restored of perceiving colour, I apprehend that it will be allowed, that now it perceives figure in the very same manner as before, with this difference only, that colour is always joined with it.

In answer, therefore, to the question proposed, there seems to be no sensation that is appropriated to visible figure, or whose office it is to suggest it. It seems to be suggested immediately by the material impression upon the organ, of which we are not conscious: and why may not a material impression upon the *retina* suggest visible figure, as well as the material impression made upon the hand, when we grasp a ball, suggests real figure? In the one case, one and the same material impression, suggests both colour and visible figure; and in the other case, one and the same material impression suggests hardness, heat, or cold, and real figure, all at the same time.

We shall conclude this section with another question upon this subject. Since the visible figure of bodies is a real and external object to the eye, as their tangible figure is to the touch, it may be asked, Whence arises the difficulty of attending to the first, and the facility of attending to the last? It is certain that the first is more frequently presented to the eye, than the last is to the touch; the first is as distinct and determinate an object as the last, and seems in its own nature as proper for speculation. Yet so little hath it been attended to, that it never had a name in any language, until Bishop Berkeley gave it that which we have used after his example, to distinguish it from the figure which is the object of touch.

The difficulty of attending to the visible figure of bodies, and making it an object of thought, appears so similar to that which we find in attending to our sensations, that both have probably like causes. Nature intended the visible figure as a sign of the tangible figure and situation of bodies, and hath taught us, by a kind of instinct, to put it always to this use. Hence it happens, that the mind passes over it with a rapid motion, to attend to the things signified by it. It is as unnatural to the mind to stop at the visible figure, and attend to it, as it is to a spherical body to stop upon an inclined plane. There is an inward principle, which constantly carries it forward, and which cannot be overcome but by a contrary force.

There are other external things which nature intended for signs, and we find this common to them all, that the mind is disposed to overlook them, and to attend only to the things signified by them. Thus there are certain modifications of the human face, which are natural signs of the present disposition of the mind. Every man understands the meaning of these signs, but not one of a hundred ever attended to the signs themselves, or knows anything about them. Hence you may find many an excellent practical physiognomist who knows nothing of the proportions of a face, nor can delineate or describe the expression of any one passion.

An excellent painter or statuary can tell, not only what are the proportions of a good face, but what changes every passion makes in it. This, however, is one of the chief mysteries of his art, to the acquisition of which infinite labour and attention, as well as a happy genius, are required; but when he puts his art in practice, and happily expresses a passion by its proper signs, every one understands the meaning of these signs, without art, and without reflection.

What has been said of painting, might easily be applied to all the fine arts. The difficulty in them all consists in knowing and attending to those natural signs whereof every man understands the meaning.

We pass from the sign to the thing signified, with ease, and by natural impulse; but to go backward from the thing signified to the sign, is a work of labour and difficulty. Visible figure, therefore, being intended by nature to be a sign, we pass on immediately to the thing signified, and cannot easily return to give any attention to the sign.

Nothing shews more clearly our indisposition to attend to visible figure and visible extension than this—that, although mathematical reasoning is no less applicable to them, than to tangible figure and extension, yet they have entirely escaped the notice of mathematicians. While that figure and that extension which are objects of touch, have been tortured ten thousand ways for twenty centuries, and a very noble system of science has been drawn out of them, not a single proposition do we find with regard to the figure and extension which are the immediate objects of sight!

When the geometrician draws a diagram with the most perfect accuracy—when he keeps his eye fixed upon it, while he goes through a long process of reasoning, and demonstrates the relations of the several parts of his figure—he does not consider that the visible figure presented to his eye, is only the representative of a tangible figure, upon which all his attention is fixed; he does not consider that these two figures have really different properties; and that, what he demonstrates to be true of the one, is not true of the other. . . .

Section XIII: Of Seeing Objects Single With Two Eyes

Another phaenomenon of vision which deserves attention, is our seeing objects single with two eyes. There are two pictures of the object, one on each *retina*, and each picture by itself makes us see an object in a certain direction from the eye; yet both together commonly make us see only one object. . . .

1. We find that, when the eyes are sound and perfect, and the axes of both directed to one point, an object placed in that point is seen single—and here we observe, that in this case the two pictures which shew the object single, are in the centres of the *retina*. When two pictures of a small object are formed upon points of the *retina*, if they show the object single, we shall, for the sake of perspicuity, call such two points of the *retina*, *corresponding points;* and where the object is seen double, we shall call the points of the *retina* on which the pictures are formed, *points that do not correspond.* Now, in this first phae nomenon, it is evident, that the two centres of the *retina* are corresponding points.

2. Supposing the same things as in the last phaenomenon, other objects at the same distance from the eyes as that to which their axes are directed, do also appear single. Thus, if I direct my eyes to a candle placed at the distance of ten feet, and, while I look at this candle, another stands at the same distance from my eyes, within the field of vision, I can, while I look at the first candle, attend to the appearance which the second makes to the eye; and I find that in this case it always appears single. It is here to be observed, that the pictures of the second candle do not fall upon the centres of the *retinae*, but they both fall upon the same side of the centres—that is, both to the right, or both to the left; and both are at the same distance from the centres. This might easily be demonstrated from the principles of optics. Hence it appears, that in this second phaenomenon of single vision, the corresponding points are points of the two *retinae*, which are similarly situate with respect to the two centres, being both upon the same side of the centre, and at the same distance from it. It appears likewise, from this phaenomenon, that every point in one *retina* corresponds with that which is similarly situate in the other.

3. Supposing still the same things, objects which are much nearer to the eyes, or much more distant from them, than that to which the two eyes are directed, appear double. Thus, if the candle is placed at the distance of ten feet, and I hold my finger at arms-length between my eyes and the candle—when I look at the candle, I see my finger double; and when I look at my finger, I see the candle double; and the same thing happens with regard to all other objects at like distances which fall within the sphere of vision. In this phaenomenon, it is evident to those who understand the principles of optics, that the pictures of the objects which are seen double, do not fall upon points of the *retinae* which are similarly situate, but that the pictures of the objects seen single do fall upon points similarly situate. Whence we infer, that, as the points of the two *retinae*, which are similarly situate with regard to the centres, do correspond, so those which are dissimilarly situate do not correspond.

4. It is to be observed, that, although, in such cases as are mentioned in the last phaenomenon, we have been accustomed from infancy to see objects double which we know to be single; yet custom, and experience of the unity of the object, never take away this appearance of duplicity.

5. It may, however, be remarked that the custom of attending to visible appearances has a considerable effect, and makes the phaenomenon of double vision to be more or less observed and remembered. Thus you may find a man that can say, with a good conscience, that he never saw things double all his life; yet this very man, put in the situation above mentioned, with his finger between him and the candle, and desired to attend to the appearance of the object which he does not look at, will, upon the first trial, see the candle double, when he looks at his finger; and his finger double, when he looks at the candle. Does he now see otherwise than he saw before? No, surely; but he now attends to what he never attended to before. The same double appearance of an object

hath been a thousand times presented to his eye before now, but he did not attend to it; and so it is as little an object of his reflection and memory, as if it had never happened.

When we look at an object, the circumjacent objects may be seen at the same time, although more obscurely and indistinctly: for the eye hath a considerable field of vision, which it takes in at once. But we attend only to the object we look at. The other objects which fall within the field of vision, are not attended to; and therefore are as if they were not seen. If any of them draws our attention, it naturally draws the eyes at the same time: for, in the common course of life, the eyes always follow the attention: or if at any time, in a revery, they are separated from it, we hardly at that time see what is directly before us. Hence we may see the reason why the man we are speaking of thinks that he never before saw an object double. When he looks at any object, he sees it single, and takes no notice of other visible objects at that time, whether they appear single or double. If any of them draws his attention, it draws his eyes at the same time; and, as soon as the eyes are turned towards it, it appears single. But, in order to see things double —at least, in order to have any reflection or remembrance that he did so—it is necessary that he should look at one object, and at the same time attend to the faint appearance of other objects which are within the field of vision. This is a practice which perhaps he never used, nor attempted; and therefore he does not recollect that ever he saw an object double. But when he is put upon giving this attention, he immediately sees objects double, in the same manner, and with the very same circumstances, as they who have been accustomed, for the greatest part of their lives, to give this attention.

There are many phaenomena of a similar nature, which shew that the mind may not attend to, and thereby, in some sort, not perceive objects that strike the senses. I had occasion to mention several instances of this in the second chapter; and I have been assured, by persons of the best skill in music, that,

in hearing a tune upon the harpsichord, when they give attention to the treble, they do not hear the bass; and when they
attend to the bass, they do not perceive the air of the treble.
Some persons are so near-sighted, that, in reading, they hold
the book to one eye, while the other is directed to other objects. Such persons acquire the habit of attending, in this case,
to the objects of one eye, while they give no attention to those
of the other. . . .

We have now finished what we intended to say, both of the
visible appearances of things to the eye, and of the laws of our
constitution by which those appearances are exhibited. But it
was observed, in the beginning of this chapter, that the visible
appearances of objects serve only as signs of their distance,
magnitude, figure, and other tangible qualities. The visible
appearance is that which is presented to the mind by nature,
according to those laws of our constitution which have been
explained. But the thing signified by that appearance, is that
which is presented to the mind by custom.

When one speaks to us in a language that is familiar, we hear
certain sounds, and this is all the effect that his discourse has
upon us by nature; but by custom we understand the meaning
of these sounds; and, therefore, we fix our attention, not upon
the sounds, but upon the things signified by them. In like
manner, we see only the visible appearance of objects by nature; but we learn by custom to interpret these appearances,
and to understand their meaning. And when this visual language is learned, and becomes familiar, we attend only to the
things signified; and cannot, without great difficulty, attend to
the signs by which they are presented. The mind passes from
one to the other so rapidly and so familiarly, that no trace of
the sign is left in the memory, and we seem immediately, and
without the intervention of any sign, to perceive the thing
signified. . . .

Section XX: Of Perception in General

Sensation, and the perception of external objects by the senses, though very different in their nature, have commonly been considered as one and the same thing. The purposes of common life do not make it necessary to distinguish them, and the received opinions of philosophers tend rather to confound them; but, without attending carefully to this distinction, it is impossible to have any just conception of the operations of our senses. The most simple operations of the mind, admit not of a logical definition: all we can do is to describe them, so as to lead those who are conscious of them in themselves, to attend to them, and reflect upon them; and it is often very difficult to describe them so as to answer this intention.

The same mode of expression is used to denote sensation and perception; and, therefore, we are apt to look upon them as things of the same nature. Thus, *I feel a pain; I see a tree:* the first denoteth a sensation, the last a perception. The grammatical analysis of both expressions is the same: for both consist of an active verb and an object. But, if we attend to the things signified by these expressions, we shall find that, in the first, the distinction between the act and the object is not real but grammatical; in the second, the distinction is not only grammatical but real.

The form of the expression, *I feel pain,* might seem to imply that the feeling is something distinct from the pain felt; yet, in reality, there is no distinction. As *thinking a thought* is an expression which could signify no more than *thinking,* so *feeling a pain* signifies no more than *being pained.* What we have said of pain is applicable to every other mere sensation. It is difficult to give instances, very few of our sensations having names; and, where they have, the name being common to the sensation, and to something else which is associated with it. But, when we attend to the sensation by itself, and separate it from other things which are conjoined with it in the imagination, it appears to be something which can have no existence but in a sentient mind, no distinction from the act of the mind by which it is felt.

Perception, as we here understand it, hath always an object distinct from the act by which it is perceived; an object which may exist whether it be perceived or not. I perceive a tree that grows before my window; there is here an object which is perceived, and an act of the mind by which it is perceived; and these two are not only distinguishable, but they are extremely unlike in their natures. The object is made up of a trunk, branches, and leaves; but the act of the mind by which it is perceived hath neither trunk, branches, nor leaves. I am conscious of this act of my mind, and I can reflect upon it; but it is too simple to admit of an analysis, and I cannot find proper words to describe it. I find nothing that resembles it so much as the remembrance of the tree, or the imagination of it. Yet both these differ essentially from perception; they differ likewise one from another. It is in vain that a philosopher assures me, that the imagination of the tree, the remembrance of it, and the perception of it, are all one, and differ only in degree of vivacity. I know the contrary; for I am as well acquainted with all the three as I am with the apartments of my own house. I know this also, that the perception of an object implies both a conception of its form, and a belief of its present existence. I know, moreover, that this belief is not the effect of argumentation and reasoning; it is the immediate effect of my constitution.

I am aware that this belief which I have in perception stands exposed to the strongest batteries of scepticism. But they make no great impression upon it. The sceptic asks me, Why do you believe the existence of the external object which you perceive? This belief, sir, is none of my manufacture; it came from the mint of Nature; it bears her image and superscription; and, if it is not right, the fault is not mine: I even took it upon trust, and without suspicion. Reason, says the sceptic, is the only judge of truth, and you ought to throw off every opinion and every belief that is not grounded on reason. Why, sir, should I believe the faculty of reason more than that of perception?—they came both out of the same shop, and were made by the same artist; and if he puts one piece of false ware into my hands, what should hinder him from putting another?

Perhaps the sceptic will agree to distrust reason, rather than give any credit to perception. For, says he, since, by your own concession, the object which you perceive, and that act of your mind by which you perceive it, are quite different things, the one may exist without the other; and, as the object may exist without being perceived, so the perception may exist without an object. There is nothing so shameful in a philosopher as to be deceived and deluded; and, therefore, you ought to resolve firmly to withhold assent, and to throw off this belief of external objects, which may be all delusion. For my part, I will never attempt to throw it off; and, although the sober part of mankind will not be very anxious to know my reasons, yet, if they can be of use to any sceptic, they are these:—

First, because it is not in my power: why, then, should I make a vain attempt? It would be agreeable to fly to the moon, and to make a visit to Jupiter and Saturn; but, when I know that Nature has bound me down by the law of gravitation to this planet which I inhabit, I rest contented, and quietly suffer myself to be carried along in its orbit. My belief is carried along by perception, as irresistibly as my body by the earth. And the greatest sceptic will find himself to be in the same condition. He may struggle hard to disbelieve the informations of his senses, as a man does to swim against a torrent; but, ah! it is in vain. It is in vain that he strains every nerve, and wrestles with nature, and with every object that strikes upon his senses. For, after all, when his strength is spent in the fruitless attempt, he will be carried down the torrent with the common herd of believers.

Secondly, I think it would not be prudent to throw off this belief, if it were in my power. If Nature intended to deceive me, and impose upon me by false appearances, and I, by my great cunning and profound logic, have discovered the imposture, prudence would dictate to me, in this case, even to put up [with] this indignity done me, as quietly as I could, and not to call her an impostor to her face, lest she should be even with me in another way. For what do I gain by resenting this injury? You ought at least not to believe what she says. This indeed seems reasonable, if she intends to impose upon me. But what is the consequence? I resolve not to believe my senses. I break my nose against a post that comes in my way; I step into a dirty kennel; and, after twenty such wise rational actions, I am taken up and clapped into a mad-house. Now, I confess I would rather make one of the credulous fools whom Nature imposes upon, than of those wise and rational philosophers who resolve to withhold assent at all this expense. If a man pretends to be a sceptic with regard to the informations of sense, and yet prudently keeps out of harm's way as other men do, he must excuse my suspicion, that he either acts the hypocrite, or imposes upon himself. For, if the scale of his belief were so evenly poised as to lean no more to one side than to the contrary, it is impossible that his actions could be directed by any rules of common prudence.

Thirdly, although the two reasons already mentioned are perhaps two more than enough, I shall offer a third. I gave implicit belief to the informations of Nature by my senses, for a considerable part of my life, before I had learned so much logic as to be able to start a doubt concerning them. And now, when I reflect upon what is past, I do not find that I have been imposed upon by this belief. I find that without it I must have perished by a thousand accidents. I find that without it I should have been no wiser now than when I was born. I should not even have been able to acquire that logic which suggests these sceptical doubts with regard to my senses. Therefore, I consider this instinctive belief as one of the best gifts of Nature. I thank the Author of my being, who bestowed it upon me before the eyes of my reason were opened, and still bestows it upon me, to be my guide where reason leaves me in the dark. And now I yield to the direction of my senses, not from instinct only, but from confidence and trust in a faithful and beneficent Monitor, grounded upon the experience of his paternal care and goodness.

In all this, I deal with the Author of my being, no otherwise than I thought it reasonable to deal with my parents and tutors. I believed by instinct whatever they told me, long before I had the idea of a lie, or thought of the possibility of their deceiving me. Afterwards, upon reflection, I found they had acted like fair and honest people, who wished me well. I found that, if I had not believed what they told me, before I could give a reason of my belief, I had to this day been little better than a changeling. And although this natural credulity hath sometimes occasioned my being imposed upon by deceivers, yet it hath been of infinite advantage to me upon the whole; therefore, I consider it as another good gift of Nature. And I continue to give that credit, from reflection, to those of whose integrity and veracity I have had experience, which before I gave from instinct.

There is a much greater similitude than is commonly imagined, between the testimony of nature given by our senses, and the testimony of men given by language. The credit we give to both is at first the effect of instinct only. When we grow up, and begin to reason about them, the credit given to human testimony is restrained and weakened, by the experience we have of deceit. But the credit given to the testimony of our senses, is established and confirmed by the uniformity and constancy of the laws of nature.

Our perceptions are of two kinds: some are natural and original; others acquired, and the fruit of experience. When I perceive that this is the taste of cyder, that of brandy; that this is the smell of an apple, that of an orange; that this is the noise of thunder, that the ringing of bells; this the sound of a coach passing, that the voice of such a friend: these perceptions, and others of the same kind, are not original—they are acquired. But the perception which I have, by touch, of the hardness and softness of bodies, of their extension, figure, and motion, is not acquired—it is original.

In all our senses, the acquired perceptions are many more than the original, especially in sight. By this sense we perceive originally the visible figure and colour of bodies only, and their visible place:[13] but we learn to perceive by the eye, almost everything which we can perceive by touch. The original perceptions of this sense serve only as signs to introduce the acquired.

The signs by which objects are presented to us in perception, are the language of Nature to man; and as, in many respects, it hath great affinity with the language of man to man, so particularly in this, that both are partly natural and original, partly acquired by custom. Our original or natural perceptions are analogous to the natural language of man to man, of which we took notice in the fourth chapter; and our acquired perceptions are analogous to artificial language, which, in our mother tongue, is got very much in the same manner with our acquired perceptions—as we shall afterwards more fully explain. . . .

Perception ought not only to be distinguished from sensation, but likewise from that knowledge of the objects of sense which is got by reasoning. There is no reasoning in perception, as hath been observed. The belief which is implied in it, is the effect of instinct. But there are many things, with regard to sensible objects, which we can infer from what we perceive; and such conclusions of reason ought to be distinguished from what is merely perceived. When I look at the moon, I perceive her to be sometimes circular, sometimes horned, and sometimes gibbous. This is simple perception, and is the same in the philosopher and in the clown: but from these various appearances of her enlightened part, I infer that she is really of a spherical figure. This conclusion is not obtained by simple perception, but by reasoning. Simple perception has the same

relation to the conclusions of reason drawn from our perceptions, as the axioms in mathematics have to the propositions.
I cannot demonstrate that two quantities which are equal to
the same quantity, are equal to each other; neither can I demonstrate that the tree which I perceive, exists. But, by the
constitution of my nature, my belief is irresistibly carried along
by my apprehension of the axiom; and, by the constitution of
my nature, my belief is no less irresistibly carried along by my
perception of the tree. All reasoning is from principles. The
first principles of mathematical reasoning are mathematical
axioms and definitions; and the first principles of all our reasoning about existenses, are our perceptions. The first principles of every kind of reasoning are given us by Nature, and are
of equal authority with the faculty of reason itself, which is also
the gift of Nature. The conclusions of reason are all built upon
first principles, and can have no other foundation. Most justly,
therefore, do such principles disdain to be tried by reason, and
laugh at all the artillery of the logician, when it is directed
against them.

When a long train of reasoning is necessary in demonstrating a mathematical proposition, it is easily distinguished from
an axiom; and they seem to be things of a very different nature.
But there are some propositions which lie so near to axioms,
that it is difficult to say whether they ought to be held as
axioms, or demonstrated as propositions. The same thing
holds with regard to perception, and the conclusions drawn
from it. Some of these conclusions follow our perceptions so
easily, and are so immediately connected with them, that it is
difficult to fix the limit which divides the one from the
other. . . .

Section XXIV: Of The Analogy Between Perception and The
Credit We Give to Human Testimony[14]

The objects of human knowledge are innumerable; but the
channels by which it is conveyed to the mind are few. Among

these, the perception of external things by our senses, and the informations which we receive upon human testimony, are not the least considerable; and so remarkable is the analogy between these two, and the analogy between the principles of the mind which are subservient to the one and those which are subservient to the other, that, without further apology, we shall consider them together.

In the testimony of Nature given by the senses, as well as in human testimony given by language, things are signified to us by signs: and in one as well as the other, the mind, either by original principles or by custom, passes from the sign to the conception and belief of the things signified.

We have distinguished our perceptions into original and acquired; and language, into natural and artificial. Between acquired perception and artificial language, there is a great analogy; but still a greater between original perception and natural language.

The signs in original perception are sensations, of which Nature hath given us a great variety, suited to the variety of the things signified by them. Nature hath established a real connection between the signs and the things signified; and Nature hath also taught us the interpretation of the signs—so that, previous to experience, the sign suggests the thing signified, and create the belief of it.

The signs in natural language are features of the face, gestures of the body, and modulations of the voice; the variety of which is suited to the variety of the things signified by them. Nature hath established a real connection between these signs, and the thoughts and dispositions of the mind which are signified by them; and Nature hath taught us the interpretation of these signs; so that, previous to experience, the signs suggest the thing signified, and create the belief of it.

A man in company, without doing good or evil, without uttering an articulate sound, may behave himself gracefully, civilly, politely; or, on the contrary, meanly, rudely, and impertinently. We see the dispositions of his mind by their natural signs in his countenance and behaviour, in the same manner as we perceive the figure and other qualities of bodies by the sensations which nature hath connected with them.

The signs in the natural language of the human countenance and behaviour, as well as the signs in our original perceptions, have the same signification in all climates and in all nations; and the skill of interpreting them is not acquired, but innate.

In acquired perception, the signs are either sensations, or things which we perceive by means of sensations. The connection between the sign and the thing signified, is established by nature; and we discover this connection by experience; but not without the aid of our original perceptions, or of those which we have already acquired. After this connection is discovered, the sign, in like manner as in original perception, always suggests the things signified, and creates the belief of it.

In artificial language, the signs are articulate sounds, whose connection with the things signified by them, is established by the will of men; and, in learning our mother tongue, we discover this connection by experience; but not without the aid of natural language, or of what we had before attained of artificial language. And, after this connection is discovered, the sign, as in natural language, always suggests the thing signified, and creates the belief of it.

Our original perceptions are few, compared with the acquired; but, without the former, we could not possibly attain the latter. In like manner, natural language is scanty, compared with artificial; but, without the former, we could not possibly attain the latter.

Our original perceptions, as well as the natural language of human features and gestures, must be resolved into particular principles of the human constitution. Thus, it is by one particular principle of our constitution that certain features express anger; and, by another particular principle, that certain fea-

tures express benevolence. It is, in like manner, by one particular principle of our constitution that a certain sensation signifies hardness in the body which I handle; and it is by another
particular principle that a certain sensation signifies motion in
that body.

But our acquired perceptions, and the information we receive by means of artificial language, must be resolved into
general principles of the human constitution. When a painter
perceives that this picture is the work of Raphael, that the work
of Titian; a jeweller, that this is a true diamond, that a counter-
feit; a sailor, that this is a ship of five hundred ton, that of four
hundred; these different acquired perceptions are produced
by the same general principles of the human mind, which have
a different operation in the same person according as they are
variously applied, and in different persons according to the
diversity of their education and manner of life. In like manner,
when certain articulate sounds convey to my mind the knowledge of the battle of Pharsalia, and others, the knowledge of
the battle of Poltowa—when a Frenchman and an Englishman
receive the same information by different articulate sounds—
the signs used in these different cases, produce the knowledge
and belief of the things signified, by means of the same general
principles of the human constitution.

Now, if we compare the general principles of our constitution, which fit us for receiving information from our fellow-
creatures by language, with the general principles which fit us
for acquiring the perception of things by our senses, we shall
find them to be very similar in their nature and manner of
operation.

When we begin to learn our mother tongue, we perceive, by
the help of natural language, that they who speak to us use
certain sounds to express certain things we imitate the same
sounds when we would express the same things; and find that
we are understood.

But here a difficulty occurs which merits our attention, because the solution of it leads to some original principles of the human mind, which are of great importance, and of very extensive influence. We know by experience that men *have* used such words to express such things; but all experience is of the *past,* and can, of itself, give no notion or belief of what is *future.* How come we, then, to believe, and to rely upon it with assurance, that men, who have it in their power to do otherwise, will continue to use the same words when they think the same things? Whence comes this knowledge and belief—this foresight, we ought rather to call it—of the future and voluntary actions of our fellow-creatures? Have they promised that they will never impose upon us by equivocation or falsehood? No, they have not. And, if they had, this would not solve the difficulty; for such promise must be expressed by words or by other signs; and, before we can rely upon it, we must be assured that they put the usual meaning upon the signs which express that promise. No man of common sense ever thought of taking a man's own word for his honesty; and it is evident that we take his veracity for granted when we lay any stress upon his word or promise. I might add, that this reliance upon the declarations and testimony of men is found in children long before they know what a promise is.

There is, therefore, in the human mind an early anticipation, neither derived from experience, nor from reason, nor from any compact or promise, that our fellow-creatures will use the same signs in language, when they have the same sentiments.

This is, in reality, a kind of prescience of human actions; and it seems to me to be an original principle of the human constitution, without which we should be incapable of language, and consequently incapable of instruction.

The wise and beneficent Author of Nature, who intended that we should be social creatures, and that we should receive the greatest and most important part of our knowledge by the information of others, hath, for these purposes, implanted in our natures two principles that tally with each other.

The first of these principles is, a propensity to speak truth, and to use the signs of language so as to convey our real sentiments. This principle has a powerful operation, even in the greatest liars; for where they lie once, they speak truth a hundred times. Truth is always uppermost, and is the natural issue of the mind. It requires no art or training, no inducement or temptation, but only that we yield to a natural impulse. Lying, on the contrary, is doing violence to our nature; and is never practised, even by the worst men, without some temptation. Speaking truth is like using our natural food, which we would do from appetite, although it answered no end; but lying is like taking physic, which is nauseous to the taste, and which no man takes but for some end which he cannot otherwise attain.

If it should be objected, That men may be influenced by moral or political considerations to speak truth, and, therefore, that their doing so is no proof of such an original principle as we have mentioned—I answer, First, That moral or political considerations can have no influence until we arrive at years of understanding and reflection; and it is certain, from experience, that children keep to truth invariably, before they are capable of being influenced by such considerations. Secondly, When we are influenced by moral or political considerations, we must be conscious of that influence, and capable of perceiving it upon reflection. Now, when I reflect upon my actions most attentively, I am not conscious that, in speaking truth, I am influenced on ordinary occasions by any motive, moral or political. I find that truth is always at the door of my lips, and goes forth spontaneously, if not held back. It requires neither good nor bad intention to bring it forth, but only that I be artless and undesigning. There may indeed be temptations to falsehood, which would be too strong for the natural principle of veracity, unaided by principles of honour or virtue; but where there is no such temptation, we speak truth by instinct—and this instinct is the principle I have been explaining.

By this instinct, a real connection is formed between our words and our thoughts, and thereby the former become fit to be signs of the latter, which they could not otherwise be. And although this connection is broken in every instance of lying and equivocation, yet these instances being comparatively few, the authority of human testimony is only weakened by them, but not destroyed.

Another original principle implanted in us by the Supreme Being, is a disposition to confide in the veracity of others, and to believe what they tell us. This is the counterpart to the former; and, as that may be called *the principle of veracity*, we shall, for want of a more proper name, call this *the principle of credulity*. It is unlimited in children, until they meet with instances of deceit and falsehood; and it retains a very considerable degree of strength through life.

If Nature had left the mind of the speaker *in aequilibrio*, without any inclination to the side of truth more than to that of falsehood, children would lie as often as they speak truth, until reason was so far ripened as to suggest the imprudence of lying, or conscience, as to suggest its immorality. And if Nature had left the mind of the hearer *in aequilibrio*, without any inclination to the side of belief more than to that of disbelief, we should take no man's word until we had positive evidence that he spoke truth. His testimony would, in this case, have no more authority than his dreams; which may be true or false, but no man is disposed to believe them, on this account, that they were dreamed. It is evident that, in the matter of testimony, the balance of human judgment is by nature inclined to the side of belief; and turns to that side of itself, when there is nothing put into the opposite scale. If it was not so, no proposition that is uttered in discourse would be believed, until it was examined and tried by reason; and most men would be unable to find reasons for believing the thousandth part of what is told them. Such distrust and incredulity would deprive us of the greatest benefits of society, and place us in a worse condition than that of savages.

Children, on this supposition, would be absolutely incredulous, and, therefore, absolutely incapable of instruction: those who had little knowledge of human life, and of the manners and characters of men, would be in the next degree incredulous: and the most credulous men would be those of greatest experience, and of the deepest penetration; because, in many cases, they would be able to find good reasons for believing testimony, which the weak and the ignorant could not discover.

In a word, if credulity were the effect of reasoning and experience, it must grow up and gather strength, in the same proportion as reason and experience do. But, if it is the gift of Nature, it will be strongest in childhood, and limited and restrained by experience; and the most superficial view of human life shews, that the last is really the case, and not the first.[15]

It is the intention of Nature, that we should be carried in arms before we are able to walk upon our legs; and it is likewise the intention of Nature, that our belief should be guided by the authority and reason of others, before it can be guided by our own reason. The weakness of the infant, and the natural affection of the mother, plainly indicate the former; and the natural credulity of youth, and authority of age, as plainly indicate the latter. The infant, by proper nursing, and care, acquires strength to walk without support. Reason hath likewise her infancy, when she must be carried in arms: then she leans entirely upon authority, by natural instinct, as if she was conscious of her own weakness; and, without this support, she becomes vertiginous. When brought to maturity by proper culture, she begins to feel her own strength, and leans less upon the reason of others; she learns to suspect testimony in some cases, and to disbelieve it in others; and sets bounds to that authority to which she was at first entirely subject. But still, to the end of life, she finds a necessity of borrowing light from testimony, where she has none within herself, and of leaning, in some degree, upon the reason of others, where she is conscious of her own imbecility.

And as, in many instances, Reason, even in her maturity, borrows aid from testimony, so in others she mutually gives aid to it, and strengthens its authority. For, as we find good reason to reject testimony in some cases, so in others we find good reason to rely upon it with perfect security, in our most important concerns. The character, the number, and the disinterestedness of witnesses, the impossibility of collusion, and the incredibility of their concurring in their testimony without collusion, may give an irresistible strength to testimony, compared to which its native and intrinsic authority is very inconsiderable.

Having now considered the general principles of the human mind which fit us for receiving information from our fellow-creatures, by the means of language, let us next consider the general principles which fit us for receiving the information of Nature by our acquired perceptions.

It is undeniable, and indeed is acknowledged by all, that when we have found two things to have been constantly conjoined in the course of nature, the appearance of one of them is immediately followed by the conception and belief of the other. The former becomes a natural sign of the latter; and the knowledge of their constant conjunction in time past, whether got by experience or otherwise, is sufficient to make us rely with assurance upon the continuance of that conjunction.

This process of the human mind is so familiar that we never think of inquiring into the principles upon which it is founded. We are apt to conceive it as a self-evident truth, that what is to come must be similar to what is past. Thus, if a certain degree of cold freezes water to-day, and has been known to do so in all time past, we have no doubt but the same degree of cold will freeze water to-morrow, or a year hence. That this is a truth which all men believe as soon as they understand it, I readily admit; but the question is, Whence does its evidence arise? Not from comparing the ideas, surely. For, when I compare the idea of cold with that of water hardened into a transparent solid body, I can perceive no connection between them:

no man can shew the one to be the necessary effect of the other; no man can give a shadow of reason why Nature hath conjoined them. But do we not learn their conjunction from experience? True; experience informs us that they have been conjoined in time *past;* but no man ever had any experience of what is *future:* and this is the very question to be resolved, How we come to believe that the *future* will be like the *past?* Hath the Author of nature promised this? Or were we admitted to his council, when he established the present laws of nature, and determined the time of their continuance. No, surely. Indeed, if we believe that there is a wise and good Author of nature, we may see a good reason why he should continue the same laws of nature, and the same connections of things, for a long time: because, if he did otherwise, we could learn nothing from what is past, and all our experience would be of no use to us. But, though this consideration, when we come to the use of reason, may confirm our belief of the continuance of the present course of nature, it is certain that it did not give rise to this belief; for children and idiots have this belief as soon as they know that fire will burn them. It must, therefore, be the effect of instinct, not of reason.[16]

The wise Author of our nature intended, that a great and necessary part of our knowledge should be derived from experience, before we are capable of reasoning, and he hath provided means perfectly adequate to this intention. For, First, He governs nature by fixed laws, so that we find innumerable connections of things which continue from age to age. Without this stability of the course of nature, there could be no experience; or, it would be a false guide, and lead us into error and mischief. If there were not a principle of veracity in the human mind, men's words would not be signs of their thoughts: and if there were no regularity in the course of nature, no one thing could be a natural sign of another. Secondly, He hath implanted in human minds an original principle by which we believe and expect the continuance of the course of nature, and the continuance of those connections which we have observed in time past. It is by this general principle of our nature, that, when two things have been found connected in time past, the appearance of the one produces the belief of the other.

I think the ingenious author of the "Treatise of Human Nature" first observed, That our belief of the continuance of the laws of nature cannot be founded either upon knowledge or probability: but, far from conceiving it to be an original principle of the mind, he endeavours to account for it from his favourite hypothesis, That belief is nothing but a certain degree of vivacity in the idea of the thing believed. I made a remark upon this curious hypothesis in the second chapter, and shall now make another.

The belief which we have in perception, is a belief of the present existence of the object; that which we have in memory, is a belief of its past existence; the belief of which we are now speaking is a belief of its future existence; and in imagination there is no belief at all. Now, I would gladly know of this author, how one degree of vivacity fixes the existence of the object to the present moment; another carries it back to time past; a third, taking a contrary direction, carries it into futurity; and a fourth carries it out of existence altogether. Suppose, for instance, that I see the sun rising out of the sea: I remember to have seen him rise yesterday; I believe he will rise to-morrow near the same place; I can likewise imagine him rising in that place, without any belief at all. Now, according to this sceptical hypothesis, this perception, this memory, this foreknowledge, and this imagination, are all the same idea, diversified only by different degrees of vivacity. The perception of the sun rising is the most lively idea; the memory of his rising yesterday is the same idea a little more faint; the belief of his rising to-morrow is the same idea yet fainter; and the imagination of his rising is still the same idea, but faintest of all. One is apt to think, that this idea might gradually pass through all possible degrees of vivacity without stirring out of its place. But, if we think so, we deceive ourselves; for no sooner does it begin to grow languid than it moves backward into time past. Supposing this to be granted, we expect, at least, that, as it moves backward by the decay of its vivacity, the more that vivacity decays it will go back the farther, until it remove quite out of sight. But here we are deceived again; for there is a certain period of this declining vivacity, when, as if it had met an elastic obstacle in its motion backward, it suddenly rebounds from the past to the future, without taking the present in its way. And now, having got into the regions of futurity, we are apt to think that it has room enough to spend all its remaining vigour: but still we are deceived; for, by another sprightly bound, it mounts up into the airy region of imagination. So that ideas, in the gradual declension of their vivacity, seem to imitate the inflection of verbs in grammer. They begin with the present, and proceed in order to the preterite, the future, and the indefinite. This article of the sceptical creed is indeed so full of mystery, on whatever side we view it, that they who hold that creed are very injuriously charged with incredulity; for, to me, it appears to require as much faith as that of St Athanasius.

However, we agree with the author of the "Treatise of Human Nature," in this, That our belief of the continuance of nature's laws is not derived from reason. It is an instinctive prescience of the operations of nature, very like to that prescience of human actions which makes us rely upon the testimony of our fellow-creatures; and as, without the latter, we should be incapable of receiving information from men by language, so, without the former, we should be incapable of receiving the information of nature by means of experience.

All our knowledge of nature beyond our original perceptions, is got by experience, and consists in the interpretation of natural signs. The constancy of nature's laws connects the sign with the thing signified; and, by the natural principle just now explained, we rely upon the continuance of the connections which experience hath discovered; and thus the appearance of the sign is followed by the belief of the thing signified.

Upon this principle of our constitution, not only acquired perception, but all inductive reasoning, and all our reasoning from analogy, is grounded; and, therefore, for want of another name, we shall beg leave to call it *the inductive principle*. It is from the force of this principle that we immediately assent to that axiom upon which all our knowledge of nature is built, That effects of the same kind must have the same cause; for *effects* and *causes*, in the operations of nature, mean nothing but signs and the things signified by them. We perceive no proper causality or efficiency in any natural cause; but only a connection established by the course of nature between it and what is called its effect. Antecedently to all reasoning, we have, by our constitution, an anticipation that there is a fixed and steady course of nature: and we have an eager desire to discover this course of nature. We attend to every conjunction of things which presents itself, and expect the continuance of that conjunction. And, when such a conjunction has been often observed, we conceive the things to be naturally connected, and the appearance of one, without any reasoning or reflection, carries along with it the belief of the other.

If any reader should imagine that the inductive principle may be resolved into what philosophers usually call the *association of ideas*, let him observe, that, by this principle, natural signs are not associated with the idea only, but with the belief of the things signified. Now, this can with no propriety be called an association of ideas, unless ideas and belief be one and the same thing. A child has found the prick of a pin conjoined with pain; hence he believes, and knows, that these things are naturally connected; he knows that the one will always follow the other. If any man will call this only an association of ideas, I dispute not about words, but I think he speaks very improperly. For, if we express it in plain English, it is a prescience that things which he hath found conjoined in time past, will be conjoined in time to come. And this prescience is not the effect of reasoning, but of an original principle of human nature, which I have called *the inductive principle.*

This principle, like that of credulity, is unlimited in infancy, and gradually restrained and regulated as we grow up. It leads us often into mistakes; but is of infinite advantage upon the whole. By it, the child once burnt shuns the fire; by it, he likewise runs away from the surgeon by whom he was inoculated. It is better that he should do the last, than he should not do the first.

But the mistakes we are led into by these two natural principles, are of a different kind. Men sometimes lead us into mistakes, when we perfectly understand their language, by speaking lies. But Nature never misleads us in this way: her language is always true; and it is only by misinterpreting it that we fall into error. There must be many accidental conjunctions of things, as well as natural connections; and the former are apt to be mistaken for the latter. Thus, in the instance above mentioned, the child connected the pain of inoculation with the surgeon; whereas it was really connected with the incision only. Philosophers, and men of science, are not exempted from such mistakes; indeed, all false reasoning in philosophy is owing to them; it is drawn from experience and analogy, as well as just reasoning, otherwise it could have no verisimilitude; but the one is an unskillful and rash, the other a just and legitimate interpretation of natural signs. If a child, or a man of common understanding, were put to interpret a book of science, written in his mother-tongue, how many blunders and mistakes would he be apt to fall.into? Yet he knows as much of this language as is necessary for his manner of life.

The language of Nature is the universal study; and the students are of different classes. Brutes, idiots, and children employ themselves in this study, and owe to it all their acquired perceptions. Men of common understanding make a greater progress, and learn, by a small degree of reflection, many things of which children are ignorant . . .

From the time that children begin to use their hands, Nature directs them to handle everything over and over, to look at it while they handle it, and to put it in various positions, and at various distances from the eye. We are apt to excuse this as a childish diversion, because they must be doing something, and have not reason to entertain themselves in a more manly way. But, if we think more justly, we shall find, that they are engaged in the most serious and important study; and, if they had all the reason of a philosopher, they could not be more properly employed. For it is this childish employment that enables them to make the proper use of their eyes. They are thereby every day acquiring habits of perception, which are of greater importance than anything we can teach them. The original perceptions which Nature gave them are few, and insufficient for the purposes of life; and, therefore, she made them capable of acquiring many more perceptions by habit. And, to complete her work, she hath given them an unwearied assiduity in applying to the exercises by which those perceptions are acquired. . . .

CHAPTER 7

Conclusion: Containing Reflections Upon the Opinions of Philosophers on This Subject

There are two ways in which men may form their notions and opinions concerning the mind, and concerning its power and operations. The first is the only way that leads to truth; but it is narrow and rugged, and few have entered upon it. The second is broad and smooth, and hath been much beaten, not only by the vulgar, but even by philosophers; it is sufficient for common life, and is well adapted to the purposes of the poet and orator: but, in philosophical disquisitions concerning the mind, it leads to error and delusion.

We may call the first of these ways, *the way of reflection.* When the operations of the mind are exerted, we are conscious of them; and it is in our power to attend to them, and to reflect upon them, until they become familiar objects of thought. This is the only way in which we can form just and accurate notions of those operations. But this attention and reflection is so difficult to man, surrounded on all hands by external objects which constantly solicit his attention, that it has been very little practised, even by philosophers. In the course of this inquiry, we have had many occasions to shew how little attention hath been given to the most familiar operations of the senses.

The second, and the most common way, in which men form their opinions concerning the mind and its operations, we may call *the way of analogy.* There is nothing in the course of nature so singular, but we can find some resemblance, or at least some analogy, between it and other things with which we are acquainted. The mind naturally delights in hunting after such analogies, and attends to them with pleasure. From them, poetry and wit derive a great part of their charms; and eloquence, not a little of its persuasive force.

Besides the pleasure we receive from analogies, they are of very considerable use, both to facilitate the conception of things, when they are not easily apprehended without such a handle, and to lead us to probable conjectures about their nature and qualities, when we want the means of more direct and immediate knowledge. When I consider that the planet Jupiter, in like manner as the earth, rolls round his own axis, and revolves round the sun, and that he is enlightened by several secondary planets, as the earth is enlightened by the moon, I am apt to conjecture, from analogy, that, as the earth by these means is fitted to be the habitation of various orders of animals, so the planet Jupiter is, by the like means, fitted for the same purpose: and, having no argument more direct and conclusive to determine me in this point, I yield, to this analogical reasoning, a degree of assent proportioned to its strength. When I observe that the potato plant very much resembles the *solanum* in its flower and fructification, and am informed that the last is poisonous, I am apt from analogy to have some suspicion of the former; but, in this case, I have access to more direct and certain evidence; and, therefore, ought not to trust to analogy, which would lead me into an error.

Arguments from analogy are always at hand, and grow up spontaneously in a fruitful imagination; while arguments that are more direct and more conclusive often require painful attention and application: and therefore mankind in general have been very much disposed to trust to the former. If one attentively examines systems of the ancient philosophers, either concerning the material world, or concerning the mind, he will find them to be built solely upon the foundation of analogy. Lord Bacon first delineated the strict and severe method of induction; since his time, it has been applied with very happy success in some parts of natural philosophy—and hardly in anything else. But there is no subject in which mankind are so much disposed to trust to the analogical way of thinking and reasoning, as in what concerns the mind and its operations; because, to form clear and distinct notions of those operations in the direct and proper way, and to reason about them, requires a habit of attentive reflection, of which few are capable, and which, even by those few, cannot be attained without much pains and labour.

Every man is apt to form his notions of things difficult to be apprehended, or less familiar, from their analogy to things which are more familiar. Thus, if a man bred to the seafaring life, and accustomed to think and talk only of matters relating to navigation, enters into discourse upon any other subject, it is well known that the language and the notions proper to his own profession are infused into every subject, and all things are measured by the rules of navigation; and, if he should take it into his head to philosophize concerning the faculties of the mind, it cannot be doubted but he would draw his notions from the fabric of his ship, and would find in the mind, sails, masts, rudder, and compass.[17]

Sensible objects, of one kind or other, do no less occupy and engross the rest of mankind, than things relating to navigation the seafaring man. For a considerable part of life, we can think of nothing but the objects of sense; and, to attend to objects of another nature, so as to form clear and distinct notions of them, is no easy matter, even after we come to years of reflection. The condition of mankind, therefore, affords good reason to apprehend that their language, and their common notions concerning the mind and its operations, will be analogical, and derived from the objects of sense; and that these analogies will be apt to impose upon philosophers, as well as upon the vulgar, and to lead them to materialize the mind and its faculties: and experience abundantly confirms the truth of this.

How generally men of all nations, and in all ages of the world, have conceived the soul, or thinking principle in man, to be some subtile matter, like breath or wind, the names given to it almost in all languages sufficiently testify. We have words which are proper, and not analogical, to express the various ways in which we perceive external objects by the senses— such as *feeling, sight, taste;* but we are often obliged to use these words analogically, to express other powers of the mind which are of a very different nature. And the powers which imply some degree of reflection, have generally no names but such as are analogical. The objects of thought are said to be *in the mind*—to be *apprehended, comprehended, conceived, imagined, retained, weighted, ruminated.*

It does not appear that the notions of the ancient philosophers, with regard to the nature of the soul, were much more refined than those of the vulgar, or that they were formed in any other way. We shall distinguish the philosophy that regards our subject into the *old* and the *new*. The old reached down to Des Cartes, who gave it a fatal blow, of which it has been gradually expiring ever since, and is now almost extinct. Des Cartes is the father of the new philosophy that relates to this subject; but it hath been gradually improving since his time, upon the principles laid down by him. The old philosophy seems to have been purely analogical; the new is more derived from reflection, but still with a very considerable mixture of the old analogical notions. . . .

Plato, of the writers that are extant, first introduced the word *idea* into philosophy; but his doctrine upon this subject [was] somewhat peculiar. He agreed with the rest of the ancient philosophers in this—that all things consist of matter and form; and that the matter of which all things were made, existed from eternity, without form: but he likewise believed that there are external forms of all possible things which exist, without matter; and to these external and immaterial forms he gave the name of *ideas;* maintaining that they are the only object of true knowledge. It is of no great moment to us, whether he borrowed these notions from Parmenides, or whether they were the issue of his own creative imagination. The latter Platonists seem to have improved upon them, in conceiving those ideas, or eternal forms of things, to exist, not of themselves, but in the divine mind, and to be the models and patterns according to which all things were made.

To these Platonic notions, that of Malebranche is very nearly allied. This author seems, more than any other, to have been aware of the difficulties attending the common hypothesis concerning ideas—to wit, That ideas of all objects of thought are in the human mind; and, therefore, in order to avoid those difficulties, makes the ideas which are the immediate objects of human thought, to be the ideas of things in the Divine mind, who, being intimately present to every human mind, may discover his ideas to it, as far as pleaseth him.

The Platonists and Malebranche excepted, all other philosophers, as far as I know, have conceived that there are ideas or images of every object of thought in the human mind, or, at least, in some part of the brain, where the mind is supposed to have its residence.

Aristotle had no good affection to the word *idea*, and seldom or never uses it but in refuting Plato's notions about ideas. He thought that matter may exist without form; but that forms cannot exist without matter. But, at the same time, he taught, That there can be no sensation, no imagination, nor intellection, without forms, phantasms, or species in the mind; and that things sensible are perceived by sensible species, and things intelligible by intelligible species. His followers taught, more explicitly, that those sensible and intelligible species are sent forth by the objects, and make their impressions upon the passive intellect; and that the active intellect perceives them in the passive intellect. And this seems to have been the common opinion while the Peripatetic philosophy retained its authority.

The Epicurean doctrine, as explained by Lucretius, though widely different from the Peripatetic in many things, is almost the same in this. He affirms, that slender films or ghosts (*tenuia rerum simulacra*) are still going off from all things, and flying about; and that these, being extremely subtile, easily penetrate our gross bodies, and, striking upon the mind, cause thought and imagination.

After the Peripatetic system had reigned above a thousand years in the schools of Europe, almost without a rival, it sunk before that of Des Cartes; the perspicuity of whose writings and notions, contrasted with the obscurity of Aristotle and his commentators, created a strong prejudice in favour of this new philosophy. The characteristic of Plato's genius was sublimity, that of Aristotle's, subtilty; but Des Cartes far excelled both in perspicuity, and bequeathed this spirit to his successors. The system which is now generally received, with regard to the mind and its operations, derives not only its spirit from Des Cartes, but its fundamental principles; and, after all the improvements made by Malebranche, Locke, Berkeley, and Hume, may still be called *the Cartesian system:* we shall, therefore, make some remarks upon its spirit and tendency in general, and upon its doctrine concerning ideas in particular.

1. It may be observed, That the method which Des Cartes pursued, naturally led him to attend more to the operations of the mind by accurate reflection, and to trust less to analogical reasoning upon this subject, than any philosopher had done before him. Intending to build a system upon a new foundation, he began with a resolution to admit nothing but what was absolutely certain and evident. He supposed that his senses, his memory, his reason, and every other faculty to which we trust in common life, might be fallacious; and resolved to disbelieve everything, until he was compelled by irresistible evidence to yield assent.

In this method of proceeding, what appeared to him, first of all, certain and evident, was, that he thought—that he doubted—that he deliberated. In a word, the operations of his own mind, of which he was conscious, must be real, and no delusion; and, though all his other faculties should deceive him, his consciousness could not. This, therefore, he looked upon as the first of all truths. This was the first firm ground upon which he set his foot, after being tossed in the ocean of scepticism; and he resolved to build all knowledge upon it, without seeking after any more first principles.

As every other truth, therefore, and particularly the existence of the objects of sense, was to be deduced by a train of strict argumentation from what he knew by consciousness, he was naturally led to give attention to the operations of which he was conscious, without borrowing his notions of them from external things.

It was not in the way of analogy, but of attentive reflection, that he was led to observe, That thought, volition, remembrance and the other attributes of the mind, are altogether unlike to extension, to figure, and to all the attributes of body;

that we have no reason, therefore, to conceive thinking substances to have any resemblance to extended substances; and that, as the attributes of the thinking substance are things of which we are conscious, we may have a more certain and immediate knowledge of them by reflection, than we can have of external objects by our senses.

These observations, as far as I know, were first made by Des Cartes; and they are of more importance, and throw more light upon the subject, than all that had been said upon it before. They ought to make us diffident and jealous of every notion concerning the mind and its operations, which is drawn from sensible objects in the way of analogy, and to make us rely only upon accurate reflection, as the source of all real knowledge upon this subject.

2. I observe that, as the Peripatetic system has a tendency to materialize the mind and its operations, so the Cartesian has a tendency to spiritualize body and its qualities. One error, common to both systems, leads to the first of these extremes in the way of analogy, and to the last in the way of reflection. The error I mean is, That we can know nothing about body, or its qualities, but as far as we have sensations which resemble those qualities. Both systems agreed in this: but, according to their different methods of reasoning, they drew very different conclusions from it; the Peripatetic drawing his notions of sensation from the qualities of body; the Cartesian, on the contrary, drawing his notions of the qualities of body from his sensations.

The Peripatetic, taking it for granted that bodies and their qualities do really exist, and are such as we commonly take them to be, inferred from them the nature of his sensations, and reasoned in this manner:—Our sensations are the impressions which sensible objects make upon the mind, and may be compared to the impression of a seal upon wax: the impression is the image or form of the seal, without the matter of it; in like manner, every sensation is the image or form of some sensible quality of the object. This is the reasoning of Aristotle: and it has an evident tendency to materialize the mind and its sensations.

The Cartesian, on the contrary, thinks that the existence of body, or of any of its qualities, is not to be taken as a first principle; and that we ought to admit nothing concerning it, but what, by just reasoning, can be deduced from our sensations; and he knows that, by reflection, we can form clear and distinct notions of our sensations, without borrowing our notions of them by analogy from the objects of sense. The Cartesians, therefore, beginning to give attention to their sensations, first discovered that the sensations corresponding to secondary qualities, cannot resemble any quality of body. Hence, Des Cartes and Locke inferred, that sound, taste, smell, colour, heat, and cold, which the vulgar took to be qualities of body, were not qualities of body, but mere sensations of the mind. Afterwards, the ingenious Berkeley, considering more attentively the nature of sensation in general, discovered and demonstrated, that no sensation whatever could possibly resemble any quality of an insentient being, such as body is supposed to be; and hence he inferred, very justly, that there is the same reason to hold extension, figure, and all the primary qualities, to be mere sensations, as there is to hold the secondary qualities to be mere sensations. Thus, by just reasoning upon the Cartesian principles, matter was stripped of all its qualities; the new system, by a kind of metaphysical sublimation, converted all the qualities of matter into sensations, and spiritualized body, as the old had materialized spirit.

The way to avoid both these extremes, is to admit the existence of what we see and feel as a first principle, as well as the existence of things whereof we are conscious; and to take our notions of the qualities of body, from the testimony of our senses, with the Peripatetics; and our notions of our sensations, from the testimony of consciousness, with the Cartesians.

3. I observe, That the modern scepticism is the natural issue of the new system; and that, although it did not bring forth this monster until the year 1739,[18] it may be said to have carried it in its womb from the beginning.

The old system admitted all the principles of common sense as first principles, without requiring any proof of them; and, therefore, though its reasoning was commonly vague, analogical, and dark, yet it was built upon a broad foundation and had no tendency to scepticism. We do not find that any Peripatetic thought it incumbent upon him to prove the existence of a material world; but every writer upon the Cartesian system attempted this, until Berkeley clearly demonstrated the futility of their arguments; and thence concluded that there was no such thing as a material world; and that the belief of it ought to be rejected as a vulgar error.

The new system admits only one of the principles of common sense as a first principle; and pretends, by strict argumentation, to deduce all the rest from it. That our thoughts, our sensations, and every thing of which we are conscious, hath a real existence, is admitted in this system as a first principle; but everything else must be made evident by the light of reason. Reason must rear the whole fabric of knowledge upon this single principle of consciousness.

There is a disposition in human nature to reduce things to as few principles as possible; and this, without doubt, adds to the beauty of a system, if the principles are able to support what rests upon them. The mathematicians glory, very justly, in having raised so noble and magnificent a system of science, upon the foundation of a few axioms and definitions. This love of simplicity, and of reducing things to few principles, hath produced many a false system; but there never was any system in which it appears so remarkably as that of Des Cartes. His whole system concerning matter and spirit is built upon one axiom, expressed in one word, *cogito*. Upon the foundation of conscious thought, with ideas for his materials, he builds his system of the human understanding, and attempts to account for all its phaenomena: and having, as he imagined, from his consciousness, proved the existence of matter; upon the existence of matter, and of a certain quantity of motion originally impressed upon it, he builds his system of the material world, and attempts to account for all its phaenomena.

These principles, with regard to the material system, have been found insufficient; and it has been made evident that, besides matter and motion, we must admit gravitation, cohesion, corpuscular attraction, magnetism, and other centripetal and centrifugal forces, by which the particles of matter attract and repel each other. Newton, having discovered this, and demonstrated that these principles cannot be resolved into matter and motion, was led, by analogy and the love of simplicity, to conjecture, but with a modesty and caution peculiar to him, that all the phaenomena of the material world depended upon attracting and repelling forces in the particles of matter. But we may now venture to say, that this conjecture fell short of the mark. For, even in the unorganized kingdom, the powers by which salts, crystals, spars, and many other bodies, concrete into regular forms, can never be accounted for by attracting and repelling forces in the particles of matter. And in the vegetable and animal kingdoms, there are strong indications of powers of a different nature from all the powers of unorganized bodies. We see, then, that, although, in the structure of the material world, there is, without doubt, all the beautiful simplicity consistent with the purposes for which it was made, it is not so simple as the great Des Cartes determined it to be; nay, it is not so simple as the greater Newton modestly conjectured it to be. Both were misled by analogy, and the love of simplicity. One had been much conversant about extension, figure, and motion; the other had enlarged his views to attracting and repelling forces; and both formed their notions of the unknown parts of nature, from those with which they were acquainted. . . .

But to come to the system of Des Cartes, concerning the human understanding. It was built, as we have observed, upon consciousness as its sole foundation, and with ideas as its materials; and all his followers have built upon the same foundation and with the same materials. They acknowledge that Nature hath given us various simple ideas. These are analogous to the matter of Des Carte's physical system. They acknowledge, likewise, a natural power, by which ideas are compounded, disjoined, associated, compared. This is analogous to the original quantity of motion in Des Cartes's physical system. From these principles, they attempt to explain the phaenomena of the human understanding, just as in the physical system the phaenomena of nature were to be explained by matter and motion. It must, indeed, be acknowledged, that there is great simplicity in this system, as well as in the other. There is such a similitude between the two, as may be expected between children of the same father; but, as the one has been found to be the child of Des Cartes, and not of Nature, there is ground to think that the other is so likewise.

That the natural issue of this system is scepticism with regard to everything except the existence of our ideas, and of their necessary relations, which appear upon comparing them, is evident; for ideas, being the only objects of thought, and having no existence but when we are conscious of them, it necessarily follows that there is no object of our thought which can have a continued and permanent existence. Body and spirit, cause and effect, time and space, to which we were wont to ascribe an existence independent of our thought, are all turned out of existence by this short dilemma. Either these things are ideas of sensation or reflection, or they are not: if they are ideas of sensation or reflection, they can have no existence but when we are conscious of them; if they are not ideas of sensation or reflection, they are words without any meaning.[19]

Neither Des Cartes nor Locke perceived this consequence of

their system concerning ideas. Bishop Berkeley was the first who discovered it. And what followed upon this discovery? Why, with regard to the material world, and with regard to space and time, he admits the consequence, That these things are mere ideas, and have no existence but in our minds; but with regard to the existence of spirits or minds, he does not admit the consequence; and, if he had admitted it, he must have been an absolute sceptic. But how does he evade this consequence with regard to the existence of spirits? The expedient which the good Bishop uses on this occasion is very remarkable, and shews his great aversion to scepticism. He maintains that we have no ideas of spirits; and that we can think, and speak, and reason about them, and about their attributes, without having any ideas of them. If this is so, my Lord, what should hinder us from thinking and reasoning about bodies, and their qualities, without having ideas of them? The Bishop either did not think of this question, or did not think fit to give any answer to it. However, we may observe, that, in order to avoid scepticism, he fairly starts out of the Cartesian system, without giving any reason why he did so in this instance, and in no other. This, indeed, is the only instance of a deviation from Cartesian principles which I have met with in the successors of Des Cartes; and it seems to have been only a sudden start, occasioned by the terror of scepticism; for, in all other things, Berkeley's system is founded upon Cartesian principles.

Thus we see that Des Cartes and Locke take the road that leads to scepticism, without knowing the end of it; but they stop short for want of light to carry them farther. Berkeley, frighted at the appearance of the dreadful abyss, starts aside, and avoids it. But the author of the "Treatise of Human Nature," more daring and intrepid, without turning aside to the right hand or to the left, like Virgil's Alecto, shoots directly into the gulf.

4. We may observe, That the account given by the new

system, of that furniture of the human understanding which is the gift of Nature, and not the acquisition of our own reasoning faculty, is extremely lame and imperfect.[20]

The natural furniture of the human understanding is of two kinds: First, The *notions* or simple apprehensions which we have of things; and, secondly, The *judgments* or the belief which we have concerning them. As to our notions, the new system reduces them to two classes—*ideas of sensation,* and *ideas of reflection:* the first are conceived to be copies of our sensations, retained in the memory or imagination; the second, to be copies of the operations of our minds whereof we are conscious, in like manner retained in the memory or imagination: and we are taught that these two comprehend all the materials about which the human understanding is, or can be employed. As to our judgment of things, or the belief which we have concerning them, the new system allows no part of it to be the gift of nature, but holds it to be the acquisition of reason, and to be got by comparing our ideas, and perceiving their agreements or disagreements. Now I take this account, both of our notions, and of our judgments or belief, to be extremely imperfect; and I shall briefly point out some of its capital defects.

The division of our notions into ideas of sensation, and ideas of reflection, is contrary to all rules of logic; because the second member of the division includes the first. For, can we form clear and just notions of our sensations any other way than by reflection? Surely we cannot. Sensation is an operation of the mind of which we are conscious; and we get the notion of sensation by reflecting upon that which we are conscious of. In like manner, doubting and believing are operations of the mind whereof we are conscious; and we get the notion of them by reflecting upon what we are conscious of. The ideas of sensation, therefore, are ideas of reflection, as much as the ideas of doubting, or believing, or any other ideas whatsoever.

But, to pass over the inaccuracy of this division, it is extremely incomplete. For, since sensation is an operation of the mind, as well as all the other things of which we form our notions by reflection, when it is asserted that all our notions are either ideas of sensation or ideas of reflection, the plain English of this is, That mankind neither do nor can think of anything but of the operations of their own minds. Nothing can be more contrary to truth, or more contrary to the experience of mankind. I know that Locke, while he maintained this doctrine, believed the notions which we have of body and of its qualities, and the notions which we have of motion and of space, to be ideas of sensation. But why did he believe this? Because he believed those notions to be nothing else but images of our sensations. If, therefore, the notions of body and its qualities, of motion and space, be not images of our sensations, will it not follow that those notions are not ideas of sensation? Most certainly.

There is no doctrine in the new system which more directly leads to scepticism than this. And the author of the "Treatise of Human Nature" knew very well how to use it for that purpose; for, if you maintain that there is any such existence as body or spirit, time or place, cause or effect, he immediately catches you between the horns of this dilemma; your notions of these existences are either ideas of sensation, or ideas of reflection: if of sensation, from what sensation are they copied? if of reflection, from what operation of the mind are they copied?

It is indeed to be wished that those who have written much about sensation, and about the other operations of the mind, had likewise thought and reflected much, and with great care, upon those operations; but is it not very strange that they will not allow it to be possible for mankind to think of anything else?

The account which this system gives of our judgment and belief concerning things, is as far from the truth as the account it gives of our notions or simple apprehensions. It represents our senses as having no other office but that of furnishing the mind with notions or simple apprehensions of things; and makes our judgment and belief concerning those things to be acquired by comparing our notions together, and perceiving their agreements or disagreements.

We have shewn, on the contrary, that every operation of the senses, in its very nature, implies judgment or belief, as well as simple apprehension. Thus, when I feel the pain of the gout in my toe, I have not only a notion of pain, but a belief of its existence, and a belief of some disorder in my toe which occasions it; and this belief is not produced by comparing ideas, and perceiving their agreements and disagreements; it is included in the very nature of the sensation. When I perceive a tree before me, my faculty of seeing gives me not only a notion or simple apprehension of the tree, but a belief of its existence, and of its figure, distance, and magnitude; and this judgment or belief is not got by comparing ideas, it is included in the very nature of the perception. We have taken notice of several original principles of belief in the course of this inquiry; and when other faculties of the mind are examined, we shall find more, which have not occurred in the examination of the five senses.

Such original and natural judgments are, therefore, a part of that furniture which Nature hath given to the human understanding. They are the inspiration of the Almighty, no less than our notions or simple apprehensions. They serve to direct us in the common affairs of life, where our reasoning faculty would leave us in the dark. They are a part of our constitution; and all the discoveries of our reason are grounded upon them. They make up what is called *the common sense of mankind;* and, what is manifestly contrary to any of those first principles, is what we call *absurd.* The strength of them is *good sense,* which is often found in those who are not acute in reasoning. A remarkable deviation from them, arising from a disorder in the constitution, is what we call *lunacy;* as when a man believes that he is made of glass. When a man suffers himself to be reasoned out of the principles of common sense, by metaphysical arguments, we may call this *metaphysical lunacy;* which differs from other species of the distemper in this, that it is not continued, but intermittent: it is apt to seize the patient in solitary and speculative moments; but, when he enters into society, Common Sense recovers her authority. A clear explication and enumeration of the principles of common sense, is one of the chief *desiderata* in logic. We have only considered such of them as occurred in the examination of the five senses.

5. The last observation that I shall make upon the new system is, that, although it professes to set out in the way of reflection, and not of analogy, it hath retained some of the old analogical notions concerning the operations of the mind; particularly, that things which do not now exist in the mind itself, can only be perceived, remembered or imagined, by means of ideas or images of them in the mind, which are the immediate objects of perception, remembrance, and imagination. This doctrine appears evidently to be borrowed from the old system; which taught that external things make impressions upon the mind, like the impressions of a seal upon wax; that it is by means of those impressions that we perceive, remember, or imagine them; and that those impressions must resemble the things from which they are taken. When we form our notions of the operations of the mind by analogy, this way of conceiving them seems to be very natural, and offers itself to our thoughts; for, as everything which is felt must make some impression upon the body, we are apt to think that everything which is understood must make some impression upon the mind.

From such analogical reasoning, this opinion of the existence of ideas or images of things in the mind, seems to have taken its rise, and to have been so universally received among philosophers. It was observed already, that Berkeley, in one instance, apostatizes from this principle of the new system, by affirming that we have no ideas of spirits, and that we can think of them immediately, without ideas. But I know not whether in this he has had any followers. There is some difference, likewise, among modern philosophers with regard to the ideas or images by which we perceive, remember, or imagine sensible things. For, though all agree in the existence of such images they differ about their place; some placing them in a particular part of the brain, where the soul is thought to have her residence, and others placing them in the mind itself. Des Cartes held the first of these opinions; to which Newton seems likewise to have inclined. . . . But Locke seems to place the ideas of sensible things in the mind; and that Berkeley, and the author of the "Treatise of Human Nature," were of the same opinion, is evident. The last makes a very curious application of this doctrine, by endeavouring to prove from it, That the mind either is no substance, or that it is an extended and divisible substance; because the ideas of extension cannot be in a subject which is indivisible and unextended.

I confess I think his reasoning in this, as in most cases, is clear and strong. For whether the idea of extension be only another name for extension itself, as Berkeley and this author assert; or whether the idea of extension be an image and resemblance of extension, as Locke conceived; I appeal to any man of common sense, whether extension, or any image of extension, can be in an unextended and indivisible subject. But while I agree with him in his reasoning, I would make a different application of it. He takes it for granted, that there are ideas of extension in the mind; and thence infers, that, if it is at all a substance, it must be an extended and divisible substance. On the contrary, I take it for granted, upon the testimony of common sense, that my mind is a substance—that is, a permanent subject of thought; and my reason convinces me that it is an unextended and indivisible substance; and hence I infer that there cannot be in it anything that resembles extension. If this reasoning had occurred to Berkeley, it would probably have led him to acknowledge that we may think and reason concerning bodies, without having ideas of them in the mind, as well as concerning spirits.

I intended to have examined more particularly and fully this doctrine of the existence of ideas or images of things in the mind; and likewise another doctrine, which is founded upon it—to wit, That judgment or belief is nothing but a perception of the agreement or disagreement of our ideas; but, having already shewn, through the course of this inquiry, that the operations of the mind which we have examined, give no countenance to either of these doctrines, and in many things contradict them, I have thought it proper to drop this part of my design. It may be executed with more advantage, if it is at all necessary, after inquiring into some other powers of the human understanding.

NOTES

1. Reason is here employed, by Reid, not as a synonyme for Common Sense, (voũs, locus principiorum,) and as he himself more correctly employs it in his later works, but as equivalent to Reasoning, (διανοσα, discursus mentalis).—H.

2. *Simple Apprehension,* in the language of the Schools, has no reference to any exclusion of belief. It was merely given to the conception of simple, in contrast to the cognition of complex, terms.—H.

3. He refers to Hume.—H.

4. See note 1.

5. "The word *suggest*" (says Mr. Stewart, in reference to the preceding passage) "is much used by Berkeley, in this appropriate and technical sense, not only in his 'Theory of Vision,' but in his 'Principles of Human Knowledge,' and in his 'Minute Philosopher.' It expresses, indeed, the cardinal principle on which his 'Theory of Vision' hinges, and is now so incorporated with some of our best metaphysical speculations, that one cannot easily conceive how the use of it was so long dispensed with. Locke uses the word *excite* for the same purpose; but it seems to imply an hypothesis concerning the *mechanism* of the mind, and by no means expresses the fact in question, with the same force and precision.

"It is remarkable, that Dr Reid should have thought it incumbent on him to apologize for introducing into philosophy a word so familiar to every person conversant with Berkeley's works. 'I beg leave to make use of the word *suggestion,* because,' &c.

"So far Dr Reid's use of the word coincides exactly with that of Berkeley; but the former will be found to annex to it a meaning more extensive than the latter, by employing it to comprehend, not only those *intimations* which are the result of experience and habit; but another class of *intimations*, (quite overlooked by Berkeley,) those which result from the original frame of the human mind."—*Dissertation on the History of Metaphysical and Ethical Science.* P. 167. Second edition.

Mr. Stewart might have adduced, perhaps, a higher, and, certainly, a more proximate authority, in favour, not merely of the term in general, but of Reid's restricted employment of it, as an intimation of what he and others have designated the Common Sense of mankind. The following sentence of Tertullian contains a singular anticipation, both of the philosophy and of the philosophical phraseology of our author. Speaking of the universal belief of the soul's immortality:—"Natura pleraque *suggeruntur,* quasi de *publico sensu* quo animam Deus ditare dignatus est."—DE ANIMA, c. 2.

Some strictures on Reid's employment of the term *suggestion* may be seen in the "Versuche" of Tetens, I., p. 508, sqq.—H. . . .

6. See Stewart's "Elements of the Philosophy of the Human Mind." Vol. II,, chap. 1., § 3, last note.—H.

7. This whole doctrine of *natural signs,* on which his philosophy is in a great measure established, was borrowed by Reid, in principle, and even in expression, from Berkeley. Compare "Minute Philosopher," Dial IV., §§ 7, 11, 12; "New Theory of Vision" §§ 144, 147; "Theory of Vision Vindicated," §§ 38–43.—H.

8. On this distinction of *Primary* and *Secondary* Qualities, see "Essays on the Intellectual Powers," Essay II., chap. 17—H.

9. It has not "always been taken for granted, that the ideas of Extension, Figure, and Motion, are ideas of sensation." Even a distinguished predecessor of Reid, in his Chair at Glasgow, denied this doctrine of the sensual school, to which he generally adhered. I would not be supposed to suspect Reid of the slightest disingenuousness, but he has certainly here and elsewhere been anticipated by Hutcheson, in some of the

most important principles, no less than in some of the weaker positions of his philosophy. . . .—H.

10. The reader will again notice this and the other instances which follow, of the inaccuracy or Reid's language in his earlier work, constituting, as different, *Reason* and *Common Sense.* —H.

11. On this subject, see "Essays on the Intellectual Powers," Essay II., chap. 7–15, and the notes thereon. It is perhaps proper to recall to the reader's attention, that, by the Ideal Theory, Reid always understands the ruder form of the doctrine, which holds that ideas are entities, different both from the external object and from the percipient mind, and that he had no conception of the finer form of that doctrine, which holds that all that we are conscious of in perception, (of course also in imagination,) is only a modification of the mind itself. —H.

12. On this last, see Aristotle *De Anima,* L. III., c. 1, and *Metaph.* L. III. c. 5.—The Aristotelic distinction of *first* and *second* qualities was of another kind.—H.

13. In this passage Reid admits Figure and Place (consequently, Extension) to be *original* perceptions of vision. . . . —H.

14. Compare Mr. Stewart's "Elements," vol. 1. ch. ii., § 4, p. 247. Second edition. Campbell "On Miracles," Part 1., § 1. Smith's "Theory of Moral Sentiment," vol. II, p. 382. Sixth edition.—H.

15. See, *contra,* Priestley's "Examination," p. 86. "Brown's Lect." lect. lxxxiv.—H.

16. Compare Stewart's "Elements," vol. I., chap. iv, § 5, p. 205, sixth edition; "Philosophical Essays," p. 74, sqq., fourth edition; Royer Collard, in Jouffroy's "Oeuvres de Reid," t. IV., p. 279, sqq.; with Priestley's "Examination," p. 86, sqq. I merely refer to works relative to *Reid's* doctrine.—H.

17. See "Essays on the Intellectual Powers," Ess. VI., ch. viii., Nos. 2 and 6.—H.

18. When Hume's "Treatise of Human Nature" appeared. —H.

19. This dilemma applies to the *sensualism* of Locke, but not to the *rationalism* of Des Cartes.—H.

20. The following summary refers principally to Locke.—H.

*ESSAYS
ON THE
INTELLECTUAL POWERS
OF MAN*

ESSAY ONE / PRELIMINARY

CHAPTER 1 / EXPLICATION OF WORDS

There is no greater impediment to the advancement of knowledge than the ambiguity of words. To this chiefly it is owing that we find sects and parties in most branches of science; and disputes which are carried on from age to age, without being brought to an issue

Sophistry has been more effectually excluded from mathematics and natural philosophy than from other sciences. In mathematics it had no place from the beginning; mathematicians having had the wisdom to define accurately the terms they use, and to lay down, as axioms, the first principles on which their reasoning is grounded. Accordingly, we find no parties among mathematicians, and hardly any disputes.

In natural philosophy, there was no less sophistry, no less dispute and uncertainty, than in other sciences, until, about a century and a half ago, this science began to be built upon the foundation of clear definitions and self-evident axioms. Since that time, the science, as if watered with the dew of Heaven, hath grown apace; disputes have ceased, truth hath prevailed, and the science hath received greater increase in two centuries than in two thousand years before.

It were to be wished that this method, which hath been so successful in those branches of science, were attempted in others; for definitions and axioms are the foundations of all science. But that definitions may not be sought where no definition can be given, nor logical definitions be attempted where the subject does not admit of them, it may be proper to lay down some general principles concerning definition, for the sake of those who are less conversant in this branch of logic.

When one undertakes to explain any art or science, he will have occasion to use many words that are common to all who use the same language, and some that are peculiar to that art or science. Words of the last kind are called *terms of the art*, and ought to be distinctly explained, that their meaning may be understood.

A definition is nothing else but an explication of the meaning of a word, by words whose meaning is already known. Hence it is evident that every word cannot be defined; for the definition must consist of words; and there could be no definition, if there were not words previously understood without definition. Common words, therefore, ought to be used in their common acceptation; and, when they have different acceptations in common language, these, when it is necessary, ought to be distinguished. But they require no definition. It is sufficient to define words that are uncommon, or that are used in an uncommon meaning.

It may farther be observed, that there are many words, which, though they may need explication, cannot be logically defined. A logical definition—that is, a strict and proper definition—must express the kind [genus] of the thing defined, and the specific difference by which the species defined is distinguished from every other species belonging to that kind. It is natural to the mind of man to class things under various kinds, and again to subdivide every kind into its various species. A species may often be subdivided into subordinate species, and then it is considered as a kind.

From what has been said of logical definition, it is evident, that no word can be logically defined which does not denote

a species; because such things only can have a specific difference; and a specific difference is essential to a logical definition. On this account there can be no logical definition of
individual things, such as London or Paris. Individuals are
distinguished either by proper names, or by accidental circumstances of time or place; but they have no specific difference;
and, therefore, though they may be known by proper names,
or may be described by proper names, or may be described by
circumstances or relations, they cannot be defined. It is no less
evident that the most general words cannot be logically
defined, because there is not a more general term, of which
they are a species.

Nay, we cannot define every species of things, because it
happens sometimes that we have not words to express the
specific difference. Thus, a scarlet colour is, no doubt, a species of colour; but how shall we express the specific difference
by which scarlet is distinguished from green or blue? The
difference of them is immediately perceived by the eye; but we
have not words to express it. These things we are taught by
logic.

Without having recourse to the principles of logic, we may
easily be satisfied that words cannot be defined, which signify
things perfectly simple, and void of all composition. This observation, I think was first made by Des Cartes, and afterwards
more fully illustrated by Locke.[1] And, however obvious it appears to be, many instances may be given of great philosophers who have perplexed and darkened the subjects they
have treated, by not knowing, or not attending to it.

When men attempt to define things which cannot be
defined, their definitions will always be either obscure or false.
It was one of the capital defects of Aristotle's philosophy, that
he pretended to define the simplest things, which neither can
be, nor need to be defined—such as *time* and *motion*. Among
modern philosophers, I know none that has abused definition
so much as Carolus [Christianus] Wolfius, the famous German

philosopher, who, in a work on the human mind, called "Psychologia Empirica," consisting of many hundred propositions, fortified by demonstrations, with a proportional accompaniment of definitions, corollaries, and scholia, has given so many definitions of things which cannot be defined, and so many demonstrations of things self-evident, that the greatest part of the work consists of tautology, and ringing changes upon words.

There is no subject in which there is more frequent occasion to use words that cannot be logically defined, than in treating of the powers and operations of the mind. The simplest operations of our minds must all be expressed by words of this kind. No man can explain, by a logical definition, what it is to *think*, to *apprehend*, to *believe*, to *will*, to *desire*. Every man who understands the language, has some notion of the meaning of those words; and every man who is capable of reflection may, by attending to the operations of his own mind, which are signified by them, form a clear and distinct notion of them; but they cannot be logically defined.

Since, therefore, it is often impossible to define words which we must use on this subject, we must as much as possible use common words, in their common acceptation, pointing out their various senses where they are ambiguous; and, when we are obliged to use words less common, we must endeavour to explain them as well as we can, without affecting to give logical definitions, when the nature of the thing does not allow it.

The following observations on the meaning of certain words are intended to supply, as far as we can, the want of definitions, by preventing ambiguity or obscurity in the use of them.

1. By the *mind* of a man, we understand that in him which thinks, remembers, reasons, wills. The essence both of body and of mind is unknown to us. We know certain properties of the first, and certain operations of the last, and by these only we can define or describe them. We define body to be that which is extended, solid, moveable, divisible. In like manner,

we define mind to be that which thinks. We are conscious that we think, and that we have a variety of thoughts of different kinds—such as seeing, hearing, remembering, deliberating, resolving, loving, hating, and many other kinds of thought—all which we are taught by nature to attribute to one internal principle; and this principle of thought we call the *mind* or *soul* of a man.

2. By the *operations* of the mind, we understand every mode of thinking of which we are conscious.

It deserves our notice, that the various modes of thinking have always, and in all languages, as far as we know, been called by the name of operations of the mind, or by names of the same import. To body we ascribe various properties, but not operations, properly so called: it is extended, divisible, moveable, inert; it continues in any state in which it is put; every change of its state is the effect of some force impressed upon it, and is exactly proportional to the force impressed, and in the precise direction of that force. These are the general properties of matter, and these are not operations; on the contrary, they all imply its being a dead, inactive thing, which moves only as it is moved, and acts only by being acted upon.

But the mind is, from its very nature, a living and active being. Everything we know of it implies life and active energy; and the reason why all its modes of thinking are called its operations, is, that in all, or in most of them, it is not merely passive, as body is, but is really and properly active.

In all ages, and in all languages, ancient and modern, the various modes of thinking have been expressed by words of active signification, such as *seeing, hearing, reasoning, willing,* and the like. It seems, therefore, to be the natural judgment of mankind, that the mind is active in its various ways of thinking; and, for this reason, they are called its operations, and are expressed by active verbs.

It may be made a question, What regard is to be paid to this natural judgment? May it not be a vulgar error? Philosophers who think so have, no doubt, a right to be heard. But, until it is proved that the mind is not active in thinking, but merely passive, the common language with regard to its operations ought to be used, and ought not to give place to a phraseology invented by philosophers, which implies its being merely passive.

3. The words *power* and *faculty*, which are often used in speaking of the mind, need little explication. Every operation supposes a power in the being that operates; for to suppose anything to operate, which has no power to operate, is manifestly absurd. But, on the other hand, there is no absurdity in supposing a being to have power to operate, when it does not operate. Thus I may have power to walk, when I sit; or to speak, when I am silent. Every operation, therefore, implies power; but the power does not imply the operation.

The *faculties* of the mind, and its *powers*, are often used as synonymous expressions. But, as most synonymes have some minute distinction that deserves notice, I apprehend that the word *faculty* is most properly applied to those powers of the mind which are original and natural, and which make a part of the constitution of the mind. There are other powers, which are acquired by use, exercise, or study, which are not called faculties, but *habits*. There must be something in the constitution of the mind necessary to our being able to acquire habits —and this is commonly called *capacity*.

4. We frequently meet with a distinction in writers upon this subject, between things *in the mind*, and things *external* to the mind. The powers, faculties, and operations of the mind, are things in the mind. Everything is said to be in the mind, of which the mind is the *subject*. It is self-evident that there are some things which cannot exist without a subject to which they belong, and of which they are attributes. Thus, colour must be in something coloured; figure in something figured: thought can only be in something that thinks; wisdom and virtue cannot exist but in some being that is wise and virtuous. When,

therefore, we speak of things in the mind, we understand by this, things of which the mind is the subject. Excepting the mind itself, and things in the mind, all other things are said to be external. It ought therefore to be remembered, that this distinction between things in the mind and things external, is not meant to signify the place of the things we speak of, but their subject.

There is a figurative sense in which things are said to be in the mind, which it is sufficient barely to mention. We say such a thing was not in my mind; meaning no more than that I had not the least thought of it. By a figure, we put the thing for the thought of it. In this sense external things are in the mind as often as they are the objects of our thought.

5. *Thinking* is a very general word, which includes all the operations of our minds, and is so well understood as to need no definition.

To *perceive*, to *remember*, to be *conscious*, and to *conceive* or *imagine*, are words common to philosophers and to the vulgar. They signify different operations of the mind, which are distinguished in all languages, and by all men that think. I shall endeavour to use them in their most common and proper acceptation, and I think they are hardly capable of strict definition. But, as some philosophers, in treating of the mind, have taken the liberty to use them very improperly, so as to corrupt the English language, and to confound things which the common understanding of mankind hath always led them to distinguish, I shall make some observations on the meaning of them, that may prevent ambiguity or confusion in the use of them.

6. *First*, We are never said to *perceive* things, of the existence of which we have not a full conviction. I may *conceive* or *imagine* a mountain of gold, or a winged horse; but no man says that he perceives such a creature of imagination. Thus *perception* is distinguished from *conception* or imagination. *Secondly*, Perception is applied only to external objects, not to those that are in the mind itself. When I am pained, I do not say that I

perceive pain, but that I feel it, or that I am conscious of it. Thus, *perception* is distinguished from *consciousness*. *Thirdly*, The immediate object of perception must be something present, and not what is past. We may remember what is past, but do not perceive it. I may say, I perceive such a person has had the small-pox; but this phrase is figurative, although the figure is so familiar that it is not observed. The meaning of it is, that I perceive the pits in his face, which are certain signs of his having had the small-pox. We say we perceive the thing signified, when we only perceive the sign. But when the word *perception* is used properly, and without any figure, it is never applied to things past. And thus it is distinguished from *remembrance*.

In a word, perception is most properly applied to the evidence which we have of external objects by our senses. But, as this is a very clear and cogent kind of evidence, the word is often applied by analogy to the evidence of reason or of testimony, when it is clear and cogent. The perception of external objects by our senses, is an operation of the mind of a peculiar nature, and ought to have a name appropriated to it. It has so in all languages. And, in English, I know no word more proper to express this act of the mind than perception. Seeing, hearing, smelling, tasting, and touching or feeling, are words that express the operations proper to each sense; perceiving expresses that which is common to them all.

The observations made on this word would have been unnecessary, if it had not been so much abused in philosophical writings upon the mind; for, in other writings, it has no obscurity. Although this abuse is not chargeable on Mr Hume only, yet I think he has carried it to the highest pitch. The first sentence of his "Treatise of Human Nature" runs thus:—"All the perceptions of the human mind resolve themselves into two distinct heads, which I shall call impressions and ideas." He adds, a little after, that, under the name of impressions, he comprehends all our sensations, passions, and emotions. Here we learn that our passions and emotions are perceptions. I believe, no English writer before him ever gave the name of a perception to any passion or emotion. When a man is angry, we must say that he has the perception of anger. When he is in love, that he has the perception of love. He speaks often of the perceptions of memory, and of the perceptions of imagination; and he might as well speak of the hearing of sight, or of the smelling of touch; for, surely, hearing is not more different from sight, or smelling from touch, than perceiving is from remembering or imagining.

7. *Consciousness* is a word used by philosophers, to signify that immediate knowledge which we have of our present thoughts and purposes, and, in general, of all the present operations of our minds. Whence we may observe, that consciousness is only of things present. To apply consciousness to things past, which sometimes is done in popular discourse, is to confound consciousness with memory; and all such confusion of words ought to be avoided in philosophical discourse. It is likewise to be observed, that consciousness is only of things in the mind, and not of external things. It is improper to say, I am conscious of the table which is before me. I perceive it, I see it; but do not say I am conscious of it. As that consciousness by which we have a knowledge of the operations of our own minds, is a different power from that by which we perceive external objects, and as these different powers have different names in our language, and, I believe, in all languages, a philosopher ought carefully to preserve this distinction, and never to confound things so different in their nature.

8. *Conceiving, imagining,* and *apprehending,* are commonly used as synonymous in our language, and signify the same thing which the logicians call simple apprehension. This is an operation of the mind different from all those we have mentioned. Whatever we perceive, whatever we remember, whatever we are conscious of, we have a full persuasion or conviction of its existence. But we may conceive or imagine what has

no existence, and what we firmly believe to have no existence. What never had an existence cannot be remembered; what has no existence *at present* cannot be the object of perception or of consciousness; but what never had, nor has any existence, may be conceived. Every man knows that it is as easy to conceive a winged horse, or a centaur, as it is to conceive a horse or a man. Let it be observed, therefore, that to *conceive*, to *imagine*, to *apprehend*, when taken in the proper sense, signify an act of the mind which implies no belief or judgment at all. It is an act of the mind by which nothing is affirmed or denied, and which, therefore, can neither be true nor false.

But there is another and a very different meaning of those words, so common and so well authorized in language that it cannot easily be avoided; and on that account we ought to be the more on our guard, that we be not misled by the ambiguity. Politeness and good-breeding lead men, on most occasions, to express their opinions with modesty, especially when they differ from others whom they ought to respect. Therefore, when we would express our opinion modestly, instead of saying, "This is my opinion," or "This is my judgment," which has the air of dogmaticalness, we say, "I conceive it to be thus—I imagine, or apprehend it to be thus;" which is understood as a modest declaration of our judgment. In like manner, when anything is said which we take to be impossible, we say, "We cannot conceive it;" meaning that we cannot believe it.

Thus we see that the words *conceive, imagine, apprehend*, have two meanings, and are used to express two operations of the mind, which ought never to be confounded. Sometimes they express simple apprehension, which implies no judgment at all; sometimes they express judgment or opinion. This ambiguity ought to be attended to, that we may not impose upon ourselves or others in the use of them. The ambiguity is indeed remedied, in a great measure, by their construction. When they are used to express simple apprehension, they are followed by a noun in the *accusative case*, which signifies the object conceived; but, when they are used to express opinion or judgment, they are commonly followed by a verb, in the *infinitive mood*. "I conceive an Egyptian pyramid." This implies no judgment. "I conceive the Egyptian pyramids to be the most ancient monuments of human art." This implies judgment. When the words are used in the last sense, the thing conceived must be a proposition, because judgment cannot be expressed but by a proposition. When they are used in the first sense, the thing conceived may be no proposition, but a simple term only —as a pyramid, an obelisk. Yet it may be observed, that even a proposition may be simply apprehended, without forming any judgment of its truth or falsehood; for it is one thing to conceive the meaning of a proposition; it is another thing to judge it to be true or false.

Although the distinction between simple apprehension, and every degree of assent or judgment, be perfectly evident to every man who reflects attentively on what passes in his own mind—although it is very necessary, in treating of the powers of the mind, to attend carefully to this distinction—yet, in the affairs of common life, it is seldom necessary to observe it accurately. On this account we shall find, in all common languages, the words which express one of those operations frequently applied to the other. To think, to suppose, to imagine, to conceive, to apprehend, are the words we use to express simple apprehension; but they are all frequently used to express judgment. Their ambiguity seldom occasions any inconvenience in the common affairs of life, for which language is framed. But it has perplexed philosophers, in treating of the operations of the mind, and will always perplex them, if they do not attend accurately to the different meanings which are put upon those words on different occasions.

9. Most of the operations of the mind, from their very nature, must have objects to which they are directed, and about which they are employed. He that perceives, must perceive something; and that which he perceives is called the object of

his perception. To perceive, without having any object of perception, is impossible. The mind that perceives, the object perceived, and the *operation* of perceiving that object, are distinct things, and are distinguished in the structure of all languages. In this sentence, "I see, or perceive the moon," *I* is the person or *mind,* the active verb *see* denotes the operation of that mind, and the *moon* denotes the object. What we have said of perceiving, is equally applicable to most operations of the mind. Such operations are, in all languages, expressed by active transitive verbs; and we know that, in all languages, such verbs require a thing or person, which is the agent, and a noun following in an oblique case, which is the object. Whence it is evident, that all mankind, both those who have contrived language, and those who use it with understanding, have distinguished these three things as different—to wit, the operations of the mind, which are expressed by active verbs; the mind itself, which is the nominative to those verbs; and the object, which is, in the oblique case, governed by them.

It would have been unnecessary to explain so obvious a distinction, if some systems of philosophy had not confounded it. Mr Hume's system, in particular, confounds all distinction between the operations of the mind and their objects. When he speaks of the ideas of memory, the ideas of imagination, and the ideas of sense, it is often impossible, from the tenor of his discourse, to know whether, by those ideas, he means the operations of the mind, or the objects about which they are employed. And, indeed, according to his system, there is no distinction between the one and the other.

A philosopher is, no doubt, entitled to examine even those distinctions that are to be found in the structure of all languages; and, if he is able to shew that there is no foundation for them in the nature of the things distinguished—if he can point out some prejudice common to mankind which has led them to distinguish things that are not really different—in that case, such a distinction may be imputed to a vulgar error, which ought to be corrected in philosophy. But when, in his first setting out, he takes it for granted, without proof, that distinctions found in the structure of all languages, have no foundation in nature, this, surely, is too fastidious a way of treating the common sense of mankind. When we come to be instructed by philosophers, we must bring the old light of common sense along with us, and by it judge of the new light which the philosopher communicates to us. But when we are required to put out the old light altogether, that we may follow the new, we have reason to be on our guard. There may be distinctions that have a real foundation, and which may be necessary in philosophy, which are not made in common language, because not necessary in the common business of life. But I believe no instance will be found of a distinction made in all languages, which has not a just foundation in nature.

10. The word *idea* occurs so frequently in modern philosophical writings upon the mind, and is so ambiguous in its meaning, that it is necessary to make some observations upon it. There are chiefly two meanings of this word in modern authors—a popular and a philosophical.

First, In popular language, *idea* signifies the same thing as conception, apprehension, notion. To have an idea of anything, is to conceive it. To have a distinct idea, is to conceive it distinctly. To have no idea of it, is not to conceive it at all. It was before observed, that conceiving or apprehending has always been considered by all men as an act or operation of the mind, and, on that account, has been expressed in all languages by an active verb. When, therefore, we use the phrase of having ideas, in the popular sense, we ought to attend to this, that it signifies precisely the same thing which we commonly express by the active verbs, conceiving or apprehending.

When the word idea is taken in this popular sense, no man can possibly doubt whether he has ideas. For he that doubts must think, and to think is to have ideas.

Sometimes, in popular language, a man's ideas signify his opinions. The ideas of Aristotle, or of Epicurus, signify the opinions of these philosophers. What was formerly said of the words *imagine, conceive, apprehend*, that they are sometimes used to express judgment, is no less true of the word idea. This signification of the word seems indeed more common in the French language than in English. But it is found in this sense in good English authors, and even in Mr. Locke. Thus we see, that having *ideas*, taken in the popular sense, has precisely the same meaning with conceiving, imagining, apprehending, and has likewise the same ambiguity. It may, therefore, be doubted, whether the introduction of this word into popular discourse, to signify the operation of conceiving or apprehending, was at all necessary. For, *first*, we have, as has been shewn, several words which are either originally English, or have been long naturalized, that express the same thing; why, therefore, should we adopt a Greek word, in place of these, any more than a French or a German word? Besides, the words of our own language are less ambiguous. For the word idea, has, for many ages, been used by philosophers as a term of art; and in the different systems of philosophers means very different things.

Secondly, According to the philosophical meaning of the word idea, it does not signify that act of the mind which we call thought or conception, but some object of thought. Ideas, according to Mr Locke, (whose very frequent use of this word has probably been the occasion of its being adopted into common language,) "are nothing but the immediate objects of the mind in thinking." But of those objects of thought called ideas, different sects of philosophers have given a very different account. Bruckerus, a learned German, wrote a whole book, giving the history of ideas. . . .

Modern philosophers, as well as the Peripatetics and Epicureans of old, have conceived that external objects cannot be the immediate objects of our thought; that there must be some image of them in the mind itself, in which, as in a mirror, they are seen. And the name *idea*, in the philosophical sense of it, is given to those internal and immediate objects of our thoughts. The external thing is the remote or mediate object; but the idea, or image of that object in the mind, is the immediate object, without which we could have no perception, no remembrance, no conception of the mediate object.

When, therefore, in common language, we speak of having an idea of anything, we mean no more by that expression, but thinking of it. The vulgar allow that this expression implies a mind that thinks, an act of that mind which we call thinking, and an object about which we think. But, besides these three, the philosopher conceives that there is a fourth—to wit, the *idea*, which is the immediate object. The idea is in the mind itself, and can have no existence but in a mind that thinks; but the remote or mediate object may be something external, as the sun or moon; it may be something past or future; it may be something which never existed. This is the philosophical meaning of the word *idea;* and we may observe that this meaning of that word is built upon a philosophical opinion: for, if philosophers had not believed that there are such immediate objects of all our thoughts in the mind, they would never have used the word idea to express them.

I shall only add, on this article, that, although I may have occasion to use the word idea in this philosophical sense in explaining the opinions of others, I shall have no occasion to use it in expressing my own, because I believe *ideas*, taken in this sense, to be a mere fiction of philosophers. And, in the popular meaning of the word, there is the less occasion to use it, because the English words *thought, notion, apprehension,* answer the purpose as well as the Greek word *idea;* with this advantage, that they are less ambiguous. There is, indeed, a meaning of the word idea, which I think most agreeable to its use in ancient philosophy, and which I would willingly adopt, if use, the arbiter of language, did permit. But this will come to be explained afterwards.

11. The word *impression* is used by Mr Hume, in speaking of

the operations of the mind, almost as often as the word *idea* is by Mr Locke. What the latter calls ideas, the former divides into two classes; one of which he calls impressions, the other ideas. I shall make some observations upon Mr Hume's explication of *that* word, and then consider the proper meaning of it in the English language.

"We may divide," (says Mr Hume, "Essays," vol. II., p. 18,[2]), "all the perceptions of the human mind into two classes or species, which are distinguished by their different degrees of force and vivacity. The less lively and forcible are commonly denominated THOUGHTS or IDEAS. The other species want a name in our language, and in most others; [I suppose because it was not requisite for any but philosophical purposes to rank them under a general term or appellation.] Let us, therefore, use a little freedom, and call them IMPRESSIONS: [employing that word in a sense somewhat different from the usual.] By the term *impression*, then, I mean all our more lively perceptions, when we hear, or see, or feel, or love, or hate, or desire, or will. [And impressions are distinguished from] ideas [which] are the less lively perceptions, of which we are conscious, when we reflect on any of those sensations or movements above mentioned."

This is the explication Mr Hume hath given in his "Essays" of the term *impressions,* when applied to the mind; and his explication of it, in his "Treatise of Human Nature," is to the same purpose [Vol. I. p. 11.]

Disputes about words belong rather to grammarians than to philosophers; but philosophers ought not to escape censure when they corrupt a language, by using words in a way which the purity of the language will not admit. I find fault with Mr Hume's phraseology in the words I have quoted—

First, Because he gives the name of perceptions to every operation of the mind. Love is a perception, hatred a perception; desire is a perception, will is a perception; and, by the same rule, a doubt, a question, a command, is a perception.

This is an intolerable abuse of language, which no philosopher has authority to introduce.

Secondly, When Mr Hume says, *that we may divide all the perceptions of the human mind into two classes or speices, which are distinguished by their degrees of force and vivacity,* the manner of expression is loose and unphilosophical. To differ in species is one thing; to differ in degree is another. Things which differ in degree only must be of the same species. It is a maxim of common sense, admitted by all men, that *greater* and *less* do not make a change of species. The same man may differ in the degree of his force and vivacity, in the morning and at night, in health and in sickness; but this is so far from making him a different species, that it does not so much as make him a different individual. To say, therefore, that two different classes, or species of perceptions, are distinguished by the degrees of their force and vivacity, is to confound a difference of *degree* with a difference of *species,* which every man of understanding knows how to distinguish.

Thirdly, We may observe, that this author, having given the general name of perception to all the operations of the mind, and distinguished them into two classes or species, which differ only in degree of force and vivacity, tells us, that he gives the name of impressions to all our more lively perceptions— to wit, when we hear, or see, or feel, or love, or hate, or desire, or will. There is great confusion in this account of the meaning of the word *impression.* When I see, this is an *impression.* But why has not the author told us whether he gives the name of *impression* to the object seen, or to that act of my mind by which I see it? When I see the full moon, the full moon is one thing, my perceiving it is another thing. Which of these two things does he call an impression? We are left to guess this; nor does all that this author writes about impressions clear this point. Everything he says tends to darken it, and to lead us to think that the full moon which I see, and my seeing it, are not two things, but one and the same thing.

The same observation may be applied to every other instance the author gives to illustrate the meaning of the word *impression*. "When we hear, when we feel, when we love, when we hate, when we desire, when we will." In all these acts of the mind there must be an *object*, which is heard, or felt, or loved, or hated, or desired, or willed. Thus, for instance, I love my country. This, says Mr Hume, is an *impression*. But what is the *impression?* Is it my country, or is it the affection I bear to it? I ask the philosopher this question; but I find no answer to it. And when I read all that he has *written* on this subject, I find this word *impression* sometimes used to signify an operation of the mind, sometimes the object of the operation; but, for the most part, it is a vague and indetermined word that signifies both.

I know not whether it may be considered as an apology for such abuse of words, in an author who understood the language so well, and used it with so great propriety in writing on other subjects, that Mr Hume's system, with regard to the mind, required a language of a different structure from the common: or, if expressed in plain English, would have been too shocking to the common sense of mankind. To give an instance or two of this. If a man receives a present on which he puts a high value, if he see and handle it, and put it in his pocket, this, says Mr Hume, is an *impression*. If the man only dream that he received such a present, this is an *idea*. Wherein lies the difference between this impression and this idea— between the dream and the reality? They are different classes or species, says Mr Hume: so far all men will agree with him. But he adds that they are distinguished only by different degrees of force and vivacity. Here he insinuates a tenet of his own, in contradiction to the commonsense of mankind. Common sense convinces every man, that a lively dream is no nearer to a reality than a faint one; and that, if a man should dream that he had all the wealth of Croesus, it would not put one farthing in his pocket. It is impossible to fabricate arguments against such undeniable principles, without confounding the meaning of words.

In like manner, if a man would persuade me that the moon which I see, and my seeing it, are not two things, but one and the same thing, he will answer his purpose less by arguing this point in plain English, than by confounding the two under one name—such as that of an *impression.* For such is the power of words, that, if we can be brought to the habit of calling two things that are connected *by the same name,* we are the more easily led to believe them to be one and the same thing.

Let us next consider the proper meaning of the word *impression* in English, that we may see how far it is fit to express either the operations of the mind or their objects.

When a figure is stamped upon a body by pressure, that figure is called an *impression,* as the impression of a seal on wax, of printing-types, or of a copperplate on paper. This seems now to be the literal sense of the word; the effect borrowing its name from the cause. But, by metaphor or analogy, like most other words, its meaning is extended, so as to signify any change produced in a body by the operation of some external cause. A blow of the hand makes no impression on a stone wall; but a battery of cannon may. The moon raises a tide in the ocean, but makes no impression on rivers and lakes.

When we speak of making an impression on the mind, the word is carried still farther from its literal meaning; use, however, which is the arbiter of language, authorizes this application of it—as when we say that admonition and reproof make little impression on those who are confirmed in bad habits. The same discourse delivered in one way makes a strong impression on the hearers; delivered in another way, it makes no impression at all.

It may be observed that, in such examples, an impression made on the mind always implies some change of purpose or will; some new habit produced, or some former habit weakened; some passion raised or allayed. When such changes are produced by persuasion, example, or any external cause, we say that such causes make an impression upon the mind; but, when things are seen, or heard, or apprehended, without producing any passion or emotion, we say that they make no impression.

In the most extensive sense, an impression is a change produced in some passive subject by the operation of an external cause. If we suppose an active being to produce any change in itself by its own active power, this is never called an impression. It is the act or operation of the being itself, not an impression upon it. From this it appears, that to give the name of an impression to any effect produced in the mind, is to suppose that the mind does not act at all in the production of that effect. If seeing, hearing, desiring, willing, be operations of the mind, they cannot be impressions. If they be impressions, they cannot be operations of the mind. In the structure of all languages, they are considered as acts or operations of the mind itself, and the names given them imply this. To call them impressions, therefore, is to trespass against the structure, not of a particular language only, but of all languages.

If the word *impression* be an improper word to signify the operations of the mind, it is at least as improper to signify their objects; for would any man be thought to speak with propriety, who should say that the sun is an impression, that the earth and the sea are impressions?

It is commonly believed, and taken for granted, that every language, if it be sufficiently copious in words, is equally fit to express all opinions, whether they be true or false. I apprehend, however, that there is an exception to this general rule, which deserves our notice. There are certain common opinions of mankind, upon which the structure and grammar of all languages are founded. While these opinions are common to all men, there will be a great similarity in all languages that are to be found on the face of the earth. Such a similarity there really is; for we find in all languages the same parts of speech, the distinction of nouns and verbs, the distinction of nouns into adjective and substantive, of verbs into active and passive. In verbs we find like tenses, moods, persons, and numbers. There are general rules of grammar, the same in all languages. This similarity of structure in all languages, shews an uniformity among men in those opinions upon which the structure of language is founded.

If, for instance, we should suppose that there was a nation who believed that the things which we call attributes might exist without a subject, there would be in their language no distinction between adjectives and substantives, nor would it be a rule with them that an adjective has no meaning, unless when joined to a substantive. If there was any nation who did not distinguish between acting and being acted upon, there would in their language be no distinction between active and passive verbs; nor would it be a rule that the active verb must have an agent in the nominative case, but that, in the passive verb, the agent must be in an oblique case.

The structure of all languages is grounded upon common notions, which Mr Hume's philosophy opposes, and endeavours to overturn. This, no doubt, led him to warp the common language into a conformity with his principles; but we ought not to imitate him in this, until we are satisfied that his principles are built on a solid foundation.

12. *Sensation* is a name given by philosophers to an act of mind, which may be distinguished from all others by this, that it hath no object distinct from the act itself. Pain of every kind is an uneasy sensation. When I am pained, I cannot say that the pain I feel is one thing, and that my feeling it is another thing. They are one and the same thing, and cannot be disjoined, even in imagination. Pain, when it is not felt, has no existence. It can be neither greater nor less in degree or duration, nor anything else in kind than it is felt to be. It cannot exist by itself, nor in any subject but in a sentient being. No quality of an inanimate insentient being can have the least resemblance to it.

What we have said of pain may be applied to every other sensation. . . .

I shall add an observation concerning the word *feeling.* This word has two meanings. *First,* it signifies the perceptions we have of external objects, by the sense of touch. When we speak of feeling a body to be hard or soft, rough or smooth, hot or cold, to feel these things is to perceive them by touch. They are external things, and that act of the mind by which we feel them is easily distinguished from the objects felt. *Secondly,* the word *feeling* is used to signify the same thing as *sensation,* which we have just now explained; and, in this sense, it has no object; the feeling and the thing felt are one and the same.

Perhaps betwixt feeling, taken in this last sense, and sensation, there may be this small difference, that sensation is most commonly used to signify those feelings which we have by our external senses and bodily appetites, and all our bodily pains and pleasures. But there are *feelings* of a nobler nature accompanying our affections, our moral judgments, and our determinations in matters of taste, to which the word *sensation* is less properly applied.

I have premised these observations on the meaning of certain words that frequently occur in treating of this subject, for two reasons: *First,* That I may be the better understood when I use them; and, *Secondly,* That those who would make any progress in this branch of science, may accustom themselves to attend very carefully to the meaning of words that are used in it. They may be assured of this, that the ambiguity of words, and the vague and improper application of them, have thrown more darkness upon this subject than the subtilty and intricacy of things.

When we use common words, we ought to use them in the sense in which they are most commonly used by the best and purest writers in the language; and, when we have occasion to enlarge or restrict the meaning of a common word, or give it more precision than it has in common language, the reader ought to have warning of this, otherwise we shall impose upon ourselves and upon him.

A very respectable writer has given a good example of this kind, by explaining, in an Appendix to his "Elements of Criticism," the terms he has occasion to use. In that Appendix, most of the words are explained on which I have been making observations; and the explication I have given, I think, agrees, for the most part, with his.

Other words that need explication, shall be explained as they occur.

CHAPTER 2 / PRINCIPLES TAKEN FOR GRANTED

As there are words common to philosophers and to the vulgar, which need no explication, so there are principles common to both, which need no proof, and which do not admit of direct proof. . . .

It may, however be observed, that the first principles of natural philosophy are of a quite different nature from mathematical axioms: they have not the same kind of evidence, nor are they necessary truths, as mathematical axioms are. They are such as these: That similar effects proceed from the same or similar causes; That we ought to admit of no other causes of natural effects, but such as are true, and sufficient to account for the effects. These are principles which, though they have not the same kind of evidence that mathematical axioms have; yet have such evidence that every man of common understanding readily assents to them, and finds it absolutely necessary to conduct his actions and opinions by them, in the ordinary affairs of life.

Though it has not been usual, yet I conceive it may be useful, to point out some of those things which I shall take for granted, as first principles, in treating of the mind and its faculties. There is the more occasion for this; because very ingenious men, such as Des Cartes, Malebranche, Arnauld, Locke, and many others, have lost much labour, by not distinguishing things which require proof, from things which, though they may admit of illustration, yet, being self-evident, do not admit of proof. When men attempt to deduce such self-evident principles from others more evident, they always fall into inconclusive reasoning: and the consequence of this has been, that others, such as Berkeley and Hume, finding the arguments brought to prove such first principles to be weak and inconclusive, have been tempted first to doubt of them, and afterwards to deny them.

It is so irksome to reason with those who deny first principles, that wise men commonly decline it. Yet it is not impossible, that what is only a vulgar prejudice may be mistaken for a first principle. Nor is it impossible that what is really a first principle may, by the enchantment of words, have such a mist thrown about it, as to hide its evidence, and to make a man of candour doubt of it. Such cases happen more frequently, perhaps, in this science than in any other; but they are not altogether without remedy. There are ways by which the evidence of first principles may be made more apparent when they are brought into dispute; but they require to be handled in a way peculiar to themselves. Their evidence is not demonstrative, but intuitive. They require not proof, but to be placed in a proper point of view. This will be shewn more fully in its proper place, and applied to those very principles which we now assume. In the meantime, when they are proposed as first principles, the reader is put on his guard, and warned to consider whether they have a just claim to that character.

1. *First*, then, I shall take it for granted, that I *think*, that I *remember*, that I *reason*, and, in general, that I really perform all those operations of mind of which I am conscious.

The operations of our minds are attended with consciousness; and this consciousness is the evidence, the only evidence, which we have or can have of their existence. If a man should take it into his head to think or to say that his consciousness may deceive him, and to require proof that it cannot, I know of no proof that can be given him; he must be left to himself, as a man that denies first principles, without which there can be no reasoning. Every man finds himself under a necessity of believing what consciousness testifies, and everything that hath this testimony is to be taken as a first principle.

2. As by consciousness we know certainly the existence of our present thoughts and passions; so we know the past by remembrance. And, when they are recent, and the remembrance of them fresh, the knowledge of them, from such distinct remembrance, is, in its certainty and evidence, next to that of consciousness.

3. But it is to be observed that we are conscious of many things to which we give little or no *attention*. We can hardly attend to several things at the same time; and our attention is commonly employed about that which is the object of our thought, and rarely about the thought itself. Thus, when a man is angry, his attention is turned to the injury done him, or the injurious person; and he gives very little attention to the passion of anger, although he is conscious of it. It is in our power, however, when we come to the years of understanding, to give attention to our own thoughts and passions, and the various operations of our minds. And, when we make these the objects of our attention, either while they are present or when they are recent and fresh in our memory, this act of the mind is called *reflection.*

We take it for granted, therefore, that, by attentive reflection, a man may have a clear and certain knowledge of the operations of his own mind; a knowledge no less clear and certain than that which he has of an external object when it is set before his eyes.

This reflection is a kind of intuition, it gives a like conviction with regard to internal objects, or things in the mind, as the faculty of seeing gives with regard to objects of sight. A man must, therefore, be convinced beyond possibility of doubt, of everything with regard to the operations of his own mind, which he clearly and distinctly discerns by attentive reflection.

4. I take it for granted that all the thoughts I am conscious of, or remember, are the thoughts of one and the same thinking principle, which I call *myself*, or my *mind*. Every man has an immediate and irresistible conviction, not only of his present existence, but of his continued existence and identity, as far back as he can remember. If any man should think fit to demand a proof that the thoughts he is successively conscious of, belong to one and the 'same thinking principle—if he should demand a proof that he is the same person today as he was yesterday, or a year ago—I know no proof that can be given him: he must be left to himself, either as a man that is lunatic, or as one who denies first principles, and is not to be reasoned with.

Every man of a sound mind, finds himself under a necessity of believing his own identity, and continued existence. The conviction of this is immediate and irresistible; and, if he should lose his conviction, it would be a certain proof of insanity, which is not to be remedied by reasoning.

5. I take it for granted that there are some things which cannot exist by themselves, but must be in something else to which they belong, as qualities, or attributes.

Thus, motion cannot exist, but in something that is moved. And to suppose that there can be motion while everything is at rest, is a gross and palpable absurdity. In like manner, hardness and softness, sweetness and bitterness, are things which cannot exist by themselves; they are qualities of something which is hard or soft, sweet or bitter. That thing, whatever it be, of which they are qualities, is called their subject; and such qualities necessarily suppose a subject.

Things which may exist by themselves, and do not necessarily suppose the existence of anything else, are called substances; and, with relation to the qualities or attributes that belong to them, they are called the subjects of such qualities or attributes.

All the things which we immediately perceive by our senses, and all the things we are conscious of, are things which must be in something else, as their subject. Thus, by my senses, I perceive figure, colour, hardness, softness, motion, resistance, and such like things. But these are qualities, and must necessarily be in something that is figured, coloured, hard or soft, that moves, or resists. It is not to these qualities, but to that which is the subject of them, that we give the name of body. If any man should think fit to deny that these things are qualities, or that they require any subject, I leave him to enjoy his opinion as a man who denies first principles, and is not fit to be reasoned with. If he has common understanding, he will find that he cannot converse half an hour without saying things which imply the contrary of what he professes to believe.

In like manner, the things I am conscious of, such as thought, reasoning, desire, necessarily suppose something that thinks, that reasons, that desires. We do not give the name of mind to thought, reason, or desire; but to that being which thinks, which reasons, and which desires.

That every act or operation, therefore, supposes an agent, that every quality supposes a subject, are things which I do not attempt to prove, but take for granted. Every man of common understanding discerns this immediately, and cannot entertain the least doubt of it. In all languages, we find certain words which, by grammarians, are called adjectives. Such words denote attributes, and every adjective must have a substantive to which it belongs—that is, every attribute must have a subject. In all languages, we find active verbs which denote some action or operation; and it is a fundamental rule in the grammar of all languages, that such a verb supposes a person—that is, in other words, that every action must have an agent. We take it, therefore, as a first principle, that goodness, wisdom, and virtue, can only be in some being that is good, wise, and virtuous; that thinking supposes a being that thinks; and that every operation we are conscious of supposes an agent that operates, which we call mind.

6. I take it for granted, that, in most operations of the mind, there must be an object distinct from the operation itself. I cannot see, without seeing something. To see without having any object of sight is absurd. I cannot remember, without remembering something. The thing remembered is past, while the remembrance of it is present; and, therefore, the operation and the object of it must be distinct things. The operations of our mind are denoted, in all languages, by active transitive verbs, which, from their construction in grammar, require not only a person or agent, but likewise an object of the operation. Thus, the verb know, denotes an operation of mind. From the general structure of language, this verb requires a person—I know, you know, or he knows; but it requires no less a noun in the accusative case, denoting the thing known; for he that knows must know something; and, to know, without having any object of knowledge, is an absurdity too gross to admit of reasoning.

7. We ought likewise to take for granted, as first principles, things wherein we find an universal agreement, among the learned and unlearned, in the different nations and ages of the world. A consent of ages and nations, of the learned and vulgar, ought, at least, to have great authority, unless we can shew some prejudice as universal as that consent is, which might be the cause of it. Truth is one, but error is infinite. There are many truths so obvious to the human faculties, that it may be expected that men should universally agree in them. And this is actually found to be the case with regard to many truths, against which we find no dissent, unless perhaps that of a few sceptical philosophers, who may justly be suspected, in such cases, to differ from the rest of mankind, through pride, obstinacy, or some favourite passion. Where there is such universal consent in things not deep nor intricate, but

which lie, as it were, on the surface, there is the greatest presumption that can be, that it is the natural result of the human faculties; and it must have great authority with every sober mind that loves truth. . . .

Perhaps it may be thought that it is impossible to collect the opinions of all men upon any point whatsoever; and, therefore, that this maxim can be of no use. But there are many cases wherein it is otherwise. Who can doubt, for instance, whether mankind have, in all ages, believed the existence of a material world, and that those things which they see and handle are real, and not mere illusions and apparitions? Who can doubt whether mankind have universally believed that everything that begins to exist, and every change that happens in nature, must have a cause? Who can doubt whether mankind have been universally persuaded that there is a right and a wrong in human conduct?—some things which, in certain circumstances, they ought to do, and other things which they ought not to do? The universality of these opinions, and of many such that might be named, is sufficiently evident, from the whole tenor of men's conduct, as far as our acquaintance reaches, and from the records of history, in all ages and nations, that are transmitted to us.

There are other opinions that appear to be universal, from what is common in the structure of all languages, ancient and modern, polished and barbarous. Language is the express image and picture of human thoughts; and, from the picture, we may often draw very certain conclusions with regard to the original. We find in all languages the same parts of speech—nouns substantive and adjective, verbs active and passive, varied according to the tenses of past, present, and future; we find adverbs, prepositions, and conjunctions. There are general rules of syntax common to all languages. This uniformity in the structure of language shews a certain degree of uniformity in those notions upon which the structure of language is grounded.

We find, in the structure of all languages, the distinction of

acting and being acted upon, the distinction of action and
agent, of quality and subject, and many others of the like kind;
which shews that these distinctions are founded in the universal sense of mankind. We shall have frequent occasion to argue
from the sense of mankind expressed in the structure of language; and therefore it was proper here to take notice of the
force of arguments drawn from this topic.

8. I need hardly say that I shall also take for granted such
facts as are attested to the conviction of all sober and reasonable men, either by our senses, by memory, or by human
testimony. Although some writers on this subject have disputed the authority of the senses, of memory, and of every
human faculty, yet we find that such persons, in the conduct
of life, in pursuing their ends, or in avoiding dangers, pay the
same regard to the authority of their senses and other faculties, as the rest of mankind. By this they give us just ground
to doubt of their candour in their professions of scepticism.

This, indeed, has always been the fate of the few that have
professed scepticism, that, when they have done what they can
to discredit their senses, they find themselves, after all, under
a necessity of trusting to them. Mr Hume has been so candid
as to acknowledge this; and it is no less true of those who have
not shewn the same candour; for I never heard that any sceptic
run his head against a post, or stepped into a kennel, because
he did not believe his eyes.

Upon the whole, I acknowledge that we ought to be cautious
that we do not adopt opinions as first principles which are not
entitled to that character. But there is surely the least danger
of men's being imposed upon in this way, when such principles
openly lay claim to the character, and are thereby fairly exposed to the examination of those who may dispute their authority. We do not pretend that those things that are laid down
as first principles may not be examined, and that we ought not
to have our ears open to what may be pleaded against their
being admitted as such. Let us deal with them as an upright

judge does with a witness who has a fair character. He pays a regard to the testimony of such a witness while his character is unimpeached; but, if it can be shewn that he is suborned, or that he is influenced by malice or partial favour, his testimony loses all its credit, and is justly rejected.

ESSAY TWO / OF THE POWERS WE HAVE BY MEANS OF OUR EXTERNAL SENSES

CHAPTER 5 / OF PERCEPTION

In speaking of the impressions made on our organs in perception, we build upon facts borrowed from anatomy and physiology, for which we have the testimony of our senses. But, being now to speak of perception itself, which is solely an act of the mind, we must appeal to another authority. The operations of our minds are known, not by sense, but by consciousness, the authority of which is as certain and as irresistible as that of sense.

In order, however, to our having a distinct notion of any of the operations of our own minds, it is not enough that we be conscious of them; for all men have this consciousness. It is farther necessary that we attend to them while they are exerted, and reflect upon them with care, while they are recent and fresh in our memory. It is necessary that, by employing ourselves frequently in this way, we get the habit of this attention and reflection; and, therefore, for the proof of facts which I shall have occasion to mention upon this subject, I can only appeal to the reader's own thoughts, whether such facts are not agreeable to what he is conscious of in his own mind.

If, therefore, we attend to that act of our mind which we call the perception of an external object of sense, we shall find in it these three things:—*First,* Some conception or notion of the object perceived; *Secondly,* A strong and irresistible conviction and belief of its present existence; and, *Thirdly,* That this conviction and belief are immediate, and not the effect of reasoning.

First, It is impossible to perceive an object without having some notion or conception of that which we perceive. We may, indeed, conceive an object which we do not perceive; but, when we perceive the object, we must have some conception of it at the same time; and we have commonly a more clear and steady notion of the object while we perceive it, than we have from memory or imagination when it is not perceived. Yet, even in perception, the notion which our senses give of the object may be more or less clear, more or less distinct, in all possible degrees.

Thus we see more distinctly an object at a small than at a great distance. An object at a great distance is seen more distinctly in a clear than in a foggy day. An object seen indistinctly with the naked eye, on account of its smallness, may be seen distinctly with a microscope. The objects in this room will be seen by a person in the room less and less distinctly as the light of the day fails; they pass through all the various degrees of distinctness according to the degrees of the light, and, at last, in total darkness they are not seen at all. What has been said of the objects of sight is so easily applied to the objects of the other senses, that the application may be left to the reader.

In a matter so obvious to every person capable of reflection, it is necessary only farther to observe, that the notion which we get of an object, merely by our external sense, ought not to be confounded with that more scientific notion which a man, come to the years of understanding, may have of the same object, by attending to its various attributes, or to its various parts, and their relation to each other, and to the whole. Thus, the notion which a child has of a jack for roasting meat, will be acknowledged to be very different from that of a man who understands its construction, and perceives the relation of the parts to one another, and to the whole. The child sees the jack and every part of it as well as the man. The child, therefore, has all the notion of it which sight gives; whatever there is more in the notion which the man forms of it, must be derived from other powers of the mind, which may afterwards be explained. This observation is made here only that we may not confound the operations of different powers of the mind, which by being always conjoined after we grow up to understanding, are apt to pass for one and the same.

Secondly, In perception we not only have a notion more or less distinct of the object perceived, but also an irresistible conviction and belief of its existence. This is always the case when we are certain that we perceive it. There may be a perception so faint and indistinct as to leave us in doubt whether we perceive the object or not. Thus, when a star begins to twinkle as the light of the sun withdraws, one may, for a short time, think he sees it without being certain, until the perception acquire some strength and steadiness. When a ship just begins to appear in the utmost verge of the horizon, we may at first be dubious whether we perceive it or not; but when the perception is in any degree clear and steady, there remains no doubt of its reality; and when the reality of the perception is ascertained, the existence of the object perceived can no longer be doubted.

By the laws of all nations, in the most solemn judicial trials, wherein men's fortunes and lives are at stake, the sentence passes according to the testimony of eye or ear witnesses of good credit. An upright judge will give a fair hearing to every objection that can be made to the integrity of a witness, and allow it to be possible that he may be corrupted; but no judge will ever suppose that witnesses may be imposed upon by trusting to their eyes and ears. And if a sceptical counsel should plead against the testimony of the witnesses, that they had no other evidence for what they declared but the testimony of their eyes and ears, and that we ought not to put so much faith in our senses as to deprive men of life or fortune upon their testimony, surely no upright judge would admit a plea of this kind. I believe no counsel, however sceptical, ever dared to offer such an argument; and, if it was offered, it would be rejected with disdain.

Can any stronger proof be given that it is the universal judgment of mankind that the evidence of sense is a kind of evidence which we may securely rest upon in the most momentous concerns of mankind; that it is a kind of evidence against which we ought not to admit any reasoning; and, therefore, that to reason either for or against it is an insult to common sense?

The whole conduct of mankind in the daily occurrences of life, as well as the solemn procedure of judicatories in the trial of causes civil and criminal, demonstrates this. I know only of two exceptions that may be offered against this being the universal belief of mankind.

The first exception is that of some lunatics who have been persuaded of things that seem to contradict the clear testimony of their senses. It is said there have been lunatics and hypochondriacal persons, who seriously believed themselves to be made of glass; and, in consequence of this, lived in continual terror of having their brittle frame shivered into pieces.

All I have to say to this is, that our minds, in our present state, are, as well as our bodies, liable to strange disorders; and, as we do not judge of the natural constitution of the body from the disorders or diseases to which it is subject from accidents, so neither ought we to judge of the natural powers of the mind from its disorders, but from its sound state. It is natural to man, and common to the species, to have two hands and two feet; yet I have seen a man, and a very ingenious one, who was born without either hands or feet. It is natural to man to have faculties superior to those of brutes; yet we see some individuals whose faculties are not equal to those of many brutes; and the wisest man may, by various accidents, be reduced to this state. General rules that regard those whose intellects are sound are not overthrown by instances of men whose intellects are hurt by any constitutional or accidental disorder.

The other exception that may be made to the principle we have laid down is that of some philosophers who have maintained that the testimony of sense is fallacious, and therefore ought never to be trusted. Perhaps it might be a sufficient answer to this to say, that there is nothing so absurd which some philosophers have not maintained.[3] ·It is one thing to profess a doctrine of this kind, another seriously to believe it, and to be governed by it in the conduct of life. It is evident that a man who did not believe his senses could not keep out of harm's way an hour of his life; yet, in all the history of philosophy, we never read of any sceptic that ever stepped into fire or water because he did not believe his senses, or that shewed in the conduct of life less trust in his senses than other men have.[4] This gives us just ground to apprehend that philosophy was never·able to conquer that natural belief which men have in their senses; and that all their subtile reasonings against this belief were never able to persuade themselves.

It appears, therefore, that the clear and distinct testimony of our senses carries irresistible conviction along with it to every man in his right judgment.

I observed, *Thirdly,* That this conviction is not only irresistible, but it is immediate, that is, it is not by a train of reasoning and argumentation that we come to be convinced of the existence of what we perceive; we ask no argument for the existence of the object, but that we perceive it; perception commands our belief upon its own authority, and disdains to rest its authority upon any reasoning whatsoever.

The conviction of a truth may be irresistible, and yet not immediate. Thus, my conviction that the three angles of every plain triangle are equal to two right angles, is irresistible, but it is not immediate; I am convinced of it by demonstrative reasoning. There are other truths in mathematics of which we have not only an irresistible but an immediate conviction. Such are the axioms. Our belief of the axioms in mathematics is not grounded upon argument—arguments are grounded upon them; but their evidence is discerned immediately by the human understanding.

It is, no doubt, one thing to have an immediate conviction of a self-evident axiom; it is another thing to have an immediate conviction of the existence of what we see; but the conviction is equally immediate and equally irresistible in both cases. No man thinks of seeking a reason to believe what he sees; and, before we are capable of reasoning, we put no less confidence in our senses than after. The rudest savage is as fully convinced of what he sees, and hears, and feels, as the most expert logician. The constitution of our understanding determines us to hold the truth of a mathematical axiom as a first principle, from which other truths may be deduced, but it is deduced from none; and the constitution of our power of perception determines us to hold the existence of what we distinctly perceive as a first principle, from which other truths may be deduced; but it is deduced from none. What has been said of the irresistible and immediate belief of the existence of objects distinctly perceived, I mean only to affirm with regard to persons so far advanced in understanding as to distinguish objects of mere imagination from things which have a real existence. Every man knows that he may have a notion of Don Quixote, or of Garagantua, without any belief that such persons ever existed; and that of Julius Caesar and Oliver Cromwell, he has not only a notion, but a belief that they did really exist. But whether children, from the time that they begin to use their senses, make a distinction between things which are only conceived or imagined, and things which really exist, may be doubted. Until we are able to make this distinction, we cannot properly be said to believe or to disbelieve the existence of anything. The belief of the existence of anything seems to suppose a notion of existence—a notion too abstract, perhaps, to enter into the mind of an infant. I speak of the power of perception in those that are adult and of a sound mind, who believe that there are some things which do really exist; and that there are many things conceived by themselves, and by others, which have no existence. That such persons do invariably ascribe existence to everything which they distinctly perceive, without seeking reasons or arguments for doing so, is perfectly evident from the whole tenor of human life.

The account I have given of our perception of external objects, is intended as a faithful delineation of what every man, come to years of understanding, and capable of giving attention to what passes in his own mind, may feel in himself. In what manner the notion of external objects, and the immediate belief of their existence, is produced by means of our senses, I am not able to shew, and I do not pretend to shew. . . .

CHAPTER 10 / OF THE SENTIMENTS OF BISHOP BERKELEY

George Berkeley, afterwards Bishop of Cloyne, published his "New Theory of Vision," in 1709; his "Treatise concerning the Principles of Human Knowledge," in 1710; and his "Dialogues between Hylas and Philonous," in 1713; being then a Fellow of Trinity College, Dublin. He is acknowledged universally to have great merit, as an excellent writer, and a very acute and clear reasoner on the most abstract subjects, not to speak of his virtues as a man, which were very conspicuous; yet the doctrine chiefly held forth in the treatises above mentioned, especially in the two last, has generally been thought so very absurd, that few can be brought to think that he either believed it himself, or that he seriously meant to persuade others of its truth.

He maintains, and thinks he has demonstrated, by a variety of arguments, grounded on principles of philosophy universally received, that there is no such thing as matter in the universe; that sun and moon, earth and sea, our own bodies, and those of our friends, are nothing but ideas in the minds of those who think of them, and that they have no existence when they are not the objects of thought; that all that is in the universe may be reduced to two categories—to wit, *minds,* and *ideas in the mind.*

But, however absurd this doctrine might appear to the unlearned, who consider the existence of the objects of sense as the most evident of all truths, and what no man in his senses can doubt, the philosophers who had been accustomed to consider ideas as the immediate objects of all thought, had no title to view this doctrine of Berkeley in so unfavourable a light.

They were taught by Des Cartes, and by all that came after him, that the existence of the objects of sense is not self-evident, but requires to be proved by arguments; and, although Des Cartes, and many others, had laboured to find arguments for this purpose, there did not appear to be that force and clearness in them which might have been expected in a matter of such importance. Mr Norris had declared that, after all the arguments that had been offered, the existence of an external world is only probable, but by no means certain. Malebranche thought it rested upon the authority of revelation, and that the arguments drawn from reason were not perfectly conclusive. Others thought that the argument from revelation was a mere sophism, because revelation comes to us by our senses, and must rest upon their authority.

Thus we see that the new philosophy had been making gradual approaches towards Berkeley's opinion; and, whatever others might do, the philosophers had no title to look upon it as absurd, or unworthy of a fair examination. . . .

In the "Theory of Vision," he goes no farther than to assert that the objects of sight are nothing but ideas in the mind, granting, or at least not denying, that there is a tangible world, which is really external, and which exists whether we perceive it or not. Whether the reason of this was, that his system had not, at that time, wholly opened to his own mind, or whether he thought it prudent to let it enter into the minds of his readers by degrees, I cannot say. I think he insinuates the last as the reason, in the "Principles of Human Knowledge."

The "Theory of Vision," however, taken by itself, and without relation to the main branch of his system, contains very important discoveries, and marks of great genius. He distinguishes more accurately than any that went before him, between the immediate objects of sight, and those of the other senses which are early associated with them. He shews that distance, of itself and immediately, is not seen; but that we learn to judge of it by certain sensations and perceptions which are connected with it. This is a very important observation; and, I believe, was first made by this author. It gives much new light to the operations of our senses, and serves to account for many phaenomena in optics, of which the greatest adepts in that science had always either given a false account, or acknowledged that they could give none at all.

We may observe, by the way, that the ingenious author seems not to have attended to a distinction by which his general assertion ought to have been limited. It is true that the distance of an object from the eye is not immediately seen; but there is a certain kind of distance of one object from another which we see immediately. The author acknowledges that there is a visible extension, and visible figures, which are proper objects of sight; there must therefore be a visible distance. Astronomers call it angular distance; and, although they measure it by the angle, which is made by two lines drawn from the eye to the two distant objects, yet it is immediately perceived by sight, even by those who never thought of that angle.

He led the way in shewing how we learn to perceive the distance of an object from the eye, though this speculation was carried farther by others who came after him. He made the distinction between that extension and figure which we perceive by sight only, and that which we perceive by touch; calling the first, visible, the last, tangible extension and figure. He shewed, likewise, that tangible extension, and not visible, is the object of geometry, although mathematicians commonly use visible diagrams in their demonstrations.

The notion of extension and figure which we get from sight only, and that which we get from touch, have been so constantly conjoined from our infancy in all the judgments we form of the objects of sense, that it required great abilities to distinguish them accurately, and to assign to each sense what truly belongs to it; "so difficult a thing it is," as Berkeley justly observes, "to dissolve an union so early begun, and confirmed by so long a habit." This point he has laboured, through the whole of the essay on vision, with that uncommon penetration and judgment which he possessed, and with as great success as could be expected in a first attempt upon so abstruse a subject.

He concludes this essay, by shewing, in no less than seven sections, the notions which an intelligent being, endowed with sight, without the sense of touch, might form of the objects of sense. This speculation, to shallow thinkers, may appear to be egregious trifling.[5] To Bishop Berkeley it appeared in another light, and will do so to those who are capable of entering into it, and who know the importance of it, in solving many of the phaenomena of vision. He seems, indeed, to have exerted more force of genius in this than in the main branch of his system.

In the new philosophy, the pillars by which the existence of a material world was supported, were so feeble that it did not require the force of a Samson to bring them down; and in this we have not so much reason to admire the strength of Berkeley's genius, as his boldness in publishing to the world an opinion which the unlearned would be apt to interpret as the sign of a crazy intellect. A man who was firmly persuaded of the doctrine universally received by philosophers concerning ideas, if he could but take courage to call in question the existence of a material world, would easily find unanswerable arguments in that doctrine. "Some truths there are," says Berkeley, "so near and obvious to the mind, that a man need only open his eyes to see them. Such," he adds, "I take this important one to be, that all the choir of heaven, and furniture of the earth—in a word, all those bodies which compose the mighty frame of the world—have not any subsistence without a mind." Princ. § 6.

The principle from which this important conclusion is obviously deduced, is laid down in the first sentence of his principles of knowledge, as evident; and, indeed, it has always been acknowledged by philosophers. "It is evident," says he, "to any one who takes a survey of the objects of human knowledge, that they are either ideas actually imprinted on the senses, or else such as are perceived, by attending to the passions and operations of the mind; or, lastly, ideas formed by help of memory and imagination, either compounding, dividing, or barely representing those originally perceived in the foresaid ways."

This is the foundation on which the whole system rests. If this be true, then, indeed, the existence of a material world must be a dream that has imposed upon all mankind from the beginning of the world.

The foundation on which such a fabric rests ought to be very solid and well established; yet Berkeley says nothing more for it than that it is evident. If he means that it is self-evident, this indeed might be a good reason for not offering any direct argument in proof of it. But I apprehend this cannot justly be said. Self-evident propositions are those which appear evident to every man of sound understanding who apprehends the meaning of them distinctly, and attends to them without prejudice. Can this be said of this proposition, That all the objects of our knowledge are ideas in our own minds? I believe that, to any man uninstructed in philosophy, this proposition will appear very improbable, if not absurd. However scanty his knowledge may be, he considers the sun and moon, the earth and sea, as objects of it; and it will be difficult to persuade him that those objects of his knowledge are ideas in his own mind, and have no existence when he does not think of them. If I may presume to speak my own sentiments, I once believed this doctrine of ideas so firmly as to embrace the whole of Berkeley's system in consequence of it; till, finding other consequences to follow from it, which gave me more uneasiness than the want of a material world, it came into my mind, more than forty years ago, to put the question, What evidence have I for this doctrine, that all the objects of my knowledge are ideas in my own mind? From that time to the present I have been candidly and impartially, as I think, seeking for the evidence of this principle, but can find none, excepting the authority of philosophers.

We shall have occasion to examine its evidence afterwards. I would at present only observe, that all the arguments brought by Berkeley against the existence of a material world are grounded upon it; and that he has not attempted to give any evidence for it, but takes it for granted, as other philosophers had done before him.

But, supposing this principle to be true, Berkeley's system is impregnable. No demonstration can be more evident than his reasoning from it. Whatever is perceived is an idea, and an idea can only exist in a mind. It has no existence when it is not perceived; nor can there be anything like an idea, but an idea. . . .

Berkeley foresaw the opposition that would be made to his system, from two different quarters: *first,* from the philosophers; and, *secondly,* from the vulgar, who are led by the plain dictates of nature. The first he had the courage to oppose openly and avowedly; the second, he dreaded much more, and, therefore, takes a great deal of pains, and, I think, uses some art, to court into his party. This is particularly observable in his "Dialogues." He sets out with a declaration, Dial. 1, "That, of late, he had quitted several of the sublime notions he had got in the schools of the philosophers, for vulgar opinions," and assures Hylas, his fellow-dialogist, "That, since this revolt from metaphysical notions to the plain dictates of nature and common sense, he found his understanding strangely enlightened; so that he could now easily comprehend a great many things, which before were all mystery and riddle." Pref. to Dial. "If his principles are admitted for true, men will be reduced from paradoxes to common sense." At the same time, he acknowledges, "That they carry with them a great opposition to the prejudices of philosophers, which have so far prevailed against the common sense and natural notions of mankind."

When Hylas objects to him, Dial. 3, "You can never persuade me, Philonous, that the denying of matter or corporeal substance is not repugnant to the universal sense of mankind" —he answers, "I wish both our opinions were fairly stated, and submitted to the judgment of men who had plain common sense, without the prejudices of a learned education. Let me be represented as one who trusts his senses, who thinks he knows the things he sees and feels, and entertains no doubt of their existence.—If by material substance is meant only sensible body, that which is seen and felt, (and the unphilosophical part of the world, I dare say, mean no more,) then I am more certain of matter's existence than you or any other philosopher pretend to be. If there be anything which makes the generality of mankind averse from the notions I espouse, it is a misapprehension that I deny the reality of sensible things: but, as it is you who are guilty of that, and not I, it follows, that, in truth, their aversion is against your notions, and not mine. I am content to appeal to the common sense of the world for the truth of my notion. I am of a vulgar cast, simple enough to believe my senses, and to leave things as I find them. I cannot, for my life, help thinking that snow is white and fire hot."

These passages shew sufficiently the author's concern to reconcile his system to the plain dictates of nature and common sense, while he expresses no concern to reconcile it to the received doctrines of philosophers. He is fond to take part with the vulgar against the philosophers, and to vindicate common sense against their innovations. What pity is it that he did not carry this suspicion of the doctrine of philosophers so far as to doubt of that philosophical tenet on which his whole system is built—to wit, that the things immediately perceived by the senses are ideas which exist only in the mind!

After all, it seems no easy matter to make the vulgar opinion and that of Berkeley to meet. And, to accomplish this, he seems to me to draw each out of its line towards the other, not without some straining.

The vulgar opinion he reduces to this, that the very things which we perceive by our senses do really exist. This he grants; for these things, says he, are ideas in our minds, or complexions of ideas, to which we give one name, and consider as one thing; these are the immediate objects of sense, and these do really exist. As to the notion that those things have an absolute external existence, independent of being perceived by any mind, he thinks that this is no notion of the vulgar, but a refinement of philosophers; and that the notion of material substance, as a *substratum*, or support of that collection of sensible qualities to which we give the name of an apple or a melon, is likewise an invention of philosophers, and is not found with the vulgar till they are instructed by philosophers. The substance not being an object of sense, the vulgar never think of it; or, if they are taught the use of the word, they mean no more by it but that collection of sensible qualities which they, from finding them conjoined in nature, have been accustomed to call by one name, and to consider as one thing.

Thus he draws the vulgar opinion near to his own; and, that he may meet it half way, he acknowledges that material things have a real existence out of the mind of this or that person; but the question, says he, between the materialist and me, is, Whether they have an absolute existence distinct from their being perceived by God, and exterior to all minds? This, indeed, he says, some heathens and philosophers have affirmed; but whoever entertains notions of the Deity, suitable to the Holy Scripture, will be of another opinion.

But here an objection occurs, which it required all his ingenuity to answer. It is this: The ideas in my mind cannot be the same with the ideas of any other mind; therefore, if the objects I perceive be only ideas, it is impossible that the objects I perceive can exist anywhere, when I do not perceive them; and it is impossible that two or more minds can perceive the same object.

To this Berkeley answers, that this objection presses no less the opinion of the materialist philosopher than his. But the difficulty is to make his opinion coincide with the notions of the vulgar, who are firmly persuaded that the very identical objects which they perceive, continue to exist when they do not perceive them; and who are no less firmly persuaded that, when ten men look at the sun or the moon, they all see the same individual object.

To reconcile this repugnancy, he observes, Dial. 3—"That, if the term *same* be taken in the vulgar acceptation, it is certain (and not at all repugnant to the principles he maintains) that different persons may perceive the same thing; or the same thing or idea exist in different minds. Words are of arbitrary imposition; and, since men are used to apply the word *same*, where no distinction or variety is perceived, and he does not pretend to alter their perceptions, it follows that, as men have said before, *several saw the same thing,* so they may, upon like occasions, still continue to use the same phrase, without any deviation, either from propriety of language, or the truth of things; but, if the term *same* be used in the acceptation of philosophers, who pretend to an abstracted notion of identity, then, according to their sundry definitions of this term, (for it is not yet agreed wherein that philosophic identity consists,) it may or may not be possible for divers persons to perceive the same thing; but whether philosophers shall think fit to call a thing the *same* or no is, I conceive, of small importance. Men may dispute about identity and diversity, without any real difference in their thoughts and opinions, abstracted from names."

Upon the whole, I apprehend that Berkeley has carried this attempt to reconcile his system to the vulgar opinion farther than reason supports him; and he was no doubt tempted to do so, from a just apprehension that, in a controversy of this kind, the common sense of mankind is the most formidable antagonist.

Berkeley has employed much pains and ingenuity to shew that his system, if received and believed, would not be attended with those bad consequences in the conduct of life, which superficial thinkers may be apt to impute to it. His system does not take away or make any alteration upon our pleasures or our pains: our sensations, whether agreeable or disagreeable, are the same upon his system as upon any other. These are real things, and the only things that interest us. They are produced in us according to certain laws of nature, by which our conduct will be directed in attaining the one, and avoiding the other; and it is of no moment to us, whether they are produced immediately by the operation of some powerful intelligent being upon our minds; or by the mediation of some inanimate being which we call *matter.*

The evidence of an all-governing mind, so far from being weakened, seems to appear even in a more striking light upon his hypothesis, than upon the common one. The powers which inanimate matter is supposed to possess, have always been the stronghold of atheists, to which they had recourse in defence of their system. This fortress of atheism must be most effectually overturned, if there is no such thing as matter in the universe. In all this the Bishop reasons justly and acutely. But there is one uncomfortable consequence of his system, which he seems not to have attended to, and from which it will be found difficult, if at all possible, to guard it.

The consequence I mean is this—that, although it leaves us sufficient evidence of a supreme intelligent mind, it seems to take away all the evidence we have of other intelligent beings like ourselves. What I call a father, a brother, or a friend, is only a parcel of ideas in my own mind; and, being ideas in my mind, they cannot possibly have that relation to another mind which they have to mine, any more than the pain felt by me can be the individual pain felt by another. I can find no principle in Berkeley's system, which affords me even probable ground to conclude that there are other intelligent beings, like myself, in the relations of father, brother, friend, or fellow-citizen. I am left alone, as the only creature of God in the universe, in that forlorn state of *egoism* into which it is said some of the disciples of Des Cartes were brought by his philosophy.

Of all the opinions that have ever been advanced by philosophers, this of Bishop Berkeley, that there is no material world, seems the strangest, and the most apt to bring philosophy into ridicule with plain men who are guided by the dictates of nature and common sense. . . .

CHAPTER 14 / REFLECTIONS ON THE COMMON THEORY OF IDEAS

There remains only one other argument that I have been able to find urged against our perceiving external objects immediately. It is proposed by Mr Hume, who, in the essay already quoted, after acknowledging that it is an universal and primary opinion of all men, that we perceive external objects immediately, subjoins what follows:—

"But this universal and primary opinion of all men is soon destroyed by the slightest philosophy, which teaches us that nothing can ever be present to the mind but an image or perception; and that the senses are only the inlets through which these images are received, without being ever able to produce any immediate intercourse between the mind and the object. The table, which we see, seems to diminish as we remove farther from it: but the real table, which exists independent of us, suffers no alteration. It was, therefore, nothing but its image which was present to the mind. These are the obvious dictates of reason; and no man who reflects ever doubted that the existences which we consider, when we say *this house*, and *that tree*, are nothing but perceptions in the mind, and fleeting copies and representations of other existences, which remain uniform and independent. So far, then, we are necessitated, by reasoning, to depart from the primary instincts of nature, and to embrace a new system with regard to the evidence of our senses."

We have here a remarkable conflict between two contradictory opinions, wherein all mankind are engaged. On the one side stand all the vulgar, who are unpractised in philosophical researches, and guided by the uncorrupted primary instincts of nature. On the other side stand all the philosophers, ancient and modern; every man, without exception, who reflects. In this division, to my great humiliation, I find myself classed with the vulgar. . . .

To judge of the strength of this argument, it is necessary to attend to a distinction which is familiar to those who are conversant in the mathematical sciences—I mean the distinction between real and apparent magnitude. The real magnitude of a line is measured by some known measure of length—as inches, feet, or miles: the real magnitude of a surface or solid, by known measures of surface or of capacity. This magnitude is an object of touch only, and not of sight; nor could we even have had any conception of it, without the sense of touch; and Bishop Berkeley, on that account, calls it *tangible magnitude.*

Apparent magnitude is measured by the angle which an object subtends at the eye. Supposing two right lines drawn from the eye to the extremities of the object making an angle, of which the object is the subtense, the apparent magnitude is measured by this angle. This apparent magnitude is an object of sight, and not of touch. Bishop Berkeley calls it *visible magnitude.*

If it is asked what is the apparent magnitude of the sun's diameter, the answer is, that it is about thirty-one minutes of a degree. But, if it is asked what is the real magnitude of the sun's diameter, the answer must be, so many thousand miles, or so many diameters of the earth. From which it is evident that real magnitude, and apparent magnitude, are things of a different nature, though the name of magnitude is given to both. The first has three dimensions, the last only two; the first is measured by a line, the last by an angle.

From what has been said, it is evident that the real magnitude of a body must continue unchanged, while the body is unchanged. This we grant. But is it likewise evident, that the apparent magnitude must continue the same while the body is unchanged? So far otherwise, that every man who knows anything of mathematics can easily demonstrate, that the same individual object, remaining in the same place, and unchanged, must necessarily vary in its apparent magnitude, according as the point from which it is seen is more or less distant; and that its apparent length or breadth will be nearly in a reciprocal proportion to the distance of the spectator. This is as certain as the principles of geometry.

We must likewise attend to this—that, though the real magnitude of a body is not originally an object of sight, but of touch, yet we learn by experience to judge of the real magnitude in many cases by sight. We learn by experience to judge of the distance of a body from the eye within certain limits; and, from its distance and apparent magnitude taken together, we learn to judge of its real magnitude.

And this kind of judgment, by being repeated every hour and almost every minute of our lives, becomes, when we are grown up, so ready and so habitual, that it very much resembles the original perceptions of our senses, and may not improperly be called *acquired perception.*

Whether we call it judgment or acquired perception is a verbal difference. But it is evident that, by means of it, we often discover by one sense things which are properly and naturally the objects of another. Thus I can say, without impropriety, I hear a drum, I hear a great bell, or I hear a small bell; though it is certain that the figure or size of the sounding body is not originally an object of hearing. In like manner, we learn by experience how a body of such a real magnitude and at such a distance appears to the eye. But neither its real magnitude, nor its distance from the eye, are properly objects of sight, any more than the form of a drum or the size of a bell, are properly objects of hearing.

If these things be considered, it will appear that Mr Hume's argument hath no force to support his conclusion—nay, that it leads to a contrary conclusion. The argument is this: the table we see seems to diminish as we remove farther from it; that is, its apparent magnitude is diminished; but the real table suffers no alteration—to wit, in its real magnitude; therefore, it is not the real table we see. I admit both the premises in this syllogism, but I deny the conclusion. The syllogism has what the logicians call two middle terms: apparent magnitude is the middle term in the first premise; real magnitude in the second. Therefore, according to the rules of logic, the conclusion is not justly drawn from the premises; but, laying aside the rules of logic, let us examine it by the light of common sense.

Let us suppose, for a moment, that it is the real table we see:

Must not this real table seem to diminish as we remove farther from it? It is demonstrable that it must. How then can this apparent diminution be an argument that it is not the real table? When that which must happen to the real table, as we remove farther from it, does actually happen to the table we see, it is absurd to conclude from this, that it is not the real table we see. It is evident, therefore, that this ingenious author has imposed upon himself by confounding real magnitude with apparent magnitude, and that his argument is a mere sophism.

I observed that Mr Hume's argument not only has no strength to support his conclusion, but that it leads to the contrary conclusion—to wit, that it is the real table we see; for this plain reason, that the table we see has precisely that apparent magnitude which it is demonstrable the real table must have when placed at that distance.

This argument is made much stronger by considering that the real table may be placed successively at a thousand different distances, and, in every distance, in a thousand different positions; and it can be determined demonstratively, by the rules of geometry and perspective, what must be its apparent magnitude and apparent figure, in each of those distances and positions. Let the table be placed successively in as many of those different distances and different positions as you will, or in them all; open your eyes and you shall see a table precisely of that apparent magnitude, and that apparent figure, which the real table must have in that distance and in that position. Is not this a strong argument that it is the real table you see? . . .

Thus, I have considered every argument I have found advanced to prove the existence of ideas, or images of external things, in the mind; and, if no better arguments can be found, I cannot help thinking that the whole history of philosophy has never furnished an instance of an opinion so unanimously entertained by philosophers upon so slight grounds.

A *third* reflection I would make upon this subject is, that philosophers, notwithstanding their unanimity as to the existence of ideas, hardly agree in any one thing else concerning them. If ideas be not a mere fiction, they must be, of all objects of human knowledge, the things we have best access to know, and to be acquainted with; yet there is nothing about which men differ so much.

A *fourth* reflection is, that ideas do not make any of the operations of the mind to be better understood, although it was probably with that view that they have been first invented, and afterwards so generally received.

We are at a loss to know how we perceive distant objects; how we remember things past; how we imagine things that have no existence. Ideas in the mind seem to account for all these operations: they are all by the means of ideas reduced to one operation—to a kind of feeling, or immediate perception of things present and in contact with the percipient; and feeling is an operation so familiar that we think it needs no explication, but may serve to explain other operations.

But this feeling, or immediate perception, is as difficult to be comprehended as the things which we pretend to explain by it. Two things may be in contact without any feeling or perception; there must therefore be in the percipient a power to feel or to perceive. How this power is produced, and how it operates, is quite beyond the reach of our knowledge. As little can we know whether this power must be limited to things present, and in contact with us. Nor can any man pretend to prove that the Being who gave us the power to perceive things present, may not give us the power to perceive things that are distant, to remember things past, and to conceive things that never existed. . . .

CHAPTER 17 / OF THE OBJECTS OF PERCEPTION;
AND, FIRST, OF PRIMARY AND SECONDARY
QUALITIES

The objects of perception are the various qualities of bodies.
Intending to treat of these only in general, and chiefly with a
view to explain the notions which our senses give us of them,
I begin with the distinction between primary and secondary
qualities. These were distinguished very early. The Peripatetic
system confounded them, and left no difference. The distinction was again revived by Des Cartes and Locke, and a second
time abolished by Berkeley and Hume. If the real foundation
of this distinction can be pointed out, it will enable us to
account for the various revolutions in the sentiments of
philosophers concerning it.

Every one knows that extension, divisibility, figure, motion,
solidity, hardness, softness, and fluidity, were by Mr Locke
called *primary qualities of body;* and that sound, colour, taste,
smell, and heat or cold, were called *secondary qualities.* Is there
a just foundation for this distinction? Is there anything common to the primary which belongs not to the secondary? And
what is it?

I answer, That there appears to me to be a real foundation
for the distinction; and it is this—that our senses give us a
direct and a distinct notion of the primary qualities, and inform us what they are in themselves. But of the secondary
qualities, our senses give us only a relative and obscure notion.
They inform us only, that they are qualities that affect us in a
certain manner—that is, produce in us a certain sensation; but
as to what they are in themselves, our senses leave us in the
dark.

Every man capable of reflection may easily satisfy himself
that he has a perfectly clear and distinct notion of extension,
divisibility, figure, and motion. The solidity of a body means

no more but that it excludes other bodies from occupying the same place at the same time. Hardness, softness, and fluidity are different degrees of cohesion in the parts of a body. It is fluid when it has no sensible cohesion; soft, when the cohesion is weak; and hard, when it is strong. Of the cause of this cohesion we are ignorant, but the thing itself we understand perfectly, being immediately informed of it by the sense of touch. It is evident, therefore, that of the primary qualities we have a clear and distinct notion; we know what they are, though we may be ignorant of their causes.

I observed, farther, that the notion we have of primary qualities is direct, and not relative only. A relative notion of a thing, is, strictly speaking, no notion of the thing at all, but only of some relation which it bears to something else.

Thus, gravity sometimes signifies the tendency of bodies towards the earth; sometimes it signifies the cause of that tendency. When it means the first, I have a direct and distinct notion of gravity; I see it, and feel it, and know perfectly what it is; but this tendency must have a cause. We give the same name to the cause; and that cause has been an object of thought and of speculation. Now, what notion have we of this cause when we think and reason about it? It is evident we think of it as an unknown cause, of a known effect. This is a relative notion; and it must be obscure, because it gives us no conception of what the thing is, but of what relation it bears to something else. Every relation which a thing unknown bears to something that is known, may give a relative notion of it; and there are many objects of thought and of discourse of which our faculties can give no better than a relative notion.

Having premised these things to explain what is meant by a relative notion, it is evident that our notion of primary qualities is not of this kind; we know what they are, and not barely what relation they bear to something else.

It is otherwise with secondary qualities. If you ask me, what is that quality or modification in a rose which I call its smell,

I am at a loss to answer directly. Upon reflection, I find, that I have a distinct notion of the sensation which it produces in my mind. But there can be nothing like to this sensation in the rose, because it is insentient. The quality in the rose is something which occasions the sensation in me; but what that something is, I know not. My senses give me no information upon this point. The only notion, therefore, my senses give is this —that smell in the rose is an unknown quality or modification, which is the cause or occasion of a sensation which I know well. The relation which this unknown quality bears to the sensation with which nature hath connected it, is all I learn from the sense of smelling; but this is evidently a relative notion. The same reasoning will apply to every secondary quality.

Thus, I think it appears that there is a real foundation for the distinction of primary from secondary qualities; and that they are distinguished by this—that of the primary we have by our senses a direct and distinct notion; but of the secondary only a relative notion, which must, because it is only relative, be obscure; they are conceived only as the unknown causes or occasions of certain sensations with which we are well acquainted.

The account I have given of this distinction is founded upon no hypothesis. Whether our notions of primary qualities are direct and distinct, those of the secondary relative and obscure, is a matter of fact, of which every man may have certain knowledge by attentive reflection upon them. To this reflection I appeal, as the proper test of what has been advanced, and proceed to make some reflections on this subject.

1. The primary qualities are neither sensations, nor are they resemblances of sensations. This appears to me self-evident. I have a clear and distinct notion of each of the primary qualities. I have a clear and distinct notion of sensation. I can compare the one with the other; and, when I do so, I am not able to discern a resembling feature. Sensation is the act or the feeling (I dispute not which) of a sentient being. Figure, divisi-

bility, solidity, are neither acts nor feelings. Sensation supposes a sentient being as its subject; for a sensation that is not felt by some sentient being, is an absurdity. Figure and divisibility supposes a subject that is figured and divisible, but not a subject that is sentient.

2. We have no reason to think that any of the secondary qualities resemble any sensation. The absurdity of this notion has been clearly shewn by Des Cartes, Locke, and many modern philosophers. It was a tenet of the ancient philosophy, and is still by many imputed to the vulgar, but only as a vulgar error. It is too evident to need proof, that the vibrations of a sounding body do not resemble the sensation of sound, nor the effluvia of an odorous body the sensation of smell.

3. The distinctness of our notions of primary qualities prevents all questions and disputes about their nature. There are no different opinions about the nature of extension, figure, or motion, or the nature of any primary quality. Their nature is manifest to our senses, and cannot be unknown to any man, or mistaken by him, though their causes may admit of dispute.

The primary qualities are the object of the mathematical sciences; and the distinctness of our notions of them enables us to reason demonstratively about them to a great extent. Their various modifications are precisely defined in the imagination, and thereby capable of being compared, and their relations determined with precision and certainty.

It is not so with secondary qualities. Their nature not being manifest to the sense, may be a subject of dispute. Our feeling informs us that the fire is hot; but it does not inform us what that heat of the fire is. But does it not appear a contradiction, to say we know that the fire is hot, but we know not what that heat is? I answer, there is the same appearance of contradiction in many things that must be granted. We know that wine has an inebriating quality; but we know not what that quality is. It is true, indeed, that, if we had not some notion of what is meant by the heat of fire, and by an inebriating quality, we could affirm nothing of either with understanding. We have a notion of both; but it is only a relative notion. We know that they are the causes of certain known effects.

4. The nature of secondary qualities is a proper subject of philosophical disquisition; and in this philosophy has made some progress. It has been discovered, that the sensation of smell is occasioned by the effluvia of bodies; that of sound by their vibration. The disposition of bodies to reflect a particular kind of light, occasions the sensation of colour. Very curious discoveries have been made of the nature of heat, and an ample field of discovery in these subjects remains.

5. We may see why the sensations belonging to secondary qualities are an object of our attention, while those which belong to the primary are not.

The first are not only signs of the object perceived, but they bear a capital part in the notion we form of it. We conceive it only as that which occasions such a sensation, and therefore cannot reflect upon it without thinking of the sensation which it occasions: we have no other mark whereby to distinguish it. The thought of a secondary quality, therefore, always carries us back to the sensation which it produces. We give the same name to both, and are apt to confound them together.

But, having a clear and distinct conception of primary qualities, we have no need, when we think of them, to recall their sensations. When a primary quality is perceived, the sensation immediately leads our thought to the quality signified by it, and is itself forgot. We have no occasion afterwards to reflect upon it; and so we come to be as little acquainted with it as if we had never felt it. This is the case with the sensations of all primary qualities, when they are not so painful or pleasant as to draw our attention.

When a man moves his hand rudely against a pointed hard body, he feels pain, and may easily be persuaded that this pain is a sensation, and that there is nothing resembling it in the hard body; at the same time, he perceives the body to be hard and pointed, and he knows that these qualities belong to the body only. In this case, it is easy to distinguish what he feels from what he perceives.

Let him again touch the pointed body gently, so as to give him no pain; and now you can hardly persuade him that he feels anything but the figure and hardness of the body: so difficult it is to attend to the sensations belonging to primary qualities, when they are neither pleasant nor painful. They carry the thought to the external object, and immediately disappear and are forgot. Nature intended them only as signs; and when they have served that purpose they vanish. . . .

CHAPTER 18 / OF OTHER OBJECTS OF PERCEPTION

Besides primary and secondary qualities of bodies, there are many other immediate objects of perception. Without pretending to a complete enumeration, I think they mostly fall under one or other of the following classes. 1*st*, Certain states or conditions of our own bodies. 2*d*, Mechanical powers or forces. 3*d*, Chemical powers. 4*th*, Medical powers of virtues. 5*th*, Vegetable and animal powers.

That we perceive certain disorders in our own bodies by means of uneasy sensations, which nature hath conjoined with them, will not be disputed. Of this kind are toothache, headache, gout, and every distemper and hurt which we feel. The notions which our sense gives of these, have a strong analogy to our notions of secondary qualities. Both are similarly compounded, and may be similarly resolved, and they give light to each other.

In the toothache, for instance, there is *first*, a painful feeling; and, *secondly*, a conception and belief of some disorder in the tooth, which is believed to be the cause of the uneasy feeling.

The first of these is a sensation, the second is perception; for it includes a conception and belief of an external object. But these two things, though of different natures, are so constantly conjoined in our experience and in our imagination, that we consider them as one. We give the same name to both; for the toothache is the proper name of the pain we feel; and it is the proper name of the disorder in the tooth which causes that pain. If it should be made a question whether the toothache be in the mind that feels it, or in the tooth that is affected, much might be said on both sides, while it is not observed that the word has two meanings. But a little reflection satisfies us, that the pain is in the mind, and the disorder in the tooth. If some philosopher should pretend to have made the discovery that the toothache, the gout, the headache, are only sensations in the mind, and that it is a vulgar error to conceive that they are distempers of the body, he might defend his system in the same manner as those who affirm that there is no sound, nor colour, nor taste in bodies, defend that paradox. But both these systems, like most paradoxes, will be found to be only an abuse of words.

We say that we *feel* the toothache, not that we perceive it. On the other hand, we say that we *perceive* the colour of a body, not that we feel it. Can any reason be given for this difference of phraseology? In answer to this question, I apprehend that, both when we feel the toothache and when we see a coloured body, there is sensation and perception conjoined. But, in the toothache, the sensation being very painful, engrosses the attention; and therefore we speak of it as if it were felt only, and not perceived: whereas, in seeing a coloured body, the sensation is indifferent, and draws no attention. The quality in the body, which we call its colour, is the only object of attention; and therefore we speak of it as if it were perceived and not felt. Though all philosophers agree that, in seeing colour there is sensation, it is not easy to persuade the vulgar that, in seeing a coloured body, when the light is not too strong nor the eye inflamed, they have any sensation or feeling at all.

There are some sensations, which, though they are very often felt, are never attended to, nor reflected upon. We have no conception of them; and, therefore, in language there is neither any name for them, nor any form of speech that supposes their existence. Such are the sensations of colour, and of all primary qualities; and, therefore, those qualities are said to be perceived, but not to be felt. Taste and smell, and heat and cold, have sensations that are often agreeable or disagreeable, in such a degree as to draw our attention; and they are sometimes said to be felt, and sometimes to be perceived. When disorders of the body occasion very acute pain, the uneasy sensation engrosses the attention, and they are said to be felt, not to be perceived.

There is another question relating to phraseology, which this subject suggests. A man says, he feels pain in such a particular part of his body; in his toe for instance. Now, reason assures us that pain being a sensation, can only be in the sentient being, as its subject—that is, in the mind. And, though philosophers have disputed much about the place of the mind; yet none of them ever placed it in the toe. What shall we say then in this case? Do our senses really deceive us, and make us believe a thing which our reason determines to be impossible? I answer, *first,* That, when a man says he has pain in his toe, he is perfectly understood, both by himself and those who hear him. This is all that he intends. He really feels what he and all men call a pain in the toe; and there is no deception in the matter. Whether, therefore, there be any impropriety in the phrase or not, is of no consequence in common life. It answers all the ends of speech, both to the speaker and the hearers.

In all languages there are phrases which have a distinct meaning; while, at the same time, there may be something in the structure of them that disagrees with the analogy of grammar or with the principles of philosophy. And the reason is, because language is not made either by grammarians or philosophers. Thus, we speak of feeling pain, as if pain was something distinct from the feeling of it. We speak of pain coming and going, and removing from one place to another. Such phrases are meant by those who use them in a sense that is neither obscure nor false. But the philosopher puts them into his alembic, reduces them to their first principles, draws out of them a sense that was never meant, and so imagines that he has discovered an error of the vulgar.

I observe, *secondly*, That, when we consider the sensation of pain by itself, without any respect to its cause, we cannot say with propriety, that the toe is either the place or the subject of it. But it ought to be remembered, that, when we speak of pain in the toe, the sensation is combined in our thought, with the cause of it, which really is in the toe. The cause and the effect are combined in one complex notion, and the same name serves for both. It is the business of the philosopher to analyse this complex notion, and to give different names to its different ingredients. He gives the name of *pain* to the sensation only, and the name of *disorder* to the unknown cause of it. Then it is evident that the disorder only is in the toe, and that it would be an error to think that the pain is in it. But we ought not to ascribe this error to the vulgar, who never made the distinction, and who, under the name of pain, comprehend both the sensation and its cause.

Cases sometimes happen, which give occasion even to the vulgar to distinguish the painful sensation from the disorder which is the cause of it. A man who has had his leg cut off, many years after feels pain in a toe of that leg. The toe has now no existence; and he perceives easily, that the toe can neither be the place nor the subject of the pain which he feels; yet it is the same feeling he used to have from a hurt in the toe; and, if he did not know that his leg was cut off, it would give him the same immediate conviction of some hurt or disorder in the toe.[6]

The same phenomenon may lead the philosopher, in all cases, to distinguish sensation from perception. We say, that the man had a deceitful feeling, when he felt a pain in his toe after the leg was cut off; and we have a true meaning in saying so. But, if we will speak accurately, our sensations cannot be deceitful; they must be what we feel them to be, and can be nothing else. Where, then, lies the deceit? I answer, it lies not in the sensation, which is real, but in the seeming perception he had of a disorder in his toe. This perception, which Nature had conjoined with the sensation, was, in this instance, fallacious.

The same reasoning may be applied to every phenomenon that can, with propriety, be called a deception of sense. As when one who has the jaundice sees a body yellow, which is really white; or when a man sees an object double, because his eyes are not both directed to it: in these, and other like cases, the sensations we have are real, and the deception is only in the perception which nature has annexed to them. . . .

CHAPTER 19 / OF MATTER AND OF SPACE

The objects of sense we have hitherto considered are qualities. But qualities must have a subject. We give the names of *matter, material substance,* and *body,* to the subject of sensible qualities; and it may be asked what this *matter* is.

I perceive in a billiard ball, figure, colour, and motion; but the ball is not figure, nor is it colour, nor motion, nor all these taken together; it is something that has figure, and colour, and motion. This is a dictate of nature, and the belief of all mankind.

As to the nature of this something, I am afraid we can give little account of it, but that it has the qualities which our senses discover.

But how do we know that they are qualities, and cannot exist without a subject? I confess I cannot explain how we know that they cannot exist without a subject, any more than I can explain how we know that they exist. We have the information of nature for their existence; and I think we have the information of nature that they are qualities.

The belief that figure, motion, and colour are qualities, and require a subject, must either be a judgment of nature, or it must be discovered by reason, or it must be a prejudice that has no just foundation. There are philosophers who maintain that it is a mere prejudice; that a body is nothing but a collection of what we call sensible qualities; and that they neither have nor need any subject. This is the opinion of Bishop Berkeley and Mr Hume; and they were led to it by finding that they had not in their minds any idea of substance. It could neither be an idea of sensation or of reflection.

But to me nothing seems more absurd than that there should be extension without anything extended, or motion without anything moved; yet I cannot give reasons for my opinion, because it seems to me self-evident, and an immediate dictate of my nature.

And that it is the belief of all mankind, appears in the structure of all languages; in which we find adjective nouns used to express sensible qualities. It is well known that every adjective in language must belong to some substantive expressed or understood—that is, every quality must belong to some subject.

Sensible qualities make so great a part of the furniture of our minds, their kinds are so many, and their number so great, that, if prejudice, and not nature, teach us to ascribe them all to a subject, it must have a great work to perform, which cannot be accomplished in a short time, nor carried on to the same pitch in every individual. We should find not individuals only, but nations and ages, differing from each other in the progress which this prejudice had made in their sentiments;

but we find no such difference among men. What one man accounts a quality, all men do, and ever did.

It seems, therefore, to be a judgment of nature, that the things immediately perceived are qualities, which must belong to a subject; and all the information that our senses give us about this subject, is, that it is that to which such qualities belong. From this it is evident, that our notion of body or matter, as distinguished from its qualities, is a relative notion; and I am afraid it must always be obscure until men have other faculties.

The philosopher, in this, seems to have no advantage above the vulgar; for, as they perceive colour, and figure, and motion by their senses as well he does, and both are equally certain that there is a subject of those qualities, so the notions which both have of this subject are equally obscure. When the philosopher calls it a *substratum,* and a subject of inhesion, those learned words convey no meaning but what every man understands and expresses, by saying, in common language, that it is a thing extended, and solid, and movable.

The relation which sensible qualities bear to their subject— that is, to body—is not, however, so dark but that it is easily distinguished from all other relations. Every man can distinguish it from the relation of an effect to its cause; of a mean to its end; or of a sign to the thing signified by it.

I think it requires some ripeness of understanding to distinguish the qualities of a body from the body. Perhaps this distinction is not made by brutes, nor by infants; and if any one thinks that this distinction is not made by our senses, but by some other power of the mind, I will not dispute this point, provided it be granted that men, when their faculties are ripe, have a natural conviction that sensible qualities cannot exist by themselves without some subject to which they belong.

I think, indeed, that some of the determinations we form concerning matter cannot be deduced solely from the testimony of sense, but must be referred to some other source.

There seems to be nothing more evident than that all bodies must consist of parts; and that every part of a body is a body, and a distinct being, which may exist without the other parts; and yet I apprehend this conclusion is not deduced solely from the testimony of sense: for, besides that it is a necessary truth, and, therefore, no object of sense, there is a limit beyond which we cannot perceive any division of a body. The parts become too small to be perceived by our senses; but we cannot believe that it becomes then incapable of being farther divided, or that such division would make it not to be a body. . . .

We are next to consider our notion of *Space.* It may be observed that, although space be not perceived by any of our senses when all matter is removed, yet, when we perceive any of the primary qualities, space presents itself as a necessary concomitant; for there can neither be extension nor motion, nor figure nor division, nor cohesion of parts, without space.

There are only two of our senses by which the notion of space enters into the mind—to wit, touch and sight. If we suppose a man to have neither of these senses, I do not see how he could ever have any conception of space. Supposing him to have both, until he sees or feels other objects, he can have no notion of space. It has neither colour nor figure to make it an object of sight: it has no tangible quality to make it an object of touch. But other objects of sight and touch carry the notion of space along with them; and not the notion only, but the belief of it; for a body could not exist if there was no space to contain it. It could not move if there was no space. Its situation, its distance, and every relation it has to other bodies, suppose space.

But, though the notion of space seems not to enter, at first, into the mind, until it is introduced by the proper objects of sense, yet, being once introduced, it remains in our conception and belief, though the objects which introduced it be removed. We see no absurdity in supposing a body to be annihilated; but the space that contained it remains; and, to suppose that annihilated, seems to be absurd. It is so much allied to nothing or emptiness, that it seems incapable of annihilation or of creation.

Space not only retains a firm hold of our belief, even when we suppose all the objects that introduced it to be annihilated, but it swells to immensity. We can set no limits to it, either of extent or of duration. Hence we call it immense, eternal, immovable, and indestructible. But it is only an immense, eternal, immovable, and indestructible void or emptiness. Perhaps we may apply to it what the Peripatetics said of their first matter, that, whatever it is, it is potentially only, not actually.

When we consider parts of space that have measure and figure, there is nothing we understand better, nothing about which we can reason so clearly, and to so great extent. Extension and figure are circumscribed parts of space, and are the object of geometry, a science in which human reason has the most ample field, and can go deeper, and with more certainty, than in any other. But, when we attempt to comprehend the whole of space, and to trace it to its origin, we lose ourselves in the search. The profound speculations of ingenious men upon this subject differ so widely as may lead us to suspect that the line of human understanding is too short to reach the bottom of it.

Bishop Berkeley, I think, was the first who observed that the extension, figure, and space, of which we speak in common language, and of which geometry treats, are originally perceived by the sense of touch only; but that there is a notion of extension, figure, and space, which may be got by sight, without any aid from touch. To distinguish these, he calls the first tangible extension, tangible figure, and tangible space. The last he calls visible.

As I think this distinction very important in the philosophy of our senses, I shall adopt the names used by the inventor to express it; remembering what has been already observed—

that space, whether tangible or visible, is not so properly an object of sense, as a necessary concomitant of the objects both of sight and touch.

The reader may likewise be pleased to attend to this, that, when I use the names of tangible and visible space, I do not mean to adopt Bishop Berkeley's opinion, so far as to think that they are really different things, and altogether unlike. I take them to be different conceptions of the same thing; the one very partial, and the other more complete; but both distinct and just, as far as they reach.

Thus, when I see a spire at a very great distance, it seems like the point of a bodkin; there appears no vane at the top, no angles. But, when I view the same object at a small distance, I see a huge pyramid of several angles, with a vane on the top. Neither of these appearances is fallacious. Each of them is what it ought to be, and what it must be, from such an object seen at such different distances. These different appearances of the same object may serve to illustrate the different conceptions of space, according as they are drawn from the information of sight alone, or as they are drawn from the additional information of touch.

Our sight alone, unaided by touch, gives a very partial notion of space, but yet a distinct one. When it is considered according to this partial notion, I call it visible space. The sense of touch gives a much more complete notion of space; and, when it is considered according to this notion, I call it tangible space. Perhaps there may be intelligent beings of a higher order, whose conceptions of space are much more complete than those we have from both senses. Another sense added to those of sight and touch, might, for what I know, give us conceptions of space as different from those we can now attain as tangible space is from visible, and might resolve many knotty points concerning it, which, from the imperfection of our faculties, we cannot, by any labour, untie.

Berkeley acknowledges that there is an exact correspondence between the visible figure and magnitude of objects, and the tangible; and that every modification of the one has a modification of the other corresponding. He acknowledges, likewise, that Nature has established such a connection between the visible figure and magnitude of an object, and the tangible, that we learn by experience to know the tangible figure and magnitude from the visible. And, having been accustomed to do so from infancy, we get the habit of doing it with such facility and quickness that we think we see the tangible figure, magnitude, and distance of bodies, when, in reality, we only collect those tangible qualities from the corresponding visible qualities, which are natural signs of them.

The correspondence and connection which Berkeley shews to be between the visible figure and magnitude of objects, and their tangible figure and magnitude, is in some respects very similar to that which we have observed between our sensations and the primary qualities with which they are connected. No sooner is the sensation felt, than immediately we have the conception and belief of the corresponding quality. We give no attention to the sensation; it has not a name; and it is difficult to persuade us that there was any such thing.

In like manner, no sooner is the visible figure and magnitude of an object seen, than immediately we have the conception and belief of the corresponding tangible figure and magnitude. We give no attention to the visible figure and magnitude. It is immediately forgot, as if it had never been perceived; and it has no name in common language; and, indeed, until Berkeley pointed it out as a subject of speculation, and gave it a name, it had none among philosophers, excepting in one instance, relating to the heavenly bodies, which are beyond the reach of touch. With regard to them, what Berkeley calls visible magnitude was, by astronomers, called apparent magnitude.

There is surely an apparent magnitude, and an apparent figure of terrestrial objects, as well as of celestial; and this is what Berkeley calls their visible figure and magnitude. But this was never made an object of thought among philosophers, until that author gave it a name, and observed the correspondence and connection between it and tangible magnitude and figure, and how the mind gets the habit of passing so instantaneously from the visible figure as a sign to the tangible figure as the thing signified by it, that the first is perfectly forgot as if it had never been perceived.

Visible figure, extension, and space, may be made a subject of mathematical speculation as well as the tangible. In the visible, we find two dimensions only; in the tangible, three. In the one, magnitude is measured by angles; in the other, by lines. Every part of visible space bears some proportion to the whole; but tangible space being immense, any part of it bears no proportion to the whole.

Such differences in their properties led Bishop Berkeley to think that visible and tangible magnitude and figure are things totally different and dissimilar, and cannot both belong to the same object.

And upon this dissimilitude is grounded one of the strongest arguments by which his system is supported. For it may be said, if there be external objects which have a real extension and figure, it must be either tangible extension and figure, or visible, or both. The last appears absurd; nor was it ever maintained by any man, that the same object has two kinds of extension and figure totally dissimilar. There is then only one of the two really in the object; and the other must be ideal. But no reason can be assigned why the perceptions of one sense should be real, while those of another are only ideal; and he who is persuaded that the objects of sight are ideas only, has equal reason to believe so of the objects of touch.

This argument, however, loses all its force, if it be true, as was formerly hinted, that visible figure and extension are only a partial conception, and the tangible figure and extension a more complete conception of that figure and extension which is really in the object.

It has been proved very fully by Bishop Berkeley, that sight alone, without any aid from the informations of touch, gives us no perception, nor even conception of the distance of any object from the eye. But he was not aware that this very principle overturns the argument for his system, taken from the difference between visible and tangible extension and figure. For, supposing external objects to exist, and to have that tangible extension and figure which we perceive, it follows demonstrably, from the principle now mentioned, that their visible extension and figure must be just what we see it to be.

The rules of perspective, and of the projection of the sphere, which is a branch of perspective, are demonstrable. They suppose the existence of external objects, which have a tangible extension and figure; and, upon that supposition, they demonstrate what must be the visible extension and figure of such objects, when placed in such a position and at such a distance.

Hence, it is evident that the visible figure and extension of objects is so far from being incompatible with the tangible, that the first is a necessary consequence from the last in beings that see as we do. The correspondence between them is not arbitrary, like that between words and the thing they signify, as Berkeley thought; but it results necessarily from the nature of the two senses; and this correspondence being always found in experience to be exactly what the rules of perspective shew that it ought to be if the senses give true information, is an argument of the truth of both.

CHAPTER 20 / OF THE EVIDENCE OF SENSE, AND OF BELIEF IN GENERAL

. . . . Belief, assent, conviction, are words which I do not think admit of logical definition, because the operation of mind signified by them is perfectly simple, and of its own kind.

Nor do they need to be defined, because they are common words, and well understood.

Belief must have an object. For he that believes must believe something; and that which he believes, is called the object of his belief. Of this object of his belief, he must have some conception, clear or obscure; for, although there may be the most clear and distinct conception of an object without any belief of its existence, there can be no belief without conception.

Belief is always expressed in language by a proposition, wherein something is affirmed or denied. This is the form of speech which in all languages is appropriated to that purpose, and without belief there could be neither affirmation nor denial, nor should we have any form of words to express either. Belief admits of all degrees, from the slightest suspicion to the fullest assurance. These things are so evident to every man that reflects, that it would be abusing the reader's patience to dwell upon them.

I proceed to observe that there are many operations of mind in which, when we analyse them as far as we are able, we find belief to be an essential ingredient. A man cannot be conscious of his own thoughts, without believing that he thinks. He cannot perceive an object of sense, without believing that it exists. He cannot distinctly remember a past event, without believing that it did exist. Belief therefore is an ingredient in consciousness, in perception, and in remembrance. . . .

That men often believe what there is no just ground to believe, and thereby are led into hurtful errors, is too evident to be denied. And, on the other hand, that there are just grounds of belief can as little be doubted by any man who is not a perfect sceptic.

We give the name of evidence to whatever is a ground of belief. To believe without evidence is a weakness which every man is concerned to avoid, and which every man wishes to avoid. Nor is it in a man's power to believe anything longer than he thinks he has evidence.

What this evidence is, is more easily felt than described. Those who never reflected upon its nature, feel its influence in governing their belief. It is the business of the logician to explain its nature, and to distinguish its various kinds and degrees; but every man of understanding can judge of it, and commonly judges right, when the evidence is fairly laid before him, and his mind is free from prejudice. A man who knows nothing of the theory of vision may have a good eye; and a man who never speculated about evidence in the abstract may have a good judgment.

The common occasions of life lead us to distinguish evidence into different kinds, to which we give names that are well understood; such as the evidence of sense, the evidence of memory, the evidence of consciousness, the evidence of testimony, the evidence of axioms, the evidence of reasoning. All men of common understanding agree that each of these kinds of evidence may afford just ground of belief, and they agree very generally in the circumstances that strengthen or weaken them.

Philosophers have endeavoured, by analysing the different sorts of evidence, to find out some common nature wherein they all agree, and thereby to reduce them all to one. This was the aim of the schoolmen in their intricate disputes about the criterion of truth. Des Cartes placed this criterion of truth in clear and distinct perception, and laid it down as a maxim, that whatever we clearly and distinctly perceive to be true, is true; but it is difficult to know what he understands by clear and distinct perception in this maxim. Mr Locke placed it in a perception of the agreement or disagreement of our ideas, which perception is immediate in intuitive knowledge, and by the intervention of other ideas in reasoning.

I confess that, although I have, as I think, a distinct notion of the different kinds of evidence above-mentioned, and, perhaps, of some others, which it is unnecessary here to enumerate, yet I am not able to find any common nature to which they may all be reduced. They seem to me to agree only in this, that they are all fitted by Nature to produce belief in the human mind, some of them in the highest degree, which we call certainty, others in various degrees according to circumstances.

I shall take it for granted that the evidence of sense, when the proper circumstances concur, is good evidence, and a just ground of belief. My intention in this place is only to compare it with the other kinds that have been mentioned, that we may judge whether it be reducible to any of them, or of a nature peculiar to itself.

First, It seems to be quite different from the evidence of reasoning. All good evidence is commonly called reasonable evidence, and very justly, because it ought to govern our belief as reasonable creatures. And, according to this meaning, I think the evidence of sense no less reasonable than that of demonstration. If Nature give us information of things that concern us, by other means than by reasoning, reason itself will direct us to receive that information with thankfulness, and to make the best use of it.

But, when we speak of the evidence of reasoning as a particular kind of evidence, it means the evidence of propositions that are inferred by reasoning, from propositions already known and believed. Thus, the evidence of the fifth proposition of the first book of Euclid's Elements consists in this, That it is shewn to be the necessary consequence of the axioms, and of the preceding propositions. In all reasoning, there must be one or more premises, and a conclusion drawn from them. And the premises are called the reason why we must believe the conclusion which we see to follow from them.

That the evidence of sense is of a different kind, needs little proof. No man seeks a reason for believing what he sees or feels; and, if he did, it would be difficult to find one. But, though he can give no reason for believing his senses, his belief remains as firm as if it were grounded on demonstration.

Many eminent philosophers, thinking it unreasonable to believe when they could not shew a reason, have laboured to furnish us with reasons for believing our senses; but their reasons are very insufficient, and will not bear examination. Other philosophers have shewn very clearly the fallacy of these reasons, and have, as they imagine, discovered invincible reasons against this belief; but they have never been able either to shake it in themselves, or to convince others. The statesman continues to plod, the soldier to fight, and the merchant to export and import, without being in the least moved by the demonstrations that have been offered of the non-existence of those things about which they are so seriously employed. And a man may as soon, by reasoning, pull the moon out of her orbit, as destroy the belief of the objects of sense.

Shall we say, then, that the evidence of sense is the same with that of axioms, or self-evident truths? I answer, *First*, That, all modern philosophers seem to agree that the existence of the objects of sense is not self-evident, because some of them have endeavoured to prove it by subtle reasoning, others to refute it. Neither of these can consider it as self-evident.

Secondly, I would observe that the word *axiom* is taken by philosophers in such a sense as that the existence of the objects of sense cannot, with propriety, be called an axiom. They give the name of axiom only to self-evident truths, that are necessary, and are not limited to time and place, but must be true at all times and in all places. The truths attested by our senses are not of this kind; they are contingent, and limited to time and place.

Thus, that one is the half of two, is an axiom. It is equally true at all times and in all places. We perceive, by attending to the proposition itself, that it cannot but be true; and, therefore, it is called an eternal, necessary, and immutable truth. That there is at present a chair on my right hand, and another on my left, is a truth attested by my senses; but it is not necessary, nor eternal, nor immutable. It may not be true next minute; and, therefore, to call it an axiom would, I apprehend, be to deviate from the common use of the word.

Thirdly, If the word axiom be put to signify every truth which is known immediately, without being deduced from any antecedent truth, then the existence of the objects of sense may be called an axiom; for my senses give me as immediate conviction of what they testify, as my understanding gives of what is commonly called an axiom.

There is, no doubt, an analogy between the evidence of sense and the evidence of testimony. Hence, we find, in all languages, the analogical expressions of the *testimony of sense,* of giving *credit* to our senses, and the like. But there is a real difference between the two, as well as a similitude. In believing upon testimony, we rely upon the authority of a person who testifies; but we have no such authority for believing our senses.

Shall we say, then, that this belief is the inspiration of the Almighty? I think this may be said in a good sense, for I take it to be the immediate effect of our constitution, which is the work of the Almighty. But, if inspiration be understood to imply a persuasion of its coming from God, our belief of the objects of sense is not inspiration; for a man would believe his senses though he had no notion of a Deity. He who is persuaded that he is the workmanship of God, and that it is a part of his constitution to believe his senses, may think that a good reason to confirm his belief. But he had the belief before he could give this or any other reason for it.

If we compare the evidence of sense with that of memory, we find a great resemblance, but still some difference. I remember distinctly to have dined yesterday with such a company. What is the meaning of this? It is, that I have a distinct conception and firm belief of this past event; not by reasoning, not by testimony, but immediately from my constitution. And

I give the name of memory to that part of my constitution by which I have this kind of conviction of past events.

I see a chair on my right hand. What is the meaning of this? It is, that I have, by my constitution, a distinct conception and firm belief of the present existence of the chair in such a place and in such a position; and I give the name of seeing to that part of my constitution by which I have this immediate conviction. The two operations agree in the immediate conviction which they give. They agree in this also, that the things believed are not necessary, but contingent, and limited to time and place. But they differ in two respects:—*First,* That memory has something for its object that did exist in time past; but the object of sight, and of all the senses, must be something which exists at present;—and, *Secondly,* That I see by my eyes and only when they are directed to the object, and when it is illuminated. But my memory is not limited by any bodily organ that I know, nor by light and darkness, though it has its limitations of another kind.

These differences are obvious to all men, and very reasonably lead them to consider seeing and remembering as operations specifically different. But the nature of the evidence they give, has a great resemblance. A like difference and a like resemblance there is between the evidence of sense and that of consciousness, which I leave the reader to trace.

As to the opinion that evidence consists in a perception of the agreement or disagreement of ideas, we may have occasion to consider it more particularly in another place. Here I only observe, that, when taken in the most favourable sense, it may be applied with propriety to the evidence of reasoning, and to the evidence of some axioms. But I cannot see how, in any sense, it can be applied to the evidence of consciousness, to the evidence of memory, or to that of the senses.

When I compare the different kinds of evidence above-mentioned, I confess, after all, that the evidence of reasoning, and that of some necessary and self-evident truths, seems to be the least mysterious and the most perfectly comprehended; and therefore I do not think it strange that philosophers should have endeavoured to reduce all kinds of evidence to these.

When I see a proposition to be self-evident and necessary, and that the subject is plainly included in the predicate, there seems to be nothing more that I can desire in order to understand why I believe it. And when I see a consequence that necessarily follows from one or more self-evident propositions, I want nothing more with regard to my belief of that consequence. The light of truth so fills my mind in these cases, that I can neither conceive nor desire anything more satisfying.

On the other hand, when I remember distinctly a past event, or see an object before my eyes, this commands my belief no less than an axiom. But when, as a philosopher, I reflect upon this belief, and want to trace it to its origin, I am not able to resolve it into necessary and self-evident axioms, or conclusions that are necessarily consequent upon them. I seem to want that evidence which I can best comprehend, and which gives perfect satisfaction to an inquisitive mind; yet it is ridiculous to doubt; and I find it is not in my power. An attempt to throw off this belief is like an attempt to fly, equally ridiculous and impracticable.

To a philosopher, who has been accustomed to think that the treasure of his knowledge is the acquisition of that reasoning power of which he boasts, it is no doubt humiliating to find that his reason can lay no claim to the greater part of it.

By his reason, he can discover certain abstract and necessary relations of things; but his knowledge of what really exists, or did exist, comes by another channel, which is open to those who cannot reason. He is led to it in the dark, and knows not how he came by it.

It is no wonder that the pride of philosophy should lead some to invent vain theories in order to account for this knowledge; and others, who see this to be impracticable, to spurn at a knowledge they cannot account for, and vainly attempt to throw it off as a reproach to their understanding. But the wise and the humble will receive it as the gift of Heaven, and endeavour to make the best use of it.

ESSAY THREE / OF MEMORY

CHAPTER 1 / THINGS OBVIOUS AND CERTAIN WITH REGARD TO MEMORY

In the gradual progress of man, from infancy to maturity, there is a certain order in which his faculties are unfolded, and this seems to be the best order we can follow in treating of them.

The external senses appear first; memory soon follows—which we are now to consider.

It is by memory that we have an immediate knowledge of things past. The senses give us information of things only as they exist in the present moment; and this information, if it were not preserved by memory, would vanish instantly, and leave us as ignorant as if it had never been.

Memory must have an object. Every man who remembers must remember something, and that which he remembers is called the object of his remembrance. In this, memory agrees with perception, but differs from sensation, which has no object but the feeling itself.

Every man can distinguish the thing remembered from the remembrance of it. We may remember anything which we have seen, or heard, or known, or done, or suffered; but the remembrance of it is a particular act of the mind which now exists, and of which we are conscious. To confound these two is an absurdity, which a thinking man could not be led into, but by some false hypothesis which hinders him from reflecting upon the thing which he would explain by it.

In memory we do not find such a train of operations connected by our constitution as in perception. When we perceive an object by our senses, there is, first, some impression made by the object upon the organ of sense, either immediately, or by means of some medium. By this, an impression is made upon the nerves and brain, in consequence of which we feel some sensation; and that sensation is attended by that conception and belief of the external object which we call perception. These operations are so connected in our constitution, that it is difficult to disjoin them in our conceptions, and to attend to each without confounding it with the others. But, in the operations of memory, we are free from this embarrassment; they are easily distinguished from all other acts of the mind, and the names which denote them are free from all ambiguity.

The object of memory, or thing remembered, must be something that is past; as the object of perception and of consciousness must be something which is present. What now is, cannot be an object of memory; neither can that which is past and gone be an object of perception or of consciousness.

Memory is always accompanied with the belief of that which we remember, as perception is accompanied with the belief of that which we perceive, and consciousness with the belief of that whereof we are conscious. Perhaps in infancy, or in a disorder of mind, things remembered may be confounded with those which are merely imagined; but in mature years, and in a sound state of mind, every man feels that he must believe what he distinctly remembers, though he can give no other reason of his belief, but that he remembers the thing distinctly; whereas, when he merely imagines a thing ever so distinctly he has no belief of it upon that account.

This belief, which we have from distinct memory, we account real knowledge, no less certain than if it was grounded on demonstration; no man in his wits calls it in question, or will hear any argument against it. The testimony of witnesses in causes of life and death depends upon it, and all the knowledge of mankind of past events is built on this foundation.

There are cases in which a man's memory is less distinct and determinate, and where he is ready to allow that it may have failed him; but this does not in the least weaken its credit, when it is perfectly distinct.

Memory implies a conception and belief of past duration; for it is impossible that a man should remember a thing distinctly, without believing some interval of duration, more or less, to have passed between the time it happened, and the present moment; and I think it is impossible to shew how we could acquire a notion of duration if we had no memory. Things remembered must be things formerly perceived or known. I remember the transit of Venus over the sun in the year 1769. I must therefore have perceived it at the time it happened, otherwise I could not now remember it. Our first acquaintance with any object of thought cannot be by remembrance. Memory can only produce a continuance or renewal of a former acquaintance with the thing remembered.

The remembrance of a past event is necessarily accompanied with the conviction of our own existence at the time the event happened. I cannot remember a thing that happened a year ago, without a conviction as strong as memory can give, that I, the same identical person who now remember that event, did then exist.

What I have hitherto said concerning memory, I consider as principles which appear obvious and certain to every man who will take the pains to reflect upon the operations of his own mind. They are facts of which every man must judge by what he feels; and they admit of no other proof but an appeal to every man's own reflection. . . .

CHAPTER 2 / MEMORY AN ORIGINAL FACULTY

First, I think it appears, that memory is an original faculty, given us by the Author of our being, of which we can give no account, but that we are so made.

The knowledge which I have of things past, by my memory, seems to me as unaccountable as an immediate knowledge would be of things to come; and I can give no reason why I should have the one and not the other, but that such is the will of my Maker. I find in my mind a distinct conception, and a firm belief of a series of past events; but how this is produced I know not. I call it memory, but this is only giving a name to it—it is not an account of its cause. I believe most firmly, what I distinctly remember; but I can give no reason of this belief. It is the inspiration of the Almighty that gives me this understanding.

When I believe the truth of a mathematical axiom, or of a mathematical proposition, I see that it must be so: every man who has the same conception of it sees the same. There is a necessary and an evident connection between the subject and the predicate of the proposition; and I have all the evidence to support my belief which I can possibly conceive.

When I believe that I washed my hands and face this morning, there appears no necessity in the truth of this proposition. It might be, or it might not be. A man may distinctly conceive it without believing it at all. How then do I come to believe it? I remember it distinctly. This is all I can say. This remembrance is an act of my mind. Is it impossible that this act should be, if the event had not happened? I confess I do not see any necessary connection between the one and the other. If any man can shew such a necessary connection, then I think that belief which we have of what we remember will be fairly accounted for; but, if this cannot be done, that belief is unaccountable, and we can say no more but that it is the result of our constitution.

Perhaps it may be said, that the experience we have had of the fidelity of memory is a good reason for relying upon its testimony. I deny not that this may be a reason to those who have had this experience, and who reflect upon it. But I believe there are few who ever thought of this reason, or who found any need of it. It must be some very rare occasion that leads a man to have recourse to it; and in those who have done so, the testimony of memory was believed before the experience of its fidelity, and that belief could not be caused by the experience which came after it.

We know some abstract truths, by comparing the terms of the proposition which expresses them, and perceiving some necessary relation or agreement between them. It is thus I know that two and three make five; that the diameters of a circle are all equal. Mr Locke having discovered this source of knowledge, too rashly concluded that all human knowledge might be derived from it; and in this he has been followed very generally—by Mr Hume in particular.

But I apprehend that our knowledge of the existence of things contingent can never be traced to this source. I know that such a thing exists, or did exist. This knowledge cannot be derived from the perception of a necessary agreement between existence and the thing that exists, because there is no such necessary agreement; and therefore no such agreement can be perceived either immediately or by a chain of reasoning. The thing does not exist necessarily, but by the will and power of him that made it; and there is no contradiction follows from supposing it not to exist.

Whence I think it follows, that our knowledge of the existence of our own thoughts, of the existence of all the material objects about us, and of all past contingencies, must be derived, not from a perception of necessary relations or agreements, but from some other source.

Our Maker has provided other means for giving us the knowledge of these things—means which perfectly answer their end, and produce the effect intended by them. But in what manner they do this, is, I fear, beyond our skill to explain. We know our own thoughts, and the operations of our minds, by a power which we call consciousness: but this is only giving a name to this part of our frame. It does not explain its fabric, nor how it produces in us an irresistible conviction of its informations. We perceive material objects and their sensible qualities by our senses; but how they give us this information, and how they produce our belief in it, we know not. We know many past events by memory; but how it gives this information, I believe, is inexplicable.

It is well known what subtile disputes were held through all the scholastic ages, and are still carried on about the prescience of the Deity. Aristotle had taught that there can be no certain foreknowledge of things contingent; and in this he has been very generally followed, upon no other grounds, as I apprehend, but that we cannot conceive how such things should be foreknown, and therefore conclude it to be impossible. Hence has arisen an opposition and supposed inconsistency between divine prescience and human liberty. Some have given up the first in favour of the last, and others have given up the last in order to support the first.

It is remarkable that these disputants have never apprehended that there is any difficulty in reconciling with liberty the knowledge of what is past, but only of what is future. It is prescience only, and not memory, that is supposed to be hostile to liberty, and hardly reconcilable to it.

Yet I believe the difficulty is perfectly equal in the one case and in the other. I admit, that we cannot account for prescience of the actions of a free agent. But I maintain that we can as little account for memory of the past actions of a free agent. If any man thinks he can prove that the actions of a free agent cannot be foreknown, he will find the same arguments of equal force to prove that the past actions of a free agent cannot be remembered. It is true, that what is past did certainly exist. It is no less true that what is future will certainly exist. I know no reasoning from the constitution of the agent, or from his circumstances, that has not equal strength, whether it be applied to his past or to his future actions. The past was, but now is not. The future will be, but now is not. The present is equally connected or unconnected with both. . . .

CHAPTER 4 / OF IDENTITY

The conviction which every man has of his Identity, as far back as his memory reaches, needs no aid of philosophy to strengthen it; and no philosophy can weaken it, without first producing some degree of insanity.

The philosopher, however, may very properly consider this conviction as a phaenomenon of human nature worthy of his attention. If he can discover its cause, an addition is made to his stock of knowledge. If not, it must be held as a part of our original constitution, or an effect of that constitution produced in a manner unknown to us.

We may observe, first of all, that this conviction is indispensably necessary to all exercise of reason. The operations of reason, whether in action or in speculation, are made up of successive parts. The antecedent are the foundation of the consequent, and, without the conviction that the antecedent have been seen or done by me, I could have no reason to proceed to the consequent, in any speculation, or in any active project whatever.

There can be no memory of what is past without the conviction that we existed at the time remembered. There may be good arguments to convince me that I existed before the earliest thing I can remember; but to suppose that my memory reaches a moment farther back than my belief and conviction of my existence, is a contradiction.

The moment a man loses this conviction, as if he had drunk the water of Lethe, past things are done away; and, in his own belief, he then begins to exist. Whatever was thought, or said, or done, or suffered before that period, may belong to some other person; but he can never impute it to himself, or take any subsequent step that supposes it to be his doing.

From this it is evident that we must have the conviction of our own continued existence and identity, as soon as we are capable of thinking or doing anything, on account of what we have thought, or done, or suffered before; that is, as soon as we are reasonable creatures.

That we may form as distinct a notion as we are able of this phenomenon of the human mind, it is proper to consider what is meant by identity in general, what by our own personal identity, and how we are led into that invincible belief and conviction which every man has of his own personal identity, as far as his memory reaches.

Identity in general, I take to be a relation between a thing which is known to exist at one time, and a thing which is known to have existed at another time. If you ask whether they are one and the same, or two different things, every man of common sense understands the meaning of your question perfectly. Whence we may infer with certainty, that every man of common sense has a clear and distinct notion of identity.

If you ask a definition of identity, I confess I can give none; it is too simple a notion to admit of logical definition. I can say it is a relation; but I cannot find words to express the specific difference between this and other relations, though I am in no danger of confounding it with any other. I can say that diversity is a contrary relation, and that similitude and dissimilitude are another couple of contrary relations, which every man easily distinguishes in his conception from identity and diversity.

I see evidently that identity supposes an uninterrupted continuance of existence. That which hath ceased to exist, cannot be the same with that which afterwards begins to exist; for this would be to suppose a being to exist after it ceased to exist, and to have had existence before it was produced, which are manifest contradictions. Continued uninterrupted existence is therefore necessarily implied in identity.

Hence we may infer that identity cannot, in its proper sense, be applied to our pains, our pleasures, our thoughts, or any operation of our minds. The pain felt this day is not the same individual pain which I felt yesterday, though they may be similar in kind and degree, and have the same cause. The same may be said of every feeling and of every operation of mind: they are all successive in their nature, like time itself, no two moments of which can be the same moment.

It is otherwise with the parts of absolute space. They always are, and were, and will be the same. So far, I think, we proceed upon clear ground in fixing the notion of identity in general.

It is, perhaps, more difficult to ascertain with precision the meaning of Personality; but it is not necessary in the present subject: it is sufficient for our purpose to observe, that all mankind place their personality in something that cannot be divided, or consist of parts. A part of a person is a manifest absurdity.

When a man loses his estate, his health, his strength, he is still the same person, and has lost nothing of his personality. If he has a leg or an arm cut off, he is the same person he was before. The amputated member is no part of his person, otherwise it would have a right to a part of his estate, and be liable for a part of his engagements; it would be entitled to a share of his merit and demerit—which is manifestly absurd. A person is something indivisible, and is what Leibnitz calls *monad*.

My personal identity, therefore, implies the continued existence of that indivisible thing which I call myself. Whatever this self may be, it is something which thinks, and deliberates, and resolves, and acts, and suffers. I am not thought, I am not action, I am not feeling; I am something that thinks, and acts, and suffers. My thoughts, and actions, and feelings, change every moment—they have no continued, but a successive existence; but that *self* or *I*, to which they belong, is permanent, and has the same relation to all the succeeding thoughts, actions, and feelings, which I call mine.

Such are the notions that I have of my personal identity. But perhaps it may be said, this may all be fancy without reality. How do you know?—what evidence have you, that there is such a permanent self which has a claim to all the thoughts, actions, and feelings, which you call yours?

To this I answer, that the proper evidence I have of all this is remembrance. I remember that, twenty years ago, I conversed with such a person; I remember several things that passed in that conversation; my memory testifies not only that this was done, but that it was done by me who now remember it. If it was done by me, I must have existed at that time, and continued to exist from that time to the present: if the identical person whom I call myself, had not a part in that conversation, my memory is fallacious—it gives a distinct and positive testimony of what is not true. Every man in his senses believes what he distinctly remembers, and everything he remembers convinces him that he existed at the time remembered.

Although memory gives the most irresistible evidence of my being the identical person that did such a thing, at such a time, I may have other good evidence of things which befel me, and which I do not remember: I know who bare me and suckled me, but I do not remember these events.

It may here be observed, (though the observation would have been unnecessary if some great philosophers had not contradicted it,) that it is not my remembering any action of mine that makes me to be the person who did it. This remembrance makes me to know assuredly that I did it; but I might have done it though I did not remember it. That relation to me, which is expressed by saying that I did it, would be the same though I had not the least remembrance of it. To say that my remembering that I did such a thing, or, as some choose to express it, my being conscious that I did it, makes me to have done it, appears to me as great an absurdity as it would be to say, that my belief that the world was created made it to be created.

CHAPTER 6 / OF MR LOCKE'S ACCOUNT OF OUR PERSONAL IDENTITY

In a long chapter upon Identity and Diversity, Mr Locke has made many ingenious and just observations, and some which I think cannot be defended. I shall only take notice of the account he gives of our own *Personal Identity.* His doctrine upon this subject has been censured by Bishop Butler, in a short essay subjoined to his "Analogy," with whose sentiments I perfectly agree.

Identity, as was observed, Chap. IV. of this Essay, supposes the continued existence of the being of which it is affirmed, and therefore can be applied only to things which have a continued existence. While any being continues to exist, it is the same being: but two beings which have a different beginning or a different ending of their existence, cannot possibly be the same. To this I think Mr Locke agrees.

He observes, very justly, that to know what is meant by the same person, we must consider what the word *person* stands for; and he defines a person to be an intelligent being, endowed with reason and with consciousness, which last he thinks inseparable from thought.

From this definition of a person, it must necessarily follow, that, while the intelligent being continues to exist and to be intelligent, it must be the same person. To say that the intelligent being is the person, and yet that the person ceases to

exist, while the intelligent being continues, or that the person
continues while the intelligent being ceases to exist, is to my
apprehension a manifest contradiction.

One would think that the definition of a person should perfectly ascertain the nature of personal identity, or wherein it
consists, though it might still be a question how we come to
know and be assured of our personal identity.

Mr Locke tells us, however, "that personal identity—that is,
the sameness of a rational being—consists in consciousness
alone, and, as far as this consciousness can be extended back-
wards to any past action or thought, so far reaches the identity
of that person. So that, whatever hath the consciousness of
present and past actions, is the same person to whom they
belong."[7]

This doctrine hath some strange consequences, which the
author was aware of, Such as, that, if the same consciousness
can be transferred from one intelligent being to another,
which he thinks we cannot shew to be impossible, then two or
twenty intelligent beings may be the same person. And if the
intelligent being may lose the consciousness of the actions
done by him, which surely is possible, then he is not the person
that did those actions; so that one intelligent being may be two
or twenty different persons, if he shall so often lose the consciousness of his former actions.

There is another consequence of this doctrine, which follows no less necessarily, though Mr Locke probably did not see
it. It is, that a man may be, and at the same time not be, the
person that did a particular action.

Suppose a brave officer to have been flogged when a boy at
school, for robbing an orchard, to have taken a standard from
the enemy in his first campaign, and to have been made a
general in advanced life: Suppose also, which must be admitted to be possible, that, when he took the standard, he was
conscious of his having been flogged at school, and that when
made a general he was conscious of his taking the standard,

but had absolutely lost the consciousness of his flogging.

These things being supposed, it follows, from Mr Locke's doctrine, that he who was flogged at school is the same person who took the standard, and that he who took the standard is the same person who was made a general. Whence it follows, if there be any truth in logic, that the general is the same person with him who was flogged at school. But the general's consciousness does not reach so far back as his flogging—therefore, according to Mr Locke's doctrine, he is not the person who was flogged. Therefore, the general is, and at the same time is not the same person with him who was flogged at school. . . .[8]

ESSAY FOUR / OF CONCEPTION

CHAPTER 1 / OF CONCEPTION OR SIMPLE APPREHENSION IN GENERAL

. . . Of all the analogies between the operations of body and those of the mind, there is none so strong and so obvious to all mankind as that which there is between painting, or other plastic arts, and the power of conceiving objects in the mind. Hence, in all languages, the words by which this power of the mind and its various modifications are expressed, are analogical, and borrowed from those arts. We consider this power of the mind as a plastic power, by which we form to ourselves images of the objects of thought.

In vain should we attempt to avoid this analogical language, for we have no other language upon the subject; yet it is dangerous, and apt to mislead. All analogical and figurative words have a double meaning; and, if we are not very much upon our guard, we slide insensibly from the borrowed and figurative meaning into the primitive. We are prone to carry the parallel between the things compared farther than it will hold, and thus very naturally to fall into error.

To avoid this as far as possible in the present subject, it is proper to attend to the dissimilitude between conceiving a thing in the mind, and painting it to the eye, as well as to their similitude. The similitude strikes and gives pleasure. The dissimilitude we are less disposed to observe; but the philosopher ought to attend to it, and to carry it always in mind, in his reasonings on this subject, as a monitor, to warn him against the errors into which the analogical language is apt to draw him.

When a man paints, there is some work done, which remains when his hand is taken off, and continues to exist though he should think no more of it. Every stroke of his pencil produces an effect, and this effect is different from his action in making it; for it remains and continues to exist when the action ceases. The action of painting is one thing; the picture produced is another thing. The first is the cause, the second is the effect.

Let us next consider what is done when he only conceives this picture. He must have conceived it before he painted it; for this is a maxim universally admitted, that every work of art must first be conceived in the mind of the operator. What is this conception? It is an act of the mind, a kind of thought. This cannot be denied. But does it produce any effect besides the act itself? Surely common sense answers this question in the negative; for every one knows that it is one thing to conceive, another thing to bring forth into effect. It is one thing to project, another to execute. A man may think for a long time what he is to do, and after all do nothing. Conceiving, as well as projecting or resolving, are what the schoolmen called *immanent* acts of the mind, which produce nothing beyond themselves. But painting is a transitive act, which produces an effect distinct from the operation, and this effect is the picture. Let this, therefore, be always remembered, that what is commonly called the image of a thing in the mind, is no more than the act or operation of the mind in conceiving it.

That this is the common sense of men who are untutored by philosophy, appears from their language. If one ignorant of the language should ask, What is meant by conceiving a thing? we should very naturally answer, that it is having an image of it in the mind—and perhaps we could not explain the word better. This shews that conception, and the image of a thing in the mind, are synonymous expressions. The image in the mind, therefore, is not the object of conception, nor is it any effect produced by conception as a cause. It is conception itself. That very mode of thinking which we call conception, is by another name called an image in the mind.

Nothing more readily gives the conception of a thing than the seeing an image of it. Hence, by a figure common in language, conception is called an image of the thing conceived. But to shew that it is not a real but a metaphorical image, it is called an image of the mind. We know nothing that is properly in the mind but thought; and, when anything else is said to be in the mind, the expression must be figurative, and signify some kind of thought.

I know that philosophers very unanimously maintain, that in conception there is a real image in the mind, which is the immediate object of conception, and distinct from the act of conceiving it. I beg the reader's indulgence to defer what may be said for or against this philosophical opinion to the next chapter; intending in this only to explain what appears to me to belong to this operation of mind, without considering the theories about it. I think it appears, from what has been said, that the common language of those who have not imbibed any philosophical opinion upon this subject, authorizes us to understand *the conception of a thing, and an image of it in the mind*, not as two different things, but as two different expressions, to signify one and the same thing; and I wish to use common words in their common acceptation.

Taking along with us what is said in the last article, to guard us against the seduction of the analogical language used on this subject, we may observe a very strong analogy, not only between conceiving and painting in general, but between the different kinds of our conceptions, and the different works of the painter. He either makes fancy pictures, or he copies from the painting of others, or he paints from the life; that is, from real objects of art or nature which he has seen. I think our conceptions admit of a division very similar.

First, There are conceptions which may be called fancy pictures. They are commonly called creatures of fancy, or of imagination. They are not the copies of any original that exists, but are originals themselves. Such was the conception which Swift formed of the island of Laputa, and of the country of the Lilliputians; Cervantes of Don Quixote and his Squire; Harrington of the Government of Oceana; and Sir Thomas More of that of Utopia. We can give names to such creatures of imagination, conceive them distinctly, and reason consequently concerning them, though they never had an existence. They were conceived by their creators, and may be conceived by others, but they never existed. We do not ascribe the qualities of true or false to them, because they are not accompanied with any belief, nor do they imply any affirmation or negation.

Setting aside those creatures of imagination, there are other conceptions, which may be called copies, because they have an original or archetype to which they refer, and with which they are believed to agree; and we call them true or false conceptions, according as they agree or disagree with the standard to which they are referred. These are of two kinds, which have different standards or originals.

The *first* kind is analogous to pictures taken from the life. We have conceptions of individual things that really exist, such as the city of London, or the government of Venice. Here the things conceived are the originals; and our conceptions are called true when they agree with the thing conceived. Thus, my conception of the city of London is true, when I conceive it to be what it really is.

Individual things which really exist, being the creatures of God, (though some of them may receive their outward form from man,) he only who made them knows their whole nature; we know them but in part, and therefore our conceptions of them must in all cases be imperfect and inadequate; yet they may be true and just, as far as they reach.

The *second* kind is analogous to the copies which the painter makes from pictures done before. Such I think are the conceptions we have of what the ancients called universals; that is, of things which belong or may belong to many individuals. These are kinds and species of things; such as man or elephant, which are species of substances; wisdom or courage, which are species of qualities; equality or similitude, which are species of relations. It may be asked—From what original are these conceptions formed? And when are they said to be true or false?

It appears to me, that the original from which they are copied—that is, the thing conceived—is the conception or meaning which other men, who understand the language, affix to the same words.

Things are parcelled into kinds and sorts, not by nature, but by men. The individual things we are connected with, are so many, that to give a proper name to every individual would be impossible. We could never attain the knowledge of them that is necessary, nor converse and reason about them, without sorting them according to their different attributes. Those that agree in certain attributes are thrown into one parcel, and have a general name given them, which belongs equally to every individual in that parcel. This common name must therefore signify those attributes which have been observed to be common to every individual in that parcel, and nothing else.

That such general words may answer their intention, all that is necessary is, that those who use them should affix the same meaning or notion—that is, the same conception to them. The common meaning is the standard by which such conceptions are formed, and they are said to be true or false according as they agree or disagree with it. Thus, my conception of felony is true and just, when it agrees with the meaning of that word in the laws relating to it, and in authors who understand the law. The meaning of the word is the thing conceived; and that meaning is the conception affixed to it by those who best understand the language.

An individual is expressed in language either by a proper name, or by a general word joined to such circumstances as distinguish that individual from all others; if it is unknown, it may, when an object of sense, and within reach, be pointed out to the senses; when beyond the reach of the senses, it may be ascertained by a description, which, though very imperfect, may be true, and sufficient to distinguish it from every other individual. Hence it is, that, in speaking of individuals, we are very little in danger of mistaking the object, or taking one individual for another.

Yet, as was before observed, our conception of them is always inadequate and lame. They are the creatures of God, and there are many things belonging to them which we know not, and which cannot be deduced by reasoning from what we know. They have a real essence, or constitution of nature, from which all their qualities flow: but this essence our faculties do not comprehend. They are therefore incapable of definition; for a definition ought to comprehend the whole nature or essence of the thing defined.

Thus, Westminster Bridge is an individual object; though I had never seen or heard of it before, if I am only made to conceive that it is a bridge from Westminster over the Thames, this conception, however imperfect, is true, and is sufficient to make me distinguish it, when it is mentioned, from every other object that exists. The architect may have any adequate conception of its structure, which is the work of man; but of the materials, which are the work of God, no man has an adequate conception; and, therefore, though the object may be described, it cannot be defined.

Universals are always expressed by general words; and all the words of language, excepting proper names, are general words; they are the signs of general conceptions, or of some circumstance relating to them. These general conceptions are formed for the purpose of language and reasoning; and the object from which they are taken, and to which they are intended to agree, is the conception which other men join to the same words; they may, therefore, be adequate, and perfectly agree with the thing conceived. This implies no more than that men who speak the same language may perfectly agree in the meaning of many general words.

Thus mathematicians have conceived what they call a plane triangle. They have defined it accurately; and, when I conceive it to be a plane surface, bounded by three right lines, I have both a true and adequate conception of it. There is nothing belonging to a plane triangle which is not comprehended in this conception of it, or deducible from it by just reasoning. This definition expresses the whole essence of the thing defined, as every just definition ought to do; but this essence is only what Mr Locke very properly calls a nominal essence; it is a general conception formed by the mind, and joined to a general word as its sign.

If all the general words of a language had a precise meaning, and were perfectly understood, as mathematical terms are, all verbal disputes would be at an end, and men would never seem to differ in opinion, but when they differ in reality; but this is far from being the case. The meaning of most general words is not learned, like that of mathematical terms, by an accurate definition, but by the experience we happen to have, by hearing them used in conversation. From such experience, we collect their meaning by a kind of induction; and, as this induction is, for the most part, lame and imperfect, it happens that different persons join different conceptions to the same general word; and, though we intend to give them the meaning which use, the arbiter of language, has put upon them, this is difficult to find, and apt to be mistaken, even by the candid and attentive. Hence, in innumerable disputes, men do not really differ in their judgments, but in the way of expressing them.

Our conceptions, therefore, appear to be of *three* kinds. They are either the conceptions of individual things, the creatures of God; or they are conceptions of the meaning of general words; or they are the creatures of our own imagination; and these different kinds have different properties, which we have endeavoured to describe. . . .

The last property I shall mention of this faculty, is that which essentially distinguishes it from every other power of the mind; and it is, that it is not employed solely about things which have existence. I can conceive a winged horse or a centaur, as easily and as distinctly as I can conceive a man whom I have seen. Nor does this distinct conception incline my judgment in the least to the belief that a winged horse or a centaur ever existed.

It is not so with the other operations of our minds. They are employed about real existences, and carry with them the belief of their objects. When I feel pain, I am compelled to believe that the pain that I feel has a real existence. When I perceive any external object, my belief of the real existence of the object is irresistible. When I distinctly remember any event, though that event may not now exist, I can have no doubt but it did exist. That consciousness which we have of the operations of our own minds, implies a belief of the real existence of those operations.

Thus we see, that the powers of sensation, of perception, of memory, and of consciousness, are all employed solely about objects that do exist, or have existed. But conception is often employed about objects that neither do, nor did, nor will exist. This is the very nature of this faculty, that its object, though distinctly conceived, may have no existence. Such an object we call a creature of imagination; but this creature never was created.

That we may not impose upon ourselves in this matter, we must distinguish between the act or operation of the mind, which we call conceiving an object, and the object which we conceive. When we conceive anything, there is a real act or operation of the mind. Of this we are conscious, and can have no doubt of its existence. But every such act must have an object; for he that conceives must conceive something. Suppose he conceives a centaur, he may have a distinct conception of this object, though no centaur ever existed.

I am afraid that, to those who are unacquainted with the doctrine of philosophers upon this subject, I shall appear in a very ridiculous light, for insisting upon a point so very evident as that men may barely conceive things that never existed. They will hardly believe that any man in his wits ever doubted it. Indeed, I know no truth more evident to the common sense and to the experience of mankind. But, if the authority of philosophy, ancient and modern, opposes it, as I think it does, I wish not to treat that authority so fastidiously as not to attend patiently to what may be said in support of it.

CHAPTER 2 / THEORIES CONCERNING CONCEPTION

The theory of ideas has been applied to the conception of objects, as well as to perception and memory. Perhaps it will be irksome to the reader, as it is to the writer, to return to that subject, after so much has been said upon it; but its application to the conception of objects, which could not properly have been introduced before, gives a more comprehensive view of it, and of the prejudices which have led philosophers so unanimously into it.

There are two prejudices which seem to me to have given rise to the theory of ideas in all the various forms in which it has appeared in the course of above two thousand years; and, though they have no support from the natural dictates of our faculties, or from attentive reflection upon their operations, they are prejudices which those who speculate upon this subject are very apt to be led into by analogy.

The *first* is—That, in all the operations of the understanding, there must be some immediate intercourse between the mind and its object, so that the one may act upon the other. The *second,* That, in all the operations of understanding, there must be an object of thought, which really exists while we think of it; or, as some philosophers have expressed it, that which is not cannot be intelligible.

Had philosophers perceived that these are prejudices grounded only upon analogical reasoning, we had never heard of ideas in the philosophical sense of that word.

The *first* of these principles has led philosophers to think that, as the external objects of sense are too remote to act upon the mind immediately, there must be some image or shadow of them that is present to the mind, and is the immediate object of perception. That there is such an immediate object of perception, distinct from the external object, has been very unanimously held by philosophers, though they have differed much about the name, the nature, and the origin of those immediate objects.

We have considered what has been said in the support of this principle, Essay II. chap. 14, to which the reader is referred, to prevent repetition.

I shall only add to what is there said, That there appears no shadow of reason why the mind must have an object immediately present to it in its intellectual operations, any more than in its affections and passions. Philosophers have not said that ideas are the immediate objects of love or resentment, of esteem or disapprobation. It is, I think, acknowledged, that persons and not ideas, are the immediate objects of those affections; persons, who are as far from being immediately present to the mind as other external objects, and, sometimes, persons who have now no existence, in this world at least, and who can neither act upon the mind, nor be acted upon by it.

The *second* principle, which I conceive to be likewise a prejudice of philosophers, grounded upon analogy, is now to be considered.

It contradicts directly what was laid down in the last article of the preceding chapter—to wit, that we may have a distinct conception of things which never existed. This is undoubtedly the common belief of those who have not been instructed in philosophy; and they will think it as ridiculous to defend it by reasoning, as to oppose it.

The philosopher says, Though there may be a remote object which does not exist, there must be an immediate object which really exists; for that which is not, cannot be an object of thought. The idea must be perceived by the mind, and, if it does not exist there, there can be no perception of it, no operation of the mind about it.

This principle deserves the more to be examined, because the other before mentioned depends upon it; for, although the last may be true, even if the first was false, yet, if the last be not true, neither can the first. If we can conceive objects which have no existence, it follows that there may be objects of thought which neither act upon the mind, nor are acted upon by it; because that which has no existence can neither act nor be acted upon.

It is by these principles that philosophers have been led to think that, in every act of memory and of conception, as well as of perception, there are two objects—the one, the immediate object, the idea, the species, the form; the other, the mediate or external object. The vulgar know only of one object, which, in perception, is something external that exists; in memory, something that did exist; and, in conception, may be something that never existed. But the immediate object of the philosophers, the idea, is said to exist, and to be perceived in all these operations.

These principles have not only led philosophers to split objects into two, where others can find but one, but likewise have led them to reduce the three operations now mentioned to one, making memory and conception, as well as perception, to be the perception of ideas. But nothing appears more evident to the vulgar, than that what is only remembered, or only conceived, is not perceived; and, to speak of the perceptions of memory, appears to them as absurd as to speak of the hearing of sight.

In a word, these two principles carry us into the whole philosophical theory of ideas, and furnish every argument that ever was used for their existence. If they are true, that system must be admitted with all its consequences. If they are only prejudices, grounded upon analogical reasoning, the whole system must fall to the ground with them. . . .

If the idea of a thing means only the thought of it, or the operation of the mind in thinking about it, which is the most common meaning of the word, to think without ideas, is to think without thought, which is undoubtedly a contradiction.

But an idea, according to the definition given of it by philosophers, is not thought, but an object of thought, which really exists and is perceived. Now, whether is it a contradiction to say, that a man may think of an object that does not exist?

I acknowledge that a man cannot perceive an object that does not exist; nor can he remember an object that did not exist; but there appears to me no contradiction to his conceiving an object that neither does nor ever did exist.

Let us take an example. I conceive a centaur. This conception is an operation of the mind, of which I am conscious, and to which I can attend. The sole object of it is a centaur, an animal which, I believe, never existed. I can see no contradiction in this.

The philosopher says, I cannot conceive a centaur without having an idea of it in my mind. I am at a loss to understand what he means. He surely does not mean that I cannot conceive it without conceiving it. This would make me no wiser. What then is this idea? Is it an animal, half horse and half man? No. Then I am certain it is not the thing I conceive. Perhaps he will say, that the idea is an image of the animal, and is the immediate object of my conception, and that the animal is the mediate or remote object.

To this I answer—*First,* I am certain there are not two objects of this conception, but one only; and that one is as immediate an object of my conception as any can be.

Secondly, This one object which I conceive, is not the image of an animal—it is an animal. I know what it is to conceive an image of an animal, and what it is to conceive an animal; and I can distinguish the one of these from the other without any danger of mistake. The thing I conceive is a body of a certain figure and colour, having life and spontaneous motion. The philosopher says, that the idea is an image of the animal; but that it has neither body, nor colour, nor life, nor spontaneous motion. This I am not able to comprehend.

Thirdly, I wish to know how this idea comes to be an object of my thought, when I cannot even conceive what it means; and, if I did conceive it, this would be no evidence of its existence, any more than my conception of a centaur is of its existence. Philosophers sometimes say that we perceive ideas, sometimes that we are conscious of them. I can have no doubt of the existence of anything which I either perceive or of which I am conscious; but I cannot find that I either perceive ideas or am conscious of them.

Perception and consciousness are very different operations,

and it is strange that philosophers have never determined by which of them ideas are discerned. This is as if a man should positively affirm that he perceived an object; but whether by his eyes, or his ears, or his touch, he could not say.

But may not a man who conceives a centaur say, that he has a distinct image of it in his mind? I think he may. And if he means by this way of speaking what the vulgar mean, who never heard of the philosophical theory of ideas, I find no fault with it. By a distinct image in the mind, the vulgar mean a distinct conception; and it is natural to call it so, on account of the analogy between an image of a thing and the conception of it. On account of this analogy, obvious to all mankind, this operation is called imagination, and an image in the mind is only a periphrasis for imagination. But to infer from this that there is really an image in the mind, distinct from the operation of conceiving the object, is to be misled by an analogical expression; as if, from the phrases of deliberating and balancing things in the mind, we should infer that there is really a balance existing in the mind for weighing motives and arguments.

The analogical words and phrases used in all languages to express conception, do, no doubt, facilitate their being taken in a literal sense. But, if we only attend carefully to what we are conscious of in this operation, we shall find no more reason to think that images do really exist in our minds, than that balances and other mechanical engines do.

We know of nothing that is in the mind but by consciousness, and we are conscious of nothing but various modes of thinking; such as understanding, willing, affection, passion, doing, suffering. If philosophers choose to give the name of an idea to any mode of thinking of which we are conscious, I have no objection to the name, but that it introduces a foreign word into our language without necessity, and a word that is very ambiguous, and apt to mislead. But, if they give that name to images in the mind, which are not thought, but only objects of thought, I can see no reason to think that there are such things in nature. If they be, their existence and their nature must be more evident than anything else, because we know nothing but by their means. I may add, that, if they be, we can know nothing besides them. For, from the existence of images, we can never, by any just reasoning, infer the existence of anything else, unless perhaps the existence of an intelligent Author of them. In this, Bishop Berkeley reasoned right. . . .

If now it should be asked, What is the idea of a circle? I answer, It is the conception of a circle. What is the immediate object of this conception? The immediate and the only object of it is a circle. But where is this circle? It is nowhere. If it was an individual, and had a real existence, it must have a place; but, being an universal, it has no existence, and therefore no place. Is it not in the mind of him that conceives it? The conception of it is in the mind, being an act of the mind; and in common language, a thing being in the mind, is a figurative expression, signifying that the thing is conceived or remembered.

It may be asked, Whether this conception is an image or resemblance of a circle? I answer, I have already accounted for its being, in a figurative sense, called the image of a circle in the mind. If the question is meant in the literal sense; we must observe, that the word *conception* has two meanings. Properly it signifies that operation of the mind which we have been endeavouring to explain; but sometimes it is put for the object of conception, or thing conceived.

Now, if the question be understood in the last of these senses, the object of this conception is not an image or resemblance of a circle; for it is a circle, and nothing can be an image of itself.

If the question be—Whether the operation of mind in conceiving a circle be an image or resemblance of a circle? I think it is not; and that no two things can be more perfectly unlike, than a species of thought and a species of figure. Nor is it more strange that conception should have no resemblance to the object conceived, than that desire should have no resemblance to the object desired, or resentment to the object of resentment.

I can likewise conceive an individual object that really exists, such as St Paul's Church in London. I have an idea of it; that is, I conceive it. The immediate object of this conception is four hundred miles distant; and I have no reason to think that it acts upon me, or that I act upon it; but I can think of it notwithstanding. I can think of the first year or the last year of the Julian period.

If, after all, it should be thought that images in the mind serve to account for this faculty of conceiving things more distant in time and place, and even things which do not exist, which otherwise would be altogether inconceivable; to this I answer, that accounts of things, grounded upon conjecture, have been the bane of true philosophy in all ages. Experience may satisfy us that it is an hundred times more probable that they are false than that they are true.

This account of the faculty of conception, by images in the mind or in the brain, will deserve the regard of those who have a true taste in philosophy, when it is proved by solid arguments—*First,* That there are images in the mind, or in the brain, of the things we conceive. *Secondly,* That there is a faculty in the mind of perceiving such images. *Thirdly,* That the perception of such images produces the conception of things most distant, and even of things that have no existence. And, *fourthly,* That the perception of individual images in the mind, or in the brain, gives us the conception of universals, which are the attributes of many individuals. Until this is done, the theory of images existing in the mind or in the brain, ought to be placed in the same category with the sensible species, *materia prima* of Aristotle, and the *vortices* of Des Cartes.

ESSAY FIVE   /   OF ABSTRACTION

CHAPTER 2   /   OF GENERAL CONCEPTIONS

As general words are so necessary in language, it is natural to conclude that there must be general conceptions, of which they are the signs.

Words are empty sounds when they do not signify the thoughts of the speaker; and it is only from their signification that they are denominated general. Every word that is spoken, considered merely as a sound, is an individual sound. And it can only be called a general word, because that which it signifies is general. Now, that which it signifies, is conceived by the mind both of the speaker and hearer, if the word have a distinct meaning, and be distinctly understood. It is, therefore, impossible that words can have a general signification, unless there be conceptions in the mind of the speaker and of the hearer, of things that are general. It is to such that I give the name of general conceptions; and it ought to be observed, that they take this denomination, not from the act of the mind in conceiving, which is an individual act, but from the object or thing conceived, which is general.

We are, therefore, here to consider whether we have such general conceptions, and how they are formed.

To begin with the conceptions expressed by general terms —that is, by such general words as may be the subject or the predicate of a proposition. They are either attributes of things, or they are *genera* or *species* of things.

It is evident, with respect to all the individuals we are acquainted with that we have a more clear and distinct conception of their attributes than of the subject to which those attributes belong.

Take, for instance, any individual body we have access to

know—what conception do we form of it? Every man may know this from consciousness. He will find that he conceives it as a thing that has length, breadth, and thickness, such a figure and such a colour; that it is hard, or soft, or fluid; that it has such qualities, and is fit for such purposes. If it is a vegetable, he may know where it grew, what is the form of its leaves, and flower, and seed. If an animal, what are its natural instincts, its manner of life, and of rearing its young. Of these attributes, belonging to the individual and numberless others, he may surely have a distinct conception; and he will find words in language by which he can clearly and distinctly express each of them.

If we consider, in like manner, the conception we form of any individual person of our acquaintance, we shall find it to be made up of various attributes, which we ascribe to him; such as, that he is the son of such a man, the brother of such another; that he has such an employment or office; has such a fortune; that he is tall or short, well or ill made, comely or ill favoured, young or old, married or unmarried; to this we may add his temper, his character, his abilities, and perhaps some anecdotes of his history.

Such is the conception we form of individual persons of our acquaintance. By such attributes we describe them to those who know them not; and by such attributes historians give us a conception of the personages of former times. Nor is it possible to do it in any other way.

All the distinct knowledge we have or can attain of any individual is the knowledge of its attributes; for we know not the essence of any individual. This seems to be beyond the reach of the human faculties.

Now, every attribute is what the ancients called an universal. It is, or may be, common to various individuals. There is no attribute belonging to any creature of God which may not belong to others; and, on this account, attributes, in all languages, are expressed by general words.

It appears, likewise, from every man's experience, that he may have as clear and distinct a conception of such attributes as we have named, and of innumerable others, as he can have of any individual to which they belong. Indeed, the attributes of individuals is all that we distinctly conceive about them. It is true, we conceive a subject to which the attributes belong; but of this subject, when its attributes are set aside, we have but an obscure and relative conception, whether it be body or mind. . . .

Enough, I think, has been said, to shew, not only that we may have clear and distinct conceptions of attributes, but that they are the only things, with regard to individuals, of which we have a clear and distinct conception.

The other class of general terms are those that signify the *genera* and *species* into which we divide and subdivide things. And, if we be able to form distinct conceptions of attributes, it cannot surely be denied that we may have distinct conceptions of *genera* and *species;* because they are only collections of attributes which we conceive to exist in a subject, and to which we give a general name. If the attributes comprehended under that general name be distinctly conceived, the thing meant by the name must be distinctly conceived. And the name may justly be attributed to every individual which has those attributes.

Thus, I conceive distinctly what it is to have wings, to be covered with feathers, to lay eggs. Suppose then that we give the name of *bird* to every animal that has these three attributes. Here undoubtedly my conception of a bird is as distinct as my notion of the attributes which are common to this species: and, if this be admitted to be the definition of a bird, there is nothing I conceive more distinctly. If I had never seen a bird, and can but be made to understand the definition, I can easily apply it to every individual of the species, without danger of mistake.

When things are divided and subdivided by men of science,

and names given to the *genera* and *species*, those names are defined. Thus, the genera and species of plants, and of other natural bodies, are accurately defined by the writers in the various branches of natural history; so that, to all future generations, the definition will convey a distinct notion of the genus or species defined.

There are, without doubt, many words signifying genera and species of things, which have a meaning somewhat vague and indistinct; so that those who speak the same language do not always use them in the same sense. But, if we attend to the cause of this indistinctness, we shall find that it is not owing to their being general terms, but to this, that there is no definition of them that has authority. Their meaning, therefore, has not been learned by a definition, but by a kind of induction, by observing to what individuals they are applied by those who understand the language. We learn by habit to use them as we see others do, even when we have not a precise meaning annexed to them. A man may know that to certain individuals they may be applied with propriety; but whether they can be applied to certain other individuals, he may be uncertain, either from want of good authorities, or from having contrary authorities, which leave him in doubt.

Thus, a man may know that, when he applies the name of beast to a lion or a tiger, and the name of bird to an eagle or a turkey, he speaks properly. But whether a bat be a bird or a beast, he may be uncertain. If there was any accurate definition of a beast and of a bird, that was of sufficient authority, he could be at no loss.

It is said to have been sometimes a matter of dispute, with regard to a monstrous birth of a woman, whether it was a man or not. Although this be, in reality, a question about the meaning of a word, it may be of importance, on account of the privileges which laws have annexed to the human character. To make such laws perfectly precise, the definition of a man would be necessary, which I believe legislators have seldom or never thought fit to give. It is, indeed, very difficult to fix a definition of so common a word; and the cases wherein it would be of any use so rarely occur, that perhaps it may be better, when they do occur, to leave them to the determination of a judge or of a jury, than to give a definition, which might be attended with unforeseen consequences.

A genus or species, being a collection of attributes conceived to exist in one subject, a definition is the only way to prevent any addition or diminution of its ingredients in the conception of different persons; and when there is no definition that can be appealed to as a standard, the name will hardly retain the most perfect precision in its signification.

From what has been said, I conceive it is evident that the words which signify genera and species of things have often as precise and definite a signification as any words whatsoever; and that, when it is otherwise, their want of precision is not owing to their being general words, but to other causes.

Having shewn that we may have a perfectly clear and distinct conception of the meaning of general terms, we may, I think, take it for granted, that the same may be said of other general words, such as prepositions, conjunctions, articles. My design at present being only to shew that we have general conceptions no less clear and distinct than those of individuals, it is sufficient for this purpose, if this appears with regard to the conceptions expressed by general terms. To conceive the meaning of a general word, and to conceive that which it signifies, is the same thing. We conceive distinctly the meaning of general terms, therefore we conceive distinctly that which they signify. But such terms do not signify any individual, but what is common to many individuals; therefore, we have a distinct conception of things common to many individuals—that is, we have distinct general conceptions.

We must here beware of the ambiguity of the word *conception,* which sometimes signifies the act of the mind in conceiving, sometimes the thing conceived, which is the object of that act. If the word be taken in the first sense, I acknowledge that every act of the mind is an individual act; the universality, therefore, is not in the act of the mind, but in the object or thing conceived. The thing conceived is an attribute common to many subjects, or it is a genus or species common to many individuals.

Suppose I conceive a triangle—that is, a plain figure, terminated by three right lines. He that understands this definition distinctly, has a distinct conception of a triangle. But a triangle is not an individual; it is a species. The act of my understanding in conceiving it is an individual act, and has a real existence; but the thing conceived is general, and cannot exist without other attributes, which are not included in the definition.

Every triangle that really exists must have a certain length of sides and measure of angles; it must have place and time. But the definition of a triangle includes neither existence nor any of those attributes; and, therefore, they are not included in the conception of a triangle, which cannot be accurate if it comprehend more than the definition.

Thus, I think, it appears to be evident, that we have general conceptions that are clear and distinct, both of attributes of things, and of genera and species of things.

CHAPTER 3 / OF GENERAL CONCEPTIONS
FORMED BY ANALYSING OBJECTS

We are next to consider the operations of the understanding, by which we are enabled to form general conceptions.

These appear to me to be three:—*First,* The resolving or analysing a subject into its known attributes, and giving a name to each attribute, which name shall signify that attribute, and nothing more.

Secondly, The observing one or more such attributes to be common to many subjects. The first is by philosophers called *abstraction;* the second may be called *generalising;* but both are commonly included under the name of *abstraction.*

It is difficult to say which of them goes first, or whether they are not so closely connected that neither can claim the precedence. For, on the one hand, to perceive an agreement between two or more objects in the same attribute, seems to require nothing more than to compare them together. A savage, upon seeing snow and chalk, would find no difficulty in perceiving that they have the same colour. Yet, on the other hand, it seems impossible that he should observe this agreement without abstraction—that is, distinguishing in his conception the colour, wherein those two objects agree, from the other qualities wherein they disagree.

It seems, therefore, that we cannot generalise without some degree of abstraction; but I apprehend we may abstract without generalising. For what hinders me from attending to the whiteness of the paper before me, without applying that colour to any other object. The whiteness of this individual object is an abstract conception, but not a general one, while applied to one individual only. These two operations, however, are subservient to each other; for the more attributes we observe and distinguish in any one individual, the more agreements we shall discover between it and other individuals.

A *third* operation of the understanding, by which we form abstract conceptions, is the combining into one whole a certain number of those attributes of which we have formed abstract notions, and giving a name to that combination. It is thus we form abstract notions of the genera and species of things. These three operations we shall consider in order.

With regard to abstraction, strictly so called, I can perceive nothing in it that is difficult either to be understood or practised. What can be more easy than to distinguish the different attributes which we know to belong to a subject? In a man, for instance, to distinguish his size, his complexion, his age, his fortune, his birth, his profession, and twenty other things that belong to him. To think and speak of these things with understanding, is surely within the reach of every man endowed with the human faculties. . . .

It ought likewise to be observed, that attributes may, with perfect ease, be distinguished and disjoined in our conception, which cannot be actually separated in the subject. Thus, in a body, I can distinguish its solidity from its extension, and its weight from both. In extension I can distinguish length, breadth, and thickness; yet none of these can be separated from the body, or from one another. There may be attributes belonging to a subject, and inseparable from it, of which we have no knowledge, and consequently no conception; but this does not hinder our conceiving distinctly those of its attributes which we know.

Thus, all the properties of a circle are inseparable from the nature of a circle, and may be demonstrated from its definition; yet a man may have a perfectly distinct notion of a circle, who knows very few of those properties of it which mathematicians have demonstrated; and a circle probably has many properties which no mathematician ever dreamed of.

It is therefore certain that attributes, which in their nature are absolutely inseparable from their subject and from one another, may be disjoined in our conception; one cannot exist without the other, but one can be conceived without the other.

Having considered abstraction, strictly so called, let us next consider the operation of generalising, which is nothing but the observing one or more attributes to be common to many subjects.

If any man can doubt whether there be attributes that are really common to many individuals, let him consider whether there be not many men that are above six feet high, and many below it; whether there be not many men that are rich, and many more that are poor; whether there be not many that were born in Britain, and many that were born in France. To multiply instances of this kind, would be to affront the reader's understanding. It is certain, therefore, that there are innumerable attributes that are really common to many individuals; and if this be what the schoolmen called *universale a parte rei*, we may affirm with certainty that there are such universals.

There are some attributes expressed by general words, of which this may seem more doubtful. Such are the qualities which are inherent in their several subjects. It may be said that every subject hath its own qualities, and that which is the quality of one subject cannot be the quality of another subject. Thus the whiteness of the sheet of paper upon which I write, cannot be the whiteness of another sheet, though both are called white. The weight of one guinea is not the weight of another guinea, though both are said to have the same weight.

To this I answer, that the whiteness of this sheet is one thing, whiteness is another; the conceptions signified by these two forms of speech are as different as the expressions. The first signifies an individual quality really existing, and is not a general conception, though it be an abstract one: the second signifies a general conception, which implies no existence, but may be predicated of everything that is white, and in the same sense. On this account, if one should say that the whiteness of this sheet is the whiteness of another sheet, every man perceives this to be absurd; but when he says both sheets are white, this is true and perfectly understood. The conception of whiteness implies no existence; it would remain the same though everything in the universe that is white were annihilated.

It appears, therefore, that the general names of qualities, as well as of other attributes, are applicable to many individuals in the same sense, which cannot be if there be not general conceptions signified by such names. . . .

CHAPTER 6 / OPINIONS OF PHILOSOPHERS ABOUT UNIVERSALS

. . . . Mr Locke's doctrine about abstraction has been combated by two very powerful antagonists, Bishop Berkeley and Mr Hume, who have taken up the opinion of the Nominalists. The former thinks, "That the opinion that the mind hath a power of forming abstract ideas or notions of things, has had a chief part in rendering speculation intricate and perplexed, and has occasioned innumerable errors and difficulties in almost all parts of knowledge." That "abstract ideas are like a fine and subtile net, which has miserably perplexed and entangled the minds of men, with this peculiar circumstance, that by how much the finer and more curious was the wit of any man, by so much the deeper was he like to be ensnared, and faster held therein." That, "among all the false principles that have obtained in the world, there is none hath a more wide influence over the thoughts of speculative men, than this of abstract general ideas."

The good bishop, therefore, in twenty four pages of the introduction to his "Principles of Human Knowledge," encounters this principle with a zeal proportioned to his apprehension of its malignant and extensive influence.

That the zeal of the sceptical philosopher against abstract ideas was almost equal to that of the bishop, appears from his words, "Treatise of Human Nature," Book I. part i. § 7:—"A very material question has been started concerning abstract or general ideas—whether they be general or particular, in the mind's conception of them. A great philosopher" (he means Dr Berkeley) "has disputed the received opinion in this particular, and has asserted that all general ideas are nothing but particular ones annexed to a certain term, which gives them a more extensive signification, and makes them recall, upon occasion, other individuals which are similar to them. As I look upon this to be one of the greatest and most valuable discoveries that have been made of late years in the republic of letters, I shall here endeavour to confirm it by some arguments, which, I hope, will put it beyond all doubt and controversy."

I shall make an end of this subject, with some reflections on what has been said upon it by these two eminent philosophers.

1. *First,* I apprehend that we cannot, with propriety, be said to have abstract and general ideas, either in the popular or in the philosophical sense of that word. In the popular sense, an idea is a thought; it is the act of the mind in thinking, or in conceiving any object. This act of the mind is always an individual act, and, therefore, there can be no general idea in this sense. In the philosophical sense, an idea is an image in the mind, or in the brain, which, in Mr Locke's system, is the immediate object of thought; in the system of Berkeley and Hume, the only object of thought. I believe there are no ideas of this kind, and, therefore, no abstract general ideas. Indeed, if there were really such images in the mind or in the brain, they could not be general, because everything that really exists is an individual. Universals are neither acts of the mind, nor images in the mind.

As, therefore, there are no general ideas in either of the senses in which the word idea is used by the moderns, Berkeley and Hume have, in this question, an advantage over Mr Locke; and their arguments against him are good *ad hominem.* They saw farther than he did into the just consequences of the hypothesis concerning ideas, which was common to them and to him; and they reasoned justly from this hypothesis when they concluded from it, that there is neither a material world, nor any such power in the human mind as that of abstraction.

A triangle, in general, or any other universal, might be called an idea by a Platonist; but, in the style of modern philosophy, it is not an idea, nor do we ever ascribe to ideas the properties of triangles. It is never said of any idea, that it has three sides and three angles. We do not speak of equilateral, isosceles, or scalene ideas, nor of right-angled, acute-angled, or obtuse-angled ideas. And, if these attributes do not belong to ideas, it follows, necessarily, that a triangle is not an idea. The same reasoning may be applied to every other universal.

Ideas are said to have a real existence in the mind, at least while we think of them; but universals have no real existence. When we ascribe existence to them, it is not an existence in time or place, but existence in some individual subject; and this existence means no more but that they are truly attributes of such a subject. Their existence is nothing but predicability, or the capacity of being attributed to a subject. The name of predicables, which was given them in ancient philosophy, is that which most properly expresses their nature.

2. I think it must be granted, in the *second* place, that universals cannot be the objects of imagination, when we take that word in its strict and proper sense. "I find," says Berkeley, "I have a faculty of imagining or representing to myself the ideas of those particular things I have perceived, and of variously compounding and dividing them. I can imagine a man with two heads, or the upper parts of a man joined to the body of a horse. I can imagine the hand, the eye, the nose, each by itself, abstracted or separated from the rest of the body. But then, whatever hand or eye I imagine, it must have some particular shape or colour. Likewise, the idea of a man that I frame to myself must be either of a white, or a black, or a tawny; a straight or a crooked; a tall, or a low, or a middle-sized man."

I believe every man will find in himself what this ingenious author found—that he cannot imagine a man without colour, or stature, or shape.

Imagination, as we before observed, properly signifies a conception of the appearance an object would make to the eye if actually seen. An universal is not an object of any external sense, and therefore cannot be imagined; but it may be distinctly conceived. When Mr Pope says, "The proper study of mankind is man," I conceive his meaning distinctly, though I neither imagine a black or a white, a crooked or a straight man. The distinction between conception and imagination is real, though it be too often overlooked, and the words taken to be synonymous. I can conceive a thing that is impossible, but I cannot distinctly imagine a thing that is impossible. I can conceive a proposition or a demonstration, but I cannot imagine either. I can conceive understanding and will, virtue and vice, and other attributes of mind, but I cannot imagine them. In like manner, I can distinctly conceive universals, but I cannot imagine them.

As to the manner how we conceive universals, I confess my ignorance. I know not how I hear, or see, or remember, and as little do I know how I conceive things that have no existence. In all our original faculties, the fabric and manner of operation is, I apprehend, beyond our comprehension, and perhaps is perfectly understood by him only who made them.

But we ought not to deny a fact of which we are conscious, though we know not how it is brought about. And I think we may be certain that universals are not conceived by means of images of them in our minds, because there can be no image of an universal.

3. It seems to me, that on this question Mr Locke and his two antagonists have divided the truth between them. He saw very clearly, that the power of forming abstract and general conceptions is one of the most distinguishing powers of the human mind, and puts a specific difference between man and the brute creation. But he did not see that this power is perfectly irreconcilable to his doctrine concerning ideas.

His opponents saw this inconsistency; but, instead of rejecting the hypothesis of ideas, they explain away the power of abstraction, and leave no specific distinction between the human understanding and that of brutes.

4. Berkeley[9], in his reasoning against abstract general ideas, seems unwillingly or unwarily to grant all that is necessary to

support abstract and general conceptions.

"A man," he says, "may consider a figure merely as triangular, without attending to the particular qualities of the angles, or relations of the sides. So far he may abstract. But this will never prove that he can frame an abstract general inconsistent idea of a triangle."

If a man may consider a figure merely as triangular, he must have some conception of this object of his consideration; for no man can consider a thing which he does not conceive. He has a conception, therefore, of a triangular figure, merely as such. I know no more that is meant by an abstract general conception of a triangle.

He that considers a figure merely as triangular, must understand what is meant by the word triangular. If, to the conception he joins to this word, he adds any particular quality of angles or relation of sides, he misunderstands it, and does not consider the figure merely as triangular. Whence, I think, it is evident, that he who considers a figure merely as triangular must have the conception of a triangle, abstracting from any quality of angles or relation of sides.

The Bishop, in like manner, grants, "That we may consider Peter so far forth as man, or so far forth as animal, without framing the forementioned abstract idea, in as much as all that is perceived is not considered." It may here be observed, that he who considers Peter so far forth as man, or so far forth as animal, must conceive the meaning of those abstract general words *man* and *animal*, and he who conceives the meaning of them has an abstract general conception.

From these concessions, one would be apt to conclude that the Bishop thinks that we can abstract, but that we cannot frame abstract ideas; and in this I should agree with him. But I cannot reconcile his concessions with the general principle he lays down before. "To be plain," says he, "I deny that I can abstract one from another, or conceive separately those qualities which it is impossible should exist so separated." This appears to me inconsistent with the concessions above mentioned, and inconsistent with experience.

If we can consider a figure merely as triangular, without attending to the particular quality of the angles or relation of the sides, this, I think, is conceiving separately things which cannot exist so separated: for surely a triangle cannot exist without a particular quality of angles and relation of sides. And it is well known, from experience, that a man may have a distinct conception of a triangle, without having any conception or knowledge of many of the properties without which a triangle cannot exist.

Let us next consider the Bishop's notion of generalising.[10] He does not absolutely deny that there are general ideas, but only that there are abstract general ideas. "An idea," he says, "which, considered in itself, is particular, becomes general, by being made to represent or stand for all other particular ideas of the same sort. To make this plain by an example: Suppose a geometrician is demonstrating the method of cutting a line in two equal parts. He draws, for instance, a black line, of an inch in length. This, which is in itself a particular line, is, nevertheless, with regard to its signification, general; since, as it is there used, it represents all particular lines whatsoever; so that what is demonstrated of it, is demonstrated of all lines, or, in other words, of a line in general. And as that particular line becomes general by being made a sign, so the name *line*, which, taken absolutely, is particular, by being a sign, is made general."

Here I observe, that when a particular idea is made a sign to represent and stand for all of a sort, this supposes a distinction of things into sorts or species. To be of a sort implies having those attributes which characterise the sort, and are common to all the individuals that belong to it. There cannot, therefore, be a sort without general attributes, nor can there be any conception of a sort without a conception of those general attributes which distinguish it. The conception of a sort, therefore, is an abstract general conception.

The particular idea cannot surely be made a sign of a thing of which we have no conception. I do not say that you must have an idea of the sort, but surely you ought to understand or conceive what it means, when you make a particular idea a representative of it; otherwise your particular idea represents, you know not what.

When I demonstrate any general property of a triangle, such as, that the three angles are equal to two right angles, I must understand or conceive distinctly what is common to all triangles. I must distinguish the common attributes of all triangles from those wherein particular triangles may differ. And, if I conceive distinctly what is common to all triangles, without confounding it with what is not so, this is to form a general conception of a triangle. And without this, it is impossible to know that the demonstration extends to all triangles.

The Bishop takes particular notice of this argument, and makes this answer to it:—"Though the idea I have in view, whilst I make the demonstration, be, for instance, that of an isosceles rectangular triangle, whose sides are of a determinate length, I may nevertheless be certain that it extends to all other rectilinear triangles, of what sort or bigness soever; and that because neither the right angle, nor the equality or determinate length of the sides, are at all concerned in the demonstration."

But, if he do not, in the idea he has in view, clearly distinguish what is common to all triangles from what is not, it would be impossible to discern whether something that is not common be concerned in the demonstration or not. In order, therefore, to perceive that the demonstration extends to all triangles, it is necessary to have a distinct conception of what is common to all triangles, excluding from that conception all that is not common. And this is all I understand by an abstract general conception of a triangle.

Berkeley catches an advantage to his side of the question,

from what Mr Locke expresses (too strongly indeed) of the difficulty of framing abstract general ideas, and the pains and skill necessary for that purpose. From which the Bishop infers, that a thing so difficult cannot be necessary for communication by language, which is so easy and familiar to all sorts of men.

There may be some abstract and general conceptions that are difficult, or even beyond the reach of persons of weak understanding; but there are innumerable which are not beyond the reach of children. It is impossible to learn language without acquiring general conceptions; for there cannot be a single sentence without them. I believe the forming these, and being able to articulate the sounds of language, make up the whole difficulty that children find in learning language at first.

But this difficulty, we see, they are able to overcome so early as not to remember the pains it cost them. They have the strongest inducement to exert all their labour and skill, in order to understand and to be understood; and they no doubt do so.

The labour of forming abstract notions, is the labour of learning to speak, and to understand what is spoken. As the words of every language, excepting a few proper names, are general words, the minds of children are furnished with general conceptions, in proportion as they learn the meaning of general words. I believe most men have hardly any general notions but those which are expressed by the general words they hear and use in conversation. The meaning of some of these is learned by a definition, which at once conveys a distinct and accurate general conception. The meaning of other general words we collect, by a kind of induction, from the way in which we see them used on various occasions by those who understand the language. Of these our conception is often less distinct, and in different persons is perhaps not perfectly the same.

"Is it not a hard thing," says the Bishop, "that a couple of children cannot prate together of their sugar-plumbs and rattles, and the rest of their little trinkets, till they have first tacked together numberless inconsistencies, and so formed in their minds abstract general ideas, and annexed them to every common name they make use of?"

However hard a thing it may be, it is an evident truth, that a couple of children, even about their sugar-plumbs and their rattles, cannot prate so as to understand and be understood, until they have learned to conceive the meaning of many general words—and this, I think, is to have general conceptions. . . .

ESSAY SIX / OF JUDGMENT

CHAPTER 1 / OF JUDGMENT IN GENERAL

Judging is an operation of the mind so familiar to every man who hath understanding, and its name is so common and so well understood, that it needs no definition.

As it is impossible by a definition to give a notion of colour to a man who never saw colours; so it is impossible by any definition to give a distinct notion of judgment to a man who has not often judged, and who is not capable of reflecting attentively upon this act of his mind. The best use of a definition is to prompt him to that reflection; and without it the best definition will be apt to mislead him.

The definition commonly given of judgment, by the more ancient writers in logic, was, that it is *an act of the mind, whereby one thing is affirmed or denied of another.* I believe this is as good a definition of it as can be given. Why I prefer it to some later definitions, will afterwards appear. Without pretending to give any other, I shall make two remarks upon it, and then offer some general observations on this subject.

1. It is true that it is by affirmation or denial that we express our judgments; but there may be judgment which is not expressed. It is a solitary act of the mind, and the expression of it by affirmation or denial is not at all essential to it. It may be tacit, and not expressed. Nay, it is well known that men may judge contrary to what they affirm or deny; the definition therefore must be understood of mental affirmation or denial, which indeed is only another name for judgment.

2. Affirmation and denial is very often the expression of testimony, which is a different act of the mind, and ought to be distinguished from judgment.

A judge asks of a witness what he knows of such a matter to which he was an eye or ear-witness. He answers, by affirming or denying something. But his answer does not express his judgment; it is his testimony. Again, I ask a man his opinion in a matter of science or of criticism. His answer is not testimony; it is the expression of his judgment.

Testimony is a social act, and it is essential to it to be expressed by words or signs. A tacit testimony is a contradiction: but there is no contradiction in a tacit judgment; it is complete without being expressed.

In testimony a man pledges his veracity for what he affirms; so that a false testimony is a lie: but a wrong judgment is not a lie; it is only an error.

I believe, in all languages, testimony and judgment are expressed by the same form of speech. A proposition affirmative or negative, with a verb in what is called the indicative mood, expresses both. To distinguish them by the form of speech, it would be necessary that verbs should have two indicative moods, one for testimony and another to express judgment. I know not that this is found in any language. And the reason is—not surely that the vulgar cannot distinguish the two, for every man knows the difference between a lie and an error of judgment—but that, from the matter and circumstances, we can easily see whether a man intends to give his testimony, or barely to express his judgment.

Although men must have judged in many cases before tribunals of justice were erected, yet it is very probable that there were tribunals before men began to speculate about judgment, and that the word may be borrowed from the practice of tribunals. As a judge, after taking the proper evidence, passes sentence in a cause, and that sentence is called his judgment, so the mind, with regard to whatever is true or false, passes sentence, or determines according to the evidence that appears. Some kinds of evidence leave no room for doubt. Sentence is passed immediately, without seeking or hearing any contrary evidence, because the thing is certain and notorious. In other cases, there is room for weighing evidence on both sides, before sentence is passed. The analogy between a tribunal of justice, and this inward tribunal of the mind, is too obvious to escape the notice of any man who ever appeared before a judge. And it is probable that the word *judgment*, as well as many other words we use in speaking of this operation of mind, are grounded on this analogy.

Having premised these things, that it may be clearly understood what I mean by judgment, I proceed to make some general observations concerning it.

First, Judgment is an act of the mind, specifically different from simple apprehension, or the bare conception of a thing. It would be unnecessary to observe this, if some philosophers had not been led by their theories to a contrary opinion.

Although there can be no judgment without a conception of the things about which we judge, yet conception may be without any judgment. Judgment can expressed by a proposition only, and a proposition is a complete sentence; but simple apprehension may be expressed by a word or words, which make no complete sentence. When simple apprehension is employed about a proposition, every man knows that it is one thing to apprehend a proposition—that is, to conceive what it means—but it is quite another thing to judge it to be true or false.

It is self-evident that every judgment must be either true or false, but simple apprehension, or conception, can neither be true nor false, as was shewn before.

One judgment may be contradictory to another; and it is impossible for a man to have two judgments at the same time, which he perceives to be contradictory. But contradictory propositions may be conceived at the same time without any difficulty. That the sun is greater than the earth, and that the sun is not greater than the earth, are contradictory propositions. He that apprehends the meaning of one, apprehends the meaning of both. But it is impossible for him to judge both to be true at the same time. He knows that, if the one is true, the other must be false. For these reasons, I hold it to be certain that judgment and simple apprehension are acts of the mind specifically different. . . .

I add in general, that, without some degree of judgment, we can form no accurate and distinct notions of things; so that one province of judgment is, to aid us in forming clear and distinct conceptions of things, which are the only fit materials for reasoning.

This will probably appear to be a paradox to philosophers, who have always considered the formation of ideas of every kind as belonging to simple apprehension; and that the sole province of judgment is to put them together in affirmation or negative propositions; and therefore it requires some confirmation.

First, I think it necessarily follows, from what has been already said in this observation. For if, without some degree of judgment, a man can neither distinguish, nor divide, nor define, nor form any general notion, simple or complex, he surely, without some degree of judgment, cannot have in his mind the materials necessary to reasoning.

There cannot be any proposition in language which does not involve some general conception. The proposition, *that I exist*, which Des Cartes thought the first of all truths, and the foundation of all knowledge, cannot be conceived without the conception of existence, one of the most abstract general conceptions. A man cannot believe his own existence, or the existence of anything he sees or remembers, until he has so much judgment as to distinguish things that really exist from things which are only conceived. He sees a man six feet high; he conceives a man sixty feet high: he judges the first object to exist, because he sees it; the second he does not judge to exist, because he only conceives it. Now, I would ask, Whether he can attribute existence to the first object, and not to the second, without knowing what existence means? It is impossible.

How early the notion of existence enters into the mind, I cannot determine; but it must certainly be in the mind as soon as we can affirm of anything, with understanding, that it exists.

In every other proposition, the predicate, at least, must be a general notion—a predicable and an universal being one and the same. Besides this, every proposition either affirms or denies. And no man can have a distinct conception of a proposition, who does not understand distinctly the meaning of affirming or denying. But these are very general conceptions, and, as was before observed, are derived from judgment, as their source and origin.

I am sensible that a strong objection may be made to this reasoning, and that it may seem to lead to an absurdity or a contradiction. It may be said, that every judgment is a mental affirmation or negation. If, therefore, some previous exercise of judgment be necessary to understand what is meant by affirmation or negation, the exercise of judgment must go before any judgment which is absurd.

In like manner, every judgment may be expressed by a proposition, and a proposition must be conceived before we can judge of it. If, therefore, we cannot conceive the meaning of a proposition without a previous exercise of judgment, it follows that judgment must be previous to the conception of any proposition, and at the same time the conception of a proposition must be previous to all judgment, which is a contradiction.

The reader may please to observe, that I have limited what I have said to distinct conception, and some degree of judgment; and it is by this means I hope to avoid this labyrinth of absurdity and contradiction. The faculties of conception and judgment have an infancy and a maturity as man has. What I have said is limited to their mature state. I believe in their infant state they are very weak and indistinct; and that, by imperceptible degrees, they grow to maturity, each giving aid to the other, and receiving aid from it. But which of them first began this friendly intercourse, is beyond my ability to determine. It is like the question concerning the bird and the egg. . . .

The necessity of some degree of judgment in forming accurate and distinct notions of things will farther appear, if we consider attentively what notions we can form, without any aid of judgment, of the objects of sense, of the operations of our own minds, or of the relations of things.

To begin with the objects of sense. It is acknowledged, on all hands, that the first notions we have of sensible objects are got by the external senses only, and probably before judgment is brought forth; but these first notions are neither simple, nor are they accurate and distinct: they are gross and indistinct, and, like the *chaos*, a *rudis indigestaque moles*. Before we can have any distinct notion of this mass, it must be analysed; the heterogeneous parts must be separated in our conception, and the simple elements, which before lay hid in the common mass, must first be distinguished, and then put together into one whole.

In this way it is that we form distinct notions even of the

objects of sense; but this process of analysis and composition, by habit, becomes so easy, and is performed so readily, that we are apt to overlook it, and to impute the distinct notion we have formed of the object to the senses alone; and this we are the more prone to do because, when once we have distinguished the sensible qualities of the object from one another, the sense gives testimony to each of them.

You perceive, for instance, an object white, round, and a foot in diameter. I grant that you perceive all these attributes of the object by sense; but, if you had not been able to distinguish the colour from the figure, and both from the magnitude, your senses would only have given you one complex and confused notion of all these mingled together.

A man who is able to say with understanding, or to determine in his own mind, that this object is white, must have distinguished whiteness from other attributes. If he has not made this distinction, he does not understand what he says. . . .

CHAPTER 4 / OF FIRST PRINCIPLES IN GENERAL

. . . . Nature hath not left us destitute of means whereby the candid and honest part of mankind may be brought to unanimity when they happen to differ about first principles.

When men differ about things that are taken to be first principles or self-evident truths, reasoning seems to be at an end. Each party appeals to common sense. When one man's common sense gives one determination, another man's a contrary determination, there seems to be no remedy but to leave every man to enjoy his own opinion. This is a common observation, and, I believe, a just one, if it be rightly understood.

It is in vain to reason with a man who denies the first principles on which the reasoning is grounded. Thus, it would be in vain to attempt the proof of a proposition in Euclid to a man who denies the axioms. Indeed, we ought never to reason with men who deny first principles from obstinacy and unwillingness to yield to reason.

But is it not possible, that men who really love truth, and are open to conviction, may differ about first principles?

I think it is possible, and that it cannot, without great want of charity, be denied to be possible.

When this happens, every man who believes that there is a real distinction between truth and error, and that the faculties which God has given us are not in their nature fallacious, must be convinced that there is a defect or a perversion of judgment on the one side or the other.

A man of candour and humility will, in such a case, very naturally suspect his own judgment, so far as to be desirous to enter into a serious examination, even of what he has long held as a first principle. He will think it not impossible, that, although his heart be upright, his judgment may have been perverted, by education, by authority, by party zeal, or by some other of the common causes of error, from the influence of which neither parts nor integrity exempt the human understanding.

In such a state of mind, so amiable, and so becoming every good man, has Nature left him destitute of any rational means by which he may be enabled, either to correct his judgment if it be wrong, or to confirm it if it be right?

I hope it is not so. I hope that, by the means which nature has furnished, controversies about first principles may be brought to an issue, and that the real lovers of truth may come to unanimity with regard to them.

It is true that, in other controversies, the process by which the truth of a proposition is discovered, or its falsehood detected, is, by shewing its necessary connection with first principles, or its repugnancy to them. It is true, likewise, that, when the controversy is, whether a preposition be itself a first principle, this process cannot be applied. The truth, therefore, in controversies of this kind, labours under a peculiar disadvantage. But it has advantages of another kind to compensate this. 1. For, in the *first* place, in such controversies, every man is a competent judge; and therefore it is difficult to impose upon mankind.

To judge of first principles, requires no more than a sound mind free from prejudice, and a distinct conception of the question. The learned and the unlearned, the philosopher and the day-labourer, are upon a level, and will pass the same judgment, when they are not misled by some bias, or taught to renounce their understanding from some mistaken religious principle.

In matters beyond the reach of common understanding, the many are led by the few, and willingly yield to their authority. But, in matters of common sense, the few must yield to the many, when local and temporary prejudices are removed. No man is now moved by the subtle arguments of Zeno against motion, though, perhaps, he knows not how to answer them

2. *Secondly*, We may observe that opinions which contradict first principles, are distinguished, from other errors, by this: —That they are not only false but absurd; and, to discountenance absurdity, Nature hath given us a particular emotion— to wit, that of ridicule—which seems intended for this very purpose of putting out of countenance what is absurd, either in opinion or practice.

This weapon, when properly applied, cuts with as keen an edge as argument. Nature hath furnished us with the first to expose absurdity; as with the last to refute error. Both are well fitted for their several offices, and are equally friendly to truth when properly used.

Both may be abused to serve the cause of error; but the same degree of judgment which serves to detect the abuse of argument in false reasoning, serves to detect the abuse of ridicule when it is wrong directed. . . .

But it must be acknowledged that the emotion of ridicule,

even when most natural, may be stifled by an emotion of a contrary nature, and cannot operate till that is removed.

Thus, if the notion of sanctity is annexed to an object, it is no longer a laughable matter; and this visor must be pulled off before it appears ridiculous. Hence we see, that notions which appear most ridiculous to all who consider them coolly and indifferently, have no such appearance to those who never thought of them but under the impression of religious awe and dread.

Even where religion is not concerned, the novelty of an opinion to those who are too fond of novelties; the gravity and solemnity with which it is introduced; the opinion we have entertained of the author; its apparent connection with principles already embraced, or subserviency to interests which we have at heart; and, above all, its being fixed in our minds at that time of life when we receive implicitly what we are taught— may cover its absurdity, and fascinate the understanding for a time.

But, if ever we are able to view it naked, and stripped of those adventitious circumstances from which it borrowed its importance and authority, the natural emotion of ridicule will exert its force. An absurdity can be entertained by men of sense no longer than it wears a mask. When any man is found who has the skill or the boldness to pull off the mask, it can no longer bear the light; it slinks into dark corners for a while, and then is no more heard of, but as an object of ridicule.

Thus I conceive, that first principles, which are really the dictates of common sense, and directly opposed to absurdities in opinion, will always, from the constitution of human nature, support themselves, and gain rather than lose ground among mankind.

3. *Thirdly,* It may be observed, that, although it is contrary to the nature of first principles to admit of direct or *apodictical* proof; yet there are certain ways of reasoning even about them, by which those that are just and solid may be confirmed,

and those that are false may be detected. It may here be proper to mention some of the topics from which we may reason in matters of this kind.

First, It is a good argument *ad hominem,* if it can be shewn that a first principle which a man rejects, stands upon the same footing with others which he admits: for, when this is the case, he must be guilty of an inconsistency who holds the one and rejects the other.

Thus the faculties of consciousness, of memory, of external sense, and of reason, are all equally the gifts of nature. No good reason can be assigned for receiving the testimony of one of them, which is not of equal force with regard to the others. The greatest sceptics admit the testimony of consciousness, and allow that what it testifies is to be held as a first principle. If, therefore, they reject the immediate testimony of sense or of memory, they are guilty of an inconsistency.

Secondly, A first principle may admit of a proof *ad absurdum.*

In this kind of proof, which is very common in mathematics, we suppose the contradictory proposition to be true. We trace the consequences of that supposition in a train of reasoning; and, if we find any of its necessary consequences to be manifestly absurd, we conclude the supposition from which it followed to be false; and, therefore its contradictory to be true.

There is hardly any proposition, especially of those that may claim the character of first principles, that stands alone and unconnected. It draws many others along with it in a chain that cannot be broken. He that takes it up must bear the burden of all its consequences; and, if that is too heavy for him to bear, he must not pretend to take it up.

Thirdly, I conceive that the consent of ages and nations, of the learned and unlearned, ought to have great authority with regard to first principles, where every man is a competent judge.

Our ordinary conduct in life is built upon first principles, as well as our speculations in philosophy; and every motive to action supposes some belief. When we find a general agreement among men, in principles that concern human life, this must have great authority with every sober mind that loves truth.

It is pleasant to observe the fruitless pains which Bishop Berkeley takes to shew that his system of the non-existence of a material world did not contradict the sentiments of the vulgar, but those only of the philosophers.

With 'good reason he dreaded more to oppose the authority of vulgar opinion in a matter of this kind, than all the schools of philosophers.

Here, perhaps, it will be said, What has authority to do in matters of opinion? Is truth to be determined by most votes? Or is authority to be again raised out of its grave to tyrannise over mankind?

I am aware that, in this age, an advocate for authority has a very unfavourable plea; but I wish to give no more to authority than is its due.

Most justly do we honour the names of those benefactors to mankind who have contributed more or less to break the yoke of that authority which deprives men of the natural, the unalienable right of judging for themselves; but, while we indulge a just animosity against this authority, and against all who would subject us to its tyranny, let us remember how common the folly is, of going from one faulty extreme into the opposite.

Authority, though a very tyrannical mistress to private judgment, may yet, on some occasions, be a useful handmaid. This is all she is entitled to, and this is all I plead in her behalf.

The justice of this plea will appear by putting a case in a science, in which, of all sciences, authority is acknowledged to have least weight.

Suppose a mathematician has made a discovery in that science which he thinks important; that he has put his demonstration in just order; and, after examining it with an attentive eye, has found no flaw in it, I would ask, Will there not be still in his breast some diffidence, some jealousy, lest the ardour of invention may have made him overlook some false step? This must be granted.

He commits his demonstration to the examination of a mathematical friend, whom he esteems a competent judge, and waits with impatience the issue of his judgment. Here I would ask again, Whether the verdict of his friend, according as it is favourable or unfavourable, will not greatly increase or diminish his confidence in his own judgment? Most certainly it will, and it ought.

If the judgment of his friend agree with his own, especially if it be confirmed by two or three able judges, he rests secure of his discovery without farther examination; but, if it be unfavourable, he is brought back into a kind of suspense, until the part that is suspected undergoes a new and a more rigorous examination.

I hope what is supposed in this case is agreeable to nature, and to the experience of candid and modest men on such occasions, yet here we see a man's judgment, even in a mathematical demonstration, conscious of some feebleness in itself, seeking the aid of authority to support it, greatly strengthened by that authority, and hardly able to stand erect against it, without some new aid.

Society in judgment, of those who are esteemed fair and competent judges, has effects very similar to those of civil society: it gives strength and courage to every individual; it removes that timidity which is as naturally the companion of solitary judgment, as of a solitary man in the state of nature.

Let us judge for ourselves, therefore; but let us not disdain to take that aid from the authority of other competent judges, which a mathematician thinks it necessary to take in that science which, of all sciences, has least to do with authority.

In a matter of common sense, every man is no less a competent judge than a mathematician is in a mathematical demonstration; and there must be a great presumption that the judgment of mankind, in such a matter, is the natural issue of those faculties which God hath given them. Such a judgment can be erroneous only when there is some cause of the error, as general as the error is. When this can be shewn to be the case, I acknowledge it ought to have its due weight. But, to suppose a general deviation from truth among mankind in things self-evident, of which no cause can be assigned, is highly unreasonable.

Perhaps it may be thought impossible to collect the general opinion of men upon any point whatsoever; and, therefore, that this authority can serve us in no stead in examining first principles. But I apprehend that, in many cases, this is neither impossible nor difficult.

Who can doubt whether men have universally believed the existence of a material world? Who can doubt whether men have universally believed that every change that happens in nature must have a cause? Who can doubt whether men have universally believed, that there is a right and a wrong in human conduct; some things that merit blame, and others that are entitled to approbation?

The universality of these opinions, and of many such that might be named, is sufficiently evident, from the whole tenor of human conduct, as far as our acquaintance reaches, and from the history of all ages and nations of which we have any records.

There are other opinions that appear to be universal, from what is common in the structure of all languages.

Language is the express image and picture of human thoughts; and from the picture we may draw some certain conclusions concerning the original.

We find in all languages the same parts of speech; we find nouns, substantive and adjective; verbs, active and passive, in their various tenses, numbers, and moods. Some rules of syntax are the same in all languages.

Now, what is common in the structure of languages, indicates an uniformity of opinion in those things upon which that structure is grounded.

The distinction between substances, and the qualities belonging to them; between thought and the being that thinks; between thought and the objects of thought; is to be found in the structure of all languages. And, therefore, systems of philosophy, which abolish those distinctions, wage war with the common sense of mankind.

We are apt to imagine that those who formed languages were no metaphysicians; but the first principles of all sciences are the dictates of common sense, and lie open to all men; and every man who has considered the structure of language in a philosophical light, will find infallible proofs that those who have framed it, and those who use it with understanding have the power of making accurate distinctions, and of forming general conceptions, as well as philosophers. Nature has given those powers to all men, and they can use them when occasions require it, but they leave it to the philosophers to give names to them, and to descant upon their nature. In like manner, nature has given eyes to all men, and they can make good use of them; but the structure of the eye, and the theory of vision, is the business of philosophers.

Fourthly, Opinions that appear so early in the minds of men that they cannot be the effect of education or of false reasoning, have a good claim to be considered as first principles. Thus, the belief we have, that the persons about us are living and intelligent beings, is a belief for which, perhaps, we can give some reason, when we are able to reason; but we had this belief before we could reason, and before we could learn it by instruction. It seems, therefore, to be an immediate effect of our constitution.

The *last* topic I shall mention is, when an opinion is so necessary in the conduct of life, that, without the belief of it, a man must be led into a thousand absurdities in practice, such an opinion, when we can give no other reason for it, may safely be taken for a first principle.

Thus I have endeavoured to shew, that, although first principles are not capable of direct proof, yet differences, that may happen with regard to them among men of candour, are not without remedy; that Nature has not left us destitute of means by which we may discover errors of this kind; and that there are ways of reasoning, with regard to first principles, by which those that are truly such may be distinguished from vulgar errors or prejudices.

CHAPTER 5 / THE FIRST PRINCIPLES OF CONTINGENT TRUTHS

. . . . If all truths were necessary truths, there would be no occasion for different tenses in the verbs by which they are expressed. What is true in the present time, would be true in the past and future; and there would be no change or variation of anything in nature.

We use the present tense in expressing necessary truths; but it is only because there is no flexion of the verb which includes all times. When I say that three is the half of six, I use the present tense only; but I mean to express not only what now is, but what always was, and always will be; and so every proposition is to be understood by which we mean to express a necessary truth. Contingent truths are of another nature. As they are mutable, they may be true at one time, and not at another; and, therefore, the expression of them must include some point or period of time. . . .

As the minds of men are occupied much more about truths that are contingent than about those that are necessary, I shall first endeavour to point out the principles of the former kind.

1. *First,* then, I hold, as a first principle, the existence of everything of which I am conscious.

Consciousness is an operation of the understanding of its own kind, and cannot be logically defined. The objects of it are our present pains, our pleasures, our hopes, our fears, our desires, our doubts, our thoughts of every kind; in a word, all the passions, and all the actions and operations of our own minds, while they are present. We may remember them when they are past; but we are conscious of them only while they are present.

When a man is conscious of pain, he is certain of its existence; when he is conscious that he doubts or believes, he is certain of the existence of those operations.

But the irresistible conviction he has of the reality of those operations is not the effect of reasoning; it is immediate and intuitive. The existence therefore of those passions and operations of our minds, of which we are conscious, is a first principle, which nature requires us to believe upon her authority.

If I am asked to prove that I cannot be deceived by consciousness—to prove that it is not a fallacious sense—I can find no proof. I cannot find any antecedent truth from which it is deduced, or upon which its evidence depends. It seems to disdain any such derived authority, and to claim my assent in its own right.

If any man could be found so frantic as to deny that he thinks, while he is conscious of it, I may wonder, I may laugh, or I may pity him, but I cannot reason the matter with him. We have no common principles from which we may reason, and therefore can never join issue in an argument.

This, I think, is the only principle of common sense that has never directly been called in question. It seems to be so firmly rooted in the minds of men, as to retain its authority with the greatest sceptics. Mr Hume, after annihilating body and mind, time and space, action and causation, and even his own mind, acknowledges the reality of the thoughts, sensations, and passions of which he is conscious. . . .

As, therefore, the real existence of our thoughts, and of all the operations and feelings of our own minds, is believed by all men—as we find ourselves incapable of doubting it, and as incapable of offering any proof of it—it may justly be considered as a first principle, or dictate of common sense.

But, although this principle rests upon no other, a very considerable and important branch of human knowledge rests upon it.

For from this source of consciousness is derived all that we know, and indeed all that we can know, of the structure and of the powers of our own minds; from which we may conclude, that there is no branch of knowledge that stands upon a firmer foundation; for surely no kind of evidence can go beyond that of consciousness.

How does it come to pass, then, that in this branch of knowledge there are so many and so contrary systems? so many subtile controversies that are never brought to an issue? and so little fixed and determined? Is it possible that philosophers should differ most where they have the surest means of agreement—where everything is built upon a species of evidence which all men acquiesce in, and hold to be the most certain?

This strange phaenomenon may, I think, be accounted for, if we distinguish between consciousness and reflection, which are often improperly confounded.

The first is common to all men at all times; but is insufficient of itself to give us clear and distinct notions of the operations of which we are conscious, and of their mutual relations and minute distinctions. The second—to wit, attentive reflection upon those operations, making them objects of thought, surveying them attentively, and examining them on all sides—is so far from being common to all men, that it is the lot of very few. The greatest part of men, either through want of capacity, or from other causes, never reflect attentively upon the operations of their own minds. The habit of this reflection, even in those whom nature has fitted for it, is not to be attained without much pains and practice.

We can know nothing of the immediate objects of sight, but

by the testimony of our eyes; and I apprehend that, if mankind had found as great difficulty in giving attention to the objects of sight, as they find in attentive reflection upon the operations of their own minds, our knowledge of the first might have been in as backward a state as our knowledge of the last.

But this darkness will not last for ever. Light will arise upon this benighted part of the intellectual globe. When any man is so happy as to delineate the powers of the human mind as they really are in nature, men that are free from prejudice, and capable of reflection, will recognise their own features in the picture; and then the wonder will be, how things so obvious could be so long wrapped up in mystery and darkness; how men could be carried away by false theories and conjectures, when the truth was to be found in their own breasts if they had but attended to it.

2. Another first principle, I think, is, *That the thoughts of which I am conscious, are the thoughts of a being which I call* MYSELF, *my* MIND, *my* PERSON.

The thoughts and feelings of which we are conscious are continually changing, and the thought of this moment is not the thought of the last; but something which I call myself, remains under this change of thought. This self has the same relation to all the successive thoughts I am conscious of—they are all my thoughts; and every thought which is not my thought, must be the thought of some other person.

If any man asks a proof of this, I confess I can give none; there is an evidence in the proposition itself which I am unable to resist. Shall I think that thought can stand by itself without a thinking being? or that ideas can feel pleasure or pain? My nature dictates to me that it is impossible.

And that nature has dictated the same to all men, appears from the structure of all languages; for in all languages men have expressed thinking, reasoning, willing, loving, hating, by personal verbs, which, from their nature, require a person who thinks, reasons, wills, loves, or hates. From which it appears, that men have been taught by nature to believe that thought requires a thinker, reason a reasoner, and love a lover. . . .

3. Another first principle I take to be—*That those things did really happen which I distinctly remember.*

This has one of the surest marks of a first principle; for no man ever pretended to prove it, and yet no man in his wits calls it in question: the testimony of memory, like that of consciousness, is immediate; it claims our assent upon its own authority.

Suppose that a learned counsel, in defence of a client against the concurring testimony of witnesses of credit, should insist upon a new topic to invalidate the testimony. "Admitting," says he, "the integrity of the witnesses, and that they distinctly remember what they have given in evidence—it does not follow that the prisoner is guilty. It has never been proved that the most distinct memory may not be fallacious. Shew me any necessary connection between that act of the mind which we call memory, and the past existence of the event remembered. No man has ever offered a shadow of argument to prove such a connection; yet this is one link of the chain of proof against the prisoner; and, if it have no strength, the whole proof falls to the ground: until this, therefore, be made evident—until it can be proved that we may safely rest upon the testimony of memory for the truth of past events—no judge or jury can justly take away the life of a citizen upon so doubtful a point."

I believe we may take it for granted, that this argument from a learned counsel would have no other effect upon the judge or jury, than to convince them that he was disordered in his judgment. Counsel is allowed to plead everything for a client that is fit to persuade or to move; yet I believe no counsel ever had the boldness to plead this topic. And for what reason? For no other reason, surely, but because it is absurd. Now, what is absurd at the bar, is so in the philosopher's chair. What would be ridiculous, if delivered to a jury of honest sensible citizens, is no less so when delivered gravely in a philosophical dissertation.

Mr Hume has not, as far as I remember, directly called in

question the testimony of memory; but he has laid down the premises by which its authority is overturned, leaving it to his reader to draw the conclusion.

He labours to shew that the belief of assent which always attends the memory and senses is nothing but the vivacity of those perceptions which they present. He shews very clearly, that this vivacity gives no ground to believe the existence of external objects. And it is obvious that it can give as little ground to believe the past existence of the objects of memory.

Indeed the theory concerning ideas, so generally received by philosophers, destroys all the authority of memory, as well as the authority of the senses. Des Cartes, Malebranche, and Locke, were aware that this theory made it necessary for them to find out arguments to prove the existence of external objects, which the vulgar believe upon the bare authority of their senses; but those philosophers were not aware that this theory made it equally necessary for them to find arguments to prove the existence of things past, which we remember, and to support the authority of memory.

All the arguments they advanced to support the authority of our senses, were easily refuted by Bishop Berkeley and Mr Hume, being indeed very weak and inconclusive. And it would have been as easy to answer every argument they could have brought, consistent with their theory, to support the authority of memory.

For, according to that theory, the immediate object of memory, as well as of every other operation of the understanding, is an idea present in the mind. And, from the present existence of this idea of memory I am left to infer, by reasoning, that, six months or six years ago, there did exist an object similar to this idea.

But what is there in the idea that can lead me to this conclusion? What mark does it bear of the date of its archetype? Or what evidence have I that it had an archetype, and that it is not the first of its kind?

Perhaps it will be said, that this idea or image in the mind must have had a cause.

I admit that, if there is such an image in the mind, it must have had a cause, and a cause able to produce the effect; but what can we infer from its having a cause? Does it follow that the effect is a type, an image, a copy of its cause? Then it will follow, that a picture is an image of the painter, and a coach of the coachmaker.

A past event may be known by reasoning; but that is not remembering it. When I remember a thing distinctly, I disdain equally to hear reasons for it or against it. And so I think does every man in his senses.

4. Another first principle is, *Our own personal identity and continued existence, as far back as we remember anything distinctly.*

This we know immediately, and not by reasoning. It seems, indeed, to be a part of the testimony of memory. Everything we remember has such a relation to ourselves as to imply necessarily our existence at the time remembered. And there cannot be a more palpable absurdity than that a man should remember what happened before he existed. He must therefore have existed as far back as he remembers anything distinctly, if his memory be not fallacious. This principle, therefore, is so connected with the last mentioned, that it may be doubtful whether both ought not to be included in one. Let every one judge of this as he sees reason. The proper notion of identity, and the sentiments of Mr Locke on this subject, have been considered before, under the head of Memory.

5. Another first principle is, *That those things do really exist which we distinctly perceive by our senses, and are what we perceive them to be.*

It is too evident to need proof, that all men are by nature led to give implicit faith to the distinct testimony of their senses, long before they are capable of any bias from prejudices of education or of philosophy.

How came we at first to know that there are certain beings

about us whom we call father, and mother, and sisters, and brothers, and nurse? Was it not by the testimony of our senses? How did these persons convey to us any information or instruction? Was it not by means of our senses?

It is evident we can have no communication, no correspondence or society with any created being, but by means of our senses. And, until we rely upon their testimony, we must consider ourselves as being alone in the universe, without any fellow-creature, living or inanimate, and be left to converse with our own thoughts. . . .

We have before examined the reasons given by philosophers to prove that ideas, and not external objects, are the immediate objects of perception, and the instances given to prove the senses fallacious. Without repeating what has before been said upon those points, we shall only here observe, that, if external objects be perceived immediately, we have the same reason to believe their existence as philosophers have to believe the existence of ideas, while they hold them to be the immediate objects of perception.

6. Another first principle, I think, is, *That we have some degree of power over our actions, and the determinations of our will.*

All power must be derived from the fountain of power, and of every good gift. Upon His good pleasure its continuance depends, and it is always subject to his control.

Beings to whom God has given any degree of power, and understanding to direct them to the proper use of it, must be accountable to their Maker. But those who are intrusted with no power can have no account to make; for all good conduct consists in the right use of power; all bad conduct in the abuse of it.

To call to account a being who never was intrusted with any degree of power, is an absurdity no less than it would be to call to account an inanimate being. We are sure, therefore, if we have any account to make to the Author of our being, that we must have some degree of power, which, as far as it is properly used, entitles us to his approbation; and, when abused, renders us obnoxious to his displeasure.

It is not easy to say in what way we first get the notion or idea of *power*. It is neither an object of sense nor of consciousness. We see events, one succeeding another; but we see not the power by which they are produced. We are conscious of the operations of our minds; but power is not an operation of mind. If we had no notions but such as are furnished by the external senses, and by consciousness, it seems to be impossible that we should ever have any conception of power. Accordingly, Mr Hume, who has reasoned the most accurately upon this hypothesis, denies that we have any idea of power, and clearly refutes the account given by Mr Locke of the origin of this idea.

But it is in vain to reason from a hypothesis against a fact, the truth of which every man may see by attending to his own thoughts. It is evident that all men, very early in life, not only have an idea of power, but a conviction that they have some degree of it in themselves; for this conviction is necessarily implied in many operations of mind, which are familiar to every man, and without which no man can act the part of a reasonable being.

First, It is implied in every act of volition. "Volition, it is plain," says Mr Locke, "is an act of the mind, knowingly exerting that dominion which it takes itself to have over any part of the man, by employing it in, or withholding it from any particular action." Every volition, therefore, implies a conviction of power to do the action willed. A man may desire to make a visit to the moon, or to the planet Jupiter; but nothing but insanity could make him will to do so. And, if even insanity produced this effect, it must be by making him think it to be in his power.

Secondly, This conviction is implied in all deliberation; for no man in his wits deliberates whether he shall do what he believes not to be in his power. *Thirdly*, The same conviction is implied in every resolution or purpose formed in consequence of deliberation. A man may as well form a resolution to pull the moon out of her sphere, as to do the most insignificant action which he believes not to be in his power. The same thing may be said of every promise or contract wherein a man plights his faith; for he is not an honest man who promises what he does not believe he has power to perform.

As these operations imply a belief of some degree of power in ourselves; so there are others equally common and familiar, which imply a like belief with regard to others.

When we impute to a man any action or omission, as a ground of approbation or of blame, we must believe he had power to do otherwise. The same is implied in all advice, exhortation, command, and rebuke, and in every case in which we rely upon his fidelity in performing any engagement or executing any trust.

It is not more evident that mankind have a conviction of the existence of a material world, than that they have the conviction of some degree of power in themselves and in others; every one over his own actions, and the determinations of his will a conviction so early, so general, and so interwoven with the whole of human conduct, that it must be the natural effect of our constitution, and intended by the Author of our being to guide our actions.

It resembles our conviction of the existence of a material world in this respect also, that even those who reject it in speculation, find themselves under a necessity of being governed by it in their practice; and thus it will always happen when philosophy contradicts first principles.

7. Another first principle is— *That the natural faculties, by which we distinguish truth from error, are not fallacious.* If any man should demand a proof of this, it is impossible to satisfy him. For, suppose it should be mathematically demonstrated, this would signify nothing in this case; because, to judge of a demonstration, a man must trust his faculties, and take for granted the very thing in question.

If a man's honesty were called in question, it would be ridiculous to refer it to the man's own word, whether he be honest or not. The same absurdity there is in attempting to prove, by any kind of reasoning, probable or demonstrative, that our reason is not fallacious, since the very point in question is, whether reasoning may be trusted.

If a sceptic should build his scepticism upon this foundation, that all our reasoning and judging powers are fallacious in their nature, or should resolve at least to withold assent until it be proved that they are not, it would be impossible by argument to beat him out of this stronghold; and he must even be left to enjoy his scepticism.

Des Cartes certainly made a false step in this matter, for having suggested this doubt among others—that whatever evidence he might have from his consciousness, his senses, his memory, or his reason, yet possibly some malignant being had given him those faculties on purpose to impose upon him; and, therefore, that they are not to be trusted without a proper voucher. To remove this doubt, he endeavours to prove the being of a Deity who is no deceiver; whence he concludes, that the faculties he had given him are true and worthy to be trusted.

It is strange that so acute a reasoner did not perceive that in this reasoning there is evidently a begging of the question.

For, if our faculties be fallacious, why may they not deceive us in this reasoning as well as in others? And, if they are not to be trusted in this instance without a voucher, why not in others?

Every kind of reasoning for the veracity of our faculties, amounts to no more than taking their own testimony for their veracity; and this we must do implicitly, until God give us new faculties to sit in judgment upon the old; and the reason why Des Cartes satisfied himself with so weak an argument for the truth of his faculties, most probably was, that he never seriously doubted of it.

If any truth can be said to be prior to all others in the order of nature, this seems to have the best claim; because, in every instance of assent, whether upon intuitive, demonstrative, or probable evidence, the truth of our faculties is taken for granted, and is, as it were, one of the premises on which our assent is grounded. . . .

We may here take notice of a property of the principle under consideration, that seems to be common to it with many other first principles, and which can hardly be found in any principle that is built solely upon reasoning; and that is, that in most men it produces its effect without ever being attended to, or made an object of thought. No man ever thinks of this principle, unless when he considers the grounds of scepticism; yet it invariably governs his opinions. When a man in the common course of life gives credit to the testimony of his senses, his memory, or his reason, he does not put the question to himself, whether these faculties may deceive him; yet the trust he reposes in them supposes an inward conviction, that, in that instance at least, they do not deceive him.

It is another property of this and of many first principles, that they force assent in particular instances, more powerfully than when they are turned into a general proposition. Many sceptics have denied every general principle of science, excepting perhaps the existence of our present thoughts; yet these men reason, and refute, and prove, they assent and dissent in particular cases. They use reasoning to overturn all reasoning, and judge that they ought to have no judgment, and see clearly that they are blind. Many have in general maintained that the senses are fallacious, yet there never was found a man so sceptical as not to trust his senses in particular instances when his safety required it; and it may be observed of those who have professed scepticism, that their scepticism lies in generals, while in particulars they are no less dogmatical than others.

8. Another first principle relating to existence, is, *That there*

is life and intelligence in our fellow-men with whom we converse.

As soon as children are capable of asking a question, or of answering a question, as soon as they shew the signs of love, of resentment, or of any other affection, they must be convinced that those with whom they have this intercourse are intelligent beings.

It is evident they are capable of such intercourse long before they can reason. Every one knows that there is a social intercourse between the nurse and the child before it is a year old. It can, at that age, understand many things that are said to it.

It can by signs ask and refuse, threaten and supplicate. It clings to its nurse in danger, enters into her grief and joy, is happy in her soothing and caresses, and unhappy in her displeasure. That these things cannot be without a conviction in the child that the nurse is an intelligent being, I think must be granted.

Now, I would ask how a child of a year old comes by this conviction? Not by reasoning surely, for children do not reason at that age. Nor is it by external senses, for life and intelligence are not objects of the external senses.

By what means, or upon what occasions, Nature first gives this information to the infant mind is not easy to determine. We are not capable of reflecting upon our own thoughts at that period of life; and before we attain this capacity, we have quite forgot how or on what occasion we first had this belief; we perceive it in those who are born blind, and in others who are born deaf; and therefore Nature has not connected it solely either with any object of sight, or with any object of hearing. When we grow up to the years of reason and reflection, this belief remains. No man thinks of asking himself what reason he has to believe that his neighbour is a living creature. He would be not a little surprised if another person should ask him so absurd a question; and perhaps could not give any reason which would not equally prove a watch or a puppet to be a living creature.

But, though you should satisfy him of the weakness of the reasons he gives for his belief, you cannot make him in the least doubtful. This belief stands upon another foundation than that of reasoning; and therefore, whether a man can give good reasons for it or not, it is not in his power to shake it off.

Setting aside this natural conviction, I believe the best reason we can give, to prove that other men are living and intelligent, is, that their words and actions indicate like powers of understanding as we are conscious of in ourselves. The very same argument applied to the works of nature, leads us to conclude that there is an intelligent Author of nature, and appears equally strong and obvious in the last case as in the first; so that it may be doubted whether men, by the mere exercise of reasoning, might not as soon discover the existence of a Deity, as that other men have life and intelligence.

The knowledge of the last is absolutely necessary to our receiving any improvement by means of instruction and example; and, without these means of improvement, there is no ground to think that we should ever be able to acquire the use of our reasoning powers. This knowledge, therefore, must be antecedent to reasoning, and therefore must be a first principle.

It cannot be said that the judgments we form concerning life and intelligence in either beings are at first free from error. But the errors of children in this matter lie on the safe side; they are prone to attribute intelligence to things inanimate. These errors are of small consequence, and are gradually corrected by experience and ripe judgment. But the belief of life and intelligence in other men, is absolutely necessary for us before we are capable of reasoning; and therefore the Author of our being hath given us this belief antecedently to all reasoning.

9. Another first principle I take to be, *That certain features of the countenance, sounds of the voice, and gestures of the body, indicate certain thoughts and dispositions of mind.*

That many operations of the mind have their natural signs in the countenance, voice, and gesture, I suppose every man will admit. *Omnis enim motus animi,* says Cicero, *suum quemdam habet a natura vultum, et vocem et gestum.* The only question is, whether we understand the signification of those signs, by the constitution of our nature, by a kind of natural perception similar to the perceptions of sense; or whether we gradually learn the signification of such signs from experience, as we learn that smoke is a sign of fire, or that the freezing of water is a sign of cold? I take the first to be the truth.

It seems to me incredible, that the notions men have of the expression of features, voice, and gesture, are entirely the fruit of experience. Children, almost as soon as born, may be frighted, and thrown into fits by a threatening or angry tone of voice. I knew a man who could make an infant cry, by whistling a melancholy tune in the same or in the next room; and again, by altering his key, and the strain of his music, could make the child leap and dance for joy. . . .

Nay, I apprehend that it is impossible that this should be learned from experience.

When we see the sign, and see the thing signified always conjoined with it, experience may be the instructor, and teach us how that sign is to be interpreted. But how shall experience instruct us when we see the sign only, when the thing signified is invisible? Now, this is the case here: the thoughts and passions of the mind, as well as the mind itself, are invisible, and therefore their connection with any sensible sign cannot be first discovered by experience; there must be some earlier source of this knowledge.

Nature seems to have given to men a faculty or sense, by which this connection is perceived. And the operation of this sense is very analogous to that of the external senses.

When I grasp an ivory ball in my hand, I feel a certain sensation of touch. In the sensation there is nothing external, nothing corporeal. The sensation is neither round nor hard;

it is an act of feeling of the mind, from which I cannot, by reasoning, infer the existence of any body. But, by the constitution of my nature, the sensation carries along with it the conception and belief of a round hard body really existing in my hand.

In like manner, when I see the features of an expressive face, I see only figure and colour variously modified. But, by the constitution of my nature, the visible object brings along with it the conception and belief of a certain passion or sentiment in the mind of the person.

In the former case, a sensation of touch is the sign, and the hardness and roundness of the body I grasp is signified by that sensation. In the latter case, the features of the person is the sign, and the passion or sentiment is signified by it. . . .

For these reasons, I conceive, it must be granted, not only that there is a connection established by Nature between certain signs in the countenance, voice, and gesture, and the thoughts and passions of the mind; but also, that, by our constitution, we understand the meaning of those signs, and from the sign conclude the existence of the thing signified.

10. Another first principle appears to me to be—*That there is a certain regard due to human testimony in matters of fact, and even to human authority in matters of opinion.*

Before we are capable of reasoning about testimony or authority, there are many things which it concerns us to know, for which we can have no other evidence. The wise Author of nature hath planted in the human mind a propensity to rely upon this evidence before we can give a reason for doing so. This, indeed, puts our judgment almost entirely in the power of those who are about us in the first period of life; but this is necessary both to our preservation and to our improvement. If children were so framed as to pay no regard to testimony or to authority, they must, in the literal sense, perish for lack of knowledge. It is not more necessary that they should be fed before they can feed themselves, than that they should be instructed in many things before they can discover them by their own judgment.

But, when our faculties ripen, we find reason to check that propensity to yield to testimony and to authority, which was so necessary and so natural in the first period of life. We learn to reason about the regard due to them, and see it to be a childish weakness to lay more stress upon them than reason justifies. Yet, I believe, to the end of life, most men are more apt to go into this extreme than into the contrary; and the natural propensity still retains some force.

The natural principles, by which our judgments and opinions are regulated before we come to the use of reason, seem to be no less necessary to such a being as man, than those natural instincts which the Author of nature hath given us to regulate our actions during that period.

11. *There are many events depending upon the will of man, in which there is a self-evident probability, greater or less, according to circumstances.*

There may be in some individuals such a degree of frenzy and madness, that no man can say what they may or may not do. Such persons we find it necessary to put under restraint, that as far as possible they may be kept from doing harm to themselves or to others. They are not considered as reasonable creatures, or members of society. But, as to men who have a sound mind, we depend upon a certain degree of regularity in their conduct; and could put a thousand different cases, wherein we could venture, ten to one, that they will act in such a way, and not in the contrary.

If we had no confidence in our fellow-men that they will act such a part in such circumstances, it would be impossible to live in society with them. For that which makes men capable of living in society, and uniting in a political body under government, is, that their actions will always be regulated, in a great measure, by the common principles of human nature.

It may always be expected that they will regard their own

interest and reputation, and that of their families and friends; that they will repel injuries, and have some sense of good offices; and that they will have some regard to truth and justice, so far at least as not to swerve from them without temptation.

It is upon such principles as these, that all political reasoning is grounded. Such reasoning is never demonstrative; but it may have a very great degree of probability, especially when applied to great bodies of men.

12. The last principle of contingent truths I mention is, *That, in the phaenomena of nature, what is to be, will probably be like to what has been in similar circumstances.*

We must have this conviction as soon as we are capable of learning anything from experience; for all experience is grounded upon a belief that the future will be like the past. Take away this principle, and the experience of a hundred years makes us no wiser with regard to what is to come.

This is one of those principles which, when we grow up and observe the course of nature, we can confirm by reasoning. We perceive that Nature is governed by fixed laws, and that, if it were not so, there could be no such thing as prudence in human conduct; there would be no fitness in any means to promote an end; and what, on one occasion, promoted it, might as probably, on another occasion, obstruct it.

But the principle is necessary for us before we are able to discover it by reasoning, and therefore is made a part of our constitution, and produces its effects before the use of reason.

This principle remains in all its force when we come to the use of reason; but we learn to be more cautious in the application of it. We observe more carefully the circumstances on which the past event depended, and learn to distinguish them from those which were accidentally conjoined with it.

In order to this, a number of experiments, varied in their circumstances, is often necessary. Sometimes a single experiment is thought sufficient to establish a general conclusion.

Thus, when it was once found, that, in a certain degree of cold, quicksilver became a hard and malleable metal, there was good reason to think that the same degree of cold will always produce this effect to the end of the world.

I need hardly mention, that the whole fabric of natural philosophy is built upon this principle, and, if it be taken away, must tumble down to the foundation. . . .

I do not at all affirm, that those I have mentioned are all the first principles from which we may reason concerning contingent truths. Such enumerations, even when made after much reflection, are seldom perfect.

CHAPTER 6 / FIRST PRINCIPLES OF NECESSARY TRUTHS

About most of the first principles of necessary truths there has been no dispute, and therefore it is the less necessary to dwell upon them. It will be sufficient to divide them into different classes; to mention some, by way of specimen, in each class; and to make some remarks on those of which the truth has been called in question.

They may, I think, most properly be divided according to the sciences to which they belong.

1. There are some first principles that may be called *grammatical:* such as, *That every adjective in a sentence must belong to some substantive expressed or understood; That every complete sentence must have a verb.*

Those who have attended to the structure of language, and formed distinct notions of the nature and use of the various parts of speech, perceive, without reasoning, that these, and many other such principles, are necessarily true.

2. There are *logical* axioms: such as, *That any contexture of words which does not make a proposition, is neither true nor false; That*

every proposition is either true or false; That no proposition can be both true and false at the same time; That reasoning in a circle proves nothing; That whatever may be truly affirmed of a genus, may be truly affirmed of all the species, and all the individuals belonging to that genus.

3. Every one knows there are *mathematical* axioms. Mathematicians have, from the days of Euclid, very wisely laid down the axioms or first principles on which they reason. And the effect which this appears to have had upon the stability and happy progress of this science, gives no small encouragement to attempt to lay the foundation of other sciences in a similar manner, as far as we are able. . . .

4. I think there are axioms, even in matters of *taste.* Notwithstanding the variety found among men, in taste, there are, I apprehend, some common principles, even in matters of this kind. I never heard of any man who thought it a beauty in a human face to want a nose, or an eye, or to have the mouth on one side. How many ages have passed since the days of Homer! Yet, in this long tract of ages, there never was found a man who took Thersites for a beauty.

The *fine arts* are very properly called the *arts of taste,* because the principles of both are the same; and, in the fine arts, we find no less agreement among those who practise them than among other artists.

No work of taste can be either relished or understood by those who do not agree with the author in the principles of taste.

Homer and Virgil, and Shakespeare and Milton, had the same taste; and all men who have been acquainted with their writings, and agree in the admiration of them, must have the same taste.

The fundamental rules of poetry and music, and painting, and dramatic action and eloquence, have been always the same, and will be so to the end of the world.

The variety we find among men in matters of taste, is easily accounted for, consistently with what we have advanced.

There is a taste that is acquired, and a taste that is natural. This holds with respect both to the external sense of taste and the internal. Habit and fashion have a powerful influence upon both.

Of tastes that are natural, there are some that may be called rational, others that are merely animal.

Children are delighted with brilliant and gaudy colours, with romping and noisy mirth, with feats of agility, strength, or cunning; and savages have much the same taste as children.

But there are tastes that are more intellectual. It is the dictate of our rational nature, that love and admiration are misplaced when there is no intrinsic worth in the object.

In those operations of taste which are rational, we judge of the real worth and excellence of the object, and our love or admiration is guided by that judgment. In such operations there is judgment as well as feeling, and the feeling depends upon the judgment we form of the object.

I do not maintain that taste, so far as it is acquired, or so far as it is merely animal, can be reduced to principles. But, as far as it is founded on judgment, it certainly may.

The virtues, the graces, the muses, have a beauty that is intrinsic. It lies not in the feelings of the spectator, but in the real excellence of the object. If we do not perceive their beauty, it is owing to the defect or to the perversion of our faculties.

And, as there is an original beauty in certain moral and intellectual qualities, so there is a borrowed and derived beauty in the natural signs and expressions of such qualities.

The features of the human face, the modulations of the voice, and the proportions, attitudes, and gesture of the body, are all natural expressions of good or bad qualities of the person, and derive a beauty or a deformity from the qualities which they express.

Works of art express some quality of the artist, and often

derive an additional beauty from their utility or fitness for their end.

Of such things there are some that ought to please, and others that ought to displease. If they do not, it is owing to some defect in the spectator. But what has real excellence will always please those who have a correct judgment and a sound heart.

The sum of what has been said upon this subject is, that, setting aside the tastes which men acquire by habit and fashion, there is a natural taste, which is partly animal, and partly rational. With regard to the first, all we can say is, that the Author of nature, for wise reasons, has formed us so as to receive pleasure from the contemplation of certain objects, and disgust from others, before we are capable of perceiving any real excellence in one or defect in the other. But that taste which we may call rational, is that part of our constitution by which we are made to receive pleasure from the contemplation of what we conceive to be excellent in its kind, the pleasure being annexed to this judgment, and regulated by it. This taste may be true or false, according as it is founded on a true or false judgment. And, if it may be true or false, it must have first principles.

5. There are also first principles in *morals.*

That an unjust action has more demerit than an ungenerous one: That a generous action has more merit than a merely just one: That no man ought to be blamed for what it was not in his power to hinder: That we ought not to do to others what we would think unjust or unfair to be done to us in like circumstances. These are moral axioms, and many others might be named which appear to me to have no less evidence than those of mathematics.

Some perhaps may think that our determinations, either in matters of taste or in morals, ought not to be accounted necessary truths: That they are grounded upon the constitution of that faculty which we call taste, and of that which we call the moral sense or conscience; which faculties might have been so constituted as to have given determinations different, or even contrary to those they now give: That, as there is nothing sweet or bitter in itself, but according as it agrees or disagrees with the external sense called taste; so there is nothing beautiful or ugly in itself, but according as it agrees or disagrees with the internal sense, which we also call taste; and nothing morally good or ill in itself, but according as it agrees or disagrees with our moral sense.

This indeed is a system, with regard to morals and taste, which hath been supported in modern times by great authorities. And if this system be true, the consequence must be, that there can be no principles, either of taste or of morals, that are necessary truths. For, according to this system, all our determinations, both with regard to matters of taste, and with regard to morals, are reduced to matters of fact—I mean to such as these, that by our constitution we have on such occasions certain agreeable feelings, and on other occasions certain disagreeable feelings.

But I cannot help being of a contrary opinion, being persuaded that a man who determined that polite behaviour has great deformity, and that there is great beauty in rudeness and ill-breeding, would judge wrong, whatever his feelings were.

In like manner, I cannot help thinking that a man who determined that there is more moral worth in cruelty, perfidy, and injustice, than in generosity, justice, prudence, and temperance, would judge wrong, whatever his constitution was.

And, if it be true that there is judgment in our determinations of taste and of morals, it must be granted that what is true or false in morals, or in matters of taste, is necessarily so. For this reason, I have ranked the first principles of morals and of taste under the class of necessary truths.

6. The last class of first principles I shall mention, we may call *metaphysical.*

I shall particularly consider three of these, because they have been called in question by Mr Hume.

The *first* is, *That the qualities which we perceive by our senses must have a subject, which we call body, and that the thoughts we are conscious of must have a subject, which we call mind.*

It is not more evident that two and two make four, than it is that figure cannot exist, unless there be something that is figured, nor motion without something that is moved. I not only perceive figure and motion, but I perceive them to be qualities. They have a necessary relation to something in which they exist as their subject. The difficulty which some philosophers have found in admitting this, is entirely owing to the theory of ideas. A subject of the sensible qualities which we perceive by our senses, is not an idea either of sensation or of consciousness; therefore say they, we have no such idea. Or, in the style of Mr Hume, from what impression is the idea of substance derived? It is not a copy of any impression; therefore there is no such idea.

The distinction between sensible qualities, and the substance to which they belong, and between thought and the mind that thinks, is not the invention of philosophers; it is found in the structure of all languages, and therefore must be common to all men who speak with understanding. And I believe no man, however sceptical he may be in speculation, can talk on the common affairs of life for half an hour, without saying things that imply his belief of the reality of these distinctions. . . .

We cannot give a reason why we believe even our sensations to be real and not fallacious; why we believe what we are conscious of; why we trust any of our natural faculties. We say, it must be so, it cannot be otherwise. This expresses only a strong belief, which is indeed the voice of nature, and which therefore in vain we attempt to resist. But if, in spite of nature, we resolve to go deeper, and not to trust our faculties, without a reason to shew that they cannot be fallacious, I am afraid, that, seeking to become wise, and to be as gods, we shall become foolish, and, being unsatisfied with the lot of humanity, we shall throw off common sense.

˙ The *second* metaphysical principle I mention is—*That what-ever begins to exist, must have a cause which produced it.*

Philosophy is indebted to Mr Hume in this respect among others, that, by calling in question many of the first principles of human knowledge, he hath put speculative men upon in-quiring more carefully than was done before into the nature of the evidence upon which they rest. Truth can never suffer by a fair inquiry; it can bear to be seen naked and in the fullest light; and the strictest examination will always turn out in the issue to its advantage. I believe Mr Hume was the first who ever called in question whether things that begin to exist must have a cause.

With regard to this point, we must hold one of these three things, either that it is an opinion for which we have no evi-dence, and which men have foolishly taken up without ground; or, *secondly,* That it is capable of direct proof by argument; or, *thirdly,* That it is self-evident, and needs no proof, but ought to be received as an axiom, which cannot, by reasonable men, be called in question.

The first of these suppositions would put at end to all philosophy, to all religion, to all reasoning that would carry us beyond the objects of sense, and to all prudence in the conduct of life.

As to the second supposition, that this principle may be proved by direct reasoning, I am afraid we shall find the proof extremely difficult, if not altogether impossible.

I know only of three or four arguments that have been urged by philosophers, in the way of abstract reasoning, to prove that things which begin to exist must have a cause.

One is offered by Mr Hobbes, another by Dr Samuel Clarke, another by Mr Locke. Mr Hume, in his "Treatise of Human Nature," has examined them all; and, in my opinion, has shewn that they take for granted the thing to be proved; a kind of false reasoning, which men are very apt to fall into when they attempt to prove what is self-evident.

It has been thought, that, although this principle does not admit of proof from abstract reasoning, it may be proved from experience, and may be justly drawn by induction, from instances that fall within our observation.

I conceive this method of proof will leave us in great uncertainty, for these three reasons:

1 *st*, Because the proposition to be proved is not a contingent but a *necessary* proposition. It is not that things which begin to exist commonly have a cause, or even that they always in fact have a cause; but that they must have a cause, and cannot begin to exist without a cause.

Propositions of this kind, from their nature, are incapable of proof by induction. Experience informs us only of what *is* or *has been*, not of what *must be;* and the conclusion must be of the same nature with the premises.

For this reason, no mathematical proposition can be proved by induction. Though it should be found by experience in a thousand cases, that the area of a plane triangle is equal to the rectangle under the altitude and half the base, this would not prove that it must be so in all cases, and cannot be otherwise; which is what the mathematician affirms.

In like manner, though we had the most ample experimental proof that things which have begun to exist had a cause, this would not prove that they must have a cause. Experience may shew us what is the established course of nature, but can never shew what connections of things are in their nature necessary.

2 *dly*, General maxims, grounded on experience, have only a degree of probability proportioned to the extent of our experience, and ought always to be understood so as to leave room for exceptions, if future experience shall discover any such.

The law of gravitation has as full a proof from experience and induction as any principle can be supposed to have. Yet, if any philosopher should, by clear experiment, shew that there is a kind of matter in some bodies which does not gravitate, the law of gravitation ought to be limited by that exception.

Now it is evident that men have never considered the principle of the necessity of causes, as a truth of this kind which may admit of limitation or exception; and therefore it has not been received upon this kind of evidence.

3 *dly*, I do not see that experience could satisfy us that every change in nature actually has a cause.

In the far greatest part of the changes in nature that fall within our observation, the causes are unknown; and, therefore, from experience, we cannot know whether they have causes or not.

Causation is not an object of sense. The only experience we can have of it, is in the consciousness we have of exerting some power in ordering our thoughts and actions. But this experience is surely too narrow a foundation for a general conclusion, that all things that have had or shall have a beginning, must have a cause.

For these reasons, this principle cannot be drawn from experience, any more than from abstract reasoning.

The *third* supposition is—That it is to be admitted as a first or self-evident principle. Two reasons may be urged for this.

1. The universal consent of mankind, not of philosophers only, but of the rude and unlearned vulgar. . . .

2. A second reason why I conceive this to be a first principle, is, That mankind not only assent to it in speculation, but that the practice of life is grounded upon it in the most important matters, even in cases where experience leaves us doubtful; and it is impossible to act with common prudence if we set it aside.

In great families, there are so many bad things done by a certain personage, called *Nobody*, that it is proverbial that there is a Nobody about every house who does a great deal of mischief; and even where there is the exactest inspection and government, many events will happen of which no other author can be found; so that, if we trust merely to experience in this matter, Nobody will be found to be a very active person, and to have no inconsiderable share in the management of affairs. But whatever countenance this system may have from experience, it is too shocking to common sense to impose upon the most ignorant. A child knows that, when his top, or any of his playthings, are taken away, it must be done by somebody. Perhaps it would not be difficult to persuade him that it was done by some invisible being, but that it should be done by nobody he cannot believe. . . .

NOTES

1. This is incorrect. Des Cartes has little, and Locke no title to praise for this observation. It had been made by Aristotle, and after him by many others; while, subsequent to Des Cartes, and *previous to Locke,* Pascal and the Port Royal Logicians, to say nothing of a paper of Leibnitz, in 1684, had reduced it to a matter of commonplace. In this instance, Locke can, indeed, be *proved* a borrower. Mr Stewart ("Philosophical Essays," Note A) is wrong in thinking that, after Des Cartes, Lord Stair is the earliest philosopher by whom this logical principle was enounced; for Stair, as a writer, is subsequent to the authors adduced.—H.

2. "Enquiry concerning Human Understanding."—H.

3. A saying of Varro.—H.

4. All this we read, however, in Laërtius, of Pyrrho; and on the authority of Antigonus Carystius, the great sceptic's contemporary. Whether we are to believe the narrative is another question.—H.

5. This, I have no doubt, is in allusion to Priestley. That writer had, not very courteously, said, in his "Examination of Reid's Inquiry" "I do not remember to have seen a more *egregious piece of solemn trifling* than the chapter which our author calls the 'Geometry of Visibles,' and his account of the 'Idomenians,' as he terms those imaginary beings who had no ideas of substance but from sight."—In a note upon that chapter of "The Inquiry," I stated that the thought of a Geometry of Visibles was original to Berkeley, and I had then no recollection of Reid's acknowledgment in the present paragraph.—H.

6. This illustration is Des Cartes'.—H.

7. See *Essay,* (Book ii. ch. 27,§9.) The passage given as a quotation in the text, is the sum of Locke's doctrine, but not

exactly in his words. Long before Butler, to whom the merit is usually ascribed, Locke's doctrine of Personal Identity had been attacked and refuted. This was done even by his earliest critic, John Sergeant. . . .—H.

8. Compare Buffer's *"Traité des prémieres Véritez,"* (*Remarques sur Locke*, § 565,) who makes a similar criticism.—H.

9. On Reid's criticism of Berkeley, see Stewart, (*Elements*, II. p. 110, sq.)—H.

10. See Stewart, (*Elements*, II p. 125.)—H.

ESSAYS
ON THE
ACTIVE POWERS OF MAN

ESSAY ONE / OF ACTIVE POWER IN GENERAL

CHAPTER 1 / OF THE NOTION OF ACTIVE POWER

To consider gravely what is meant by *Active Power*, may seem altogether unnecessary, and to be mere trifling. It is not a term of art, but a common word in our language, used every day in discourse, even by the vulgar. We find words of the same meaning in all other languages; and there is no reason to think that it is not perfectly understood by all men who understand the English language.

I believe all this is true, and that an attempt to explain a word so well understood, and to shew that it has a meaning, requires an apology.

The apology is, That this term, so well understood by the vulgar, has been darkened by philosophers, who, in this as in many other instances, have found great difficulties about a thing which, to the rest of mankind, seems perfectly clear.

This has been the more easily effected, because Power is a thing so much of its own kind, and so simple in its nature, as not to admit of a logical definition.

It is well known that there are many things perfectly understood, and of which we have clear and distinct conceptions, which cannot be logically defined. No man ever attempted to define magnitude; yet there is no word whose meaning is more distinctly or more generally understood. We cannot give a

299

logical definition of thought, of duration, of number, or of motion. . . .

I shall not therefore attempt to define Active Power, that I may not be liable to the same censure; but shall offer some observations that may lead us to attend to the conception we have of it in our own minds.

1. Power is not an object of any of our external senses, nor even an object of consciousness.

That it is not seen, nor heard, nor touched, nor tasted, nor smelt, needs no proof. That we are not conscious of it, in the proper sense of that word, will be no less evident, if we reflect, that consciousness is that power of the mind by which it has an immediate knowledge of its own operations. Power is not an operation of the mind, and therefore no object of consciousness. Indeed, every operation of the mind is the exertion of some power of the mind; but we are conscious of the operation only—the power lies behind the scene; and, though we may justly infer the power from the operation, it must be remembered, that inferring is not the province of consciousness, but of reason.

I acknowledge, therefore, that our having any conception or idea of power is repugnant to Mr Locke's theory, that all our simple ideas are got either by the external senses, or by consciousness. Both cannot be true. Mr Hume perceived this repugnancy, and consistently maintained, that we have no idea of power. Mr Locke did not perceive it. If he had, it might have led him to suspect his theory; for when theory is repugnant to fact, it is easy to see which ought to yield. I am conscious that I have a *conception* or *idea* of power; but, strictly speaking, I am not conscious that I have *power*.

I shall have occasion to shew, that we have very early, from our constitution, a conviction or belief of some degree of active power in ourselves. This belief, however, is not consciousness—for we may be deceived in it; but the testimony of consciousness can never deceive. Thus, a man who is struck with a palsy in the night, commonly knows not that he has lost the power of speech till he attempts to speak: he knows not whether he can move his hands and arms till he makes the trial; and if, without making trial, he consults his consciousness ever so attentively, it will give him no information whether he has lost these powers, or still retains them.

From this we must conclude, that the powers we have are not an object of consciousness, though it would be foolish to censure this way of speaking in popular discourse, which requires not accurate attention to the different provinces of our various faculties. The testimony of consciousness is always unerring, nor was it ever called in question by the greatest sceptics, ancient or modern.

2. A *second* observation is—That, as there are some things of which we have a *direct*, and others of which we have only a *relative*, conception; Power belongs to the latter class. . . .

Of some things, we know what they are in themselves: our conception of such things I call *direct*. Of other things, we know not what they are in themselves, but only that they have certain properties or attributes, or certain relations to other things: of these our conception is only *relative*. . . .

Of this kind are our notions both of body and mind. What is body? It is, say philosophers, that which is extended, solid, and divisible. Says the querist, I do not ask what the properties of body are, but what is the thing itself; let me first know directly what body is, and then consider its properties? To this demand, I am afraid the querist will meet with no satisfactory answer; because our notion of body is not direct but relative to its qualities. We know that it is something extended, solid, and divisible, and we know no more.

Again, if it should be asked, What is mind? It is that which thinks. I ask not what it does, or what its operations are, but what it is. To this I can find no answer; our notion of mind being not direct, but relative to its operations, as our notion of body is relative to its qualities.

There are even many of the qualities of body, of which we have only a relative conception. What is heat in a body? It is a quality which affects the sense of touch in a certain way. If you want to know, not how it affects the sense of touch, but what it is in itself—this, I confess, I know not. My conception of it is not direct, but relative to the effect it has upon bodies. The notions we have of all those qualities which Mr Locke calls secondary, and of those he calls powers of bodies—such as the power of the magnet to attract iron, or of fire to burn wood—are relative.

Our conception of power is relative to its exertions or effects. Power is one thing; its exertion is another thing. It is true, there can be no exertion without power; but there may be power that is not exerted. Thus, a man may have power to speak when he is silent; he may have power to rise and walk when he sits still.

But, though it be one thing to speak, and another to have the power of speaking, I apprehend we conceive of the power as something which has a certain relation to the effect. And of every power we form our notion by the effect which it is able to produce.

3. It is evident that Power is a *quality,* and cannot exist without a subject to which it belongs.

That power may exist without any being or subject to which that power may be attributed, is an absurdity, shocking to every man of common understanding.

It is a quality which may be varied, not only in degree, but also in kind; and we distinguish both the kinds and degrees by the effects which they are able to produce.

Thus a power to fly, and a power to reason, are different kinds of power, their effects being different in kind. But a power to carry one hundred weight, and a power to carry two hundred, are different degrees of the same kind.

4. We cannot conclude the want of power from its not being exerted; nor from the exertion of a less degree of power, can

we conclude that there is no greater degree in the subject. Thus, though a man on a particular occasion said nothing, we cannot conclude from that circumstance, that he had not the power of speech; nor from a man's carrying ten pound weight, can we conclude that he had not power to carry twenty.

5. There are some qualities that have a *contrary*, others that have not: Power is a quality of the latter kind.

Vice is contrary to virtue, misery to happiness, hatred to love, negation to affirmation; but there is no contrary to power. Weakness or impotence are defects or privations of power, but not contraries to it.

If what has been said of power be easily understood, and readily assented to, by all who understand our language, as I believe it is, we may from this justly conclude, That we have a distinct notion of power, and may reason about it with understanding, though we can give no logical definition of it.

If power were a thing of which we have no idea, as some philosophers have taken much pains to prove—that is, if power were a word without any meaning—we could neither affirm nor deny anything concerning it with understanding. We should have equal reason to say that it is a substance, as that it is a quality; that it does not admit of degrees as that it does. If the understanding immediately assents to one of these assertions, and revolts from the contrary, we may conclude with certainty, that we put some meaning upon the word *power* —that is, that we have some idea of it. And it is chiefly for the sake of this conclusion, that I have enumerated so many obvious things concerning it.

The term *active power* is used, I conceive to distinguish it from *speculative powers*. As all languages distinguish action from speculation, the same distinction is applied to the powers by which they are produced. The powers of seeing, hearing, remembering, distinguishing, judging, reasoning, are speculative powers; the power of executing any work of art or labour is active power. . . .

CHAPTER 5 / WHETHER BEINGS THAT HAVE NO WILL NOR UNDERSTANDING MAY HAVE ACTIVE POWER

That active power is an attribute, which cannot exist but in some being possessed of that power, and the subject of that attribute, I take for granted as a self-evident truth. Whether there can be active power in a subject which has no thought, no understanding, no will, is not so evident.

The ambiguity of the words *power, cause, agent,* and of all the words related to these, tends to perplex this question. The weakness of human understanding, which gives us only an indirect and relative conception of power, contributes to darken our reasoning, and should make us cautious and modest in our determinations.

We can derive little light in this matter from the events which we observe in the course of nature. We perceive changes innumerable in things without us. We know that those changes must be produced by the active power of some agent; but we neither perceive the agent nor the power, but the change only. Whether the things be active, or merely passive, is not easily discovered. And though it may be an object of curiosity to the speculative few, it does not greatly concern the many.

To know the event and the circumstances that attended it, and to know in what circumstances like events may be expected, may be of consequence in the conduct of life; but to know the real efficient, whether it be matter or mind, whether of a superior or inferior order, concerns us little.

Thus it is with regard to all the effects we ascribe to nature.

Nature is the name we give to the efficient cause of innumerable effects which fall daily under our observation. But, if it be asked what nature is—whether the first universal cause or a subordinate one, whether one or many, whether intelligent or unintelligent—upon these points we find various conjectures and theories, but no solid ground upon which we can rest. And I apprehend the wisest men are they who are sensible that they know nothing of the matter.

From the course of events in the natural world, we have sufficient reason to conclude the existence of an eternal intelligent First Cause. But whether He acts immediately in the production of those events, or by subordinate intelligent agents, or by instruments that are unintelligent, and what the number, the nature, and the different offices, of those agents or instruments may be—these I apprehend to be mysteries placed beyond the limits of human knowledge. We see an established order in the succession of natural events, but we see not the bond that connects them together.

Since we derive so little light, with regard to efficient causes and their active power, from attention to the natural world, let us next attend to the moral, I mean to human actions and conduct. . . .

When I observe a plant growing from its seed to maturity, I know that there must be a cause that has power to produce this effect. But I see neither the cause nor the manner of its operation.

But, in certain motions of my body and directions of my thought, I know not only that there must be a cause that has power to produce these effects, but that I am that cause; and I am conscious of what I do in order to the production of them.

From the consciousness of our own activity, seems to be derived not only the clearest, but the only conception we can form of activity, or the exertion of active power.

As I am unable to form a notion of any intellectual power different in kind from those I possess, the same holds with respect to active power. If all men had been blind, we should have had no conception of the power of seeing, nor any name for it in language. If man had not the powers of abstraction and reasoning, we could not have had any conception of these operations. In like manner, if he had not some degree of active power, and if he were not conscious of the exertion of it in his voluntary actions, it is probable he could have no conception of activity, or of active power.

A train of events following one another ever so regularly, could never lead us to the notion of a cause, if we had not, from our constitution, a conviction of the necessity of a cause to every event.

And of the manner in which a cause may exert its active power, we can have no conception, but from consciousness of the manner in which our own active power is exerted.

With regard to the operations of nature, it is sufficient for us to know, that, whatever the agents may be, whatever the manner of their operation or the extent of their power, they depend upon the First Cause, and are under his control; and this indeed is all that we know; beyond this we are left in darkness. But, in what regards human actions, we have a more immediate concern.

It is of the highest importance to us, as moral and accountable creatures, to know what actions are in our own power, because it is for these only that we can be accountable to our Maker, or to our fellow-men in society; by these only we can merit praise or blame; in these only all our prudence, wisdom, and virtue must be employed; and, therefore, with regard to them, the wise Author of nature has not left us in the dark.

Every man is led by nature to attribute to himself the free determinations of his own will, and to believe those events to be in his power which depend upon his will. On the other hand, it is self-evident, that nothing is in our power that is not subject to our will.

We grow from childhood to manhood, we digest our food, our blood circulates, our heart and arteries beat, we are sometimes sick and sometimes in health; all these things must be done by the power of some agent; but they are not done by our power. How do we know this? Because they are not subject to our will. This is the infallible criterion by which we distinguish what is our doing from what is not; what is in our power from what is not.

Human power, therefore, can only be exerted by will, and we are unable to conceive any active power to be exerted without will. Every man knows infallibly that what is done by his conscious will and intention, is to be imputed to him, as the agent or cause; and that whatever is done without his will and intention, cannot be imputed to him with truth.

We judge of the actions and conduct of other men by the same rule as we judge of our own. In morals, it is self-evident that no man can be the object either of approbation or of blame for what he did not. But how shall we know whether it is his doing or not? If the action depended upon his will, and if he intended and willed it, it is his action in the judgment of all mankind. But if it was done without his knowledge, or without his will and intention, it is as certain that he did it not, and that it ought not to be imputed to him as the agent.

When there is any doubt to whom a particular action ought to be imputed, the doubt arises only from our ignorance of facts; when the facts relating to it are known, no man of understanding has any doubt to whom the action ought to be imputed.

The general rules of imputation are self-evident. They have been the same in all ages, and among all civilized nations. No man blames another for being black or fair, for having a fever or the falling sickness; because these things are believed not to be in his power; and they are believed not to be in his power, because they depend not upon his will. We can never conceive that a man's duty goes beyond his power, or that his power goes beyond what depends upon his will.

Reason leads us to ascribe unlimited power to the Supreme Being. But what do we mean by unlimited power? It is power to do whatsoever he wills. To suppose him to do what he does not will to do, is absurd.

The only distinct conception I can form of active power is,

that it is an attribute in a being by which he can do certain things if he wills. This, after all, is only a relative conception. It is relative to the effect, and to the will of producing it. Take away these, and the conception vanishes. They are the handles by which the mind takes hold of it. When they are taken away, our hold is gone. The same is the case with regard to other relative conceptions. . . .

If it be so that the conception of an efficient cause enters into the mind, only from the early conviction we have that we are the efficients of our own voluntary actions, (which I think is most probable,) the notion of efficiency will be reduced to this, That it is a relation between the cause and the effect, similar to that which is between us and our voluntary actions. This is surely the most distinct notion, and, I think, the only notion we can form of real efficiency.

Now it is evident, that, to constitute the relation between me and my action, my conception of the action, and will to do it, are essential. For what I never conceived nor willed, I never did.

If any man, therefore, affirms, that a being may be the efficient cause of an action, and have power to produce it, which that being can neither conceive nor will, he speaks a language which I do not understand. If he has a meaning, his notion of power and efficiency must be essentially different from mine; and, until he conveys his notion of efficiency to my understanding, I can no more assent to his opinion than if he should affirm that a being without life may feel pain.

It seems, therefore, to me most probable, that such beings only as have some degree of understanding and will, can possess active power; and that inanimate beings must be merely passive, and have no real activity. Nothing we perceive without us affords any good ground for ascribing active power to any inanimate being; and everything we can discover in our own constitution, leads us to think that active power cannot be exerted without will and intelligence.

CHAPTER 6 / OF THE EFFICIENT CAUSES OF THE PHAENOMENA OF NATURE

If active power, in its proper meaning, requires a subject endowed with will and intelligence, what shall we say of those active powers which philosophers teach us to ascribe to matter —the powers of corpuscular attraction, magnetism, electricity, gravitation, and others? Is it not universally allowed, that heavy bodies descend to the earth by the power of gravity; that, by the same power, the moon, and all the planets and comets, are retained in their orbits? Have the most eminent natural philosophers been imposing upon us, giving us words instead of real causes?

In answer to this, I apprehend, that the principles of natural philosophy have, in modern times, been built upon a foundation that cannot be shaken, and that they can be called in question only by those who do not understand the evidence on which they stand. But the ambiguity of the words *cause, agency, active power*, and the other words related to these, has led many to understand them, when used in natural philosophy, in a wrong sense, and in a sense which is neither necessary for establishing the true principles of natural philosophy, nor was ever meant by the most enlightened in that science.

To be convinced of this, we may observe that those very philosophers who attribute to matter the power of gravitation, and other active powers, teach us, at the same time, that matter is a substance altogether inert, and merely passive; that gravitation, and the other attractive or repulsive powers which they ascribe to it, are not inherent in its nature, but impressed upon it by some external cause, which they do not pretend to know or to explain. Now, when we find wise men ascribing action and active power to a substance which they expressly teach us to consider as merely passive and acted upon by some unknown cause, we must conclude that the action and active power ascribed to it are not to be understood strictly, but in some popular sense.

It ought likewise to be observed, that although philosophers, for the sake of being understood must speak the language of the vulgar—as when they say, the sun rises and sets, and goes through all the signs of the zodiac—yet they often think differently from the vulgar. . . .

In all languages, action is attributed to many things which all men of common understanding believe to be merely passive. Thus, we say the wind blows, the rivers flow, the sea rages, the fire burns, bodies move, and impel other bodies.

Every object which undergoes any change must be either active or passive in that change. This is self-evident to all men from the first dawn of reason; and, therefore, the change is always expressed in language, either by an active or a passive verb. Nor do I know any verb, expressive of a change, which does not imply either action or passion. The thing either changes, or it is changed. But it is remarkable in language, that when an external cause of the change is not obvious, the change is always imputed to the thing changed, as if it were animated, and had active power to produce the change in itself. So we say, the moon changes, the sun rises and goes down.

Thus active verbs are very often applied, and active power imputed to things, which a little advance in knowledge and experience teaches us to be merely passive. This property, common to all languages, I endeavoured to account for in the second chapter of this Essay, to which the reader is referred.

A like irregularity may be observed in the use of the word signifying *cause*, in all languages, and of the words related to it. . . .

In common language, we give the name of a *cause* to a reason, a motive, an end, to any circumstance which is connected with the effect, and goes before it.

Aristotle, and the schoolmen after him, distinguished four

kinds of causes—the Efficient, the Material, the Formal, and the Final. This, like many of Aristotle's distinctions, is only a distinction of the various meanings of an ambiguous word; for the Efficient, the Matter, the Form, and the End, have nothing common in their nature, by which they may be accounted species of the same *genus;* but the Greek word which we translate *cause*, had these four different meanings in Aristotle's days, and we have added other meanings. We do not indeed call the matter or the form of a thing its cause; but we have final causes, instrumental causes, occasional causes, and I know not how many others.

Thus the word *cause* has been so hackneyed, and made to have so many different meanings in the writings of philosophers, and in the discourse of the vulgar, that its original and proper meaning is lost in the crowd.

With regard to the phaenomena of nature, the important end of knowing their causes, besides gratifying our curiosity, is, that we may know when to expect them, or how to bring them about. This is very often of real importance in life; and this purpose is served by knowing what, by the course of nature, goes before them and is connected with them; and this, therefore, we call the *cause* of such a phaenomenon.

If a magnet be brought near to a mariner's compass, the needle, which was before at rest, immediately begins to move, and bends its course towards the magnet, or perhaps the contrary way. If an unlearned sailor is asked the cause of this motion of the needle, he is at no loss for an answer. He tells you it is the magnet; and the proof is clear; for, remove the magnet, and the effect ceases; bring it near, and the effect is again produced. It is, therefore, evident to sense, that the magnet is the cause of this effect.

A Cartesian philosopher enters deeper into the cause of this phaenomenon. He observes, that the magnet does not touch the needle, and therefore can give it no impulse. He pities the ignorance of the sailor. The effect is produced, says he, by magnetic effluvia, or subtile matter, which passes from the magnet to the needle, and forces it from its place. He can even shew you, in a figure, where these magnetic effluvia issue from the magnet, what round they take, and what way they return home again. And thus he thinks he comprehends perfectly how, and by what cause, the motion of the needle is produced.

A Newtonian philosopher inquires what proof can be offered for the existence of magnetic effluvia, and can find none. He therefore holds it as a fiction, a hypothesis; and he has learned that hypotheses ought to have no place in the philosophy of nature. He confesses his ignorance of the real cause of this motion, and thinks that his business, as a philosopher, is only to find from experiment the laws by which it is regulated in all cases.

These three persons differ much in their sentiments with regard to the real cause of this phaenomenon; and the man who knows most is he who is sensible that he knows nothing of the matter. Yet all the three speak the same language, and acknowledge that the cause of this motion is the attractive or repulsive power of the magnet.

What has been said of this, may be applied to every phaenomenon that falls within the compass of natural philosophy. We deceive ourselves if we conceive that we can point out the real efficient cause of any one of them.

The grandest discovery ever made in natural philosophy, was that of the law of gravitation, which opens such a view of our planetary system that it looks like something divine. But the author of this discovery was perfectly aware, that he discovered no real cause, but only the law or rule, according to which the unknown cause operates.

Natural philosophers, who think accurately, have a precise meaning to the terms they use in the science; and, when they pretend to shew the cause of any phaenomenon of nature, they mean by the cause, a law of nature of which that phaenomenon is a necessary consequence.

The whole object of natural philosophy, as Newton expressly teaches, is reducible to these two heads: first, by just induction from experiment and observation, to discover the laws of nature; and then, to apply those laws to the solution of the phaenomena of nature. This was all that this great philosopher attempted, and all that he thought attainable. And this indeed he attained in a great measure, with regard to the motions of our planetary system, and with regard to the rays of light.

But supposing that all the phaenomena that fall within the reach of our senses, were accounted for from general laws of nature, justly deduced from experience—that is, supposing natural philosophy brought to its utmost perfection—it does not discover the efficient cause of any one phaenomenon in nature.

The laws of nature are the rules according to which the effects are produced; but there must be a cause which operates according to these rules. The rules of navigation never navigated a ship; the rules of architecture never built a house.

Natural philosophers, by great attention to the course of nature, have discovered many of her laws, and have very happily applied them to account for many phaenomena; but they have never discovered the efficient cause of any one phaenomenon; nor do those who have distinct notions of the principles of the science make any such pretence.

Upon the theatre of nature we see innumerable effects, which require an agent endowed with active power; but the agent is behind the scene. Whether it be the Supreme Cause alone, or a subordinate cause or causes; and if subordinate causes be employed by the Almighty, what their nature, their number, and their different offices may be—are things hid, for wise reasons without doubt, from the human eye.

It is only in human actions, that may be imputed for praise or blame, that it is necessary for us to know who is the agent; and in this, nature has given us all the light that is necessary for our conduct.

ESSAY THREE, PART III / OF THE RATIONAL PRINCIPLES OF ACTION

CHAPTER 5 / OF THE NOTION OF DUTY, RECTITUDE, MORAL OBLIGATION

A BEING endowed with the animal principles of action only, may be capable of being trained to certain purposes by discipline, as we see many brute-animals are, but would be altogether incapable of being governed by law.

The subject of law must have the conception of a general rule of conduct, which, without some degree of reason, he cannot have. He must likewise have a sufficient inducement to obey the law, even when his strongest animal desires draw him the contrary way.

This inducement may be a sense of *interest,* or a sense of *duty,* or both concurring.

These are the only principles I am able to conceive, which can reasonably induce a man to regulate all his actions according to a certain general rule or law. They may therefore be justly called the *rational* principles of action, since they can have no place but in a being endowed with reason, and since it is by them only that man is capable either of political or of moral government.

Without them human life would be like a ship at sea without hands, left to be carried by winds and tides as they happen. It belongs to the rational part of our nature to intend a certain port, as the end of the voyage of life; to take the advantage of winds and tides when they are favourable, and to bear up against them when they are unfavourable.

A sense of interest may induce us to do this, when a suitable reward is set before us. But there is a nobler principle in the constitution of man, which, in many cases, gives a clearer and more certain rule of conduct, than a regard merely to interest would give, and a principle, without which man would not be a moral agent.

A man is prudent when he consults his real interest; but he cannot be virtuous, if he has no regard to duty.

I proceed now to consider this *regard to Duty* as a rational principle of action in man, and as that principle alone by which he is capable either of virtue or vice.

I shall first offer some observations with regard to the *general notion of duty, and its contrary, or of right and wrong in human conduct,* and then consider, *how we come to judge and determine certain things in human conduct to be right, and others to be wrong.*

With regard to the *notion* or *conception* of Duty, I take it to be too simple to admit of a logical definition.

We can define it only by synonymous words or phrases, or by its properties and necessary concomitants, as when we say that it is *what we ought to do—what is fair and honest—what is approvable—what every man professes to be the rule of his conduct— what all men praise—*and, *what is in itself laudable, though no man should praise it.*

I observe, in the *next* place, That the notion of duty cannot be resolved into that of interest, or what is most for our happiness.

Every man may be satisfied of this who attends to his own conceptions, and the language of all mankind shews it. When I say, This is my interest, I mean one thing; when I say, It is my duty, I mean another thing. And, though the same course of action, when rightly understood, may be both my duty and my interest, the conceptions are very different. Both are reasonable motives to action, but quite distinct in their nature.

I presume it will be granted, that, in every man of real worth, there is a principle of honour, a regard to what is honourable or dishonourable, very distinct from a regard to his interest. It is folly in a man to disregard his interest, but to do what is dishonourable, is baseness. The first may move our pity, or, in some cases, our contempt; but the last provokes our indignation.

As these two principles are different in their nature, and not resolvable into one, so the principle of honour is evidently superior in dignity to that of interest.

No man would allow him to be a man of honour who should plead his interest to justify what he acknowledged to be dishonourable; but to sacrifice interest to honour never costs a blush.

It likewise will be allowed by every man of honour, that this principle is not to be resolved into a regard to our reputation among men, otherwise the man of honour would not deserve to be trusted in the dark. He would have no aversion to lie or cheat, or play the coward, when he had no dread of being discovered.

I take it for granted, therefore, that every man of real honour feels an abhorrence of certain actions, because they are in themselves base, and feels an obligation to certain other actions, because they are in themselves what honour requires, and this independently of any consideration of interest or reputation.

This is an immediate moral obligation. This principle of honour, which is acknowledged by all men who pretend to character, is only another name for what we call a regard to duty, to rectitude, to propriety of conduct. It is a moral obligation which obliges a man to do certain things because they are right, and not to do other things because they are wrong.

Ask the man of honour why he thinks himself obliged to pay a debt of honour? The very question shocks him. To suppose that he needs any other inducement to do it but the principle of honour, is to suppose that he has no honour, no worth, and deserves no esteem.

There is, therefore, a principle in man, which, when he acts according to it, gives him a consciousness of worth, and, when he acts contrary to it, a sense of demerit.

From the varieties of education, of fashion, of prejudices, and of habits, men may differ much in opinion with regard to the extent of this principle, and of what it commands and forbids, but the notion of it, as far as it is carried, is the same in all. It is that which gives a man real worth, and is the object of moral approbation.

Men of rank call it *honour,* and too often confine it to certain virtues that are thought most essential to their rank. The vulgar call it *honesty, probity, virtue, conscience.* Philosophers have given it the names of *the moral sense, the moral faculty, rectitude.*

The universality of this principle in men that are grown up to years of understanding and reflection, is evident. The words that express it, the names of the virtues which it commands, and of the vices which it forbids, the *ought* and *ought not* which express its dictates, make an essential part of every language. The natural affections of respect to worthy characters, of resentment of injuries, of gratitude for favours, of indignation against the worthless, are parts of the human constitution which suppose a right and wrong in conduct. Many transactions that are found necessary in the rudest societies go upon the same supposition. In all testimony, in all promises, and in all contracts, there is necessarily implied a moral obligation on one party, and a trust in the other, grounded upon this obligation.

The variety of opinions among men in points of morality, is not greater, but, as I apprehend, much less than in speculative points; and this variety is as easily accounted for, from the common causes of error, in the one case as in the other; so that it is not more evident, that there is a real distinction between true and false, in matters of speculation, than that there is a real distinction between right and wrong in human conduct. . . .

If we examine the abstract notion of Duty, or Moral Obligation, it appears to be neither any real quality of the action considered by itself, nor of the agent considered without respect to the action, but a certain relation between the one and the other.

When we say a man ought to do such a thing, the *ought*, which expresses the moral obligation, has a respect, on the one hand, to the person who ought; and, on the other, to the action which he ought to do. Those two correlates are essential to every moral obligation; take away either, and it has no existence. So that, if we seek the place of moral obligation among the categories, it belongs to the category of *relation*.

There are many relations of things, of which we have the most distinct conception, without being able to define them logically. Equality and proportion are relations between quantities, which every man understands, but no man can define.

Moral obligation is a relation of its own kind, which every man understands, but is, perhaps, too simple to admit of logical definition. Like all other relations, it may be changed or annihilated by a change in any of the two related things—I mean the agent or the action.

Perhaps it may not be improper to point out briefly the circumstances, both in the action and in the agent, which are necessary to constitute moral obligation. The universal agreement of men in these, shews they have one and the same notion of it.

With regard to the action, it must be a voluntary action, or prestation of the person obliged, and not of another. There can be no moral obligation upon a man to be six feet high. Nor can I be under a moral obligation that another person should do such a thing. His actions must be imputed to himself, and mine only to me, either for praise or blame.

I need hardly mention, that a person can be under a moral obligation, only to things within the sphere of his natural power.

As to the party obliged, it is evident there can be no moral obligation upon an inanimate thing. To speak of moral obligation upon a stone or a tree is ridiculous, because it contradicts every man's notion of moral obligation.

The person obliged must have understanding and will, and some degree of active power. He must not only have the natural faculty of understanding, but the means of knowing his obligation. An invincible ignorance of this destroys all moral obligation.

The opinion of the agent in doing the action gives it its moral denomination. If he does a materially good action, without any belief of its being good, but from some other principle, it is no good action in him. And if he does it with the belief of its being ill, it is ill in him.

Thus, if a man should give to his neighbour a potion which he really believes will poison him, but which, in the event, proves salutary, and does much good; in moral estimation, he is a poisoner, and not a benefactor.

These qualifications of the action and of the agent, in moral obligation, are self-evident; and the agreement of all men in them shews that all men have the same notion, and a distinct notion of moral obligation.

CHAPTER 6 / OF THE SENSE OF DUTY

We are next to consider, how we learn to judge and determine, that this is right, and that is wrong.

The abstract notion of moral good and ill would be of no use to direct our life, if we had not the power of applying it to particular actions, and determining what is morally good, and what is morally ill.

Some philosophers, with whom I agree, ascribe this to an original power or faculty in man, which they call the *Moral Sense*, the *Moral Faculty*, *Conscience*. Others think that our moral sentiments may be accounted for without supposing any original sense or faculty appropriated to that purpose, and go into very different systems to account for them.

I am not, at present, to take any notice of those systems,

because the opinion first mentioned seems to me to be the truth; to wit, That, by an original power of the mind, when we come to years of understanding and reflection, we not only have the notions of right and wrong in conduct, but perceive certain things to be right, and others to be wrong.

The name of the *Moral Sense,* though more frequently given to Conscience since Lord Shaftesbury and Dr Hutcheson wrote, is not new. The *sensus recti et honesti,* is a phrase not unfrequent among the ancients; neither is the *sense of duty,* among us.

It has got this name of *sense,* no doubt, from some analogy which it is conceived to bear to the external senses. And, if we have just notions of the office of the external senses, the analogy is very evident, and I see no reason to take offence, as some have done, at the name of the *moral sense. . . .*

In its dignity it is, without doubt, far superior to every other power of the mind; but there is this analogy between it and the external senses, That, as by them we have not only the original conceptions of the various qualities of bodies, but the original judgment that this body has such a quality, that such another; so by our moral faculty, we have both the original conceptions of right and wrong in conduct, of merit and demerit, and the original judgments that this conduct is right, that is wrong; that this character has worth, that demerit.

The testimony of our moral faculty, like that of the external senses, is the testimony of nature, and we have the same reason to rely upon it.

The truths immediately testified by the external senses are the first principles from which we reason, with regard to the material world, and from which all our knowledge of it is deduced.

The truths immediately testified by our moral faculty, are the first principles of all moral reasoning, from which all our knowledge of our duty must be deduced.

By moral reasoning, I understand all reasoning that is

brought to prove that such conduct is right, and deserving of moral approbation; or that it is wrong; or that it is indifferent, and, in itself, neither morally good nor ill.

I think, all we can properly call moral judgments, are reducible to one or other of these, as all human actions, considered in a moral view, are either good, or bad, or indifferent.

I know the term *moral reasoning* is often used by good writers in a more extensive sense; but, as the reasoning I now speak of is of a peculiar kind, distinct from all others, and, therefore, ought to have a distinct name, I take the liberty to limit the name of *moral reasoning* to this kind.

Let it be understood, therefore, that in the reasoning I call *moral*, the conclusion always is, That something in the conduct of moral agents is good or bad, in a greater or a less degree, or indifferent.

All reasoning must be grounded on first principles. This holds in moral reasoning, as in all other kinds. There must, therefore, be in morals, as in all other sciences, first or self-evident principles, on which all moral reasoning is grounded, and on which it ultimately rests. From such self-evident principles, conclusions may be drawn synthetically with regard to the moral conduct of life; and particular duties or virtues may be traced back to such principles, analytically. But, without such principles, we can no more establish any conclusion in morals, than we can build a castle in the air, without any foundation.

An example or two will serve to illustrate this.

It is a first principle in morals, That we ought not do to another what we should think wrong to be done to us in like circumstances. If a man is not capable of perceiving this in his cool moments, when he reflects seriously, he is not a moral agent, nor is he capable of being convinced of it by reasoning.

From what topic can you reason with such a man? You may possibly convince him by reasoning, that it is his interest to observe this rule; but this is not to convince him that it is his duty. To reason about justice with a man who sees nothing to be just or unjust, or about benevolence with a man who sees nothing in benevolence preferable to malice, is like reasoning with a blind man about colour, or with a deaf man about sound.

It is a question in morals that admits of reasoning, Whether, by the law of nature, a man ought to have only one wife?

We reason upon this question, by balancing the advantages and disadvantages to the family, and to society in general, that are naturally consequent both upon monogamy and polygamy. And, if it can be shewn that the advantages are greatly upon the side of monogamy, we think the point is determined.

But, if a man does not perceive that he ought to regard the good of society, and the good of his wife and children, the reasoning can have no effect upon him, because he denies the first principle upon which it is grounded.

Suppose, again, that we reason for monogamy from the intention of nature, discovered by the proportion of males and of females that are born—a proportion which corresponds perfectly with monogamy, but by no means with polygamy—this argument can have no weight with a man who does not perceive that be ought to have a regard to the intention of nature.

Thus we shall find that all moral reasonings rest upon one or more first principles of morals, whose truth is immediately perceived without reasoning, by all men come to years of understanding. . . .

The first principles of morals are the immediate dictates of the moral faculty. They shew us, not what man is, but what he ought to be. Whatever is immediately perceived to be just, honest, and honourable, in human conduct, carries moral obligation along with it, and the contrary carries demerit and blame; and, from those moral obligations that are immediately perceived, all other moral obligations must be deduced by reasoning.

He that will judge of the colour of an object, must consult his eyes, in a good light, when there is no medium or contiguous objects that may give it a false tinge. But in vain will he consult every other faculty in this matter.

In like manner, he that will judge of the first principles of morals, must consult his conscience, or moral faculty, when he is calm and dispassionate, unbiased by interest, affection, or fashion.

As we rely upon the clear and distinct testimony of our eyes, concerning the colours and figures of the bodies about us, we have the same reason to rely with security upon the clear and unbiased testimony of our conscience, with regard to what we ought and ought not to do. In many cases moral worth and demerit are discerned no less clearly by the last of those natural faculties, than figure and colour by the first.

The faculties which nature hath given us, are the only engines we can use to find out the truth. We cannot indeed prove that those faculties are not fallacious, unless God should give us new faculties to sit in judgment upon the old. But we are born under a necessity of trusting them. . . .

ESSAY FOUR / OF THE LIBERTY OF MORAL AGENTS

CHAPTER 1 / THE NOTIONS OF MORAL LIBERTY AND NECESSITY STATED

By the *Liberty of a Moral Agent,* I understand, *a power over the determinations of his own Will.*

If, in any action, he had power to will what he did, or not to will it, in that action he is free. But if, in every voluntary action, the determination of his will be the necessary consequence of something involuntary in the state of his mind, or of something in his external circumstances, he is not free; he has not what I call the Liberty of a Moral Agent, but is subject to Necessity.

This Liberty supposes the agent to have Understanding and Will; for the determinations of the will are the sole object about which this power is employed; and there can be no will without such a degree of understanding, at least, as gives the conception of that which we will.

The liberty of a moral agent implies, not only a *conception* of what he wills, but some degree of practical *judgment* or *reason*.

For, if he has not the judgment to discern one determination to be preferable to another, either in itself or for some purpose which he intends, what can be the use of a power to determine? His determinations must be made perfectly in the dark, without reason, motive, or end. They can neither be right nor wrong, wise nor foolish. Whatever the consequences may be, they cannot be imputed to the agent, who had not the capacity of foreseeing them, or of perceiving any reason for acting otherwise than he did.

We may, perhaps, be able to conceive a being endowed with power over the determinations of his will, without any light in his mind to direct that power to some end. But such power would be given in vain. No exercise of it could be either blamed or approved. As nature gives no power in vain, I see no ground to ascribe a power over the determinations of the will to any being who has no judgment to apply it to the direction of his conduct, no discernment of what he ought or ought not to do.

For that reason, in this Essay, I speak only of the Liberty of Moral Agents, who are capable of acting well or ill, wisely or foolishly, and this, for distinction's sake, I shall call *Moral Liberty.*

What kind or what degree of liberty belongs to brute animals, or to our own species, before any use of reason, I do not know. We acknowledge that they have not the power of self-government. Such of their actions as may be called *voluntary* seem to be invariably determined by the passion, or appetite, or affection, or habit, which is strongest at the time.

This seems to be the law of their constitution, to which they yield, as the inanimate creation does, without any conception of the law, or any intention of obedience.

But of civil or moral government, which are addressed to the rational powers, and require a conception of the law and an intentional obedience, they are, in the judgment of all mankind, incapable. Nor do I see what end could be served by giving them a power over the determinations of their own will, unless to make them intractable by discipline, which we see they are not.

The effect of moral liberty is, *That it is in the power of the agent to do well or ill.* This power, like every other gift of God, may be abused. The right use of this gift of God is to do well and wisely, as far as his best judgment can direct him, and thereby merit esteem and approbation. The abuse of it is to act contrary to what he knows or suspects to be his duty and his wisdom, and thereby justly merit disapprobation and blame.

By *Necessity*, I understand the want of that moral liberty which I have above defined.

If there can be a better and a worse in actions on the system of Necessity, let us suppose a man necessarily determined in all cases to will and to do what is best to be done, he would surely be innocent and inculpable. But, as far as I am able to judge, he would not be entitled to the esteem and moral approbation of those who knew and believed this necessity. What was, by an ancient author, said of Cato, might, indeed, be said of him: *He was good because he could not be otherwise.* But this saying, if understood literally and strictly, is not the praise of Cato, but of his constitution, which was no more the work of Cato than his existence.

On the other hand, if a man be necessarily determined to do ill, this case seems to me to move pity, but not disapprobation. He was ill, because he could not be other wise. Who can blame him? Necessity has no law. . . .

Such are my notions of moral liberty and necessity, and of the consequences inseparably connected with both the one and the other.

This moral liberty a man may have, though it do not extend to all his actions, or even to all his voluntary actions. He does many things by instinct, many things by the force of habit, without any thought at all, and consequently without will. In the first part of life, he has not the power of self-government any more than the brutes. That power over the determinations of his own will, which belongs to him in ripe years, is limited, as all his powers are; and it is, perhaps, beyond the reach of his understanding to define its limits with precision. We can only say, in general, that it extends to every action for which he is accountable.

This power is given by his Maker, and at his pleasure whose gift it is it may be enlarged or diminished, continued or withdrawn. No power in the creature can be independent of the Creator. His hook is in its nose; he can give it line as far as he sees fit, and, when he pleases, can restrain it, or turn it whithersoever he will. Let this be always understood when we ascribe liberty to man, or to any created being.

Supposing it therefore to be true, *That man is a free agent*, it may be true, at the same time, that his liberty may be impaired or lost, by disorder of body or mind, as in melancholy, or in madness; it may be impaired or lost by vicious habits; it may, in particular cases, be restrained by divine interposition.

We call man a *free* agent in the same way as we call him a *reasonable* agent. In many things he is not guided by reason, but by principles similar to those of the brutes. His reason is weak at best. It is liable to be impaired or lost, by his own fault, or by other means. In like manner, he may be a free agent, though his freedom of action may have many similar limitations.

The liberty I have described has been represented by some philosophers as inconceivable, and as involving an absurdity.

"Liberty, they say, consists only in a power to act as we will; and it is impossible to conceive in any being a greater liberty than this. Hence it follows, that liberty does not extend to the determinations of the will, but only to the actions consequent to its determination, and depending upon the will. To say that we have power to will such an action, is to say, that we may will it, if we will. This supposes the will to be determined by a prior will; and, for the same reason, that will must be determined by a will prior to it, and so on in an infinite series of wills, which is absurd. To act freely, therefore, can mean nothing more than to act voluntarily; and this is all the liberty that can be conceived in man, or in any being."

This reasoning—first, I think, advanced by Hobbes—has been very generally adopted by the defenders of necessity. It is grounded upon a definition of liberty totally different from that which I have given, and therefore does not apply to moral liberty, as above defined.

But it is said that this is the only liberty that is possible, that is conceivable, that does not involve an absurdity.

It is strange, indeed, if the word *Liberty* has no meaning but this one. I shall mention *three*, all very common. The objection applies to one of them, but to neither of the other two.

Liberty is sometimes opposed to external force or confinement of the body. Sometimes it is opposed to obligation by law, or by lawful authority. Sometimes it is opposed to necessity.

1. It is opposed to confinement of the body by superior force. So we say a prisoner is set at liberty when his fetters are knocked off, and he is discharged from confinement. This is the liberty defined in the objection; and I grant that this liberty extends not to the will, neither does the confinement, because the will cannot be confined by external force.

2. Liberty is opposed to obligation by law, or lawful authority. This liberty is a right to act one way or another, in things which the law has neither commanded nor forbidden; and this liberty is meant when we speak of a man's natural liberty, his civil liberty, his Christian liberty. It is evident that this liberty, as well as the obligation opposed to it, extends to the will: For it is the will to obey that makes obedience; the will to transgress that makes a transgression of the law. Without will there can be neither obedience nor transgression. Law supposes a power to obey or to trangress; it does not take away this power, but proposes the motives of duty and of interest, leaving the power to yield to them, or to take the consequence of transgression.

3. Liberty is opposed to Necessity, and in this sense it extends to the determinations of the will only, and not to what is consequent to the will.

In every voluntary action, the determination of the will is the first part of the action, upon which alone the moral estimation of it depends. It has been made a question among philosophers, *Whether, in every instance, this determination be the necessary consequence of the constitution of the person, and the circumstances in which he is placed; or whether he had not power, in many cases, to determine this way or that?*

This has, by some, been called the *philosophical* notion of liberty and necessity; but it is by no means peculiar to philosophers. The lowest of the vulgar have, in all ages, been prone to have recourse to this necessity, to exculpate themselves or their friends in what they do wrong, though, in the general tenor of their conduct, they act upon the contrary principle.

Whether this notion of moral liberty be *conceivable* or not, every man must judge for himself. To me there appears no difficulty in conceiving it. I consider the determination of the will as an effect. This effect must have a cause which had power to produce it; and the cause must be either the person himself, whose will it is, or some other being. The first is as easily conceived as the last. If the person was the cause of that determination of his own will, he was free in that action, and it is justly imputed to him, whether it be good or bad. But, if another being was the cause of this determination, either by producing it immediately, or by means and instruments under his direction, then the determination is the act and deed of that being, and is solely imputable to him.

But it is said—"That nothing is in our power but what depends upon the will, and therefore, the will itself cannot be in our power."

I answer—That this is a fallacy arising from taking a common saying in a sense which it never was intended to convey, and in a sense contrary to what it necessarily implies.

In common life, when men speak of what is, or is not, in a man's power, they attend only to the external and visible effects, which only can be perceived, and which only can affect them. Of these, it is true that nothing is in a man's power but what depends upon his will, and this is all that is meant by this common saying.

But this is so far from excluding his will from being in his power, that it necessarily implies it. For to say that what depends upon the will is in a man's power, but the will is not in his power, is to say that the end is in his power, but the means necessary to that end are not in his power, which is a contradiction.

In many propositions which we express universally, there is an exception necessarily implied, and, therefore, always understood. Thus, when we say that all things depend upon God, God himself is necessarily excepted. In like manner, when we say, that all that is in our power depends upon the will, the will itself is necessarily excepted: for, if the will be not, nothing else can be in our power. Every effect must be in the power of its cause. The determination of the will is an effect, and, therefore, must be in the power of its cause, whether that cause be the agent himself, or some other being.

From what has been said in this chapter, I hope the notion of moral liberty will be distinctly understood, and that it appears that this notion is neither inconceivable, nor involves any absurdity or contradiction.

CHAPTER 2 / OF THE WORDS CAUSE AND EFFECT, ACTION, AND ACTIVE POWER

The writings upon Liberty and Necessity have been much darkened by the ambiguity of the words used in reasoning upon that subject. The words *cause* and *effect*, *action* and *active power*, *liberty* and *necessity*, are related to each other: The meaning of one determines the meaning of the rest. When we attempt to define them, we can only do it by synonymous words which need definition as much. There is a strict sense in which those words must be used, if we speak and reason clearly about moral liberty; but to keep to this strict sense is difficult, because, in all languages, they have, by custom, got a great latitude of signification.

As we cannot reason about moral liberty without using those ambiguous words, it is proper to point out, as distinctly as possible, their proper and original meaning in which they ought to be understood in treating of this subject, and to shew from what causes they have become so ambiguous in all languages as to darken and embarrass our reasonings upon it.

Everything that begins to exist, must have a cause of its existence, which had power to give it existence. And everything that undergoes any change, must have some cause of that change.

That neither existence, nor any mode of existence, can begin without an efficient cause, is a principle that appears very early in the mind of man; and it is so universal, and so firmly rooted in human nature, that the most determined scepticism cannot eradicate it.

It is upon this principle that we ground the rational belief of a deity. But that is not the only use to which we apply it. Every man's conduct is governed by it, every day, and almost every hour, of his life. And if it were possible for any man to root out this principle from his mind, he must give up everything that is called common prudence, and be fit only to be confined as insane.

From this principle it follows, *That everything which undergoes any change, must either be the efficient cause of that change in itself, or it must be changed by some other being.*

In the *first* case, it is said to have *active power*, and to *act* in producing that change. In the *second* case, it is merely *passive*, or is *acted upon*, and the active power is in that being only which produces the change.

The name of a *cause* and of an *agent*, is properly given to that being only, which, by its active power, produces some change in itself, or in some other being. The change, whether it be of thought, of will, or of motion, is the *effect*. Active power, therefore, is a quality in the cause, which enables it to produce the effect. And the exertion of that active power in producing the effect, is called *action, agency, efficiency.*

In order to the production of any effect, there must be in the cause, not only power, but the *exertion of that power;* for power that is not exerted produces no effect.

All that is necessary to the production of any effect, is power in an efficient cause to produce the effect, and the exertion of that power; for it is a contradiction to say, that the cause has power to produce the effect, and exerts that power, and yet the effect is not produced. The effect cannot be in his power unless all the means necessary to its production be in his power.

It is no less a contradiction to say, that a cause has power to produce a certain effect, but that he cannot exert that power; for power which cannot be exerted is no power, and is a contradiction in terms.

To prevent mistake, it is proper to observe, That a being may have a power at one time which it has not at another. It may commonly have a power, which, at a particular time, it has not. Thus, a man may commonly have power to walk or to run; but he has not this power when asleep, or when he is confined by superior force. In common language, he may be said to have a power which he cannot then exert. But this popular expression means only that he commonly has this power, and will have it when the cause is removed which at present deprives him of it; for, when we speak strictly and philosophically, it is a contradiction to say that he has this power, at that moment when he is deprived of it.

These, I think, are necessary consequences from the principle first mentioned—That every change which happens in nature must have an efficient cause which had power to produce it.

Another principle, which appears very early in the mind of man, is, *That we are efficient causes in our deliberate and voluntary actions.*

We are conscious of making an exertion, sometimes with difficulty, in order to produce certain effects. And exertion made deliberately and voluntarily, in order to produce an effect, implies a conviction that the effect is in our power. No man can deliberately attempt what he does not believe to be in his power. The language of all mankind, and their ordinary conduct in life, demonstrate that they have a conviction of some active power in themselves to produce certain motions in their own and in other bodies, and to regulate and direct their own thoughts. This conviction we have so early in life, that we have no remembrance when, or in what way, we acquired it.

That such a conviction is at first the necessary result of our constitution, and that it can never be entirely obliterated, is, I think, acknowledged by one of the most zealous defenders of Necessity. "Free Discussion, &c.," p. 298. "Such are the influences to which all mankind, without distinction, are exposed that they necessarily refer actions (I mean refer them ultimately) first of all to themselves and others; and it is a long time before they begin to consider themselves and others as instruments in the hand of a superior agent. Consequently, the associations which refer actions to themselves get so confirmed that they are never entirely obliterated; and therefore the common language, and the common feelings, of mankind, will be adapted to the first, the limited and imperfect, or rather erroneous, view of things."

It is very probable that the very conception or idea of active power, and of efficient causes, is derived from our voluntary exertions in producing effects; and that, if we were not conscious of such exertion, we should have no conception at all of a cause, or of active power, and consequently no conviction of the necessity of a cause of every change which we observe in nature.

It is certain that we can conceive no kind of active power but what is similar or analogous to that which we attribute to ourselves; that is, a power which is exerted by will and with understanding. Our notion, even of Almighty power, is derived from the notion of human power, by removing from the former those imperfections and limitations to which the latter is subjected.

It may be difficult to explain the origin of our conceptions and belief concerning efficient causes and active power. The common theory, that all our ideas are ideas of Sensation or Reflection, and that all our belief is a perception of the agreement or the disagreement of those ideas, appears to be repugnant, both to the idea of an efficient cause, and to the belief of its necessity.

An attachment to that theory has led some philosophers to deny that we have any conception of an efficient cause, or of active power, because efficiency and active power are not ideas, either of sensation or reflection. They maintain, therefore, that a Cause is only *something prior to the effect, and constantly conjoined with it.* This is Mr Hume's notion of a cause, and seems to be adopted by Dr Priestley, who says, "That a cause cannot be defined to be any thing, but *such previous circumstances as are constantly followed by a certain effect,* the constancy of the result making us conclude that there must be a *sufficient reason,* in the nature of the things, why it should be produced in those circumstances." *[Doctrine of Philosophical Necessity,* p. 11.*]*

But theory ought to stoop to fact, and not fact to theory. Every man who understands the language knows that neither priority, nor constant conjunction, nor both taken together, imply efficiency. . . .

The very dispute, whether we have the conception of an efficient cause, shews that we have. For, though men may dispute about things which have no existence, they cannot dispute about things of which they have no conception.

What has been said in this chapter is intended to shew— That the conception of causes, of action and of active power, in the strict and proper sense of these words, is found in the minds of all men very early, even in the dawn of their rational life. It is therefore probable, that, in all languages, the words by which these conceptions were expressed were at first distinct and unambiguous, yet it is certain that, among the most enlightened nations, these words are applied to so many things of different natures, and used in so vague a manner, that it is very difficult to reason about them distinctly.

This phaenomenon, at first view, seems very unaccountable. But a little reflection may satisfy us, that it is a natural consequence of the slow and gradual progress of human knowledge. . . .

CHAPTER 4 / OF THE INFLUENCE OF MOTIVES

The modern advocates for the doctrine of Necessity lay the stress of their cause upon the influence of *motives.*

"Every deliberate action, they say, must have a motive. When there is no motive on the other side, this motive must determine the agent: When there are contrary motives, the strongest must prevail. We reason from men's motives to their actions, as we do from other causes to their effects. If man be a free agent, and be not governed by motives, all his actions must be mere caprice, rewards and punishments can have no effect, and such a being must be absolutely ungovernable."

In order, therefore, to understand distinctly, in what sense we ascribe moral liberty to man, it is necessary to understand what influence we allow to motives. . . .

I grant that all rational beings are influenced, and ought to be influenced, by motives. But the influence of motives is of a very different nature from that of efficient causes. They are neither causes nor agents. They suppose an efficient cause, and can do nothing without it. We cannot, without absurdity, suppose a motive either to act, or to be acted upon; it is equally incapable of action and of passion; because it is not a thing that exists, but a thing that is conceived; it is what the schoolmen called an *ens rationis*. Motives, therefore, may *influence* to action, but they do not act. They may be compared to advice, or exhortation, which leaves a man still at liberty. For in vain is advice given when there is not a power either to do or to forbear what it recommends. In like manner, motives suppose liberty in the agent, otherwise they have no influence at all.

It is a law of nature with respect to matter, That every motion and change of motion, is proportional to the force impressed, and in the direction of that force. The scheme of necessity supposes a similar law to obtain in all the actions of intelligent beings; which, with little alteration, may be expressed thus:—Every action, or change of action, in an intelligent being, is proportional to the force of motives impressed, and in the direction of that force.

The law of nature respecting matter, is grounded upon this principle: That matter is an inert, inactive substance, which does not act, but is acted upon; and the law of necessity must be grounded upon the supposition, That an intelligent being is an inert, inactive substance, which does not act, but is acted upon. . . .

The arguments to prove that man is endowed with moral liberty, which have the greatest weight with me, are three: *first*, Because he has a natural conviction or belief, that, in many cases, he acts freely; *secondly*, Because he is accountable; and, *thirdly*, Because he is able to prosecute an end by a long series of means adapted to it.

CHAPTER 6 / FIRST ARGUMENT

We have, by our constitution a natural conviction or belief, that we act freely—a conviction so early, so universal, and so necessary in most of our rational operations, that it must be the result of our constitution, and the work of Him that made us.

Some of the most strenuous advocates for the doctrine of necessity acknowledge that it is impossible to act upon it. They say that we have a natural sense or conviction that we act freely; but that this is a fallacious sense.

This doctrine is dishonourable to our Maker, and lays a foundation for universal scepticism. It supposes the Author of our being to have given us one faculty on purpose to deceive us, and another by which we may detect the fallacy, and find that he imposed upon us.

If any one of our natural faculties be fallacious, there can be no reason to trust to any of them; for He that made one made all. . . .

Passing this opinion, therefore, as shocking to an ingenuous mind, and, in its consequences, subversive of all religion, all morals, and all knowledge, let us proceed to consider the evidence of our having a natural conviction that we have some degree of active power.

The very conception or idea of active power must be derived from something in our own constitution. It is impossible to account for it otherwise. We see events, but we see not the power that produces them. We perceive one event to follow another, but we perceive not the chain that binds them together. The notion of power and causation, therefore, cannot be got from external objects.

Yet the notion of causes, and the belief that every event must have a cause which had power to produce it, is found in every human mind so firmly established, that it cannot be rooted out.

This notion and this belief must have its origin from something in our constitution; and that it is natural to man, appears from the following observations.

1. We are conscious of many voluntary exertions, some easy, others more difficult, some requiring a great effort. These are exertions of power. And, though a man may be unconscious of his power when he does not exert it, he must have both the conception and the belief of it, when he knowingly and willingly exerts it, with intention to produce some effect.

2. Deliberation about an action of moment, whether we shall do it or not, implies a conviction that it is in our power. To deliberate about an end, we must be convinced that the means are in our power; and to deliberate about the means, we must be convinced that we have power to choose the most proper.

3. Suppose our deliberation brought to an issue, and that we resolve to do what appeared proper, can we form such a resolution or purpose, without any conviction of power to execute it? No; it is impossible. A man cannot resolve to lay out a sum of money which he neither has nor hopes ever to have.

4. Again, when I plight my faith in any promise or contract, I must believe that I shall have power to perform what I promise. Without this persuasion, a promise would be downright fraud.

There is a condition implied in every promise, *if we live* and *if God continue with us the power which he hath given us.* Our conviction, therefore, of this power derogates not in the least from our dependence upon God. The rudest savage is taught by nature to admit this condition in all promises, whether it be expressed or not. For it is a dictate of common sense, that we can be under no obligation to do what it is impossible for us to do.

If we act upon the system of necessity, there must be another condition implied in all deliberation, in every resolution, and in every promise; and that is, *if we shall be willing.* But the will not being in our power, we cannot engage for it.

If this condition be understood, as it must be understood if we act upon the system of necessity, there can be no deliberation, or resolution, nor any obligation in a promise. A man might as well deliberate, resolve, and promise, upon the actions of other men as upon his own.

It is no less evident that we have a conviction of power in other men, when we advise or persuade, or command, or conceive them to be under obligation by their promises.

5. Is it possible for any man to blame himself for yielding to necessity? Then he may blame himself for dying, or for being a man. Blame supposes a wrong use of power; and, when a man does as well as it was possible for him to do, wherein is he to be blamed? Therefore, all conviction of wrong conduct, all remorse and self-condemnation, imply a conviction of our power to have done better. Take away this conviction, and there may be a sense of misery, or a dread of evil to come; but there can be no sense of guilt or resolution to do better.

Many who hold the doctrine of necessity, disown these consequences of it, and think to evade them. To such, they ought not to be imputed; but their inseparable connection with that doctrine appears self-evident; and, therefore, some late patrons of it have had the boldness to avow them. "They cannot accuse themselves of having done anything wrong, in the ultimate sense of the words. In a strict sense, they have nothing to do with repentance, confession, and pardon—these being adapted to a fallacious view of things."

Those who can adopt these sentiments, may, indeed, celebrate, with high encomiums, *"the great and glorious doctrine of necessity."* It restores them, in their own conceit, to the state of innocence. It delivers them from all the pangs of guilt and remorse, and from all fear about their future conduct, though not about their fate. They may be as secure that they shall do nothing wrong as those who have finished their course. A doctrine so flattering to the mind of a sinner, is very apt to give strength to weak arguments.

After all, it is acknowledged, by those who boast of this glorious doctrine, "That every man, let him use what efforts he can, will necessarily feel the sentiments of shame, remorse, and repentance, and, oppressed with a sense of guilt, will have recourse to that mercy of which he stands in need."

The meaning of this seems to me to be, That, although the doctrine of necessity be supported by invincible arguments, and though it be the most consolatory doctrine in the world; yet no man, in his most serious moments, when he sits himself before the throne of his Maker, can possibly believe it, but must then necessarily lay aside this glorious doctrine, and all its flattering consequences, and return to the humiliating conviction of his having made a bad use of the power which God had given him.

If the belief of our having active power be necessarily implied in those rational operations we have mentioned, it must be coeval with our reason; it must be as universal among men, and as necessary in the conduct of life, as those operations are.

We cannot recollect by memory when it began. It cannot be a prejudice of education, or of false philosophy. It must be a part of our constitution, or the necessary result of our constitution and therefore the work of God.

It resembles, in this respect, our belief of the existence of a material world; our belief that those we converse with are living and intelligent beings; our belief that those things did really happen, which we distinctly remember; and our belief that we continue the same identical persons.

We find difficulty in accounting for our belief of these things; and some philosophers think that they have discovered good reasons for throwing it off. But it sticks fast, and the greatest sceptic finds that he must yield to it in his practice, while he wages war with it in speculation.

If it be objected to this argument, That the belief of our acting freely cannot be implied in the operations we have mentioned, because those operations are performed by them who believe that we are, in all our actions, governed by necessity—the answer to this objection is, That men in their practice may be governed by a belief which in speculation they reject.

However strange and unaccountable this may appear, there are many well-known instances of it.

I knew a man who was as much convinced as any man of the folly of the popular belief of apparitions in the dark; yet he could not sleep in a room alone, nor go alone into a room in the dark. Can it be said, that his fear did not imply a belief of danger? This is impossible. Yet his philosophy convinced him that he was in no more danger in the dark when alone, than with company.

Here an unreasonable belief, which was merely a prejudice of the nursery, stuck so fast as to govern his conduct, in opposition to his speculative belief as a philosopher and a man of sense.

There are few persons who can look down from the battlement of a very high tower without fear, while their reason convinces them that they are in no more danger than when standing upon the ground.

There have been persons who professed to believe that there is no distinction between virtue and vice, yet in their practice they resented injuries, and esteemed noble and virtuous actions.

There have been sceptics who professed to disbelieve their senses and every human faculty; but no sceptic was ever known, who did not, in practice, pay a regard to his senses and to his other faculties.

There are some points of belief so necessary, that, without them, a man would not be the being which God made him. These may be opposed in speculation, but it is impossible to root them out. In a speculative hour they seem to vanish, but in practice they resume their authority. This seems to be the case of those who hold the doctrine of necessity, and yet act as if they were free.

This natural conviction of some degree of power in ourselves and in other men, respects voluntary actions only. For, as all our power is directed by our will, we can form no conception of power, properly so called, that is not under the direction of will. And therefore our exertions, our deliberations, our purposes, our promises, are only in things that depend upon our will. Our advices, exhortations, and commands, are only in things that depend upon the will of those to whom they are addressed. We impute no guilt to ourselves, nor to others, in things where the will is not concerned.

But it deserves our notice, that we do not conceive everything, without exception, to be in a man's power which depends upon his will. There are many exceptions to this general rule. The most obvious of these I shall mention, because they both serve to illustrate the rule, and are of importance in the question concerning the liberty of man.

In the rage of madness, men are absolutely deprived of the power of self-government. They act voluntarily, but their will is driven as by a tempest, which, in lucid intervals, they resolve to oppose with all their might, but are overcome when the fit of madness returns.

Idiots are like men walking in the dark, who cannot be said to have the power of choosing their way, because they cannot distinguish the good road from the bad. Having no light in their understanding, they must either sit still, or be carried on by some blind impulse.

Between the darkness of infancy, which is equal to that of

idiots, and the maturity of reason, there is a long twilight, which, by insensible degrees, advances to the perfect day.

In this period of life, man has but little of the power of self-government. His actions, by nature, as well as by the laws of society, are in the power of others more than in his own. His folly and indiscretion, his levity and inconstancy, are considered as the fault of youth, rather than of the man. We consider him as half a man and half a child, and expect that each by turns should play its part. He would be thought a severe and unequitable censor of manners, who required the same cool deliberation, the same steady conduct, and the same mastery over himself, in a boy of thirteen, as in a man of thirty.

It is an old adage, That violent anger is a short fit of madness. If this be literally true in any case, a man, in such a fit of passion, cannot be said to have the command of himself. If real madness could be proved, it must have the effect of madness while it lasts, whether it be for an hour or for life. But the madness of a short fit of passion, if it be really madness, is incapable of proof; and therefore is not admitted in human tribunals as an exculpation. And, I believe, there is no case where a man can satisfy his own mind that his passion, both in its beginning and in its progress, was irresistible. The Searcher of hearts alone knows infallibly what allowance is due in cases of this kind.

But a violent passion, though it may not be irresistible, is difficult to be resisted: And a man, surely, has not the same power over himself in passion, as when he is cool. On this account it is allowed by all men to alleviate, when it cannot exculpate; and has its weight in criminal courts, as well as in private judgment.

It ought likewise to be observed, That he who has accustomed himself to restrain his passions, enlarges by habit his power over them, and consequently over himself. When we consider that a Canadian savage can acquire the power of defying death in its most dreadful forms, and of braving the most exquisite torment for many long hours, without losing the command of himself; we may learn from this, that, in the constitution of human nature, there is ample scope for the enlargement of that power of self-command without which there can be no virtue nor magnanimity.

There are cases, however, in which a man's voluntary actions are thought to be very little, if at all, in his power, on account of the violence of the motive that impels him. The magnanimity of a hero, or of a martyr, is not expected in every man, and on all occasions.

If a man trusted by the government with a secret which it is high treason to disclose, be prevailed upon by a bribe, we have no mercy for him, and hardly allow the greatest bribe to be any alleviation of his crime.

But, on the other hand, if the secret be extorted by the rack, or by the dread of present death, we pity him more than we blame him, and would think it severe and unequitable to condemn him as a traitor.

What is the reason that all men agree in condemning this man as a traitor in the first place, and, in the last, either exculpate him, or think his fault greatly alleviated? If he acted necessarily in both cases, compelled by an irresistible motive, I can see no reason why we should not pass the same judgment on both.

But the reason of these different judgments is evidently this —That the love of money, and of what is called a man's interest, is a cool motive, which leaves to a man the entire power over himself; but the torment of the rack, or the dread of present death, are so violent motives that men who have not uncommon strength of mind, are not masters of themselves in such a situation, and, therefore, what they do is not imputed, or is thought less criminal.

If a man resist such motives, we admire his fortitude, and think his conduct heroical rather than human. If he yields, we impute it to human frailty, and think him rather to be pitied than severely censured.

Inveterate habits are acknowledged to diminish very considerably the power a man has over himself. Although we may think him highly blameable in acquiring them, yet, when they are confirmed to a certain degree, we consider him as no longer master of himself, and hardly reclaimable without a miracle.

Thus we see that the power which we are led, by common sense, to ascribe to man respects his voluntary actions only, and that it has various limitations even with regard to them. Some actions that depend upon our will are easy, others very difficult, and some, perhaps, beyond our power. In different men, the power of self-government is different, and in the same man at different times. It may be diminished, or perhaps lost, by bad habits; it may be greatly increased by good habits.

These are facts attested by experience, and supported by the common judgment of mankind. Upon the system of Liberty they are perfectly intelligible; but, I think, irreconcileable to that of Necessity; for, How can there be an easy and a difficult in actions equally subject to necessity?—or, How can power be greater or less, increased or diminished, in those who have no power?

This natural conviction of our acting freely, which is acknowledged by many who hold the doctrine of necessity, ought to throw the whole burden of proof upon that side; for, by this, the side of liberty has what lawyers call a *jus quaesitum*, or a right of ancient possession, which ought to stand good till it be overturned. If it cannot be proved that we always act from necessity, there is no need of arguments on the other side to convince us that we are free agents.

To illustrate this by a similar case:—If a philosopher would persuade me that my fellow-men with whom I converse are not thinking, intelligent beings, but mere machines, though I might be at a loss to find arguments against this strange opinion, I should think it reasonable to hold the belief which nature gave me before I was capable of weighing evidence, until convincing proof is brought against it.

CHAPTER 7 / SECOND ARGUMENT

That there is a real and essential distinction between right and wrong conduct, between just and unjust—That the most perfect moral rectitude is to be ascribed to the Deity—That man is a moral and accountable being, capable of acting right and wrong, and answerable for his conduct to Him who made him, and assigned him a part to act upon the stage of life; are principles proclaimed by every man's conscience—principles upon which the systems of morality and natural religion, as well as the system of revelation, are grounded, and which have been generally acknowledged by those who hold contrary opinions on the subject of human liberty. I shall therefore here take them for granted.

These principles afford an obvious, and, I think, an invincible argument, that man is endowed with Moral Liberty.

Two things are implied in the notion of a moral and accountable being—*Understanding* and *Active Power.*

First, He must *understand the law to which he is bound, and his obligation to obey it.* Moral obedience must be voluntary, and must regard the authority of the law. I may command my horse to eat when he hungers, and drink when he thirsts. He does so; but his doing it is no moral obedience. He does not understand my command, and therefore can have no will to obey it. He has not the conception of moral obligation, and therefore cannot act from the conviction of it. In eating and drinking, he is moved by his own appetite only, and not by my authority.

Brute-animals are incapable of moral obligation, because they have not that degree of understanding which it implies. They have not the conception of a rule of conduct and of obligation to obey it, and therefore, though they may be noxious, they cannot be criminal.

Man, by his rational nature, is capable both of understanding the law that is prescribed to him, and of perceiving its obligation. He knows what it is to be just and honest, to injure no man, and to obey his Maker. From his constitution, he has an immediate conviction of his obligation to these things. He has the approbation of his conscience when he acts by these rules; and he is conscious of guilt and demerit when he transgresses them. And, without this knowledge of his duty and his obligation, he would not be a moral and accountable being.

Secondly, Another thing implied in the notion of a moral and accountable being, is *power to do what he is accountable for.*

That no man can be under a moral obligation to do what it is impossible for him to do, or to forbear what it is impossible for him for forbear, is an axiom as self-evident as any in mathematics. It cannot be contradicted, without overturning all notion of moral obligation; nor can there be any exception to it, when it is rightly understood. . . .

Active power, therefore, is necessarily implied in the very notion of a moral accountable being. And if man be such a being, he must have a degree of active power proportioned to the account he is to make. He may have a model of perfection set before him which he is unable to reach; but, if he does to the utmost of his power, this is all he can be answerable for. To incur guilt, by not going beyond his power, is impossible.

What was said, in the first argument, of the limitation of our power, adds much strength to the present argument. A man's power, it was observed, extends only to his voluntary actions, and has many limitations, even with respect to them.

His *accountableness* has the same extent and the same limitations.

In the rage of madness he has no power over himself, neither is he accountable, or capable of moral obligation. In ripe age, man is accountable in a greater degree than in non-age, because his power over himself is greater. Violent passions and violent motives alleviate what is done through their influence, in the same proportion as they diminish the power of resistance.

There is, therefore, a perfect correspondence between *power*, on the one hand, and *moral obligation* and *accountableness*, on the other. They not only correspond in general, as they respect voluntary actions only, but every limitation of the first produces a corresponding limitation of the two last. This, indeed, amounts to nothing more than that maxim of common sense, confirmed by Divine authority, "That to whom much is given, of him much will be required."

The sum of this argument is—that a certain degree of active power is the talent which God hath given to every rational accountable creature, and of which he will require an account. If man had no power, he would have nothing to account for. All wise and all foolish conduct, all virtue and vice, consist in the right use or in the abuse of that power which God hath given us. If man had no power, he could neither be wise nor foolish, virtuous nor vicious.

If we adopt the system of necessity, the terms *moral obligation* and *accountableness, praise* and *blame, merit* and *demerit, justice* and *injustice, reward* and *punishment, wisdom* and *folly, virtue* and *vice,* ought to be disused, or to have new meanings given to them when they are used in religion, in morals, or in civil government; for, upon that system, there can be no such thing as they have been always used to signify.

CHAPTER 8 / THIRD ARGUMENT

That man has power over his own actions and volitions appears, because he is capable of carrying on, wisely and prudently, a system of conduct, which he has before conceived in his mind, and resolved to prosecute.

I take it for granted, that, among the various characters of men, there have been some who, after they came to years of understanding, deliberately laid down a plan of conduct, which they resolve to pursue through life; and that of these, some have steadily pursued the end they had in view, by the proper means.

It is of no consequence in this argument, whether one has made the best choice of his main end or not; whether his end be riches, or power, or fame, or the approbation of his Maker. I suppose only, that he has prudently and steadily pursued it; that, in a long course of deliberate actions, he has taken the means that appeared most conducive to his end, and avoided whatever might cross it.

That such conduct in a man demonstrates a certain degree of wisdom and understanding, no man ever doubted; and I say it demonstrates, with equal force, a certain degree of power over his voluntary determinations.

This will appear evident, if we consider, that understanding without power may project, but can execute nothing. A regular plan of conduct, as it cannot be contrived without understanding, so it cannot be carried into execution without power; and, therefore, the execution, as an effect, demonstrates, with equal force, both power and understanding in the cause. Every indication of wisdom, taken from the effect, is equally an indication of power to execute what wisdom planned. And if we have any evidence that the wisdom which formed the plan is in the man, we have the very same evidence that the power which executed it is in him also.

In this argument, we reason from the same principles as in demonstrating the being and perfections of the First Cause of all things.

The effects we observe in the course of nature require a cause. Effects wisely adapted to an end, require a wise cause. Every indication of the wisdom of the Creator is equally an indiction of His power. His wisdom appears only in the works done by his power; for wisdom without power may speculate, but it cannot act; it may plan, but it cannot execute its plans.

The same reasoning we apply to the works of men. In a stately palace we see the wisdom of the architect. His wisdom contrived it, and wisdom could do no more. The execution required both a distinct conception of the plan, and power to operate according to that plan.

Let us apply these principles to the supposition we have made—That a man, in a long course of conduct, has determined and acted prudently in the prosecution of a certain end. If the man had both the wisdom to plan this course of conduct, and that power over his own actions that was necessary to carry it into execution, he is a free agent, and used his liberty, in this instance, with understanding.

But, if all his particular determinations, which concurred in the execution of this plan were produced, not by himself, but by some cause acting necessarily upon him, then there is no evidence left that he contrived this plan, or that he ever spent a thought about it.

The cause that directed all these determinations so wisely, whatever it was, must be a wise and intelligent cause; it must have understood the plan, and have intended the execution of it.

If it be said that all this course of determination was produced by Motives, motives, surely, have not understanding to receive a plan, and intend its execution. We must, therefore, go back beyond motives to some intelligent being who had the power of arranging those motives, and applying them in their proper order and season, so as to bring about the end.

This intelligent being must have understood the plan, and intended to execute it. If this be so, as the man had no hand in the execution, we have not any evidence left that he had any hand in the contrivance, or even that he is a thinking being.

If we can believe that an extensive series of means may conspire to promote an end without a cause that intended the end, and had power to choose and apply those means for the purpose, we may as well believe that this world was made by a fortuitous concourse of atoms, without an intelligent and powerful cause.

If a lucky concourse of motives could produce the conduct

of an Alexander or a Julius Caesar, no reason can be given why a lucky concourse of atoms might not produce the planetary system.

If, therefore, wise conduct in a man demonstrates that he has some degree of wisdom, it demonstrates, with equal force and evidence, that he has some degree of power over his own determinations.

All the reason we can assign for believing that our fellow-men think and reason, is grounded upon their actions and speeches. If they are not the cause of these, there is no reason left to conclude that they think and reason.

Des Cartes thought that the human body is merely an engine, and that all its motions and actions are produced by mechanism. If such a machine could be made to speak and to act rationally, we might, indeed, conclude with certainty, that the maker of it had both reason and active power; but, if we once knew that all the motions of the machine were purely mechanical, we should have no reason to conclude that the man had reason or thought.

The conclusion of this argument is—That, if the actions and speeches of other men give us sufficient evidence that they are reasonable beings, they give us the same evidence, and the same degree of evidence, that they are free agents.

There is another conclusion that may be drawn from this reasoning, which it is proper to mention.

Suppose a Fatalist, rather than give up the scheme of necessity, should acknowledge that he has no evidence that there is thought and reason in any of his fellow-men, and that they may be mechanical engines for all that he knows, he will be forced to acknowledge that there must be active power, as well as understanding, in the maker of those engines, and that the first cause is a free agent. We have the same reason to believe this as to believe his existence and his wisdom. And, if the Deity acts freely, every argument brought to prove that freedom of action is impossible, must fall to the ground.

The First Cause gives us evidence of his power by every effect that gives us evidence of his wisdom. And, if he is pleased to communicate to the work of his hands some degree of his wisdom, no reason can be assigned why he may not communicate some degree of his power, as the talent which wisdom is to employ.

That the first motion, or the first effect, whatever it be, cannot be produced necessarily, and, consequently, that the First Cause must be a free agent, has been demonstrated so clearly and unanswerably by Dr Clarke, both in his "Demonstration of the Being and Attributes of God," and in the end of his "Remarks on Collins's Philosophical Enquiry concerning Human Liberty," that I can add nothing to what he has said; nor have I found any objection made to his reasoning, by any of the defenders of necessity.

ESSAY FIVE / OF MORALS

CHAPTER 1 / OF THE FIRST PRINCIPLES OF MORALS

Morals, like all other sciences, must have *first principles*, on which all moral reasoning is grounded.

In every branch of knowledge where disputes have been raised, it is useful to distinguish the first principles from the superstructure. They are the foundation on which the whole fabric of the science leans; and whatever is not supported by this foundation can have no stability.

In all rational belief, the thing believed is either itself a first principle, or it is by just reasoning deduced from first principles. When men differ about deductions of reasoning, the appeal must be to the rules of reasoning, which have been very unanimously fixed from the days of Aristotle. But when they differ about a first principle, the appeal is made to another tribunal—to that of *Common Sense*. . . .

I propose, therefore, in this chapter, to point out some of the first principles or morals, without pretending to a complete enumeration.

The principles I am to mention, relate either [A] to *virtue in general*, or [B] to the different *particular branches of virtue*, or [C] to the *comparison of virtues* where they seem to interfere.

[A] 1. *There are some things in human conduct that merit approbation and praise, others that merit blame and punishment; and different degrees either of approbation or of blame, are due to different actions.*

2. *What is in no degree voluntary, can neither deserve moral approbation nor blame.*

3. *What is done from unavoidable necessity may be agreeable or disagreeable, useful or hurtful, but cannot be the object either of blame or of moral approbation.*

4. *Men may be highly culpable in omitting what they ought to have done, as well as in doing what they ought not.*

5. *We ought to use the best means we can to be well informed of our duty*—by serious attention to moral instruction; by observing what we approve, and what we disapprove, in other men, whether our acquaintance, or those whose actions are recorded in history; by reflecting often, in a calm and dispassionate hour, on our own past conduct, that we may discern what was wrong, what was right, and what might have been better; by deliberating coolly and impartially upon our future conduct, as far as we can foresee the opportunities we may have of doing good, or the temptations to do wrong; and by having this principle deeply fixed in our minds, that, as moral excellence is the true worth and glory of a man, so the knowledge of our duty is to every man, in every station of life, the most important of all knowledge.

6. *It ought to be our most serious concern to do our duty as far as we know it, and to fortify our minds against every temptation to deviate from it*—by maintaining a lively sense of the beauty of right conduct, and of its present and future reward, of the turpitude of vice, and of its bad consequences here and hereafter; by having always in our eye the noblest examples; by the habit of subjecting our passions to the government of reason; by firm purposes and resolutions with regard to our conduct; by avoiding occasions of temptation when we can; and by imploring the aid of Him who made us, in every hour of temptation.

These principles concerning virtue and vice *in general*, must appear self-evident to every man who hath a conscience, and who hath taken pains to exercise this natural power of his mind. I proceed to others that are *more particular*.

[B] 1. *We ought to prefer a greater good, though more distant, to a less; and a less evil to a greater.*

A regard to our own good, though we had no conscience, dictates this principle; and we cannot help disapproving the man that acts contrary to it, as deserving to lose the good which he wantonly threw away, and to suffer the evil which he knowingly brought upon his own head. . . .

Let a man's moral judgment be ever so little improved by exercise, or ever so much corrupted by bad habits, he cannot be indifferent to his own happiness or misery. When he is become insensible to every nobler motive to right conduct, he cannot be insensible to this. And though to act from this motive solely may be called *prudence* rather than *virtue*, yet this prudence deserves some regard upon its own account, and much more as it is the friend and ally of virtue, and the enemy of all vice; and as it gives a favourable testimony of virtue to those who are deaf to every other recommendation.

If a man can be induced to do his duty even from a regard to his own happiness, he will soon find reason to love virtue for her own sake, and to act from motives less mercenary.

I cannot therefore approve of those moralists who would

banish all persuasives to virtue taken from the consideration of private good. In the present state of human nature these are not useless to the best, and they are the only means left of reclaiming the abandoned.

2. *As far as the intention of nature appears in the constitution of man, we ought to comply with that intention, and to act agreeably to it.*

The Author of our being hath given us not only the power of acting within a limited sphere, but various principles or springs of action, of different nature and dignity, to direct us in the exercise of our active power.

From the constitution of every species of the inferior animals, and especially from the active principles which nature has given them, we easily perceive the manner of life for which nature intended them; and they uniformly act the part to which they are led by their constitution, without any reflection upon it, or intention of obeying its dictates. Man only, of the inhabitants of this world, is made capable of observing his own constitution, what kind of life it is made for, and of acting according to that intention, or contrary to it. He only is capable of yielding an intentional obedience to the dictates of his nature, or of rebelling against them.

In treating of the principles of action in man, it has been shewn, that, as his natural instincts and bodily appetites are well adapted to the preservation of his natural life, and to the continuance of the species; so his natural desires, affections, and passions, when uncorrupted by vicious habits, and under the government of the leading principles of reason and conscience, are excellently fitted for the rational and social life. Every vicious action shews an excess, or defect, or wrong direction of some natural spring of action, and therefore may, very justly, be said to be unnatural. Every virtuous action agrees with the uncorrupted principles of human nature.

The Stoics defined Virtue to be *a life according to nature.* Some of them more accurately, *a life according to the nature of man, in so far as it is superior to that of brutes.* The life of a brute is according to the nature of the brute; but it is neither virtuous nor vicious. The life of a moral agent cannot be according to his nature, unless it be virtuous. That conscience which is in every man's breast, is the law of God written in his heart, which he cannot disobey without acting unnaturally, and being self-condemned.

The intention of nature, in the various active principles of man—in the desires of power, of knowledge, and of esteem, in the affection to children, to near relations, and to the communities to which we belong, in gratitude, in compassion, and even in resentment and emulation—is very obvious, and has been pointed out in treating of those principles. Nor is it less evident, that reason and conscience are given us to regulate the inferior principles, so that they may conspire, in a regular and consistent plan of life, in pursuit of some worthy end.

3. *No man is born for himself only.* Every man, therefore, ought to consider himself as a member of the common society of mankind, and of those subordinate societies to which he belongs, such as family, friends, neighbourhood, country, and to do as much good as he can, and as little hurt to the societies of which he is a part.

This axiom leads directly to the practice of every social virtue, and indirectly to the virtues of self-government, by which only we can be qualified for discharging the duty we owe to society.

4. *In every case, we ought to act that part towards another, which we would judge to be right in him to act toward us, if we were in his circumstances and he in ours;* or, more generally—*What we approve in others, that we ought to practise in like circumstances, and what we condemn in others we ought not to do.*

If there be any such thing as right and wrong in the conduct of moral agents, it must be the same to all in the same circumstances.

We stand all in the same relation to Him who made us, and will call us to account for our conduct; for with Him there is no respect of persons. We stand in the same relation to one another as members of the great community of mankind. The duties consequent upon the different ranks and offices and relations of men are the same to all in the same circumstances.

It is not want of judgment, but want of candour and impartiality, that hinders men from discerning what they owe to others. They are quicksighted enough in discerning what is due to themselves. When they are injured, or ill-treated, they see it, and feel resentment. It is the want of candour that makes men use one measure for the duty they owe to others, and another measure for the duty that others owe to them in like circumstances. That men ought to judge with candour, as in all other cases, so especially in what concerns their moral conduct, is surely self-evident to every intelligent being. The man who takes offence when he is injured in his person, in his property, in his good name, pronounces judgment against himself if he act so toward his neighbour.

As the equity and obligation of this rule of conduct is self-evident to every man who hath a conscience; so it is, of all the rules of morality, the most comprehensive, and truly deserves the encomium given it by the highest authority, that *"it is the law and the prophets."*

It comprehends every rule of justice without exception. It comprehends all the relative duties, arising either from the more permanent relations of parent and child, of master and servant, of magistrate and subject, of husband and wife, or from the more transient relations of rich and poor, of buyer and seller, of debtor and creditor, of benefactor and beneficiary, of friend and enemy. It comprehends every duty of charity and humanity, and even of courtesy and good manners.

Nay, I think, that, without any force or straining, it extends even to the duties of self-government. For, as every man approves in others the virtues of prudence, temperance, self-command, and fortitude, he must perceive that what is right in others must be right in himself in like circumstances.

To sum up all, he who acts invariably by this rule will never deviate from the path of his duty, but from an error of judgment. And, as he feels the obligation that he and all men are under to use the best means in his power to have his judgment well-informed in matters of duty, his errors will only be such as are invincible.

It may be observed, that this axiom supposes a faculty in man by which he can distinguish right conduct from wrong. It supposes also, that, by this faculty, we easily perceive the right and the wrong in other men that are indifferent to us; but are very apt to be blinded by the partiality of selfish passions when the case concerns ourselves. Every claim we have against others is apt to be magnified by self-love, when viewed directly. A change of persons removes this prejudice, and brings the claim to appear in its just magnitude.

5. *To every man who believes the existence, the perfections, and the providence of God, the veneration and submission we owe to him is self-evident.* Right sentiments of the Deity and of his works, not only make the duty we owe to him obvious to every intelligent being, but likewise add the authority of a Divine law to every rule of right conduct.

[C.] There is another class of axioms in morals, by which, when there seems to be an *opposition* between the actions that different virtues lead to, we determine to which the *preference* is due.

Between the several virtues, as they are dispositions of mind, or determinations of will, to act according to a certain general rule, there can be no opposition. They dwell together most amicably, and give mutual aid and ornament, without the possibility of hostility or opposition, and, taken altogether, make one uniform and consistent rule of conduct. But, between particular external actions, which different virtues would lead to, there may be an opposition. Thus, the same man may be in his heart, generous, grateful, and just. These dispositions strengthen, but never can weaken one another.

Yet it may happen, that an external action which generosity or gratitude solicits, justice may forbid.

That in all such cases, *unmerited generosity should yield to gratitude, and both to justice,* is self-evident. Nor is it less so, that *unmerited beneficence to those who are at ease should yield to compassion to the miserable,* and *external acts of piety to works of mercy,* because God loves mercy more than sacrifice.

At the same time, we perceive, that those acts of virtue which ought to yield in the case of a competition, have most intrinsic worth when there is no competition. Thus, it is evident that there is more worth in pure and unmerited benevolence than in compassion, more in compassion than in gratitude, and more in gratitude than in justice.

I call these *first principles,* because they appear to me to have in themselves an intuitive evidence which I cannot resist. I find I can express them in other words. I can illustrate them by examples and authorities, and perhaps can deduce one of them from another; but I am not able to deduce them from other principles that are more evident. And I find the best moral reasonings of authors I am acquainted with, ancient and modern, Heathen and Christian, to be grounded upon one or more of them.

The evidence of mathematical axioms is not discerned till men come to a certain degree of maturity of understanding. A boy must have formed the general conception of *quantity,* and of *more* and *less* and *equal,* of *sum* and *difference;* and he must have been accustomed to judge of these relations in matters of common life, before he can perceive the evidence of the mathematical axiom—that equal quantities, added to equal quantities, make equal sums.

In like manner, our Moral Judgment or Conscience, grows to maturity from an imperceptible seed, planted by our Creator. When we are capable of contemplating the actions of other men, or of reflecting upon our own calmly and dispassionately, we begin to perceive in them the qualities of honest and dishonest, of honourable and base, of right and wrong, and to feel the sentiments of moral approbation and disapprobation.

These sentiments are at first feeble, easily warped by passions and prejudices, and apt to yield to authority. By use and time, the judgment, in morals, as in other matters, gathers strength, and feels more vigour. We begin to distinguish the dictates of passion from those of cool reason, and to perceive that it is not always safe to rely upon the judgment of others. By an impulse of nature, we venture to judge for ourselves, as we venture to walk by ourselves.

There is a strong analogy between the progress of the body from infancy to maturity, and the progress of all the powers of the mind. This progression in both is the work of nature, and in both may be greatly aided or hurt by proper education. It is natural to a man to be able to walk, or run, or leap; but, if his limbs had been kept in fetters from his birth, he would have none of those powers. It is no less natural to a man trained in society, and accustomed to judge of his own actions and those of other men, to perceive a right and a wrong, an honourable and a base, in human conduct; and to such a man, I think, the principles of morals I have above mentioned will appear self-evident. Yet there may be individuals of the human species so little accustomed to think or judge of anything but of gratifying their animal appetites, as to have hardly any conception of right or wrong in conduct, or any moral judgment; as there certainly are some who have not the conceptions and the judgment necessary to understand the axioms of geometry.

From the principles above mentioned, the whole system of moral conduct follows so easily, and with so little aid of reasoning, that every man of common understanding, who wishes to know his duty, may know it. That path of duty is a plain path, which the upright in heart can rarely mistake. Such it must be, since every man is bound to walk in it. There are some intricate cases in morals which admit of disputation; but these seldom occur in practice; and, when they do, the learned disputant has no great advantage: for the unlearned man, who uses the best means in his power to know his duty, and acts according to his knowledge, is inculpable in the sight of God and man. He may err, but he is not guilty of immorality.

CHAPTER 7 / THAT MORAL APPROBATION IMPLIES A REAL JUDGMENT

The approbation of good actions, and disapprobation of bad, are so familiar to every man come to years of understanding, that it seems strange there should be any dispute about their nature.

Whether we reflect upon our own conduct, or attend to the conduct of others with whom we live, or of whom we hear or read, we cannot help approving of some things, disapproving of others, and regarding many with perfect indifference.

These operations of our minds we are conscious of every day and almost every hour we live. Men of ripe understanding are capable of reflecting upon them, and of attending to what passes in their own thoughts on such occasions; yet, for half a century, it has been a serious dispute among philosophers, what this approbation and disapprobation is, *Whether there be a real judgment included in it, which, like all other judgments, must be true or false; or, Whether it include no more but some agreeable or uneasy feeling, in the person who approves or disapproves.*

Mr Hume observes very justly, that this is a controversy *started of late.* Before the modern system of Ideas and Impressions was introduced, nothing would have appeared more absurd than to say, that when I condemn a man for what he has done, I pass no judgment at all about the man, but only express some uneasy feeling in myself.

Nor did the new system produce this discovery at once, but gradually, by several steps, according as its consequences were more accurately traced, and its spirit more thoroughly imbibed by successive philosophers.

Des Cartes and Mr Locke went no farther than to maintain that the Secondary Qualities of body—Heat and Cold, Sound, Colour, Taste, and Smell—which we perceive and judge to be in the external object, are mere feelings or sensations in our minds, there being nothing in bodies themselves to which these names can be applied; and that the office of the external senses is not to judge of external things, but only to give us ideas of sensations, from which we are by reasoning to deduce the existence of a material world without us, as well as we can.

Arthur Collier and Bishop Berkeley discovered, from the same principles, that the Primary, as well as the Secondary, Qualities of bodies, such as Extension, Figure, Solidity, Motion, are only sensations in our minds; and, therefore, that there is no material world without us at all.

The same philosophy, when it came to be applied to matters of taste, discovered that beauty and deformity are not anything in the objects, to which men, from the beginning of the world, ascribed them, but certain feelings in the mind of the spectator.

The next step was an easy consequence from all the preceding, that Moral Approbation and Disapprobation are not Judgments, which must be true or false, but barely agreeable and uneasy Feelings or Sensations.

Mr Hume made the last step in this progress, and crowned the system by what he calls his *hypothesis*—to wit, That Belief is more properly an act of the Sensitive then of the Cogitative part of our nature.

Beyond this I think no man can go in this track; sensation or feeling is all, and what is left to the cogitative part of our nature, I am not able to comprehend.

I have had occasion to consider each of these paradoxes,

excepting that which relates to morals, in "Essays on the Intellectual Powers of Man;" and, though they be strictly connected with each other, and with the system which has produced them, I have attempted to shew that they are inconsistent with just notions of our intellectual powers, no less than they are with the common sense and common language of mankind. And this, I think, will likewise appear with regard to the conclusion relating to morals—to wit, That moral approbation is only an agreeable feeling, and not a real judgment.

To prevent ambiguity as much as possible, let us attend to the meaning of *Feeling* and of *Judgment*. These operations of the mind, perhaps, cannot be logically defined; but they are well understood, and easily distinguished, by their properties and adjuncts.

Feeling, or sensation, seems to be the lowest degree of animation we can conceive. We give the name of *animal* to every being that feels pain and pleasure; and this seems to be the boundary between the inanimate and animal creation.

We know no being of so low a rank in the creation of God as to possess this animal power only without any other.

We commonly distinguish *Feeling* from *Thinking*, because it hardly deserves the name; and though it be, in a more general sense, a species of thought, is least removed from the passive and inert state of things inanimate.

A feeling must be agreeable, or uneasy, or indifferent. It may be weak or strong. It is expressed in language either by a single word, or by such a contexture of words as may be the subject or predicate of a proposition, but such as cannot by themselves make a proposition. For it implies neither affirmation nor negation; and therefore cannot have the qualities of true or false, which distinguish propositions from all other forms of speech, and judgments from all other acts of the mind.

That I have such a feeling, is indeed an affirmative proposition, and expresses testimony grounded upon an intuitive judgment. But the feeling is only one term of this proposition; and it can only make a proposition when joined with another term, by a verb affirming or denying.

As feeling distinguishes the animal nature from the inanimate; so judging seems to distinguish the rational nature from the merely animal.

Though judgment in general is expressed by one word in language, as the most complex operations of the mind may be; yet a particular judgment can only be expressed by a sentence, and by that kind of sentence which logicians call a *proposition*, in which there must necessarily be a verb in the indicative mood, either expressed or understood.

Every judgment must necessarily be true or false, and the same may be said of the proposition which expresses it. It is a determination of the understanding, with regard to what is true, or false, or dubious.

In judgment, we can distinguish the object about which we judge, from the act of the mind in judging of that object. In mere feeling there is no such distinction. The object of judgment must be expressed by a proposition; and belief, disbelief, or doubt, always accompanies the judgment we form. If we judge the proposition to be true, we must believe it; if we judge it to be false, we must disbelieve it; and if we be uncertain whether it be true or false, we must doubt.

The *toothache*, the *headache*, are words which express uneasy feelings; but to say that they express a judgment would be ridiculous.

That the sun is greater than the earth, is a proposition, and therefore the object of judgment; and, when affirmed or denied, believed or disbelieved, or doubted, it expresses judgment; but to say that it expresses only a feeling in the mind of him that believes it, would be ridiculous.

These two operations of mind, when we consider them separately, are very different, and easily distinguished. When we feel without judging, or judge without feeling, it is impossible, without very gross inattention, to mistake the one for the other.

But in many operations of the mind, both are inseparably conjoined under one name; and when we are not aware that the operation is complex, we may take one ingredient to be the whole, and overlook the other.

In former ages, that moral power by which human actions ought to be regulated, was called *Reason,* and considered, both by philosophers and by the vulgar, as the power of judging what we ought and what we ought not to do.

This is very fully expressed by Mr Hume, in his "Treatise of Human Nature," Book II. Part iii. § 3. "Nothing is more usual in philosophy, and even in common life, than to talk of the combat of passion and reason, to give the preference to reason, and assert that men are only so far virtuous as they conform themselves to its dictates. Every rational creature, 'tis said, is obliged to regulate his actions by reason; and, if any other motive or principle challenge the direction of his conduct, he ought to oppose it, till it be entirely subdued, or, at least, brought to a conformity to that superior principle. On this method of thinking, the greatest part of moral philosophy, ancient and modern, seems to be founded."

That those philosophers attended chiefly to the judging power of our moral faculty, appears from the names they gave to its operations, and from the whole of their language concerning it.

The modern philosophy has led men to attend chiefly to their sensations and feelings, and thereby to resolve into mere feeling, complex acts of the mind, of which feeling is only one ingredient.

I had occasion, in the preceding Essays, to observe, that several operations of the mind, to which we give one name, and consider as one act, are compounded of more simple acts inseparably united in our constitution, and that, in these, sensation or feeling often makes one ingredient.

Thus, the appetites of hunger and thirst are compounded of an uneasy sensation, and the desire of food or drink. In our benevolent affections, there is both an agreeable feeling, and a desire of happiness to the object of our affection; and malevolent affections have ingredients of a contrary nature.

In these instances, sensation or feeling is inseparably conjoined with desire. In other instances, we find sensation inseparably conjoined with judgment or belief, and that in two different ways. In some instances, the judgment or belief seems to be the consequence of the sensation, and to be regulated by it. In other instances, the sensation is the consequence of the judgment.

When we perceive an external object by our senses, we have a sensation conjoined with a firm belief of the existence and sensible qualities of the external object. Nor has all the subtilty of metaphysics been able to disjoin what nature has conjoined in our constitution. Des Cartes and Locke endeavoured, by reasoning, to deduce the existence of external objects from our sensations, but in vain. Subsequent philosophers, finding no reason for this connection, endeavoured to throw off the belief of external objects as being unreasonable; but this attempt is no less vain. Nature has doomed us to believe the testimony of our senses, whether we can give a good reason for doing so or not.

In this instance, the belief or judgment is the consequence of the sensation, as the sensation is the consequence of the impression made on the organ of sense.

But in most of the operations of mind in which judgment or belief is combined with feeling, the feeling is the consequence of the judgment, and is regulated by it.

Thus, an account of the good conduct of a friend at a distance gives me a very agreeable feeling, and a contrary account would give me a very uneasy feeling; but these feelings depend entirely upon my belief of the report.

In hope, there is an agreeable feeling, depending upon the

belief or expectation of good to come: fear is made up of contrary ingredients; in both, the feeling is regulated by the degree of belief.

In the respect we bear to the worthy, and in our contempt of the worthless, there is both judgment and feeling, and the last depends entirely upon the first.

The same may be said of gratitude for good offices and resentment of injuries.

Let me now consider how I am affected when I see a man exerting himself nobly in a good cause. I am conscious that the effect of his conduct on my mind is complex, though it may be called by one name. I look up to his virtue, I approve, I admire it. In doing so, I have pleasure indeed, or an agreeable feeling; this is granted. But I find myself interested in his success and in his fame. This is affection; it is love and esteem, which is more than mere feeling. The man is the object of this esteem; but in mere feeling there is no object.

I am likewise conscious that this agreeable feeling in me, and this esteem of him, depend entirely upon the judgment I form of his conduct. I judge that this conduct merits esteem; and, while I thus judge, I cannot but esteem him, and contemplate his conduct with pleasure. Persuade me that he was bribed, or that he acted from some mercenary or bad motive, immediately my esteem and my agreeable feeling vanish.

In the approbation of a good action, therefore, there is feeling indeed, but there is also esteem of the agent; and both the feeling and the esteem depend upon the judgment we form of his conduct.

When I exercise my moral faculty about my own actions or those of other men, I am conscious that I judge as well as feel. I accuse and excuse, I acquit and condemn, I assent and dissent, I believe and disbelieve, and doubt. These are acts of judgment, and not feelings.

Every determination of the understanding, with regard to what is true or false, is judgment. That I ought not to steal, or to kill, or to bear false witness, are propositions, of the truth of which I am as well convinced as of any proposition in Euclid. I am conscious that I judge them to be true propositions; and my consciousness makes all other arguments unnecessary, with regard to the operations of my own mind.

That other men judge, as well as feel, in such cases, I am convinced, because they understand me when I express my moral judgment, and express theirs by the same terms and phrases.

Suppose that, in a case well known to both, my friend says —*Such a man did well and worthily, his conduct is highly approvable.* This speech, according to all rules of interpretation, expresses my friend's judgment of the man's conduct. This judgment may be true or false, and I may agree in opinion with him, or I may dissent from him without offence, as we may differ in other matters of judgment.

Suppose, again, that, in relation to the same case, my friend says—*The man's conduct gave me a very agreeable feeling.*

This speech, if approbation be nothing but an agreeable feeling, must have the very same meaning with the first, and express neither more nor less. But this cannot be, for two reasons.

First, Because there is no rule in grammar or rhetoric, nor any usage in language, by which these two speeches can be construed so as to have the same meaning. The *first* expresses plainly an opinion or judgment of the conduct of the man, but says nothing of the speaker. The *second* only testifies a fact concerning the speaker—to wit, that he had such a feeling.

Another reason why these two speeches cannot mean the same thing is, that the first may be contradicted without any ground of offence, such contradiction being only a difference of opinion, which, to a reasonable man, gives no offence. But the second speech cannot be contradicted without an affront: for, as every man must know his own feelings, to deny that a man had a feeling which he affirms he had, is to charge him with falsehood.

If moral approbation be a real judgment, which produces an

agreeable feeling in the mind of him who judges, both speeches are perfectly intelligible, in the most obvious and literal sense. Their meaning is different, but they are related, so that the one may be inferred from the other, as we infer the effect from the cause, or the cause from the effect. I know, that what a man judges to be a very worthy action, he contemplates with pleasure; and what he contemplates with pleasure must, in his judgment, have worth. But the judgment and the feeling are different acts of his mind, though connected as cause and effect. He can express either the one or the other with perfect propriety; but the speech, which expresses his feeling, is altogether improper and inept to express his judgment, for this evident reason, that judgment and feeling, though in some cases connected, are things in their nature different.

If we suppose, on the other hand, that moral approbation is nothing more than an agreeable feeling, occasioned by the contemplation of an action, the second speech, above mentioned, has a distinct meaning, and expresses all that is meant by moral approbation. But the first speech either means the very same thing, (which cannot be, for the reasons already mentioned,) or it has no meaning.

Now, we may appeal to the reader, whether, in conversation upon human characters, such speeches as the first are not as frequent, as familiar, and as well understood, as anything in language; and whether they have not been common in all ages that we can trace, and in all languages? . . . .